ANY GIVEN SUNDAY

ANY GIVEN SUNDAY

The NFL's Epic 100-Year History in 20 Games

Matthew Sherry

WEIDENFELD & NICOLSON

First published in Great Britain in 2020 by Weidenfeld & Nicolson
an imprint of The Orion Publishing Group Ltd
Carmelite House, 50 Victoria Embankment
London EC4Y 0DZ

An Hachette UK Company

1 3 5 7 9 10 8 6 4 2

A CIP catalogue record for this book is
available from the British Library.

ISBN Hardback 978 1 4746 1 3644
ISBN Trade Paperback 978 1 4746 1 3651
ISBN eBook 978 1 4746 3675

Typeset by Input Data Services Ltd, Somerset

Printed and bound in Great Britain by Clays Ltd, Elcograf S.p.A.

www.weidenfeldandnicolson.co.uk

CONTENTS

PROLOGUE

To drive into Canton, Ohio, is to witness true American heart-lands. Rocking chairs hypnotically sway back and forth on the porches of archetypal US houses. Truck drivers pass by on tiny roads, bleary-eyed amid yet another graveyard shift through the country's seemingly endless lands, passing on their way the farm-ers who shift hay and equipment on battered RVs.

This is small-town America, 'Meat and Potatoes Land'; the liv-ing antithesis of the excessive metropolises such places surround. Driving in as I did from Pittsburgh, a city gradually shedding its rough-around-the-edges feel, offers a view into the soul of this gargantuan nation, to the places time has left behind, where those written off as simple folk get on with their simple lives.

The reality isn't so, well, simple. For these lands are the oil that drives the engine. More often than not, lying deep beneath the surface-level clichés, are hidden treasures – of rich histories and stories from years past; of dramatic country- and world-altering moments that took place here.

In Canton, the treasure is not so much hidden as it is written on every sign, all pointing to its Mecca: the Pro Football Hall of Fame. To new football fans, this tiny speck on the map, home to just 70,000 people, seems an unusual setting for *the* museum dedicated to the world's most lucrative sports league. But Canton, as any local will quickly tell you, is special in a manner that belies its size. It is the birthplace of the National Football League.

Until the last quarter-century, during which the NFL has risen in prominence at a mind-blowing rate, there was much conjecture over just when the league formed. Barstool arguments, at least in the watering holes frequented by historians, debated the merits of multiple dates – and it's true that the history is sketchy. However, by the time 2019 and the NFL's centenary campaign rolled around, disagreements had long been placed in the rear-view mirror. For the league had acknowledged 1920 as being its inaugural season.

As such, it is now undeniable that the actions of seven men in a very undistinguished setting – the office at Ralph Hay's Canton Hupmobile agency – began to lay the path towards a multi-billion-dollar behemoth.

Present on 20 August 1920 were representatives of four teams from the pre-eminent regional football organisation of its time, the Ohio League: the Canton Bulldogs' Hay and Jim Thorpe, Cleveland Tigers' Jimmy O'Donnell and Stan Cofall, Dayton Tri-angles' Carl Storck and Frank Nied, and Akron Pros' Art Ranney. They attended as kindred spirits increasingly concerned by opportunists taking advantage of the dishevelled mess that was pro football.

To understand the necessity of this meeting of minds, you have to understand the professional game's place in American society at that time. It was, for all intents and purposes, the ugly sister to college football. Football, to the vast majority, started and finished with the purity of the college game – with the lack of interest in a professional version demonstrated by the many failed leagues that disappeared as quickly as they arrived.

Amid this backdrop, pro football existed in pockets of society, a regional game operating in loose professional groups within territories. It was a lawless land, where teams' willingness to steal a rival's player by offering more money saw salaries spiral. Clubs would also lure local college stars into playing, as explained by the *Dayton Herald* in 1920:

Last season there were quite a number of intercollegiate stars who padded their bankrolls by slipping away on a Sunday, per-forming with a pro team using every name under the sun but their own to hide their identity. Some startling disclosures came later that brought the wrath of the intercollegiate heads down on the pro game.

Unpicking what occurred inside the walls of Hay's office is tricky. There were no official minutes taken, so the only way to develop an understanding is by looking back at the few newspapers that covered the event. Most homed in on the issues mentioned previously. *The Canton Repository* noted the teams agreed to 'eliminate bidding for players between rival clubs and to secure cooperation in the formation of schedules, at least for the bigger teams'; the *Dayton Herald* said they 'voted unanimously not to seek the services of any undergraduate college player'; and the *Canton Daily News* suggested 'business representatives of the elevens came to an understanding on financial terms of players' contracts'.

It is the last point that is perhaps most noteworthy historically, for it foreshadows a development that wouldn't come to fruition for nearly 75 years: the introduction of a salary cap. That it didn't immediately owed much to the fact that agreement between a quartet of Ohio teams wasn't enough. The American Professional Football Conference, as it was named, needed other members, all of whom would likely have their own opinions.

Of the men from that initial assembly, Thorpe's name is immediately the most recognisable. When you enter the Hall of Fame, it's his statue, the All-American hero whose combover nestles beneath a leather helmet, that fills the centre of the room. He was, and is still remembered as, pro football's first true superstar. Yet the role of his boss and paymaster Hay was most significant. After the 'Ohio Four' left that room with broad agreement between themselves about the fledgling league's future direction, Hay's resourcefulness lured other cities and teams around the table.

By the second meeting, which took place less than a month later on 17 September 1920, four became 12, such swelling numbers meaning it took place in Hay's dealership itself, rather than his office, with the Hupmobiles' running boards providing seats. Not all were present – the Buffalo All-Americans, Rochester Jeffersons and Hammond Pros couldn't make it but allegedly sent Hay a letter stating their intention to join – while another squad would never even play a league down.

That club, the Massillon Tigers – an Ohio League powerhouse whose rivalry with Canton was legendary – were the first order of business. Hay and Thorpe, knowing enmity made the teams' contests a rare commercial success, spent many hours trying to find a new backer, and Vernon Maginnis, – who managed the Akron Indians, a local pro club, in 1919 – had stepped forward. But his representatives were not admitted to the meeting, so Hay, having appointed himself spokesman for the now-defunct Tigers, began business by announcing Massillon were withdrawing from professional football for 1920.

There were multiple reasons for this: nobody liked the idea, proposed by Maginnis, of a travelling team trading falsely under the Tigers' name; the owners of Akron's new squad, the Pros, had personal quarrels with Maginnis having partnered with him at the helm of the 1919 Indians; and Hay potentially calculated the move would disenfranchise Massillon, an integral part of his Hupmobiles customer base. Any hopes Maginnis had of circum-venting those present were extinguished by Hay, who issued a diktat: 'Do not schedule any other Massillon team.'

Massillon ceased action altogether from that point forward, but technically – having been present in the meeting through Hay – could be considered one of the NFL's charter members.

The waters are less muddied for the others in Canton that day, who enjoyed the trappings laid on by their summoner. Hay had thought of everything, including – in the era of prohibition – furnishing his guests with several buckets of beer to combat the summer weather, raising the interesting question of whether the NFL would exist had the police turned up. Thankfully, they didn't and, by the time everybody left Hay's place at 8.15 p.m., much was agreed. Representatives from the Rock Island Independents, Muncie Flyers, Decatur Staleys and Racine Cardinals had decided to join, and it was determined there would be a small change in the league's name to the American Professional Football Association (APFA).

Also approved was the management structure: Thorpe was named the league's first president. Most in the room urged Hay to take the role, but Thorpe boasted popularity and pull. The appointment brought more coverage than if the title had been given to a car salesman, even if Thorpe was just a figurehead. Cofall and Ranney were elected vice-president and secretary-treasurer respectively.

Ironically, according to the meeting minutes, none of the three issues that brought the Ohio quartet around the table – salaries, team jumping and college players – were addressed. Reports indicate some of these points were raised, and agreed to, in communications prior to 17 September – although not all three. In particular, no salary cap was ever introduced. One team, the Decatur Staleys, assembled easily the most expensive squad, what with players doubling up as employees for the Staley Starch Company. The man behind that club would have a wider impact than anybody else in the room: George Halas.

At some point during the season that ensued, the 11 playing teams either present or not present on 17 September were joined by three others – the Detroit Heralds, Columbus Panhandles and Chicago Tigers. Hence there are 14 'charter' members of what we now know as the NFL.

THE FOUNDING FOUR

Akron Pros
Canton Bulldogs
Cleveland Tigers
Dayton Triangles

SECOND-MEETING ATTENDEES

Decatur Staleys
Chicago Racine Cardinals
Muncie Flyers
Rock Island Independents

THREE ADDED BY LETTER

Rochester Jeffersons
Hammond Pros
Buffalo All-Americans

POST-MEETING ADDITIONS

Detroit Heralds
Columbus Panhandles
Chicago Tigers

There is no official record of exactly when the Heralds, Panhandles and Tigers arrived, for the humble first year barely warranted a mention in newspapers. It wasn't until the next league meeting – held three months later than scheduled on 30 April 1921 in Akron's Portage Hotel – that their involvement became common knowledge.

Confusing? Absolutely. But this is how the all-singing, all-dancing, all-conquering National Football League began. As a ramshackle operation orchestrated out of a car dealership in small-town Ohio.

Let the games begin . . .

1

A Season of Firsts

DAYTON TRIANGLES 14
COLUMBUS PANHANDLES 0

---

3 October 1920
Triangle Park, Dayton

For 4,000 supporters packed into the bleachers nestled against a hill surrounding the gridiron, enthusiasm was tangible. They represented, according to the *Dayton Daily News*, 'the biggest crowd that ever witnessed the opening of the professional grid season'.

Each spectator had paid $1.75 to see the local Dayton Triangles open their campaign at the home venue that provided their nickname. Triangle Park – called as such because of its shape, created by the intersection of the Great Miami and Stillwater rivers – was primarily used for baseball, as evidenced by the presence of a diamond in the south end zone. Yet the only show in town on 3 October 1920 was the Triangles' meeting with the Columbus Panhandles. It's improbable the attendance owed anything to the club's place in a precocious new football league – the likelihood of word of Ralph Hay's creation reaching Dayton's residents was about as high as the mediocre Triangles' chances of actually winning the American Professional Football Association's inaugural season.

Unbeknown to those in attendance, they were participating in the latest seminal moment for a small town boasting an already rich history. For Triangle Park lay just a few miles from McCook Field, where the local Wright Brothers first began experimenting with flying machines. As a local park ranger told me 100 years on: 'You can't throw a stone around here without hitting a bit of history.'

And so it came to pass that those people bore witness to one of the most significant moments in the USA's cultural folklore. Seventeen years after Orville and Wilbur's life's work bore fruit, residents of Dayton, Ohio, watched as the American Professional Football Association took flight.

It is fitting that the opening contest took place in Ohio. After all, it was the question of pro football's survival there that had brought about the APFA's necessity in the first place. Sensing increased interest from bigger markets such as Chicago and New York, Hay opened his doors in an act that was as motivated by self-preservation as any ambition of unifying the nation.

Whatever the motives behind clubs joining the league – most simply wanted a crack at Jim Thorpe and Hay's Canton Bulldogs, a well-known outfit who drew large crowds – a league it was. In name at least.

Despite these first steps, the pro-football landscape remained disjointed. There was nothing close to a set schedule, and teams were responsible for arranging their own games. As such, franchises' diaries featured a mix of match-ups between league members as well as against teams outside the structure. Even so, the 14 clubs within the system were competing for a silver trophy, showcased at the conclusion of Hay's second meeting, named the Brunswick-Balke Collender Cup, and the first blows were thrown on 26 September, although only one APFA member – the Rock Island Independents – actually played that day. Their opening foray was much like many of their rivals': an easy thumping of an overmatched team that allowed the players to settle into the campaign. Some might argue their 48–0 destruction of the St. Paul Ideals was, in fact, the first APFA/NFL game, a case given weight by meetings with non-league teams counting in that year's standings. But, officially, first-game honours go to the following week's battle at Triangle Park, a privilege it enjoys by virtue of an hour. There were two proper APFA games on 3 October: Dayton versus Columbus, and Rock Island against the Muncie Flyers. For all the former may lay claim to being the opening fixture, the latter almost certainly saw the league's first points scored.

While Dayton and Columbus were grinding through a scoreless first half, Rock Island – buoyed by their exploits the week before – began in more explosive fashion. A Muncie three-and-out* forced an immediate punt that tackle Ed Shaw exploded off the line to block, the ball bobbling into the arms of Arnie Wyman – who rumbled in for a touchdown from 35 yards. It may not have felt significant at the time, but Wyman had just scored, most likely, the first points in NFL history.

If not Wyman, the league's maiden score goes to Dayton's Lou Partlow, who broke the deadlock in the third quarter of a tense contest by living up to his nickname as the 'West Carrollton Battering Ram', powering over from seven yards. His touchdown was complemented by a Frank Bacon punt-return score as the Triangles ran out 14–0 victors, leaving the impressive audience convinced their tickets had been money well spent. Which is more than can be said for the 3,100 spectators at Illinois' Douglas Park, who saw a 45–0 drubbing for Rock Island against an out-of-their-depth Flyers team. In fact, the only place Muncie were flying, after a game in which they managed a paltry three first downs, was out of favour. So poor was their showing that Decatur manager George Halas cancelled the contest with his Staleys the following week. In two years, the Flyers would play just three games against APFA opposition. Although, in fairness, that's still three more than the Massillon Tigers.

The other squads to turn out on opening weekend fared better, each going on to play at least nine games. The best of the quartet were undoubtedly Dayton, who – by the campaign's mid-point – were one of only four unbeaten teams, alongside Halas' Staleys, the Buffalo All-Americans and Akron Pros.

Decatur's start seemed to have been written in the stars. Player-manager Halas was a former University of Illinois great who had spent the previous season as a member of the $20,000 Hammond Bobcats – a name bestowed upon a star-studded team because of the money spent putting it together. A 1919 spring-training member of the New York Yankees before hip issues ended hopes on the diamond, Halas was recruited by A.E. Staley to play for the company's baseball team. He parlayed this chance by starting a football club with immediate advantages over its competitors: by offering jobs with the starch works for the players as well as practices on the company's time and dime, he tabled a proposition few teams could match. Almost immediately, Halas boasted an enviable line-up, featuring future Hall-of-Fame centre George Trafton, ex-Illinois teammate Ed 'Dutch' Sternaman and, crucially, Canton's star end Guy Chamberlin.

'Crucially' because that move might explain how Halas so quickly found his upstart team in the APFA. His snaffling of Chamberlin wouldn't have escaped the attention of Canton's wily owner Hay, who recognised that bringing Halas into the league fold, with its aim of adding rules to lawless lands, might prevent a repeat.

Over the opening campaign, however, there was little Hay could do but watch as Chamberlin starred with Decatur, while his own team – despite boasting the all-conquering, pre-eminent athlete of his time – failed to scale previous heights.

Born in Oklahoma during the late nineteenth century, James Francis 'Jim' Thorpe lived a nomadic childhood, running away from home and returning at various junctures. He eventually settled where his legend would be crafted – Carlisle, Pennsylvania – at the age of 16, two years after his mother had passed away. Just months later, he was orphaned when father Hiram died from gangrene poisoning contracted while hunting.

Thorpe was an athlete built the old-fashioned way, from a Native American life spent undertaking hard labour in the Oklahoma wilderness. His early childhood honed the skills needed in that terrain – hunting, riding, trapping and fishing – alongside Hiram, a horse breeder and bootlegger, but Thorpe's sporting diversity provided a route to superstardom.

The scale of that athletic potential wasn't recognised until he returned to Carlisle Indian Industrial School in 1907, having worked on the farm following his dad's death. Legend suggests Thorpe gained attention by spotting pupils doing the high jump, joining in and immediately clearing a school-record 5ft 9in despite standing only 5ft 8in and wearing street clothes. Based on his subsequent achievements, it isn't farfetched.

The man to refine Thorpe's brilliance was equally renowned. Carlisle coach Glenn Scobey 'Pop' Warner was forging a career that led him to be an inaugural inductee into the College Football Hall of Fame and someone whose name is still synonymous with the youth football league he created: Pop Warner Little Scholars.

Thorpe, too, earned a place in the College Football Hall, as well as pro football's, as an original inductee. But his journey into the game was initially blocked because Warner, enamoured by Thorpe's track-and-field prowess, worried the rigours of football were too great a risk. As such, Thorpe's early 20s were spent focusing on athletics. The upshot? He earned gold medals in both the decathlon and pentathlon at the 1912 Stockholm Olympics, winning eight of 15 individual segments. His 1,500-metre time in the former wouldn't be matched until 1972. 'Sir, you are the greatest athlete in the world,' said Sweden's King Gustav V upon handing over Thorpe's second medal; he didn't know even the half of it. The unassuming Thorpe replied, 'Thanks King,' and set about leaving an indelible mark on other sporting disciplines.

Upon returning from Sweden, Thorpe headed back to Carlisle, scoring 25 touchdowns and 198 points in a season for the ages. He might also have been the first 2,000-yard single-season rusher in history; we know Thorpe produced 1,869 in 191 attempts, but two games from that 1912 campaign are unaccounted for. Ken Strong, of New York University in 1928, is the inaugural man to officially cross the barrier.

Not that Thorpe is short of accolades. He played Major League Baseball – reaching a World Series with the New York Giants – and lacrosse to a high level, while competing in hockey, handball, tennis and boxing. Thorpe even won a national ballroom-dancing contest. In 1950, the Associated Press (AP) named him the 'Greatest Athlete of the First Half of the Century'.

In football terms, Thorpe was brilliant. Future President Dwight D. Eisenhower, who played against him during that epic 1912 campaign, said in a 1961 speech: 'Here and there, there are some people who are supremely endowed. My memory goes back to Jim Thorpe. He never practiced in his life, and could do anything better than any other football player I ever saw.'

By 1920, the 33-year-old – whose multifaceted excellence on the football field was a microcosm of his wider athletic genius – had faded. He still had many strings to his bow, as a running back, defensive back, placekicker and punter, but mostly operated as coach–captain.

The team he oversaw bore few resemblances with the Canton squads that had captured Ohio League titles in 1916, '17 and '19 (they didn't play in '18). The ultimate confirmation of their decline came on Halloween, when the Bulldogs suffered their first defeat in three years at the hands of the league's original Cinderella Story.

To say Akron were more than the sum of their parts is quite the understatement. They were largely made up of journeymen from fragmented football associations with one exception: Fritz

6

Pollard. Pollard's impact on the NFL remains significant to this day through the Fritz Pollard Alliance, a group that promotes minority hires throughout the NFL and whose name owes to him being the league's first black coach in 1921. Yet before blazing that trail, Pollard had already left an indelible mark as the star player on Akron's energetic 1920 squad. Utilising what grandson Steven Towns described as 'the speed of Tony Dorsett, elusiveness of Barry Sanders, and tenacity of Walter Payton' when Pollard was inducted into the Hall of Fame, Pollard quickly became one of the APFA's most-feared 'backs.

For all his excellence, Akron's journey through the campaign owed more to an outstanding defensive unit's ability to shut out opponent after opponent. The landmark defeat inflicted upon Canton came via Karl 'Pike' Johnson's pick-six* on a tipped pass, setting the tone for an astonishing run through a murderer's row of opponents. By Thanksgiving, the day on which they effectively ended Hay and Thorpe's chances with a second victory over the Bulldogs, Akron were one of just two unbeaten teams, alongside Decatur.

With Akron sitting at nine wins, no losses and one tie (9-0-1) and Decatur at 10-0-1, only one other club stood a realistic chance of winning the opening championship: an All-Americans side whose 7-1 record was particularly impressive given most of their players turned out for Philadelphia-based The Unions on Saturday and in All-American colours on Sundays.

A key moment in the campaign came just after 'Turkey Day', when the Chicago Cardinals inflicted a monumental blow on the team who would eventually drive them out of the Windy City. The Cardinals were a middle-of-the-road outfit, despite boasting arguably the campaign's best player in triple-threat stud 'Paddy' Driscoll, a quarterback–halfback who was also considered the best kicker in football. So important was he to Cardinal fortunes that owner Chris O'Brien cancelled their Thanksgiving game rather than playing without Driscoll after his father died. He was back three days later, much to the chagrin of the Staleys, who were beaten 7–6 in a contest where the *Chicago Tribune* declared Driscoll 'the big star'.

The Staleys avenged the loss in a hastily arranged rematch, winning 10–0 before an impressive 11,000 people, but the damage was done and, suddenly, all competitors were jostling to set up more games in the hopes of securing enough wins to be crowned champions. Both Buffalo and Decatur agreed 'home' games against Akron – the Staleys' was at Chicago's Cubs Park, which later became their base – knowing victory would strengthen any claim on the crown.

The All-Americans were up first. Prior to kickoff, the teams executed the first-ever league trade when Akron sold Buffalo the rights to end 'Nasty' Nash's contract for $300 and five per cent of the gate. In an illustration of the title race's failure to capture the public's imagination, only 3,000 spectators showed up. Those who stayed away were proven right: the game ended 0–0.

When it came to the Staleys' chance against Akron – a contest which would surely determine the winner of the cup, with Buffalo now out of the picture – Halas had an ace up his sleeve. Taking advantage of league rules (or lack thereof), he and the Staleys arrived at Cubs Park with a new, albeit familiar, face: Driscoll, the Cardinals star, who was 'hired' for a one-off Staleys outing. However, neither that trick, nor a crowd which was some 12,000 strong, could penetrate the Pros' championship resolve. Just like the All-Americans before them, the Staleys were unable to break through in another scoreless tie that gave Pollard and his Pros a clear run at the title.

If those results sound too mind-blowing to be true – at the beginning of the 2020 campaign, the NFL's most recent scoreless game was in 1943 – it's worth considering how different this version of football was. The one-platoon era saw every player play both offense and defense, while the game itself was more like a version of rugby than what we know today – the ball was shaped as such and proved too big and rough to throw consistently. The forward pass had been legal for nearly 15 years, but there was little incentive to use something considered a gimmick by purists, and many reasons not to. All balls had to be thrown from at least five yards behind the line of scrimmage, incompletions into the end zone were ruled as turnovers and plays started where they last ended – if the ball was downed out of bounds, the action resumed just one yard in from the sideline. Such was the difficulty that only around a third of passes were complete, with roughly 20 per cent being intercepted.

Creative coaches found ways to move the ball, at least. Warner invented the single wing* at the turn of the century and had perfected it by the time Thorpe was hurtling at defenders for his Carlisle team. The coach implemented sweeps*, reverses* and, occasionally, forward passes to keep defenses off-balance – but there was only so much window dressing you could do against good teams. Quarterbacks were not as we now know them – in those days, they called signals and blocked for the other 'backs. As such, games were three-yards-and-a-cloud-of-dust wars of attrition, players running into walls of bodies, rising to their feet and doing it all over again.

All of which, combined with a league searching for its identity, meant a veteran group of grizzled defenders and one bona fide offensive superstar could stand above the pack. In all, the 1920 Akron Pros played 12 games, posted 11 shutouts and finished 9-0-3, giving up just seven points (in their 7–7 tie with a loaded Cleveland Tigers squad that flattered to deceive all year). The phrase 'defense wins championships' would be popularised much later but was most certainly true of the NFL's first victors. Even if it took a while for the Pros to be crowned.

Football followers might have justly wondered, as Akron's defensive masterpieces became increasingly distant memories, whether the Pros would ever enjoy recognition as league champions. The matter of crowning a victor and determining whether this whole venture would last beyond Year 1 was planned for January, yet didn't actually take place until 30 April 1921.

Not that those supposedly at the top of the APFA seemed too bothered. Neither president Thorpe nor vice-president Stan Cofall were in attendance as the APFA addressed its agenda, beginning with determining the 1920 champions. Surprisingly, there were plenty of teams who put forward a case: Buffalo claimed their tie with Akron should be enough for the prize, as did Decatur. In the end, the voice of reason was that of Columbus manager Joe Carr. He moved that the group award 'the world's Professional Football Championship to Akron Pros'. The motion was agreed, though this somehow got left out of the league's history books. The NFL subsequently claimed the inaugural campaign was undecided before finally correcting themselves a half-decade later.

That the league was still in operation by that stage was thanks, in no small part, to another decision made at Akron's Portage Hotel. With Thorpe having illustrated his ambivalence towards an ambassadorial role, it was time for the APFA to appoint a proper leader – and the man they settled upon was the same person who'd shown an assured hand in helping determine Akron as victors.

An unassuming, bespectacled son of an Irish shoemaker, Carr was a former machinist for the Pennsylvania Railroad who side-gigged as a reporter and got into team ownership when setting up a baseball club from his company's Panhandle division in the early 1900s, naming it the Famous Panhandle White Sox. Carr's team developed a reputation as one of baseball's best semi-pro outfits, but the orchestrator also had longing eyes for pro football and originally formed his team in 1904. He saved on expenses by fielding Panhandle employees, who could travel by rail for free, and only playing road games. Of the group, his most illustrious players were the Nesser family, six brothers who enjoyed legend-ary local status for their gridiron exploits. In 1921, Ted Nesser and his son Charles played in the same game, making the pair the only father–son combination to feature in an NFL line-up.

Those in the room likely didn't know what they were getting when Carr was elected, but it proved a masterful decision. The owners appointed a smart, intelligent and steely leader who immediately set about professionalising a discombobulated operation. 'He had what the rest of us lacked, and that was real business sense,' remarked Halas. 'All we were interested in was winning games. He was a born organiser. It was Joe who said our real concern should be the future of the sport.'

The move brought a bright ending to a bittersweet campaign for Carr. His Panhandles had continued their campaign in much the same way they started it, only beating out Muncie in the APFA rankings. Sandwiching that disappointment, though, were two moments that made league history. Having led his unfancied team into the first-ever APFA game, Carr was now tasked with shepherding an embryonic organisation operating firmly on the margins – of society and the balance sheet.

2

Red 77

CHICAGO BEARS 19
NEW YORK GIANTS 7

---

6 December 1925
The Polo Grounds, New York

They arrived in their droves, thousands upon thousands rumbling through the turnstiles of the Polo Grounds. Those not among the lucky 60,000 with tickets found another way, clambering over wooden fences surrounding the ballpark nestled at Eighth Avenue and West 155th street, all desperate for just a solitary glance at the man behind the myth.

Among the attendees was the 'Biggest Show in Town': Babe Ruth, the superstar outfielder and pitcher who had already helped the New York Yankees to four of the seven titles that created his enduring legend in this iconic town. But even Bambino couldn't steal the limelight because, on this day, he wasn't the star attraction.

'I'll have to sue that bum,' joked Babe. 'They're my photographers.' All lenses were focused not on the icon in the stands, but the one on the field, capturing the chiselled jaw, bulging biceps and golden smile of the red-haired thoroughbred resplendent in his mud-splatted Chicago Bears uniform. So, too, were the eyes of everyone occupying the bleachers, who waited with bated breath to see, in the flesh, the boy behind the stories.

They knew every single one: how Red marked his University of Illinois debut with 208 yards and three touchdowns; how Red, in his second year, took the opening kickoff against Michigan to the house* then ran in scores of 67, 56 and 44 yards inside the first 12 minutes; how Red became a three-time All-American with three touchdowns versus Penn.

All those tales paled in comparison to what they would witness on this day, when the 'Galloping Ghost', Harold Edward 'Red' Grange, brought his talents to New York City.

That the most-coveted free agent of a brave, new professional football league joined the Bears was unsurprising. In the venture's early years, there was one man, and one team, that stood above the rest. They may not have won everything on the field, but it was a different story in the stands and – for any franchise operating precariously, year to year, and counting on gate receipts to keep their heads above water – that was where it really mattered.

The man was George Halas and the team were, originally, the Decatur Staleys. Midway through the Staleys' second APFA campaign, Halas claimed financer A.E. Staley called him into his office and suggested, because of the recession and players spending more time playing rather than processing corn, he could no longer underwrite the team's costs. Staley advised Halas, by that point more invested in football than work, to move the franchise to Chicago, a bigger market capable of sufficiently supporting a sports team.

In making his offer, Staley gave Halas $5,000 start-up cash, asking only that the team retain the name 'Staleys' for the rest of the year, save advertising space for the company in their 50,000 game programmes and drum up local media interest that 'reflected credit on the company'.

Edward 'Dutch' Sternaman – who Halas asked to partner in

13

the venture but often left out of his later tales on account of their subsequent falling out – corroborated the story. However, one piece of evidence indicates it isn't quite as told: Halas was scheduling games in Chicago as early as August, when the deal was apparently formulated in October.

Whatever the reality, Staley's request was obliged and, on 16 October 1921, the team opened their season at Cubs Park, Halas having made an agreement with the baseball club's owner William Veeck. Everybody won: Staley's company profited from advertising in a bigger market while Halas relocated to a city befitting his ambitions, all without involving the league office.

The boon extended to the field too. Attendances were strong in comparison with other clubs – they had an average gate of 8,400 from 1921 to 1925 – as was their play. The latter hit its crescendo during that maiden campaign in the Windy City. The Bears – led by their brilliant duo of ends, Halas and Guy Chamberlin – rattled off two straight wins at Decatur's Staley Field, albeit one against non-league opposition, which, following the standings disputes of Year 1, no longer counted. It was the same story in Chicago, too, as the Rochester Jeffersons, Dayton Triangles, Detroit Tigers, Rock Island Independents and Cleveland Indians were all overmatched.

Their efforts set up a showdown, perceived to be for the league title, with a Buffalo All-Americans team that had endured a share of strife over the season. The game was up for All-Americans players continuing to represent the Unions on Saturday and Buffalo on Sunday. Their coach Frank McNeil, reacting badly to a tie he put down to fatigue against an Akron Pros squad failing to match the previous year's heroics, whistle-blew to the league office when he discovered the Canton Bulldogs had scheduled back-to-back games against the Unions and Buffalo the following week. Bulldogs owner Ralph Hay claimed not to know of the player share, even though his team had played both sides during the previous campaign.

It seemed like the move had backfired spectacularly when five of McNeil's stars opted only to play for Philadelphia, but the cunning coach had a plan. How he managed it is unknown but, by the time the next game came around, Buffalo's roster was replenished with a quintet of Detroit Tigers. The team from Motor City, minus their star players and mired in financial difficulty, folded after the year.

When the All-Americans reached Chicago on Thanksgiving, they did so with an excellent team ready to prevail 7–6 on the back of Tommy Hughitt's 40-yard touchdown pass to Waddy Kuehl, which, unlike Chicago's score on the opening drive, was successfully converted. The All-Americans, at least in their own mind, were APFA champions.

But there were still games to be played. Chicago bounced back with a shutout victory over some new team from a small town in Wisconsin that few gave any hope of surviving beyond one season: the Green Bay Packers were brushed aside 21–0. Buffalo, meanwhile, furnished their season with victories over Dayton and Akron.

And then they made their fatal mistake. McNeil, buoyed by the performances of his new team, decided to play another game in Chicago, on the basis it was an exhibition. Somewhere along the way, this information was lost on Halas. The Bears played as if their season depended upon it, edging out a Buffalo team that had travelled on an all-night train from Akron after their game the previous day.

The All-Americans, convinced their league crown had been in the bag since Thanksgiving, disbanded for the season and patted themselves on the back. With no end to the year enforced by the league, Halas continued scheduling games to ensure Chicago's record was better than Buffalo's. They beat Canton 10–0 and, a week later, took on their Chicago rivals, the Cardinals, in a game masquerading as a city championship that Halas hoped would give them one more win over Buffalo. Instead, it finished 0–0.

For all Halas' plan hadn't worked, he and the Staleys claimed the championship anyway. Much like its inaugural year, the APFA season ended with multiple teams arguing their title credentials. The decision, once again, would be made by the league.

The 1922 league meetings saw the APFA return to its spiritual home, Canton, with Hay's car dealership traded for a richer setting: the Courtland Hotel. Before those involved could get on with settling the trivial matter of the previous year's champion, they first had to answer another question: who owned the Chicago Staleys? Legally, despite Halas and Sternaman operating the Staleys in 1921 and assuming any losses, the team was still Staley's. He was finished with professional football – which meant that, when the team's registration fee wasn't paid, they would cease to exist.

Halas and Dutch were forced to reapply for the right to operate a Chicago team and encountered further complications in the form of a rival bid from none other than a trio of their own players! Chic Harley, 'Tarzan' Taylor and Gaylord Stinchcomb were Ohio State teammates who had joined forces for Halas' Staleys. Now they were pursuing a Chicago franchise, fronted by Harley's brother, a veteran promoter who had brokered Chic's Staleys deal. The contract stipulated Harley was paid based on a percentage of profits, which the brothers claimed amounted to an ownership stake.

It says much about league business in those days that the dispute was settled with Halas and Dutch in the room throughout. A call was made to Staley, and the subsequent vote brought an emphatic result: Halas and Dutch had their team. As for Harley, he unsuccessfully attempted to wrestle away a piece of the pie in court years later.

Halas and Dutch paid the league their $100 fee to register the new franchise and established it with a capital stock of $15,000. Now they just needed a team name. The pair contemplated Cubs – replicating baseball was common – but Halas famously stated that 'football players are bigger than baseball players so, if baseball players are cubs, then football players must be bears'. Thus the Chicago Bears – and Halas' own nickname, Papa Bear – were born.

Next came the matter of naming the 1921 champion. In Buffalo, it's known as the 'Staley Swindle'. The powers-that-be – which now, of course, included Halas – decided that not only did the second contest between Buffalo and Chicago count in the standings, but that they'd also initiate the commonly used tie-breaker rule that stated the most recent game carried more weight. Even though the Bears played every game at home, had an almost identical record (9-1-1 to Buffalo's 9-1-2) and lost the perceived championship game, Halas and his Staleys were victorious. In the annals of NFL history, 1921 is remembered as the Chicago Bears' first championship season.

If those events gave Halas delusions of grandeur about his standing, he was quickly cut down to size. It is true the league needed Halas, his Bears and the money that came with them, but that didn't stop other owners triumphing in the true battleground for this start-up enterprise: meetings. There, facing the collective might of his peers, Halas watched the passing of a new rule, stolen from baseball, known as the reserve clause. A wider-ranging franchise tag,* it meant that teams reserved the right to re-sign any member of the previous year's roster on a one-year deal with the same terms. This had the happy coincidence of scuppering Halas' latest plot – he'd agreed a deal with Cardinals star Paddy Driscoll. The player lost out, too, for the contract on the table included an ownership clause. He eventually joined the Bears in 1926, but only as a lowly player.

Worse was to come for Halas. Not content with preventing him from grabbing their players, the other owners set about stealing his by way of some sneaky semantics. The main beneficiary, by complete coincidence, was the league's original architect, Hay, who spent two frustrating years watching his brainchild come to life without ever enjoying the fruits of victory. He helped determine that because Halas' Staleys moved from Decatur to Chicago, and had been forced to reapply to start a new franchise, the original team officially ceased to exist. Thus the Bears were forced to operate from scratch, unable to enforce a reserve clause for their own players.

This left all members of the Staleys' championship-winning squad as free agents, and Hay was only too happy to offer open arms to Chamberlin, who rejoined Canton as player–coach, shepherding a rebuilt team formed around himself and fellow future Hall of Famers Wilbur 'Pete' Henry and Roy 'Link' Lyman, both two-way linemen. Henry was a portly tackle whose diminutive stature belied deceptive speed – he could run 100 metres in just over 11 seconds – and road-grading power as a blocker. The former came in useful on trick tackle-eligible plays* in which he caught passes. Henry doubled up as a star on defense and, if all else failed, was also a wonderfully effective punter and drop-kicker.*

Lyman may not have been quite so versatile but was a multi-faceted force. Arguably the first defensive-line technician in football, the Nebraska alumnus joined Canton in 1922 and is credited with pioneering shifts.* He also impressed on offense, but it was alongside Chamberlin where his best work was done; the duo wreaked havoc on offensive linemen.

Chamberlin was the jewel in the crown. An able blocker and pass-catcher on offense, those efforts paled in comparison to his work on defense. Perhaps his greatest influence on Canton, however, was in the locker room. As coach, he galvanised the Bulldogs and delivered on the vision Hay had foreseen when first summoning those Ohio teams to his office. Chamberlin stewarded Canton to a championship in 1922, continuing a personal streak that would reach five in six years.

Such success did not stop costs spiralling out of control and, after a 1923 campaign that brought Canton's second APFA crown and first without Hay at the helm (after losses persuaded him to sell), the team was purchased by local jeweller Samuel Deutsch, who moved the Bulldogs to Cleveland. Henry sought pastures new, but Chamberlin and Lyman remained in place, and the result was the same: the Bulldogs, while officially a different team, won their third successive championship in 1924 – albeit only after yet another dressing down in the league office for Halas.

Having seen his Bears lose their first meeting with Cleveland that year, Halas returned to the 1921 playbook and scheduled a rematch that his team won. The Bears, therefore, claimed victory on the basis that their 7 December match-up was, as it had been billed in the press, for the 'championship'. The situation created a challenge for the league office. The Bulldogs, despite their on-field success and move to Cleveland, were continuing to fail at the gates, while the Bears were undoubtedly the league's biggest commercial draw. As such, it would have been easy for Joe Carr to simply side with Chicago and disregard the rule passed prior to that campaign – ironically put forward by Halas – that the season began on 27 September and concluded at November's end. However, in an illustration of the fundamental fairness that exemplified his tenure, Carr opted against awarding the crown to the league's most lucrative franchise and honoured the initial directive.

Although the Bulldogs triumphed on that occasion, Chicago won in the long run. The club's stay in Cleveland lasted just one year, with a consortium of players – including Lyman and Henry – buying back the team and returning 'home' to Canton. Henry – having spent the intervening year winning another pro title, the Anthracite League, with the Pottsville Maroons – headed back to Ohio. The old band was not completely back together, though, as Chamberlin joined the Frankford Yellows Jackets, a Philadelphia-based club who joined the ranks in 1924.

Without their inspirational coach and end, Canton never rediscovered the winning formula. While Chamberlin was continuing an astonishing run of success with Frankford – after his injury derailed a promising first season, the Yellow Jackets went 14-1-2 to win the 1926 title – Canton followed a 4-4 year by going 1-9-3.

So precipitous was their slip that, when the league purged a whopping 10 teams after the 1927 season, Canton and fellow Founding Four members Akron and the Hammond Pros were among the teams to go. Just a few years after establishing themselves as the organisation's first truly great team, the Canton Bulldogs ceased to exist.

That cull signified a league growing in confidence. It had been a steady progression from that first meeting, when some willing lads, a pigskin and home field was enough to earn membership. Although many seasons were enmeshed in controversy and some teams went as quickly as they came (35 folded in the opening decade), the APFA was making progress.

Central to that was the man appointed president, as much because he bothered to attend the 1921 meetings as his credentials. Carr's first orders of business were creating a standardised player contract, introducing the reserve clause and putting together the constitution that nobody got around to in 1920. The latter would feature multiple rules developed over the course of several years: team colours were introduced; 15 per cent of players' salaries were withheld until the season's end to prevent them from turning out for independent, non-league squads; franchise entry fees were enforced; roster sizes were standardised at 16 per game; and, perhaps most pertinently, in 1922 the American Professional Football Association had the name bestowed upon it that still exists today: the National Football League.

Though the administration was strengthening, the league would live or die on its ability to attract teams that could capture the imaginations of spectators. On this front, it was intermittently successful: 1921 brought the Packers' introduction, and the Yellow Jackets – buoyed by an impressive 6-2-1 record versus NFL opposition the previous two seasons – joined three years later.

The Yellow Jackets epitomised Carr's vision, a big-market team who drew great crowds and became a destination for western franchises that could finally make money on their travels. Better yet, they succeeded on the field, recruiting Chamberlin in 1925 and winning a championship the following year. That feat was all the more impressive because the team often played back-to-back on Saturdays and Sundays; Pennsylvania's Blue Laws – in place for religious reasons – meant no games could take place in the area on Sundays, so they were usually at home on Saturday, then on the road the next day.

The next year brought an additional three esteemed eastern teams into the fold. The aforementioned Maroons and Providence Steam Roller were established outfits that moved into the expanding NFL, while the New York Giants were the brainchild of Carr – desperate for a presence in the Big Apple – and Tim Mara.

Of those clubs, it is the Giants everybody recognises today. They were founded by Mara, a self-made, notoriously honest man who'd risen from poverty to make his fortune as a bookmaker (at the time legal). The 38-year-old knew little about football but considered the tiny entry fee – now $500 – a small price to pay for any New York franchise. Given the Giants' worth today stands at around $3 billion, it proved a wise decision. Mara's Giants were something of a resurrection. The Brickley Giants played unsuccessfully in 1921 under the stewardship of Billy Gibson, who introduced Mara to Carr. The difference this time was in name: the New York Football Giants were born and captured the first of Big Blue's eight titles in their third NFL campaign in 1927.

The most established of the league's new trio at the time was a Providence squad that filled their bleachers and were the previous year's unofficial 'undisputed champion of the northeast'. Yet they had to wait a little longer to make their mark on the league, going 6-5-1 in 1925, 5-7-1 in '26 and 8-5-1 in '27, before triumphing at 8-1-2 the following campaign. They are the last now-defunct team to win an NFL Championship, as well as the hosts of the league's first night game, against the Cardinals on 6 November 1929.

For all their subsequent efforts, neither the Giants nor the Steam Roller could match the exploits of the third notable eastern team to enter the fray in 1925: Pottsville, whose maiden NFL campaign was a story in and of itself.

The Maroons played in a small stadium, Minersville Park, perfectly befitting a tiny mining town with a population of around 25,000. Admittance to the NFL wasn't so much about their own pedigree as it was proximity to Frankford and the Yellow Jackets. Teams, mostly situated in the Midwest, could schedule back-to-back games over a weekend, doubling their returns on a long trip. Yet the Maroons entered the NFL with an impressive track record, as evidenced by their Anthracite League title the previous year.

Nobody, though, expected much from the newcomers, especially when Henry and several other stars returned to more established franchises. But Dr Striegel, the club's owner and manager, built a strong, young team bonded by his insistence they live in the town during the campaign. This allowed the Maroons to practise each day, with the players still better off than most people living in Pottsville on the strength of their $100-per-game salary.

It proved the perfect formula as the Maroons upset the applecart by starting 6-1 before losing to local rivals Frankford. If most people thought their hopes died there, they were quickly proved wrong as Pottsville avenged that defeat with a 49–0 stomping of the Yellow Jackets, coming off a tough loss to Green Bay the previous day. That set up an unlikely showdown for the championship versus a Cardinals squad, led by the indomitable Driscoll, that were stepping out of their city rivals' shadow. Even the local press – perhaps at the encouragement of owner O'Brien, who desperately needed added gate receipts – billed it as a game for all the marbles.

On a snowy day, plucky Pottsville rode into Comiskey Park

and overcame the fancied Cardinals. In doing so, they sealed the NFL's 1925 championship. Except, if you look in any history book, that title belongs not to the Maroons but to the Cardinals.

The Maroons' downfall was heralded by Philadelphia promoter Frank Schumann, who arranged for the NFL's leading eastern team to play an all-star squad of former Notre Dame players in December at Shibe Park. Knowing the Fighting Irish were the biggest draw in football not named Red Grange, everybody signed up for a *guaranteed* money-spinner. Prevailing wisdom suggested that the 'leading eastern team' would be Frankford – only for Pottsville's victory in the second game to flip the script.

The story thereafter becomes complex and convoluted, changing depending on whose version you're reading. What we do know is that, one week after believing they had sealed the NFL title, the Maroons met a squad that included the famous Four Horsemen – Harry Stuhldreher, Jim Crowley, Don Miller and Elmer Layden – who had led Notre Dame to Rose Bowl and National Championship glory in 1924. They did so as planned at Shibe Park, which was located within the market of Frankford – who were playing the Cleveland Bulldogs nearby in a game that drew just 8,000 fans, half their usual attendance. This infuriated Frankford, so they complained to Carr that playing in the area on the same day as a Yellow Jackets outing circumvented league rules. Which it did.

This is where the story becomes murky. Pottsville's version is that Carr instructed the Cardinals to schedule two other games – cupcakes against Hammond and the Milwaukee Badgers – to furnish their record, while also stripping the Maroons of their championship, and that Dr Striegel only agreed to play the Notre Dame game after being given permission by the league's president.

Unfortunately, though it makes for a great conspiracy theory, it's revisionist. Newspaper articles from the time show Carr issued not one but three warnings that Pottsville would be expelled from the league – and therefore lose any claim upon the title – should they play the exhibition game. And so, on 12 December 1925, after Pottsville beat the Notre Dame All-Stars 9–7, they received a telegram advising of a $500 fine and the franchise's forfeiture.

Were the Maroons the best team in the NFL that year? The win against Notre Dame offers compelling evidence to counter the argument that most of their games were on Sundays against teams who'd played the previous day. What's certain is that, although Frankford's complaints owed much to sour grapes, the Maroons only had themselves to blame. The bitter irony was that the Notre Dame contest flopped and was played in front of just 8,000 fans – a number they could have fit into Pottsville's own stadium. Which would have removed the thorny issue of playing in another team's territory and changed the annals of NFL history.

Instead, the 1925 championship went to the Cardinals – not that they were overly excited. It wasn't even scant consolation to O'Brien, who had seen a grand plan of his own fall flat, just not the one Pottsville accused him of. It is true the owner hastily scheduled games towards the year's end, but that wasn't against NFL rules. By this point, most of the schedule was published prior to the campaign, but not all of it. In 1925, the final set of games were listed as being on 6 December, but the end of the season was given as 20 December, allowing teams in the hunt to organise further contests over the final fortnight.

Which is exactly what O'Brien did, only the gold at the end of the rainbow wasn't the league championship – it was Grange and the thousands of spectators who would turn up just to see him play.

'Football isn't a game to play for money,' said Bob Zuppke, Illinois' head coach.

'You get paid for coaching,' replied Grange. 'Why should it be wrong for me to get paid for playing?'

The immortal words that changed pro football for ever. By that stage, the Galloping Ghost's head had been turned by promoter C.C. Pyle, the man nicknamed 'Cash and Carry', having promised Grange untold fortunes. 'I would have been thought more of had I joined the Capone mob in Chicago rather than played professional football,' Grange later remarked, 'but I made a few bucks and had fun playing my favourite game.'

More than a few. Before his final down at Illinois, Grange's services upon the campaign's conclusion had been sold to every team under the snowy skies of America's Midwest and beyond. The Giants reportedly offered Pyle $40,000, but the wily 'agent' knew more could be made and, within hours of Grange's 192-yard college finale versus Ohio State, the pair were aboard a train bound for Chicago, Red donning a black wig to avoid chaos.

Such was the buzz that, days later, 3,000 fans stormed the field just to grab a closer look at Grange as he sat watching the Bears' thrashing of Green Bay from the bench. Later that week, he was in uniform, the star attraction for a Thanksgiving tilt with the Bears' city rival Cardinals at Wrigley Field. Red's pro debut should have been a win–win for everybody, yet O'Brien – battling spiralling losses – foolishly opted for the minimum guaranteed payment of $1,200 rather than taking a share of what turned out to be the 36,000-strong gate, 14,000 fewer than the number who braved snowstorms to try to get in.

Burnt by that experience, he hatched his plan. Knowing a return to the summit of the NFL standings would aid his case for a rematch with the Bears on the league's final date, O'Brien arranged the fixtures with Hammond and Milwaukee. His ploy was going along swimmingly until Grange injured his arm in Pittsburgh. The Cardinals owner didn't even bother to schedule an alternative game. It would just have cost him more money.

And so O'Brien was left with second prize: the 1925 NFL Championship – a 'prize' the Cardinals refused to accept, even if the league's and club's records now recognise their title. Because for all NFL football would come to be defined by champions, its early years were defined by money – or, more pertinently, making enough to survive.

Thanks to Grange, plenty did just that in 1925. Those Thanks-giving crowds in Chicago were a harbinger for the remainder of Red's barnstorming, 10-game, 18-day tour. Twenty-eight-thousand more turned out at the same venue on Sunday 29 November for a tilt with the Columbus Tigers, in which he ran for 140 yards and threw a touchdown pass. Wednesday brought 8,000 to St. Louis for a meeting with the Donnelly All-Stars in temperatures hover-ing at minus-11 Celsius, while Saturday saw the crowd hit 35,000 in Philadelphia, where Grange scored both touchdowns in a 14–0 win over Frankford.

By the following Sunday, tour day number 10 and a game against the Giants, fever pitch had hit. Red, perhaps sensing the enormity of the occasion, didn't disappoint, delivering a 35-yard pick-six to help the Bears to victory. A scarcely believable 73,651 packed a stadium whose capacity was 57,000, as well as – crucially – 125 reporters. In the process, the economy of 'Red Enterpris-es' saw a significant boost; he profited to the tune of a reported $90,000 from the tour – $1.2 million in today's money – for less than three weeks' work.

Yet perhaps the biggest economic impact, indirectly, was local. Giants owner Mara had been contemplating selling the team, his accounts being as red as Grange himself. But he didn't make the same mistake as the Cardinals by taking the minimum guarantee, and instead Big Blue saw losses of $35,000 quickly turn to profit on the back of a $143,000 gate.

Mara – whose descendants still own the team – unsurprisingly thought much the same as everybody else there that day: maybe, just maybe, there is something in this pro football lark.

3

A Stinkin' Circus

---

18 December 1932

Chicago Stadium, Chicago

'Stinker' feels a most apt description of the NFL's first playoff game, and not just because of a surface comprised of manure and dirt, whose stench was so bad at least one player vomited. 'It was stinking and dirty,' said Chicago Bears centre Charles Miller.

The *field* was certainly a key issue; in an era of playing conditions being far from ideal, those at Chicago Stadium represented the nadir. The Bears and Portsmouth Spartans were forced to settle the league's 13th campaign on a brown pit, which many claim was left behind by the circus that departed two days previous. In reality, the carnival didn't show up until two weeks after Chicago and Portsmouth did battle, although their game provided a suitable appetiser. Fans witnessed a blur of white Bear and purple Spartan jerseys, stumbling around to deliver something masquerading as football but bearing little resemblance to an actual contest.

The Windy City had lived up to its name, an Arctic blast rendering the outdoors inhospitable. The white stuff at Wrigley

27

Field, the original venue for this showpiece, lay waist deep and prompted the league to seek an alternative. Their choice was far from ideal. Chicago Stadium was the world's largest indoor sports arena, a suitable home to the National Hockey League's Blackhawks – but not football. It was 45 yards wide and 80 long – 60 yards separated the two goallines – with rounding corners creating half-moon end zones.

Its dimensions didn't mean a game was impossible, though. Bears owner George Halas had taken his team there for an exhibition against the Chicago Cardinals two years earlier, so it could be done. And if the game didn't happen that week, it probably wouldn't at all. Already hastily arranged, the encounter was never planned. But Portsmouth and Chicago tied atop the NFL's standings with a .857 winning percentage,* meaning the championship's destination needed to be settled as soon as possible. After all, the Spartans – a lowly team that faced such crippling losses they often practised in public areas like Central Park and bussed the long journey from Ohio – were already in town. At least most were. Portsmouth took the 'field' – if it could be called that – without All-Pro Earl 'Dutch' Clark, who – not expecting the campaign to go beyond its planned end – was contracted to begin a new job as Colorado College's basketball coach. They wouldn't release him; it was only a bloody football game.

Even that was a loose description. Football, but not as people knew it. The tiny field meant a host of for-one-game-only rules: kickoffs were from the 10-yard line, which is also where teams took possession following touchbacks; if either team passed midfield, they were pushed back 20 yards; there were no field goals; and, due to the narrow pitch being surrounded by a fence, teams brought the ball in 10 yards from the boundary if the previous play ended near the sidelines or out of bounds, at the cost of a down.

It made for quite the spectacle, taken in – remarkably given the conditions outside – by a near-capacity 11,198 crowd. With sure footing virtually impossible, big running plays were a pipe dream, while five completions to eight interceptions tells its own story of the passing game. Having been scoreless most of the way – threatening the league's first overtime – it was settled by a controversy that, along with the unusual backdrop, changed the face of football. In the moment, though, those in attendance were merely pleased to crown a new champion after the three previous campaigns were won by a team who became the NFL's first true dynasty.

Forecasts of demise surrounded the Green Bay Packers from the moment they joined the APFA in 1921. Up until that point, the team from a tiny industrial town on the banks of the Bay Lake were like many others: an independent entity finding games wherever they could locally. But the Packers, named due to their backers being a local meat-packing company, harboured ambitions that outweighed their humble surrounds. Green Bay opted to join the new league at probably the first opportunity; they, like most others, are unlikely to have known about Ralph Hay's meetings the previous year.

By their time of entry, the Packers were in the third year of operation, stewarded by a curly haired 22-year-old named Earl Lambeau, who briefly played for legendary college coach Knute Rockne's first Notre Dame team before dropping out and returning home. There, Lambeau worked for the Indian Packing Company, but a burning desire for football still existed. 'Curly' was an industrious type and started a club alongside *Green Bay Press-Gazette* sports editor George Whitney Calhoun, persuading his employers to pay for their uniforms.

The operation was running smoothly by the time Green Bay were rolled into the APFA. The Pack had accrued 10-1 and 9-1-1 records against local sides and were ready for the step up. Contrary to popular belief, and the NFL's own official statistics, Lambeau operated not as head coach but playing captain – which, in fairness, carried most of the key responsibilities in those days – for the first three years. William Ryan was the club's first coach in 1919, Jack Dalton in '20 and Joe Hoeffel in '21.

Many in the APFA doubted the franchise's sustainability. Had you told those who accepted the Packers' application in 1921 that Green Bay would be the most successful team in the league's opening century, it would have drawn more laughs than the idea of pro football one day trumping Major League Baseball in popularity. It's tough to know which notion would have been deemed more fanciful: the APFA lasting 100 years or the Packers winning 13 titles.

Neither seemed on the horizon immediately after Green Bay's debut campaign, in which the Packers played six APFA games for a 3-2-1 record while joining their contemporaries in the ongoing struggle for solvency. Although that mark was respectable, the season's end brought with it what so many predicted 12 months earlier: the Pack were sent packing. Only the reason wasn't quite as anticipated.

On the day end-of-season meetings began – 28 January 1922 – national headlines were dominated by football. Unsurprisingly, this had nothing to do with the APFA, which was still overshadowed by college football; surprisingly, it did involve the pros, at a level a couple of rungs below. The teams in question were outfits from rural Illinois towns whose bitter rivalry spiralled out of control. The folk of Carlinville were the instigators, having hatched a plan to recruit college boys for the annual clash with Taylorville. The players – from the era's powerhouse Notre Dame – provided such a guarantee of victory that it was worth the whole population betting everything they had on the outcome. Word spread like wildfire, which is probably what the locals felt like starting afterwards. For every granny dusting off notes plucked from under the mattress, there was a family man pleading with the bank for just another buck. In all, $50,000 was staked in Carlinville alone – $629,280 in today's money – according to the AP, although the overall amount wagered was rumoured to be double.

What the locals hadn't counted on was Taylorville's own residents catching wind of the ploy and recruiting some college boys of their own, from the University of Illinois. It set up a fascinating phenomenon, of a local derby taking place between players nobody in the stands knew. Per the AP: 'When the Carlinville 11 came on the field the visiting rooters rose to cheer. "What are we yelling for? That's the Taylorville team," said a Carlinville woman. "Oh no, that's Carlinville," replied a Taylorville policeman. "I guess I know our boys and not one of those fellows is from Carlinville," indignantly replied the woman.'

Carlinville lost 10–7, a result that brings into question whether they were duped twice, for it feels bizarre that a side laden with stars from Notre Dame's 10-1-0 group were beaten by counterparts from Illinois, who finished 3-4. Either way, they were undoubtedly the whole affair's biggest losers. Closely followed, it seemed, by that plucky pro club nearly 450 miles away in Wisconsin.

News of the scandal prompted the APFA's power brokers to take a look internally. Rumours abounded that its teams still fielded college players under false names, despite the practice having been outlawed as one of the league's founding principles. Accusing fingers were pointed, the first – ironically – at Hay. His Canton Bulldogs had, in fact, utilised a college star, Notre Dame's Heartley 'Hunk' Anderson, but – he argued – only in exhibition games. Those in the room accepted the explanation and moved on, perhaps due to his hosting the meeting.

But it was a different story when suspicious glances moved the modest Packers' way. The league's more powerful owners were like wolves around a carcass, happy to scapegoat an expendable squad in the name of some good PR. Green Bay fessed up without argument – they had fielded multiple Notre Dame players – and accepted banishment. In the pure world of the APFA, there was no place for such practices.

*

What is remarkable about scandals is how they seem the most important matter in the world at the time and then fade into footnotes just as quickly. That was certainly true of the one that robbed Green Bay of their APFA status. On 24 June 1922, owners and league officials reconvened, this time in Cleveland's Hollenden Hotel. It was a momentous day on two counts: the APFA became the NFL, and what would become its most successful franchise rose like a phoenix from still-warm ashes.

Lambeau fronted the bid to repurchase the franchise, which proved surprisingly acceptable to Joe Carr. The Packers had gone a whole five months out of the fold as punishment, during which time no APFA games had been played. In any case, this was a different team altogether: the Green Bay Blues. That everybody continued to call them the Packers wasn't the league's fault.

Whether this was the plan all along is unknown; all that's certain is everybody benefitted. The NFL was seen, at the peak of coverage, as fighters in the glorious battle to stop an underhand habit, while the Packers missed no game time. That their original owner, J. Emmett Clair, withdrew the team in January without fuss lends credence to a theory of something more calculated, as does the fact nobody investigated who was responsible for those Notre Dame lads representing Green Bay in the first place: the former Fighting Irish player in Lambeau, or Clair – who had no affiliation to the university.

Perhaps the biggest impact of their brief exile was the myths that surrounded it locally. It became a common yarn to suggest the instigator was Halas which, at the very least, helped further spice the clubs' burgeoning mutual disdain. Despite the meeting's official minutes showing Halas formally moved for Green Bay's banishment, the claim simply isn't true – but it doesn't take much for a story to become accepted fact.

Halas' early influence on Green Bay was actually incredibly positive. That 1921 campaign saw him extend the team an olive branch by agreeing to play what became the first instalment of their epic rivalry. Sure, he did it to furnish the Bears' own record in the midst of a title tilt, but the game also provided a key show-case for the Pack to illustrate their potential. It didn't go unnoticed that Green Bay pulled up in the city accompanied by a rough-and-ready band and 500 travelling fans, displaying pageantry that had long been a staple of high-school and college football, but not the pros. It suggested an ability to capture the local imagination. Yes, that locale was small, but merely having a fanbase was more than could be said for other clubs, many of whom operated in more favourable locations. That same community spirit rescued the Packers again a year later, when the crisis many originally anticipated actually hit.

With Indian Packing not involved in the reborn club, the Packers were suddenly run by a private company, Green Bay Football Club, with Lambeau as chairman. By Thanksgiving, financial turmoil hit, largely due to torrential rain meaning their 5 November game with the Columbus Panhandles was ruined. Fans started a fundraising drive for their holiday clash with the Duluth Kelleys, enlisting support from city officials and efforts were productive until calamity struck once more. Another day of biblical rain meant they contemplated cancelling the game, only for *Press-Gazette* owner Andrew Turnbull to persuade Lambeau to proceed on the promise he would help drum up support from local businesses to get the team on track for the following year.

A week later, more than 150 people attended a meeting called by Turnbull and, come 1923, the face of the Packers changed again. They became a community-supported public corporation, with 14 major shareholders helping to raise over $5,000. The structure exists to this day, albeit with considerably more shareholders (360,760), making Green Bay unique among all major American sports franchises. The practice is now outlawed in the NFL, and the Packers remain an exception.

In the moment, it gave Green Bay the muscle to punch above

their weight and this, more than any old wives' tales surrounding Halas, lit the fuse of theirs and the Bears' rivalry.

Come 1926, the Packers were progressing steadily year on year, going 3-2-1 in 1921, 4-3-3 in '22, 7-2-1 in '23, 7-4 in '24 and 8-5 in '25. Yet the subsequent campaign would be one in which the greatest importance was placed upon the NFL's collective spirit, as opposed to individual clubs' on-field exploits.

That situation was due to Red Grange, who had turned from enlightener to enemy following his dramatic arrival onto the pro-football scene. Unable to agree financial terms with Chicago after a second successful barnstorming tour alongside the Bears, this one hitting the two coasts either side of a trip to New Orleans, he and C.C. Pyle demanded their own team, based out of New York's Yankee Stadium, for which they held a five-year lease. But Giants owner Tim Mara owned exclusive rights to New York and disdained 'Cash and Carry' Pyle. His refusal, which wasn't necessarily supported by other owners keen to acquiesce to Pyle's demands, persuaded Grange to set up his own organisation.

What followed was a war that had more bark than bite, much like Grange's new American Football League. For all Grange and Pyle enjoyed some victories, such as luring Dutch Sternaman's brother Joey as owner, coach and player for their Chicago Bulls team and persuading the Rock Island Independents to jump ship, the AFL flopped. Five of nine teams folded by November, and the NFL – thanks to strong leadership from Carr, the newly named Duluth Eskimos' shrewd acquisition of Ernie Nevers (the biggest draw other than Grange) and, most importantly, experience – saw off the challenge in a year.

The episode left Carr with a problem. In battling Pyle and Grange's upstart, he allowed franchise numbers to swell to an unsustainable 22. With big-market teams like the Bears, Giants and Frankford Yellow Jackets losing money, fat would have to be trimmed and small clubs, such as the Packers, were in the spotlight. The resulting cull reduced franchise numbers to 12, including the AFL's New York Yankees – who were folded into the NFL under the ownership of Mara. He in turn rented the team to Pyle; the Giants supremo, it seemed, could accept two New York clubs if the money was going to him.

Among those also surviving, remarkably, were the Packers. Green Bay had a few factors in their favour: they could draw solid crowds versus big opponents, such as the Bears, had been competitive from day one and, perhaps most importantly, opponents and league officials liked visiting the town. The latter sounds implausible, but in the era of prohibition, trips to a place where the laws weren't stringently enforced were so welcome that many squads arrived early and left late. Interestingly, one of three meetings determining who would be expelled took place in Green Bay.

The Packers weren't just winning off the field. In Lambeau, they boasted a fine coach who was the first to implement daily practices and a pioneer, in pro football at least, when it came to expanding use of forward passes, often thrown by his own hand. Yet his ability throwing the football paled in comparison to pro football's first great passer.

Just as Green Bay were happy to break trends by throwing, so too were the Giants, and their chief thrower – former Michigan star Benny Friedman – was so good that Mara bought a full Detroit Wolverines franchise for $10,000 just to acquire his rights. Somehow, Friedman repaid the faith. In an era when some clubs went whole campaigns without a touchdown pass, he averaged one per game over a four-season run from 1927. The best year came in 1929 when Friedman delivered – albeit unofficially, given the league didn't start tracking statistics until 1932 – 1,500 passing yards and 20 touchdowns, a mark that wouldn't be beaten for a decade. Not exempt from one platoon, Friedman tripled up as a kicker and defensive back.

The only man making a greater impact than Friedman for his team was Nevers, now starring for a Cardinals squad under new ownership. The question was not what Nevers did, but what he didn't do. He ran, passed, kicked, played defense and called plays. At a time when the NFL was growing in strength, Nevers might have been its best player.

Its best team, though, were the Packers. Two factors were key to their run of success: Lambeau's tactical prowess and several new additions. Green Bay had a fine roster in 1928 but needed that little bit extra – and Lambeau recognised it. In the same offseason, he recruited Cal Hubbard, Mike Michalske and Johnny Blood, all of whom would be enshrined in the Hall of Fame. Hubbard essentially became football's first linebacker during a stint with the Giants but starred at end for Lambeau opposite Michalske. The latter was even better on offense, opening holes at guard for Blood, an electrifying runner and the best pass-catcher of his day.

Collectively, they joined forces with several other stars – from punter Verne Lewellen, who settled more plays with his boot than as a halfback or impressive defensive player, to superb two-way end LaVern 'Lavvie' Dilweg – to form the first truly dominant NFL team. The formula won three titles in a row – a feat the Packers have accomplished twice when no other club have even done so once.

Green Bay looked set to make it four on the spin in 1932, with Arnie Herber – a local boy returning home following a brief spell at Regis College – establishing himself as the league's new brilliant deep-ball passer following Friedman's retirement. But having already beaten their main rivals – the Spartans and Bears – the Packers lost in front of 30,000 fans at the Polo Ground to a Giants squad that was nowhere near as good as Friedman's ilk. Worse was to come.

Still a game ahead in the standings, knowing victory would secure another crown, Green Bay slumped to a 19–0 humiliation at the hands of Portsmouth – whose 11 starters played the whole game – then lost 9–0 amid a snowstorm at Wrigley Field to the Bears. The game was notable for two reasons: first, Halas famously couldn't pay the full $2,500 game guarantee and wrote Packers president Lee Joannes an IOU for $1,500 that was remunerated the next year; and second, it ended Green Bay's hopes of an unprecedented 'four-peat'.

Victory also justified Halas' pragmatism years earlier. Rumours of him and Sternaman being at loggerheads had circulated for some time – but it reached breaking point in 1929 when their disagreements on playing philosophy led to the worst Bears outfit ever fielded. Their lowest point saw Nevers accrue a record that will surely never be broken by accounting for every Cardinals point in their 40–6 win against the Bears to back up the claim that Chicago's other team really were a one-man show. A 4-9-2 record became the owners' come-to-Jesus moment; with no agreement on how they should coach, both relinquished the reins.

They brought in a familiar face. Ralph Jones had enjoyed a successful college career with Lake Forest, having previously coached Halas and Sternaman under Bob Zuppke at Illinois. He brought with him a T-formation offense* showing minor tweaks that laid the foundation for an offensive revolution down the line, and no shortage of confidence. Jones promised to deliver a championship within three years and, after guiding the Bears to 9-4-1 and 8-5 records in his first two, the bill was due in 1932.

Portsmouth, meanwhile, were diametric opposites to the Bears. Still a relatively new club, they operated out of a tiny market – the town of 42,000 made Green Bay look big. Their place in the NFL owed to geography, what with the NFL's revolving door leaving six clubs situated on the East Coast and four in the Midwest ahead of the 1930 campaign. The Spartans – an independent squad nestled nicely in the middle – were welcomed with open arms after tabling their application.

It might have been a different story had the established order realised how game they would be. After going 5-6-3 in Year 1, Portsmouth shocked the football world by being 11-3 the next year and were robbed of a chance to win it all by the continued farce of NFL scheduling. With their title seemingly in the bag, Green Bay had two final games planned: against Chicago and Portsmouth. But knowing back-to-back defeats would open the door to the latter having a claim on the championship, Lambeau decided the Pack would only face the Spartans if they beat the Bears. Green Bay didn't, and the second game never took place despite protests. There was some good that came from the episode: Carr formed a three-man committee to close that loophole – although setting the schedule would remain a fractious issue for years to come.

Portsmouth got their revenge on Green Bay 12 months later, though. They finished 6-1-4, while the Bears ended 6-1-6, meaning the clubs were equal on winning percentage and, crucially, ahead of the 10-3-1 Packers. Under modern rules, whereby a tie counts as a half win, Green Bay would have triumphed; at the time, winning percentage was the tiebreaker. There was only one thing left for it: Chicago and Portsmouth would settle matters on the field.

Halas recognised a problem early in the week. Unrelenting snow left Wrigley Field buried and meant the much-anticipated contest would be a financial disaster if an alternative wasn't found. By Friday, with the game just three days away, a decision was made: Chicago Stadium it was.

Whatever the conditions, it was time for the Bears' coach to make good on his promise. One of the revolutionaries of his era, Jones had not only turned Chicago around, but also set NFL coaching on a new course. He was the first man to put together game-specific plans that players were taught during the week and also implemented changes to the T-formation that became a foundation built upon by Halas and Clark Shaughnessy nearly 10 years later. By widening the splits of linemen and 'backs, while adding a man in motion, Jones reduced some of the compactness that made the T so easy to defend. The scheme also took advantage of his two star 'backs: Grange, having returned to Chicago after two campaigns with the now-defunct Yankees, and brilliant youngster Bronko Nagurski. No longer the Galloping Ghost of old due to a serious leg injury, Grange was nevertheless still effective, especially alongside Nagurski – who capped a brilliant campaign by powering through blizzards and Green Bay's brilliant defensive line to score the touchdown that set up the shotgun season finale.

The indoor game was settled by both of the Bears' stars. After intercepting Ace Gutowsky and returning the ball 10 yards, Dick Nesbitt was knocked out of bounds at the seven. The ball, due to the special regulations, was brought in 10 yards, costing the Bears a down and making it second-and-goal. Enter Nagurski, who gained six yards to leave Chicago on the brink of a score that would surely bring the club its second championship.

Stonewalled on his next try, losing one yard and setting up a tantalising fourth-and-goal from the two, Nagurski's number was called again. All the 'back could see was a haze of purple, the Spartans' defenders leaving not a glimmer of daylight between their impressive wall. Freestyling, Nagurski retreated ever so slightly, rose from his feet and threw a little pop pass that nestled into the hands of Grange. Infuriated Portsmouth coach George 'Potsy' Clark charged onto the playing area, urging referee Bobby Cahn to change his touchdown signal on the grounds Nagurski – to his eye – hadn't been the requisite five yards behind the line of scrimmage. 'He wasn't anywhere near five yards back,' said Spartans halfback Glenn Presnell, who replaced 'Dutch' Clark in the line-up. 'It was an illegal pass, but they counted it anyway.'

Protests fell on deaf ears. Halas and the Bears won their second title, one that was every bit as controversial as the first, and the NFL enjoyed its own measure of success. At a time when the Great Depression had contracted team numbers to eight, a record low, the $15,000 gate receipts were most welcome.

The impact of a championship game – which attracted increased media coverage and fan interest – saw the hierarchy implement a change first suggested a decade earlier. The NFL was split into eastern and western divisions, with the victors of each to meet in a similar contest at the end of every season. Lessons were learnt elsewhere, too: scoring was at a six-year low in 1932, an average of just 16.4 points per game, while 10 contests ended in ties with four scoreless. The on-field product, simply put, had to improve.

Taking heed from the finale, the NFL retained the rule of play beginning 10 yards from the sideline but removed the loss of a down – signalling the introduction of hash marks – and also abandoned passing only being allowed five yards behind the line of scrimmage to further open up the game. Finally, goalposts were put on the goalline, rather than at the back of the end zone, to encourage field-goal kicking (they weren't moved back until 1974). 'We think we have overcome the balance previously held by the defense,' said Carr. 'In fact, if we can give the offense a slight edge, it doubtless would improve the game for players and spectators.'

Within a year, the Bears beat the Giants 23–21 in the first official NFL Championship Game, featuring six lead changes, over 600 yards of offense and ending with Grange making a game-saving tackle that prevented Morris 'Red' Badgro lateralling to an open teammate. More importantly, their battle for the new Ed Thorp Memoiral Trophy – named after a noted rules expert and referee who boasted many friends among the league's ownership circle – it garnered national media attention and brought 25,000 fans to Wrigley Field.

By accident, the NFL had stumbled upon a better, vibrant new path, all thanks to what the *Portsmouth Times* succinctly described as a 'Sham Battle on Tom Thumb Gridiron'.

4

Makings of Monsters

NFL Championship Game

CHICAGO BEARS 73
WASHINGTON REDSKINS 0

---

8 December 1940

Griffith Stadium, Washington, D.C.

'The Bears are a bunch of cry-babies.'

In the days when attaining significant media coverage was still an ongoing battle for the NFL, bulletin-board material didn't really exist. At least until the Washington Redskins' controversial owner George Preston Marshall sent a genre-creating grenade the way of George Halas' Chicago Bears. 'They're frontrunners,' continued Marshall. 'They can't take defeat . . . The Bears are quitters.'

One thing Marshall couldn't be accused of was misreading the pulse of his city. The Bears' train rolled into town the day before gameday and, after a brief workout on the field at Griffith Stadium, Halas and players retreated to their hotel, nestled in the shadows of the White House. Each squad member was greeted by a copy of the sports pages in their room at the Mayflower with the incendiary headline: 'Gutless Bears Hit Capitol'.

It illustrated the confidence permeating D.C. The teams had met three weeks earlier, with Chicago living up to their status as a rough-and-ready outfit who operated firmly on the line of legality. One-hundred-and-ninety yards of penalties racked up by Halas' crew told its own story, but it was Papa Bear crying foul after the game.

Down 7–3 with seconds remaining, the Bears were on the opposing six-yard line facing one final chance to score. Sid Luckman, Chicago's second-year quarterback sensation, took the snap from under centre and threw for glory. Bill Osmanski homed in on the ball, only for his attempted catch to be thwarted by grappling from Washington rookie Bob Titchenal. The pigskin hit the fullback's chest and dropped to the ground, leaving Halas screaming interference.

Subsequent complaints from the Bears supremo prompted Marshall to call 'sour grapes' and sent Washington into hysteria. It took just three and a half hours for the return fixture to sell out, with 35,752 of the league's most ardent fanbase purchasing tickets amid expectation their Redskins would repeat the feat of three years previous, when they overcame Chicago 28–21 in the 1937 Championship Game.

The outside belief was, like the prior meeting, it would be a closely fought meeting of teams with contrasting styles. The game, in theory, was a battle between new and old, the Bears' outdated T-formation attack tackling the Redskins' in-vogue single-wing offense. It would pit the first man operating as what became a 'traditional' quarterback, Luckman, against Washington's running-back slinger Sammy Baugh, who piloted the NFL's best offense three years after announcing himself as a future star with his league-record 335-yard passing display in that previous title-game match-up.

Such a backdrop created palpable hostility. The atmosphere was intoxicatingly fervent ahead of kickoff, backing up pregame media hype of the 'bitterest championship game since the playoff began'. As his charges waited to leave the locker room, desperate to exact revenge, Halas pointed to press clippings adorning the wall. 'Gentlemen, this is what Mr Marshall thinks of you,' he said, voice shaking and eyes watering. 'I know you are the greatest football team in America. I know it and you know it. I want you to prove that to Mr Marshall, the Redskins and, above all, the nation.'

The Bears' players smashed down the door en route to the field, ready to meet the wall of vitriol from the stands, ready for the rowdiest atmosphere in pro-football history. And then, within 56 seconds of kickoff, the air lifted out of the stadium.

For Halas, realisation hit slightly earlier. 'We got 'em,' he screamed after the first play, George McAfee's seven-yard scramble that confirmed Washington were deploying the same 5-3-3 defense* they rode to victory on in the last meeting. For everyone else, including the outspoken Skins owner watching from the stands, it came on the next play, when Luckman retreated from under centre and handed the ball to Osmanski, running a sweep from right to left. The fullback crossed the left side of the line, following closely behind George Wilson, whose block sent Ed Justice and Charley Malone crashing into one another and to the ground. From there, it was daylight. Osmanski – the man Halas claimed had been unfairly felled in the end zone 21 days previous – raced in untouched.

Marshall's entry to the NFL, ironically, owed everything to Halas. The pair collaborated on a failed basketball venture, alongside league president Joe Carr, at the end of which Chicago's owner suggested Marshall get involved in their little pro-football operation.

Such an opportunity interested the laundry magnate – an avid, lifelong sports fan who routinely attended college games – and by the conclusion of his first trip to a pro game, he was hooked. 'In 1931, I went with a party of friends to a great Giants–Bears game in New York,' Marshall remembered, 'and afterwards Vincent Bendix and my other friends were clamouring for a franchise.'

The clamour among those who set up the Boston Braves – Marshall, Bendix, Jay O'Brien and Dorland Doyle – dissipated after a year, in which the team lost $46,000 and three of their four-man ownership group. The one who remained was Marshall, despite knowing the shaky foundations on which the NFL was built. 'The first year I was in the NFL, the loose coordination of the 22-team circuit was startling to anyone with business training. There was no balance of schedules; contracts were variable and leaky; the players were given few, if any, incentives. The few good teams played more exhibition games than league games. The teams were poorly uniformed, stayed in cheap hotels, carried their own equipment in duffle bags. Sometimes players got all the money promised to them.'

These were stark realisations for Marshall, a career entrepreneur who began making money selling rabbits as a child before amassing his fortune through a string of laundrettes in Washington, D.C., where his NFL franchise soon relocated. Boston, unlike nowadays, was a college football hotbed in the 1930s, as passionate for the amateur game as those in the southern lands Marshall hailed from are today. In Harvard, Yale and Brown, the city's residents had football powers on their doorsteps, and the pro game was unable to establish itself in the town. In 1937, just after losing the previous year's NFL Championship Game 21–6 to the Green Bay Packers, the Boston Redskins – as they were renamed in Marshall's first year of sole ownership – moved to the capital.

That the city immediately took to their new club was thanks to Marshall, who made the shrewd appointment of Ray Flaherty as head coach and accepted the future Hall of Famer's insistence he stay out of decisions. It yielded outstanding returns, Flaherty amassing a 54-21-3 record across six seasons, featuring league championships in 1937 and 1942.

Such results tied in beautifully with the owner's carefully managed PR machine – the first of its kind in football – that turned Baugh into the league's biggest star before he played a snap and made Redskins games 'events' beyond just the action. Washington became the first team to employ their own band, which took part in gala halftime shows that fostered a fanbase so rabid the Redskins took 10,000 travelling supporters to New York for a meeting with the Giants in their first year.

More significant than Marshall's imprint on the city were the indelible marks he left on the league, both good and bad. The good was being a leading voice in instigating the key rule changes that resulted from the 1932 indoor playoff. At Marshall's funeral in 1969, then-NFL commissioner Pete Rozelle said: 'Mr Marshall was an outspoken foe of the status quo when most were content with it. His fertile imagination and vision brought vital improvements to the structure and presentation of the game. Pro football today does in many ways reflect his personality. It has his imagination, style, zest, dedication, openness, brashness, strength and courage.'

Unfortunately, pro football also reflected the murky side of Marshall's personality, his arrival coinciding with the league segregating. Marshall was the unspoken rule's biggest champion, illustrated by his refusal to sign a black player until 1962, 16 years after the league reintegrated, and only following the intervention of the White House.

His voice was a significant one in an era when seven owners stood above the rest. There was the old guard – Halas, 'Curly' Lambeau and Tim Mara – joined by the new: Marshall, Charles Bidwill, Art Rooney and De Benneville 'Bert' Bell. Bidwill was a Chicago businessman who made his name as a lawyer before branching out into racetrack and printing-company ownership. He actually helped save the Bears in 1932, assuming a vice-president role in the team before purchasing the city rival Cardinals for $50,000.

Entering the NFL at the same time as Bidwill were Rooney and

Bell, with the pair taking advantage of Pennsylvania's religious Blue Laws finally being relaxed to introduce the Pittsburgh Pirates and Philadelphia Eagles (rebranded from the Frankford Yellow Jackets) respectively. Their joint entrance wasn't the only thing tying together pro football's odd couple, though. They originally met in the late 1920s at the racetrack, Bell the aristocrat playboy who spent his formative years enjoying trappings of the 'Roaring Twenties' and Rooney the son of a tavern owner who starred as a boxer and baseball player before becoming Pennsylvania's pre-eminent sports promoter. For all they appeared an improbable double act, the reality was very different. Bell, who encouraged people to call him Bert rather than De Benneville, was a man more at home in Saratoga and saloons than the surrounds in which he grew up. 'He was born with the silver spoon in his mouth,' reveals his son Upton, 'but people would say he talked like a dock-walloper.' Becoming involved in pro football was far from the path set out for him – so much so that he had to borrow the money from his movie-star wife Frances Upton rather than dip into the family coffers. But Bell had played in college and loved it dearly.

He completed a septet of men who fought like brothers but banded together like them too and led the NFL into a brighter future. It was a mix of dreamers and devotees, gamblers and goliaths, all unified by their deep-rooted love of pro football and willingness to innovate in the quest to ensure its survival. Of the many advances they oversaw, Bell's creation of a player-selection weekend – in 1936 – was easily the most significant, to such an extent that it eventually became arguably the crowning achievement of the league's opening century.

In 2017, the NFL Draft returned to its original location. The three-day bonanza drew a collective crowd greater than 200,000, all of whom gleefully filled the vast area around Philadelphia's Museum of Art, made famous by the iconic image of Rocky Balboa climbing its steps.

During the day, they enjoyed the NFL Experience, the league's travelling amusement park, taking pictures with the Vince Lombardi Trophy one moment and undertaking the challenges at Combine Corner – a homage to one of many sub-industries created by this event – the next. At night, their eyes, like those of the 30 million people watching on TV, were transfixed by the spectacular stage erected where Balboa completed his run, ready to boo and cheer as it was graced by a suited man reading out names.

That their everyday lives were impacted to make it happen was of little concern to locals. For downtown might as well have been NFL Town – even city hall was emblazoned with a banner. The league shut down whole streets for an entire month, during which time their spectacular amphitheatre was erected.

Full marks for marketing gimmickry. You can see the scene playing out, of some immaculately dressed executive dropping another idea grenade into the thought pool: 'Hey, why don't we have it on the Rocky Steps?' In normal organisations, they would have been laughed out of the room: an outdoor draft in Philadelphia . . . in April?

By this stage, however, the NFL had long since shed its lowly underdog status, having risen to the summit of the American sporting picture as a shimmering monument for the profit principle. And the draft, which represents the epicentre of their continued ability to maintain year-round interest in a five-month season, might well be its most audacious racket. Charles Davis, one of several NFL Network analysts employed to scout the event, says: 'It's just more presence for the league, and it keeps football out there all the time. We didn't used to talk football in the off-season; we talked baseball. Football has superseded that because it's a 24/7, 365-day-a-year operation.'

The league's network had more than 100 employees on-site in Philadelphia, documenting the fortunes of players whose tension was palpable as they strode the red carpet to the dreaded green room, their outward smiles belying internal turmoil. All of which

47

owed everything to the knowledge the next few nights were make or break, the culmination of 20 years' blood, sweat and tears.

They knew what could happen. For every person who'd gone earlier than expected in the selection weekend's history, there were others who endured the dreaded slip. Some, like safety Tony Jefferson, slid all the way from a prospective second-round selection to undrafted: 'I had loads of people around me, and it was just so embarrassing,' he admits. 'I still think about it every day.'

Just after 8 p.m., the waiting was over. Commissioner Roger Goodell stepped on stage and announced, simply: 'With the first pick of the 2017 NFL Draft, the Cleveland Browns select Myles Garrett, defensive end, Texas A&M.' After showing some highlights of his career, TV coverage panned to Arlington, Texas, where Garrett – surrounded by around 100 friends, family members and handlers – celebrated a dream coming true. 'It was such a blessing,' says Garrett. 'It was stressful waiting for that call, but I achieved one of my huge goals.'

The same could not be said for Jay Berwanger, whose selection as the first number-one pick was confirmed just over two miles from the stage on which Goodell stood, at Philadelphia's Ritz-Carlson hotel, 81 years previous. Holding that pick was the man whose brainchild the whole process was: Eagles owner Bell.

Berwanger – like almost everybody else – had no idea what the draft was or that it was even taking place. 'The first draft, nobody from the media was there,' says Upton Bell. 'It wasn't written about until two weeks later. But I remember my dad saying that the media interest would come.'

Berwanger also didn't have any desire to play pro football for the sums offered. When he couldn't come to terms with the 1935 Heisman Trophy winner, Bell traded the player's rights to the Bears – but even Halas was unable to agree a deal. Berwanger never played an NFL down and took a job with a rubber company. At least the Bears gleaned some returns from the rest of their class, including first- and ninth-round future Hall of Famers Joe

Stydahar and Dan Fortmann. Overall, 53 of 81 draftees never played, including all nine Eagles picks.

Yet the fact that the event took place was a victory for Bell, an illustration of a deft ability to unify the NFL's ownership base that later became his hallmark. Bell's call to implement the system could easily be considered selfish, what with Philadelphia having delivered records of 3-5-1, 4-7 and 2-9 in their first three years. The idea – a nine-round selection process in which picks were awarded in reverse order to the standings – would positively influence his Eagles while negatively impacting teams that were financially better off.

Bell's ability to persuade his contemporaries could best be explained by the analogy which informed many of his decisions over an outstanding administrative career. 'The league is like a chain,' he told the owners. 'It's no stronger than its weakest link.' Those in the room, including power brokers from the quartet of clubs he subsequently focused on, were listening. 'Every year, the rich get richer,' he continued, 'and the poor get poorer. Four teams control the championship. Because they are successful, they keep attracting the best college players in the open market, which makes them more successful.'

The Eagles, despite operating in a big city, were losing money each year, while the league-title race was becoming predictable. In the first 10 NFL Championship Games, 19 of 20 places were taken up by the Packers, Bears, Giants and Redskins, with the sole exception seeing the Detroit Lions – a team spawned from the Portsmouth Spartans in 1934 – winning the 1935 crown by overcoming Big Blue 26–7.

It was to the eternal credit of Halas, Lambeau, Marshall and Mara that they agreed and, while parity was not immediately forthcoming, the draft is one of two revolutions that ensure it exists today. 'If he hadn't founded the draft, we wouldn't be talking today,' says Upton Bell. 'Pro football was going out of business. It wouldn't exist without the draft.'

What those in the room could never have foreseen – perhaps with the exception of Bell – was its development from an unknown entity taking place in snug hotel conference rooms to what is arguably America's second-biggest sporting occasion. The draft's development is a microcosm of the league itself: a behemoth rising from the humblest of beginnings. The only resemblance between that opening selection process and those today is that it remains such a maddeningly inexact science. Although, in those days, that was a little more understandable. 'My first draft with the Cowboys was in 1960,' says lengendary former scout Gil Brandt. 'We drafted straight after the NFL Championship Game, in a parlour at Philadelphia's Warwick Hotel. There were tables set up, and we were so close that you could almost touch each other.

'People would come in with rolls of quarters because we didn't have credit-card calling in those days. A guy would go over and call, for example, Pappy Lewis at West Virginia, and an operator would say: "That's $3.75." He'd drop in that many quarters: clang, clang, clang. "Hey, Pappy, we've gotta draft a tackle. Who's the best guy you played against?" Or: "Who is the best guy on your team?" People came in with a Street & Smith's football magazine to find names to draft. There was no preparation or anything at all. We didn't go see prospects so didn't know their measurements.'

Nowadays, teams employ dozens of people year-round specifically to scout the draft, all of whose livelihoods depend on projecting college players' ability to play and handle the trappings of professional football. And they are not the only ones analysing it – so too are devoted employees of every major media operation. 'In 1960, we had six writers,' adds Brandt. 'Now, there are over 2,500.'

And an array of armchair analysts from home. Davis adds: 'Any time somebody on a platform like mine opens their mouth, somebody at home tells them: "You don't know what you're talking about. I know more." In the past, we could just say: "I've watched the All-22 tape," but now they have as well. The interest and knowledge is incredible.'

Opportunities to scout talent are plentiful. The NFL Combine, where the best of each year's class convene in Indianapolis to be put through athletic testing and interviews with teams, began in 1982 and now attracts millions of viewers on NFL Network and ABC. Moreover, the Pro Day circuit – in which prospects showcase their athleticism on their college campus – is unrecognisable from years past. 'There are over 300 pro days now,' says Brandt. 'Places like Shepherd University, South Dakota State and Montana State have them.'

Yet there are still countless stories like that of Jefferson, who overcame his draft status to sit among the highest-paid safeties in the NFL, while fellow defensive back Dee Milliner – the ninth pick of that class – found himself out of football after three years. It's an intoxicating mix that brings millions of viewers to an event originally operated with no fanfare. 'It's the biggest event, attendance-wise, in NFL history,' enthuses Upton Bell. 'My dad would have liked that.'

'It's become like a city of hope,' says Brandt. 'Everybody in the world dreams of their team getting better because of the draft, and it's now the second most talked-about part of football. And it's year-round. It's gone from being like a one-storey motel in Montana to the 97-storey Sirius building that's still growing.'

That it has risen to such a remarkable point of intrigue – where attention dwarfs that enjoyed by other major sports' actual games – is rooted in the explosion of interest in football itself. Its inception coincided with an era in which the on-field action was becoming unrecognisable from what preceded it.

League-wide parity might not have immediately resulted from Bell's idea, but there was a semblance of it among the NFL's best teams, who entertained the masses with a brave, new brand of play.

Though they failed to repeat the dominant run that so spectacularly captured the imagination at the turn of the decade, the Packers were chief among those changing the face of football. Not least because they secured a once-in-a-lifetime player in 1935.

It took just one play of his first start for Don Hutson to announce himself. The consensus All-American from Alabama's 1934 National Championship team lined up at split end on the left side opposite Beattie Feathers, who, like his Bears teammates, was focused on stopping Green Bay's star halfback Johnny Blood. Only what he, and the rest of Chicago's defense, didn't realise was that a different, better player was about to emerge in front of their eyes. As Arnie Herber faked a hand-off, Hutson languidly moved off the line, stopping briefly and turning to the passer. Feathers, fatally, did likewise and, utilising the quickness of foot honed during a childhood spent catching snakes in the boy scouts, Hutson was gone for an 83-yard touchdown.

For Lambeau, it was an immediate validation of his decision to pursue the player so vigorously after college. 'I started before they had a draft,' remembered Hutson. 'After Alabama, I had letters from maybe 10 pro clubs. I ended up signing for Green Bay because the Packers offered me the most money – $300 per game. That was far and above what they ever paid a player. Each week they'd give me a cheque for $150 from one bank and $150 from another so nobody knew.'

In Hutson, Lambeau saw the final piece of a passing attack he utilised when others considered throwing to be a dastardly act. Combining with Herber, who belied his sideways grip to star, and later Cecil Isbell, Hutson went on a scarcely believable, decade-long reign of terror, leading the league in receptions eight times, yards seven, receiving touchdowns nine and scoring five. He was voted All-Pro on eight occasions, MVP twice and ended up being a charter member of the College and Pro Football Halls of Fame. Asked how to stop Hutson, Giants head coach Steve Owen once replied: 'A double-barrelled shotgun.'

Hutson, also an effective punter and safety who once led the league in interceptions, starred in the title-winning teams of 1936, '39 and '44. Having beaten Washington for the first of those titles, Green Bay overcame the Giants, 27–0 and 14–7 respectively, for the others. The most impressive team was probably the '39 group, with the Pack fielding both Herber and Isbell, two of the finest passers in early football history. But more significant than Hutson's influence on the Pack was how he revolutionised NFL pass-catching. The receiver – who ended his career with 18 league records, including receptions, yards and touchdowns – is credited with inventing passing routes.*

As Hutson set about for ever changing the face of his position, so too did Washington signal-caller Baugh. Signed ostensibly to create a splash in D.C. after the Redskins' move, he was lured away from a fledgling baseball career by Marshall's offer of a contract rumoured to have been worth anything from $5,000 to $15,000. Whatever the number, it proved a worthwhile investment.

Baugh paired beautifully with Flaherty. The man on the side-lines provided no shortage of innovation – inventing the screen pass* in Baugh's rookie year – while his passer delivered the ball with unerring accuracy. During one exchange, Flaherty was diagramming a play on the chalkboard and told his charge: 'When the receiver gets to this point, you hit him in the eye.' Baugh replied: 'Which one?'

Baugh didn't shrink from backing up his words. A star from the moment he was selected with the sixth pick in the opening NFL Draft, he followed up his rookie-campaign title with another in 1942 and enjoyed a thrilling 16-year career as a passer and punter (his average mark in the latter, of 45.1 yards, is still second all-time). Of his passing stats, Baugh completing a ridiculous 70.3 per cent of throws in 1945 stands out; the mark wasn't broken until Ken Anderson's 70.6 per cent in 1982, still sat tied ninth all-time entering the 2020 campaign and, most remarkably, was way ahead of second-placed Luckman's 53.9 per cent that campaign.

Although Baugh secured victory over the Chicago passer on that score, it was a different story in the 1940 Championship Game due to the era's other significant innovator rebooting an archaic scheme.

'Not since the British sacked this city more than a 100 years ago has Washington seen such a rout,' summarised the *Chicago Tribune*'s Wilfrid Smith.

The origins of the Bears' remarkable beatdown can be traced back to 1935 when Halas, in sole ownership of the team having bought out Dutch Sternaman and back at the helm as head coach, first met then-University of Chicago head coach Clark Shaughnessy at a civic dinner. The union seemed like happenstance, but in actuality the men rearranged the place cards to make it happen, and their partnership would serve to revitalise the T-formation.

Halas' relationship with the scheme dated back to his days in the great Bob Zuppke's 1914 University of Illinois team, but its place in the modern game – even after tweaks from Ralph Jones – was under threat. 'When George Halas didn't laugh at me or my theories,' said Shaughnessy, 'I naturally warmed up to him.'

So willing that Halas paid football's original mad scientist $2,000 for a consultancy role in 1937, with the promise he would expound upon his ideas of implementing a T-formation with 'hidden-ball stuff, but power'. It was win–win. Shaughnessy, who didn't boast the quality of player to implement the schemes in his main job, gained a testing ground, and Halas could reinvent the only offensive system he knew. 'Before we began collaborating,' said Halas, 'our T-formation had two major weaknesses. We had only two end runs . . . Thanks to Shaughnessy we had 22. Second, the majority of our plays went to the side of the line of the man in motion. Shaughnessy designed ground gainers that ran to the side opposite. Those counter plays were honeys.'

In Shaughnessy's T, the quarterback's responsibility was passing and directing the offense, while two of the three 'backs were

54

primary ball-carriers and the other a pass-catcher. Key, though, was the passer, and Luckman, whom Shaughnessy scouted with Halas prior to his selection with the second pick of the 1939 draft, proved perfect.

The innovations were in the details. Linemen who always operated in the power game, taking on one man until the play was dead, began brush blocking, instigating initial contact with the defensive player to create a hole before moving on to the second level, while the other 'backs were no longer asked to lead block. Commonplace now, but alien at the time. When first told, Luckman said to Halas: 'You're nuts. How can you send a halfback into the line alone, without a 'back to block for him?'

They could do so due to the scheme's key facet: deception. 'It's a breakaway from the old power game,' wrote Shaughnessy in 1942:

> Concealment of the ball by the quarterback turning around instantly sets the stage for a finesse, deceptive-speed type of attack. The direct pass to the 'back of the other systems reveals where the ball is. This type of play literally opens up the play, just as the swiftness of the airplane and light tanks has opened up the threat of attack in a war. Our quick, shifty, speedy men with their fast getaway and quick turns and side thrusts can threaten the defensive line from sideline to sideline constantly, thus opening up a wider territory for attack. We threaten continuously the entire width of the field.

By the 1940 NFL Championship Game, everything was in place. Ten Bears combined to score 11 touchdowns, delivering a victory margin that still stands as the largest in league history. The *Tribune* continued:

> From the moment Bill Osmanski broke away for sixty-eight yards and a touchdown on the third play of the game, until

little Harry Clarke popped through a hole as wide as a bleacher exit for his second and the Bears' last touchdown late in the fourth period, there was no question in the minds of the 36,034 jammed into Griffith Stadium that the colossus from the west, this day at least, was a super team.

Team is the operative word, because just crediting the offense is disingenuous given Chicago also collected eight interceptions, returning three to the house. It was a perfect storm of an incredibly talented squad with a schematic edge putting their opponents in a position they weren't equipped to handle. The T created Chicago's lead and Washington's own system wasn't built to play from behind.

The day shepherded in a new/old era of offensive football. Most thought the T-formation should be left behind with the Great Depression, but Shaughnessy changed the landscape, with further validation coming weeks after the Bears' triumph when, in his new role as Stanford's leading man, the coach completed an unbeaten National Championship campaign with a team who had won just one game the previous year.

Shaughnessy's enduring impact on the pros was in the creation of the modern quarterback. By 1945, even Slingin' Sammy was operating in the T, starring in the position's first real period of prosperity. A game that was more open and entertaining also created similar yields off the field. Events at Griffith Stadium were transmitted around the United States in the first nationwide radio broadcast of an NFL Championship Game and delivered record playoff gate receipts of $112,508, one year after the NFL hit 1 million fans viewing games in a single campaign and broadcast its first TV contest.

While the commercial success could be considered a positive by-product of Marshall's jabs at Halas and his Bears, which undoubtedly added interest, the on-field humiliation was undoubtedly a negative. Certainly, his crestfallen players were striking a very different tone. When Baugh, having been reduced to a footnote whose most notable contributions came as Washington's punter, was asked whether it might have been different if Malone didn't shell one of his passes in the end zone at 7–0, he replied matter-of-factly: 'Yep, it would have been 73–7.'

For he knew what Marshall had completely failed to anticipate when uttering his now-infamous words: the 1940 Chicago Bears – with Luckman, halfback McAfee and linemen Bulldog Turner, Stydahar, Dan Fortmann and George Musso – were peerless.

Victory set in motion a run that saw Chicago defend their title the following year, a 10-1 record preceding their 37–9 Championship Game hammering of the Giants, and a three-peat looked on the cards when the Bears went through the next regular season unbeaten. Chicago reaching that point was remarkable considering they did so without Halas coaching after the opening five games, the owner having joined many of his players – including McAfee and Stydahar – by joining the Second World War effort. Without his and many star players' presence, Chicago lost a tight Championship Game 14–6 to Washington. They avenged that the following year, however, by winning the 1943 campaign's finale 41–21, having lured Bronko Nagurski out of retirement due to their depleted numbers. One final championship for the group came in 1946, the Bears overcoming the Giants 24–14, but even four in seven years wasn't wholly satisfying. When asked by McAfee how many titles that Bears team might have won had the war not intervened, Halas simply sighed.

Despite what might have been, though, the group's place as not only the masterpiece of their tireless owner and eternal cheerleader, but also one of the greatest teams in NFL history is unquestioned. This fact is summed up by the iconic nickname bestowed upon them, one taken from the nearby University of Illinois's famous squads. Halas' boys of the 1940s were, and always will be, the Bears' original 'Monsters of the Midway'.

5

Brown's Browns

Week 1

CLEVELAND BROWNS 35
PHILADELPHIA EAGLES 10

---

16 September 1950

Philadelphia Municipal Stadium, Philadelphia

A buzz descended from the 71,237 in the stands of Philadelphia's Municipal Stadium before kickoff, that unmistakable hushed murmur which precedes only the most anticipated sporting contests. This would be a doozy, the game to settle barstool debates four years in the arguing, pro football's equivalent of the Rocky Marciano–Joe Louis fight that took place just over a year later.

For Greasy Neale, Philadelphia's revered coach coming off leading the Eagles to back-to-back NFL titles, the surroundings were familiar. He stood on the sidelines in the accustomed garments, sporting his lucky chequered suit and straw hat, ready for the Eagles to back up his pregame confidence. 'Mine is the best team ever put together,' he had said. 'Who is there to beat us?'

The words weren't anything new. Throughout the Cleveland Browns' four-year domination of the All-America Football Conference (AAFC), the first relatively successful league to rival the NFL since its inception in 1920, doubters had been vocal. Their quartet of titles, including an unbeaten campaign in 1948, were discredited because, in the words of the older organisation's chief trash-talker George Preston Marshall: 'The worst team in our league could beat the best in theirs.'

Through it all, as their achievements were downplayed, Cleveland coach Paul Brown stayed publicly silent. 'Coach Brown should've been a general,' said Otto Graham, the Browns' brilliant quarterback. 'For four years, he never said a word, just kept putting that stuff on the bulletin board.'

But now, with a merger (of sorts) between new and old league agreed, the time for talking was almost over. In the Cleveland locker room, sage words came from an unlikely source. 'I've seen what you can do,' Bert Bell, the indefatigable NFL commissioner responsible for scheduling this mouth-watering Week 1 match-up, told the Browns. 'Show them they can be beaten.' Afterwards, it was Brown's turn. There were no grand gestures, just the simplified truth, delivered in the coach's signature all-business manner: 'Remember, the worst thing one can do to an opponent is defeat him. Nothing hurts as bad as losing.'

In reality, no words were needed. 'We were so fired up,' admitted Graham. 'We would've played them anywhere, anytime – for a keg of beer or a chocolate milkshake. It didn't matter.' The game, of course, meant a whole lot more than beer or milkshake, for the legacy of the Browns – and, indeed, their original league's existence – was on the line.

The NFL thought it had seen off its biggest challenge by 1945. American involvement in the Second World War became inevitable two weeks before the Chicago Bears' Monsters of the Midway captured their second successive NFL crown with victory over the New York Giants in front of just 13,341 spectators. Japan's bombing of Pearl Harbor altered society for ever, and pro football – unlike baseball – wasn't exempt.

While President Franklin D. Roosevelt decreed action on the diamond should continue, he didn't give the NFL a second thought. Within 12 months, 20 years' hard-earned growth was threatening to unravel. Nearly a third of the league's players were called up, while average attendances dipped from more than 20,000 in 1941 to a little over 16,000 in '42. The 1943 campaign was similarly taxing: the Cleveland Rams didn't play on account of their owners being in service, only seven people reported to the Brooklyn Dodgers' training camp and the Bears were forced to lure Bronko Nagurski out of a six-year retirement.

The latter speaks to the resourcefulness and comradeship that wartime brings out in everybody, and that was certainly true of pro football. The same year, the Philadelphia Eagles and Pittsburgh Steelers merged to create the 'Steagles'. Pittsburgh repeated the trick with the Chicago Cardinals the next season, forming 'Card-Pitt' (which became 'Carpets' when they went 0-10), while the Boston Yanks and Brooklyn were 'Yanks' in '45. Even then, the Steagles – amid simmering hostility between Neale and Pittsburgh counterpart Walt Kiesling – only opted to carry 25 players of the available 28 due to the absence of quality available. Such was the struggle that when tackle Al Wistert limped to the sidelines complaining of a suspected broken leg, Neale replied: 'Well, get back out there and find out for sure.'

Players accepted less trappings around gameday, travelling on public transport and shunning hotels, while the NFL reduced rosters and schedules. Similarly, the introduction of substitutions – implemented due to contracted numbers – would unexpectedly set a new course, for it spelled the beginning of the end for one-platoon football's 'Iron Men'. In all, more than 1,000 players, coaches and owners served during the war, with 22 current and former NFL men passing away.

For all the strife endured, though, the league emerged from the conflict stronger. It not only continued uninterrupted but thrived to such an extent that attendances rebounded to hit all-time highs in 1943 (1,115,154) and 1944 (1,234,750). That it did so amid an internal leadership void following Joe Carr's death in May 1939 was thanks to the NFL's close-knit ownership conclave.

Unfortunately, this same close-knit group gave rise to another conflict; one that, from the outset, it wasn't clear the NFL would weather. For it was the same togetherness that allowed choppy wartime waters to be navigated that sparked the creation of the AAFC. The NFL's main power brokers banding like brothers also led to an old-boys'-club mentality and reticence to both outsiders and change.

All of which came to a head when debonair Hollywood star Don Ameche was introduced to the group by influential *Chicago Tribune* sports editor Arch Ward, the man responsible for Major League Baseball and college football's All-Star games, as well as the Golden Gloves amateur boxing tournament. Ameche's intention was to create a Los Angeles club that would play in Buffalo during the war then move west afterwards. In Ward, who the owners previously tried to appoint as its president, he enjoyed an influential champion. But the NFL's heavy hitters balked at the idea of introducing a West Coast club, seemingly due to the prospect of greater travel costs, and short-sightedly refused Ameche's advances. 'We owners were a tight little group,' admitted Halas. 'We had gone through a lot together and liked things the way they were. Looking back, I can see how our closed door was certain sooner or later to produce trouble.'

A furious Ward was not about to let sleeping dogs lie. With an array of other prospective owners spurned at the NFL altar over the years, the industrious editor gathered some at a St. Louis hotel, and the AAFC was formed within a month.

While not the first competition the NFL had faced – the brief Red Grange Wars of 1926 were followed by two other reboots of the American Football League – it was easily the most serious. As if the names involved, most of whom boasted wealth dwarfing the NFL's owners, weren't jarring enough, the AAFC quickly captured attention by appointing an Ohio legend as coach of its Cleveland team.

Hiring Brown seemed a masterstroke for deep-pocketed owner Arthur McBride. It took a perfect storm of factors to do it: the coach, amid a wartime stint at Great Lakes Navy in which he went 15-5-2 and signed off with a 39–7 victory over Notre Dame, received a lukewarm reception from Ohio State regarding an anticipated return to his actual job. 'I needed more than that,' he admitted. 'I needed to be pampered a bit. Someone had to say: "Gee, we'll really be looking forward to getting you back." No one said that, and it only added to my hurt feelings.' As such, an incredible offer from McBride – $25,000 salary, five per cent ownership stake and $1,500 monthly wartime stipend – was too good to refuse.

Brown had never been a proponent of the pro game, having fallen into coaching accidentally at Maryland's Severn Prep. An English teacher who agreed to help out, he took the reins because the head coach fell ill and went 16-1-1, before returning home and turning Massillon into Ohio's high-school powerhouse across nine seasons. A remarkable 80-8-2 record was somehow less impressive than Brown unifying the community behind his Tigers. Their 10 games in his final season, which brought a sixth successive state title, were attended by more than 180,000 fans. From there, he moved to Ohio State – who had been encouraged to hire him by the area's other high-school coaches – and lifted a National Championship in the second of his three campaigns before the war intervened.

Were it not for the global conflict, Brown might never have made his landscape-altering voyage into pro football. But he did, and that initially gave the NFL a problem that their current president, Elmer Layden, didn't seem equipped to handle.

*

The death of Carr, the NFL's venerable president of 17 years, was devastating and caused problems that took nearly a decade to solve. The first to try to fill his shoes had the physical size to fill most footwear. Carl Storck, a rough-and-ready CEO who'd send Don Draper running for the nearest hill, lasted two years. Layden proved equally unsuccessful. He stuck around three years longer, but struggled to leave any lasting imprint outside of his college pedigree bringing the NFL some further legitimacy. His death knell was a dreadful reaction to the AAFC, whose president was Layden's former Notre Dame teammate Jim Crowley – the pair were two of the Fighting Irish's famous Four Horsemen.

'There is nothing for the National Football League to talk about as far as new leagues are concerned until someone gets a football and plays a game,' condescended Layden – the first NFL head who used the title 'commissioner' – when asked about the AAFC. If those comments felt like a man whistling past the graveyard, they were. Soon after, Layden was relieved of his duties, the owners aware that another battle loomed, especially after Brooklyn defected to the AAFC under the commissioner's nose. A new, more hardened leader was needed.

The NFL settled upon a familiar face. Despite an ownership record that was as poor as his 10-46-2 coaching mark – the two weren't mutually exclusive – Bell had the respect of his peers for his tireless work ethic, deep-rooted passion and problem-solving skills. He was a desperately needed unifying force whose commitment to the league and its teams was unmatched.

Despite his exhaustive efforts – it wasn't unknown for Bell to sell tickets to passers-by in cars during rush hour – the Eagles had never captured Philadelphia's imagination. In 1941, he reached breaking point and formulated a deal with friend Art Rooney in which Pittsburgh's owner sold the Steelers to New York millionaire Alexis Thompson and utilised the money to buy a half-share in the Eagles. Bizarrely, the parties subsequently swapped teams so, by the time Bell rose to the NFL's commissionership, he was a part-owner of the Steelers, while Thompson controlled the Eagles.

The episode was an illustration of Bell's resourcefulness and resilience, qualities so badly sought by the league. But he was also indisputably pugnacious. Recognised once as he entered Philadelphia's Vesper Club after an Eagles defeat, the then-owner was greeted by a shout of: 'The Eagles stink.' Bell appeared not to have heard the insult and entered, seated his wife and two guests, then excused himself. Soon after, there was a commotion outside and, sure enough, there was Bell, rolling on the floor fighting the heckler.

The marriage of those traits – savvy yet scrappy – made him perfect for an increasingly demanding role. It being so challenging owed much to the AAFC, but there were other difficulties that provided an early test of his leadership credentials. When word reached Bell of an attempt to fix the 1946 NFL Championship Game, he reacted decisively, banning Giants running back Merle Hapes. In the league meetings following that campaign, Bell insisted upon powers to suspend any player or official involved in match-fixing. Hapes and Big Blue quarterback Frank Filchock, who later admitted to being approached, were the first punished. Bell's actions played well in the court of public opinion. Soon after, he implemented a diktat that all injured players would be listed prior to each game, helping create what eventually became the extensive injury reports released today.

Although his public persona was a large part of the job, internal disputes remained at the forefront. It was here where Bell really shone, turning owners' meetings that had become more confrontational and less productive by the year into fruitful affairs. He did so by undertaking a task that, even following Carr's decision to set up a dedicated committee and the NFL's move to a two-division system, remained as contentious as ever: creating the schedule. The only rule in place was that teams must arrange home and road games versus each club in their section, meaning disputes continued to rage annually. As such, Bell began formulating each team's slate entirely on his own, a remarkable feat given the operation is now performed by hundreds of computers that throw out more than 50,000 options before a four-person team settles on one.

Bell spent weeks working at it on the homemade grid that adorned his dining table, a system of trial and error that required incredible patience. 'He would get home from a full day at the office,' remembers Upton Bell, 'take off his shirt and tie and put on a grey sweatshirt. It was like a boxer going into training. He walked into the drawing room, closed the doors to shut out the noise, sat by his table, and began moving his pieces around on his giant grid with the teams at the top and dates down the side.

'At that time, most teams played in baseball stadiums, and the NFL season only ran until December, meaning there was a huge overlap with baseball. It wasn't just a case of scheduling the games when he wanted. He had to also work around baseball. It was like watching a chess master.'

Bell was helping to shut down a different chess game among owners, whose suspicions of one another had turned schedule creation into an arduous game of politicking. Bell, operating by the doctrine of his chain analogy that the league is only as strong as its weakest link, was a leader in whom there existed implicit trust. 'He would schedule the weak against the weak and strong against the strong early in the season so everybody had things to play for by mid-season,' reveals Upton Bell.

A new recruit among that group of proprietors provided another of Bell's first major challenges as commissioner. As a true football obsessive in the mould of Bell, George Halas, Curly Lambeau, et al., Dan Reeves fit the NFL ownership circle like a ball to Sammy Baugh's hand. Asked upon purchasing the Cleveland Rams in 1941 for his reasons, Reeves replied, without irony: 'Doesn't everyone dream of owning a football team?'

Reeves' plan upon entering the NFL was to own a Los Angeles franchise, but that ambition was put on hold during the war. Not that his team were held back in Cleveland, outside of a year in which they were given special permission not to play (1943) due to, among other factors, Reeves partaking in the war effort. By 1945, the Rams boasted an outstanding squad led by handsome, Hall-of-Fame quarterback Bob Waterfield, who turned the club into champions courtesy of a 15–14 win over the Washington Redskins. The scoreline is significant, given the ludicrousness of the Rams' first score: a safety resulting from Redskins quarterback Baugh attempting a throw from his own end zone that rattled the crossbar and dropped to the ground.

Their title was still shimmering when, on 12 January 1946, Reeves announced it was time to hit Hollywood. The move, in reality, had been in Reeves' planning from the beginning, but there were two additional factors that increased his urgency: the previous campaign, though victorious, had brought financial losses that would only worsen with the competition from Brown's club, and the AAFC having two California teams – the San Francisco 49ers and Los Angeles Dons – meant the NFL surely required one of their own. Both were outstanding arguments that fell on deaf ears. With owners reticent to undertake the travel costs – termed 'financial lunacy' in the room – and seemingly happy to operate in their pocket of the USA, Reeves failed to garner the necessary eight votes. 'You call this a NATIONAL league,' he fumed at the owners. 'Consider the Cleveland Rams out of pro football.'

With the defection of Brooklyn still raw, Bell sprang into action, acting as conciliator. Hours later, Reeves agreed to pay each visiting outfit an additional $5,000 on top of the $10,000 guarantee, and a deal was agreed.

Attaining approval of ownership was only half the battle, though. Reeves needed to convince the city of Los Angeles, perturbed by the NFL's continued segregation, to allow him to use the Coliseum. The crucial sweetener was Reeves permitting general manager Chile Walsh to commit to signing former UCLA Bruin

Kenny Washington, a black star the NFL ignored after he left college in 1940. Reeves won approval and Washington, alongside Pacific Coast League teammate Woody Strode, joined the Rams. With one move, the NFL eliminated an unwritten segregation policy and truly lived up to its name for the first time by having a footprint in the west.

Such positives didn't earn any victories in the PR battle. The AAFC, in the eyes of those not privy to Reeves' long-term plan, had seemingly forced the NFL's champion out of Cleveland without even having played a game. Considering the men bankrolling the operation – ranging from Ameche to MGM owner Louis B. Mayer – many felt it foreshadowed a future in which the new league would prove too powerful. What those assumptions ignored is the established league owners' ongoing stomach for a fight. Ward and co. probably underestimated that factor, as well as the respect built over the course of the NFL's first quarter-decade – especially in remaining active during the war.

The AAFC enjoyed a measure of success on and off the field, galvanising impressive interest with the Bills in Buffalo, capturing the San Francisco imagination with an exciting 49ers team and posting profits in Cleveland with the Browns. The same couldn't be said in NFL-dominated markets. Brooklyn and the New York Yankees hurt the Giants but couldn't gain any real foothold in the city, while the Chicago Rockets were no match for the Bears and Cardinals. The AAFC's losses spiralled year on year, totalling $11 million at the point of its eventual deal with the NFL.

In the older league, amid swelling salaries, losses also mounted – but its owners were in it for the long haul, knowing their product was better. The NFL enjoyed an era of greater parity, during which previous basement dwellers such as the Cardinals and Eagles won titles. The Cards sealed the 1947 crown – their second and still most recent – with a 28–21 win over Philadelphia, who gained revenge in a 7–0 rematch the following campaign and then overcame the Rams 14–0 to make it back-to-back championships.

All of which coincided with the AAFC being staggeringly predictable. Because the beast built to make the new league would eventually break it: nobody could compete with Brown's remarkable programme.

Having shelved his previous disdain and accepted the dollar of pro football, Brown set about the task that most attracted him: putting together the perfect squad. The planned use of a T-formation attack that placed an even greater emphasis on throwing than others meant a passer with whom he was painfully familiar topped his wish list.

Brown would never forget the day that led him to the player with whom he formed one of the most significant head coach–quarterback tandems in NFL history. The 33-year-old Brown was in his first year coaching at Ohio State, attempting to convert legendary status in high-school circles to big-time college 'ball at the helm of a Buckeye squad considered National Championship favourites. At 3-0, though, they fell to injury-depleted Northwestern's unknown tailback.

Graham didn't even join the Wildcats to play football. He was a star basketball scholar at Northwestern, whose football coach Lynn 'Pappy' Waldorf saw him tossing passes by happenstance. But, like many athletes who reach the highest level, he possessed an enviable ability to turn his hand to anything, boasting a repertoire ranging from the hard wood to ping-pong to French horn. Unfortunately for Brown, come 25 October 1941, he wasn't bad on the gridiron either.

Graham's two touchdown passes earned the Wildcats a 14–7 victory over Ohio State, and he inflicted another defeat on his future boss two years later. In between, Brown led the Buckeyes to college football's biggest prize – but Graham left an ineradicable memory.

When it came to putting together a championship-calibre squad, Brown turned to the man who had denied him previously.

68

The former Wildcats star was one of several players stationed around the world to receive letters from the coach in 1945: Graham in Carolina, Mac Speedie in Wyoming and Lou 'The Toe' Groza in the Philippine island of Mindoro, as well as Dante Lavelli and Frank Gatski in Europe, to name the future Hall of Famers. Included in their correspondence from Brown were unique contracts featuring $250 retainers for the remainder of the war and salaries ranging from $2,500 to $7,500.

The military provided ideal preparation for those who accepted his overtures, for Brown's methods wouldn't have looked out of place at their former bases. An insight into his exacting standards was provided the moment players reported to Bowling Green University's campus in the summer of 1946. If training camp at most pro clubs represented a glorified summer camp, Brown's was more like boot camp.

There the players were introduced to Brown's doctrine. Each was handed a binder that would become their playbooks. In it, they were expected to compile copious notes and diagrams as plays were installed. 'I will call in notebooks without warning,' he advised his team. 'They will be graded. A sloppy notebook means a sloppy player. Star or rookie, you will be gone.'

Players left as dazed as they were at 7 a.m. the next morning when the fire bell awoke everybody for the meticulously planned day that followed: breakfast at 7.30 a.m.; practice at 9.30 a.m.; lunch at midday; practice at 3.30 p.m.; dinner at 6.15 p.m., with meetings afterwards; players to their dorms at 10 p.m.; lights out at 10.30 p.m. If that didn't give an indication of the strict expectations, Brown wasn't shy in reminding his troops. On occasions that players laughed during film sessions, the coach turned on the lights and growled: 'Ain't nothing funny about football.'

Each day of camp saw Brown introduce a run in the morning and a pass in the afternoon. Beforehand, every individual element of that specific design – from each lineman's stance to the quarterback's footwork – was drilled. 'The laws of learning,' said

Brown, 'were the same for football as they were in my English and history classrooms. A person's attention span lasts no more than 60 to 90 minutes, after which he begins to drift. Our practices were never longer than 90 minutes. If we were not finished, I told the players it was the coaches' fault for not organising ourselves.'

What followed was a cycle of this routine, interspersed with the odd written test, overseen by Brown and his league-biggest six-man coaching staff. All with one simple goal. 'I want this team to be a darling of professional football,' Brown told his players. 'When you think of baseball, you think of the New York Yankees. When you think of boxing, it's Joe Louis. One of these days when people think of football, I want them to think of the Cleveland Browns.'

Tales of such bluntness and unfathomable intensity suggest Brown was the living embodiment of what pop culture would have you believe an old 'ball coach is: the shouty caricature who frightens his charges into obedience. In reality, nothing could be further from the truth. At heart, Brown was still the English teacher who first began at Severn – the only differences were the age of his pupils and curriculum. What he required was men with a thirst to learn and willingness to subjugate personal ambition for the collective. Anybody who didn't fit that brief was surplus to requirements.

'Brown put teaching into coaching,' said Don Shula, who played for him in the early 1950s. 'He brought the classroom into pro football. You'd learn by listening, reading, writing and reviewing, and then practise on the practice field in order to be ready to utilise your skills.'

Those who got with the programme reaped untold rewards, for Brown altered the course of pro football – but in a manner different to the day's other geniuses. While the likes of Clark Shaughnessy were evolving the game only through schematic ingenuity, Brown did so by defining what became its most important position, alongside quarterback. Not only was he pro football's first true head coach, Brown was the man who created the blueprint of how one should operate. 'There's nobody I have more respect for,' said Bill Belichick. 'Fifty years later, we're basically just doing the same thing.'

He innovated, too, probably more than anybody in the game's history. As well as being the original implementer of individual playbooks and extensive coaching staffs, Brown boasted an array of other firsts: calling plays from the sideline by using messenger guards prior to introducing the first radio earpiece for Graham (which was banned until it became commonplace); utilising the 40- rather than 100-yard dash to determine speed, believing it a better gauge for football; introducing game film as a coaching tool; and statistically analysing his and opposing teams' tendencies, a task undertaken by the staff he, unlike other coaches of the day, appointed year-round. Brown also invented the pocket in which a quarterback throws by having his tackles block outwards rather than in a straight line, single-bar facemasks, draw plays,* zone defense* and option routes.* Simply put, if you switch on any NFL game today, you will see multiple innovations that can be traced back to Brown. 'When I think of Paul Brown,' added Belichick, 'I really think of him as the father of professional football.'

The core of Brown's programme was teaching. His players didn't practise on Mondays or Tuesdays of gameweek, instead getting up to speed on the gameplan, which was more detailed than other clubs' due to one of his assistants, Red Conkright, attending their next opponent's fixtures. When they did practice, the physicality paled in comparison to other outfits. (There was also no physical exertion from Tuesday onwards in players' home lives, either, what with the coach implementing a no-sex policy.) 'A coach who scrimmages doesn't know how to teach,' he said.

From fundamentals through to X's and O's, Brown was a moulder of men. His team in Cleveland was a medley of guys he previously coached or faced at all levels. Brown possessed intimate knowledge of each and fitted them together like pieces in a jigsaw. By the end of that first camp, the quintet of aforementioned Hall of Famers were joined by two more: Marion Motley and Bill Willis, whose delay in signing owed to them being black at a time when uncertainty surrounded whether the AAFC would be integrated.

Collectively, they formed a super team that ensured the fervour whipped up in Cleveland eventually turned to indifference. Brown's boys were so exceptional, winning 52 of 59 games across four title-winning campaigns, the AAFC's seasons became boring and the league increasingly unsustainable. As such, something labelled a 'merger' was agreed, although it amounted to three AAFC teams – the Baltimore Colts, 49ers and Browns – being rolled into the NFL. Even a planned name change to the National-American Football League was shelved.

The question, therefore, became: 'Could the Browns win in the NFL too?'

Buoyed by the personal triumph of stabilising his league and defeating its valiant rival, Bell delivered another masterstroke when the NFL's 31st season – and first with the three former AAFC teams in the fold – began with a Saturday-night fixture that had the sporting world buzzing.

The motive, Brown told his players, was clear. The NFL scheduled the jewel in its crown against the AAFC's to inflict a final humiliation. Many of its owners believed the AAFC a 'cheese league' and Brown a glorified high-school coach who had no business going up against Neale's Eagles. Some, including Philadelphia's latest supremo James Clark, fought the addition of Cleveland, San Francisco and Baltimore for this reason.

Certainly, Clark didn't believe the Browns belonged on the same field as his two-time champion Eagles, even if star halfback Steve van Buren was sidelined. 'We felt cocky,' admitted Bosh Pritchard, one of those tasked with filling in for his illustrious teammate. 'We thought this was a team from a bush league. Greasy thought

Paul Brown was a high-school coach. We didn't really scout them.'

Realisation came on Philadelphia's opening two plays, when Willis manhandled Chuck Bednarik, the brilliant Eagles centre and linebacker nicknamed 'Concrete Charlie' who went on to become a 10-time first-team All-Pro, Hall of Famer and member of the NFL's 75th Anniversary All-Time Team. 'He jumped on me like a cat,' said Bednarik.

Philadelphia settled into their work and led 3–0 towards the end of the opening quarter amid Graham starting with three incompletions. If that seemingly backed up Greasy's pregame words, he was soon eating them.

The hallmark of the Browns' brilliance in the AAFC was that while other teams were reticent to throw inside their own territory, Cleveland weren't. Their passing attack, featuring route concepts never before seen, was more advanced than any in pro football, directed from the sidelines by Brown and executed by his brilliant field marshal.

Graham assembled the troops in the huddle and listened as one of his pass-catchers, Dub Jones, identified Eagles linebacker Russ Craft as being unable to handle his speed. 'He's ready for it,' whispered Jones. 'We knew we had them,' admitted Graham. The signal-caller stood under centre as halfback Rex Bumgardner went into motion, creating the match-up he desired. Craft was left to cover Jones and looked to be doing a good job when the 'back broke towards the sideline on an out pattern.* Craft, seeing Graham begin his wind up, bit hard for the interception and, in the blink of an eye, Jones executed the double move and was gone. Graham, with a pass-rusher bearing down on him, completed his pump fake, delivered the ball off his back foot and hit the receiver perfectly in-stride for the 59-yard touchdown.

Philadelphia initially showed their own championship resolve in response, stripping the ball from Motley and marching to the Browns' six-yard line. But the brilliant halfback atoned for his error, coming in at linebacker and stuffing the Eagles four straight times. Suddenly, it was 21–3, Graham hitting Lavelli for 26 yards and the aptly named Speedie for 12. 'I never saw a team with so many guns,' admitted Neale afterwards.

A victory set up by the passing game – Graham threw for 346 yards – was closed on the ground. Brown instructed his linemen – without the outstanding Groza, who suffered an injury on the first play to leave 'Chubby' Grigg to kick extra points – to split a fraction further on each play to open up holes for Motley and co. later in the game. Much like everything else, it worked a treat, overpowering Neale's ballyhooed 5-2 Eagle defense* and completing a 25-point drubbing that provided the ultimate justification of Brown's methods. 'There are times I've wanted to shoot him,' admitted Graham. 'But nobody ever outcoached him.'

While the NFL's owners were deflated, its commissioner struck a different tone. 'Cleveland is the best-coached football team I have ever seen,' enthused Bell. It's a point they proved emphatically over ensuing months spent dishing out extra servings of humble pie. After the Week 1 humiliation, Neale suggested Brown 'may as well be a basketball coach because all he does is put the ball in the air'. His words set up the ultimate ignominy later in the campaign as Brown's men overcame his Eagles 13–7 without throwing a pass.

Neale was not the only one without answers. The Browns finished their inaugural campaign with a 30–28 victory over the Rams to win a maiden NFL title in the first of six successive trips to the Championship Game, with three victories – they beat the Detroit Lions 56–10 in 1954 and Rams 38–14 the following year.

The final of those represented Graham's last outing, capping a 10-year career in which he went to 10 title games. In actuality, he was 11 for 11 because, in the time between leaving service and pro football, Graham spent a campaign in the American Basketball League, which would later become the National Basketball Association, for the Rochester Royals. They won the championship.

Brown finished the 1955 season requiring a replacement for

his outgoing star. One of the options was a kid he'd received a call about from Rooney the year previous at the behest of his son Dan. 'I drafted a guy I knew from my playing days in Pittsburgh in the ninth round against the will of our coach Walt Kiesling,' remembered Dan Rooney. 'Coach had made up his mind on him before training camp started. He would turn up on time every day, learn the plays, work after practice and throw the ball better than anybody else – his accuracy was incredible – but there was no persuading Kiesy.'

Lost amid a four-way battle for the position in Pittsburgh, the youngster – now a free agent – telegrammed Brown in the 1954 offseason and the coach replied that Graham would be returning for one final campaign, but he was welcome to their training camp the following year.

Buoyed, the 21-year-old found work in a steel mill and spent his Thursday nights playing semi-pro ball for $6 a game. Word of his exploits spread to Baltimore, now under the stewardship of Brown's old assistant Weeb Ewbank and general manager Don Kellett. In February 1956, after finishing another day of grind, the passer received a call that cost 84 cents from Kellett offering a try-out and the prospect of a $7,000 contract.

Having not heard from Brown since the previous summer, Johnny Unitas headed to Baltimore.

6

Johnny, U the Man

NFL Championship Game

BALTIMORE COLTS 23
NEW YORK GIANTS 17

---

28 December 1958

Yankee Stadium, New York

Puffs of breath filled the icy air as supporters roared a thrilling NFL Championship Game towards its conclusion. If the explosion of noise delivered by those from the five boroughs filling Yankee Stadium was familiar, then the object of their affections wasn't. For, on this day, the 'House That Ruth Built' was, ironically, providing the finishing touches to the castle from which pro football would thereafter look down upon baseball, and most of 64,185 people in the bleachers were rousing those in dirt-stained all-blue New York Giants uniforms rather than pristine Yankees pinstripes.

The tension was no less palpable for the 45 million watching on NBC, escalated by those inside the iconic arena providing a soundtrack for the anticipated crescendo of a sloppy-yet-captivating title game. Big Blue broke the offensive huddle just four yards from a first down that would all but secure a second NFL Championship in three years, sitting 17–14 ahead with just over two minutes remaining. Vince Lombardi, their brilliant offensive coordinator, made the call that would be the hallmark of his legendary career: a power sweep.*

That the play would send Frank Gifford in the direction of Gino Marchetti, the best defensive end in football, was of little concern. Lombardi constructed his offense on execution and, if his charges delivered, they would win. Gifford, the outstanding running back who caught the go-ahead touchdown, took the ball from Charlie Conerly, followed his pulling guards and crashed into two Colt defenders. The crack was as audible as it was sickening, and the three players were left sprawled on the floor, surrounded by a familiar cloud of dust.

Marchetti lay stricken, and shouting, on the ground. Tackling Gifford alongside Gene Lipscomb had resulted in a snapped ankle, which buckled under the weight of a teammate nicknamed 'Big Daddy'. 'If I wasn't a big guy, I'd have cried,' remembered Marchetti. 'I really played it badly. I tried to outrun Frank. If I'd have played it as I should have, I wouldn't have got hurt.'

Whatever the quality of his decision-making, Marchetti put his body on the line at a crucial time and saved the game. As he was being carted off on a stretcher, the referee spotted the ball inches short of the line to gain. Big Blue would punt, leaving their hopes in the hands of a defensive coordinator every bit as good as his offensive counterpart.

As Gifford raged on the sideline, convinced he had gained enough for the first, Tom Landry went to work, encouraging a league-best defense led by Andy Robustelli, Sam Huff and Emlen Tunnell to continue harassing the Baltimore Colts' quarterback. For this crucial series, Landry installed a new wrinkle, advising linebacker Harland Svare to shade the right side with the sole intention of stopping two men whose unique chemistry was about to change the face of football.

77

*

They came together in the summer of 1956, an improbable union of unlikely football players fighting an uphill battle to make the Colts' roster. The first was Johnny Unitas, whose hunched back, gaunt face, matchstick frame and crew cut belied a toughness built in Pittsburgh's ghettos, but explained why he was playing sandlot football in the city after failing to catch on with the Pittsburgh Steelers two years previously. And the other was Raymond Berry, the slow, unathletic end with one leg longer than the other and eyesight so bad he wasn't too far from being clinically blind.

That a key tenet of football scouting became not judging a player on what he can't do but what he can is easily traced back to the ultimate deadly duo. In the case of Unitas, the cosmetic physical limitations and unusual throwing motion, from the elongated pull-back through to the wrist snap that sent the ball spinning through the air, concealed deadly accuracy. As for Berry, obsessions over his legs and eyes drew the focus from giant hands that would pluck balls from the sky and surrender just one career fumble, not to mention the nimble feet, body twitches and brain honed to outmanoeuvre defensive players whose speed he couldn't match. Where the rubber met the road for one of the greatest passer–catcher relationships in history was internally, in the mutual obsession with their craft that turned both into legends and catapulted Baltimore into the NFL's elite.

Berry, a 20th-round draft pick, arrived at his first camp in 1955. He was greeted warmly by Colts ends coach Charley Winner: 'Hey, Ray, welcome to training camp. We're glad to have you.' The reply – 'My name is Raymond' – heralded a difficult opening campaign, in which Berry snagged just 13 balls and struggled to fit in, that left his future precarious.

The youngster was an embodiment of everything a 1950s football player wasn't. While those with more natural ability enjoyed the trappings of growing fame and salaries, Berry was teetotal and spent his wages on contact lenses, a fitted mouthguard and lighter gamepants (which he hand-washed daily). Berry stood not in bars or ballrooms, but at the foot of his own 16 millimetre projector, poring over film of the era's best receivers and jotting tiny, illegible observations into notebooks. The practice gathered momentum during the 1956 offseason, as did Berry refining his body through homemade weight exercises using rope and a tree, as well as whole simulated games.

All Berry lacked when he arrived at his second camp was a key ingredient noticed during those hours watching tape: the symbiotic relationship with his quarterback. That man, ostensibly, would be George Shaw, the previous year's first overall pick from Oregon, but Berry's after-practice efforts were spent sharpening his skills alongside someone fully aware he, too, had arrived at the last-chance saloon.

Unitas, whose Lithuanian coal-driving father died when he was five and mother worked two jobs to support her five children through an impoverished childhood, stood on the precipice of being resigned to the blue-collar life of Pittsburgh's construction industry. Such contemplations fostered the determination that made him a willing thrower for Berry, and the hypnotic sound of his voice simulating calls, followed by the thud of ball hitting hand, could be heard hours after Weeb Ewbank's sessions wrapped.

They were kindred spirits. Within months, Berry regularly dined at the Unitas family home, then spent hours learning to see the game through the same eyes. From the moment Unitas got his opportunity, via a broken leg suffered by Shaw, their synergy blossomed and neither looked back.

During one after-dinner film session, the pair spotted a team shading their linebacker to one side to help double-cover a wide receiver. If they ever encountered it, both agreed, Berry would fake the out and, utilising the feints that bamboozled defenders throughout a 12-year Hall-of-Fame career, flip his hips to run a quick slant and capitalise on the open middle of the field. Which is how, when Landry thought he had the pair fooled in the 1958 championship game, the result was a 25-yard gain that left Huff running in the opposite direction.

Confidence gleaned from Berry's notes on which routes worked against each Giants defender, a pregame inspection of the field that revealed the slippery spots and hours spent catching Unitas' passes was paying dividends. The second of three grabs on this crucial drive was a slant in which Berry boxed out Carl Karilivacz to snaffle the ball out of the sky, while the next saw the end grab an out route, quickly turn up field and move the ball to the Big Blue 13-yard line. On each occasion, Berry was split out alone on the left, in what would become the traditional wide receiver position as pro football's evolution continued apace.

For pro-football historians, the 1950s are known as the 'Golden Age'. It was a decade free from the conflicts that preceded and followed it, in which games entertained and crucial ingredients to success were defined. By the end of that period, it was also becoming increasingly clear the blueprint for success featured two key facets: coaching and scouting.

Just as Paul Brown set the course for the former, another visionary catapulted the latter into a new era. Dan Reeves' obsession with winning was as absolute as his ownership contemporaries', but they couldn't match his foresight. Spotting a gap in the haphazard process of assessing college prospects, Reeves filled it by employing a full-time scout. Eddie Kotal spent 200 days per year on the road visiting colleges – from spring practices until the season's end – and turned the procurement of draft talent into something more organised.

The efforts didn't end there. The Rams enlisted college assistant coaches as stringers to file scouting reports for $100 apiece, sent questionnaires to prospects and – at the suggestion of a young executive called Tex Schramm – delivered letters asking coaches of smaller colleges to name the best players they faced under the ruse of putting together 'Tom Harmon's Little All-America Team'

– Harmon was a former first overall pick from Michigan who spent two campaigns with the Rams from 1946.

The data comprised football's first true scouting network, and the results were clear. The questionnaires brought word that Norm Van Brocklin was on course to graduate a year early, allowing the Rams to select Oregon's superstar passer before he was on any other club's radar, while Robustelli and Dick 'Night Train' Lane were by-products of Harmon's 'team'. Amid the rest of football throwing darts at a wall, the Rams hit bullseyes.

Their coaching would become similarly scientific, what with football's nutty professor back in the pro laboratory. Reeves became so enamoured with Clark Shaughnessy during a stint as a team consultant that he fired Bob Snyder and turned the reins over to the schematic whizz in 1948. Within two years, Los Angeles were in the NFL Championship Game, and only a shocking rainstorm stopped the Rams winning the 1949 title, nullifying the speed on which they were built and helping secure victory for the Philadelphia Eagles.

That Shaughnessy so quickly turned around a sliding team was thanks to the players acquired by Reeves, Kotal and Schramm, as well as his ability to evolve systems to fit their skillsets. Realising that lightning-fast halfback Elroy 'Crazy Legs' Hirsch would be more effective as a pass-catcher, Shaughnessy moved him to flanker and began utilising three-receiver sets* as his base concept, turning the Rams offense from moribund to magical and once again sparking an offensive revolution.

Theoretically, Shaughnessy and Reeves were a match made in heaven. While the former continued to move the needle on the field, the latter did so off it: from scouting to introducing logos on helmets, to an impressive eye for talent that provided Schramm and Pete Rozelle's introductions to football. But Shaughnessy was notoriously difficult to work with, a recluse most comfortable analysing game film, where social interaction wasn't necessary. After two years, Reeves and players weighed down by the increasing complexity of Shaughnessy's schemes grew tired. In the end, a Rams team directed towards the throne by him were crowned under Joe Stydahar in 1951, avenging their previous year's Championship Game loss to Brown's Cleveland squad by winning 24–17 with Hall-of-Famers Van Brocklin and Bob Waterfield rotating at quarterback. It completed a particularly remarkable year for Van Brocklin, who set a single-game passing-yardage record that still stands with 554 against the New York Yanks in Week 1.

So began a frustrating trend for Shaughnessy, who subsequently spent 11 years as the Chicago Bears' defensive coordinator – easily the longest tenure of his career – only to see the club win their last NFL title under George Halas in 1963, the year after he departed. His time in the Windy City was also transformative, as Shaughnessy proved equally adept scheming the other side of the ball, utilising a 5-3-3 defense to shut down his own T-formation, as well as an early iteration of the shotgun.*

The latter came in 1961 when Chicago faced a San Francisco 49ers outfit stewarded by an eccentric schemer of their own, Red Hickey. The coach's shotgun attack, featuring option looks, dominated football over the campaign's opening weeks, his team heading to Wrigley Field having scored 49, 35 and 38 points in the previous three games. Against the Bears, however, they were on the receiving end of a 31–0 beatdown that was every bit as ingenious and transformative as the 73–0 1940 title game. It would be nearly 15 years before the shotgun returned in earnest.

That proved Shaughnessy's last role in the NFL, but his legacy lives on to this day. His impact wasn't just on the teams he coached, but the many that copied his methods. If imitation is the sincerest form of flattery, Shaughnessy was permanently honoured. No less so than during the drive that left the Colts on the brink of levelling in Yankee Stadium.

After Berry's third catch, Steve Myhra raced onto the field to attempt a 20-yard field goal – no sure thing for anyone not named

Lou Groza and certainly not the inconsistent Colts kicker. But he stepped forward in a straight line, as was the way in those days, before toe-poking over to spark uncertainty. 'What do we do now?' asked the Giants' Kyle Rote.

'I think we play on,' replied kicker Pat Summerall. He was right, only most didn't know it. The NFL had initiated sudden-death overtime for playoff games as far back as 1941, but it hadn't been required.

Unlike currently, sudden death meant sudden death. So, when Big Blue won the coin toss, their equation was simple: score and win to cap perhaps the franchise's most incredible campaign yet.

From their inception, the Giants were among football's most consistent teams without ever building a dynasty, à la the Monsters of the Midway or Curly Lambeau's Green Bay Packers. Reaching the 1958 title game represented their 10th appearance since the contest was introduced in 1933, a league-high mark. Yet they had just three titles, won via 30–13 and 47–7 wins over the Bears in 1934 and '56, which sandwiched a 23–17 triumph over Green Bay in '38. Combined with their 1927 crown, the Giants had four titles, compared to seven apiece for the Packers and Bears.

Yet there was a feeling Big Blue, just two years removed from their latest triumph, were entering halcyon days. No longer requiring the name New York Football Giants after the New York Baseball Giants headed to San Francisco in 1957, they entered 1958 with perhaps their finest roster. On offense, Conerly earned huge respect for fighting the tide of criticism that followed his initial inability to follow up a Rookie-of-the-Year campaign by establishing himself as one of the game's best – he won MVP the following year – while Gifford proved a dynamic weapon in the running and passing game. The defense was driven by the brilliant pass-rush of Robustelli, marshalled by roving middle linebacker Huff and protected by safety Tunnell.

Just as impressive were the men on the sideline. Except,

ironically, head coach Jim Lee Howell. 'All he did was blow the whistle and say: "Everyone on the bus,"' said Gifford.

Howell joined in 1954, tasked with following the irreplaceable Steve Owen, whose run in New York spanned 23 years, 155 victories and two championships. Moreover, Owen played a wider role in football schematics by implementing the A-formation* on offense, and umbrella* on defense. The latter proved the most effective counter to Brown and Otto Graham's brilliant passing game, famously shutting out Cleveland in Week 3 of their opening NFL campaign.

Owen's fingerprints were on the 1958 squad, too, in the form of Landry. The defensive coordinator spent five seasons as a defensive back for Owen and became so reliable that when the coach devised the umbrella, he explained the scheme to Landry and advised him to teach the rest of the team.

The talent Owen spotted and honed in Landry was on full display during the Giants' run to Yankee Stadium. What the apprentice took from his master, as well as emphasis on fundamentals, was the importance of thinking outside the box. Until that point, most defenses featured at least five linemen, one of whom started directly over the centre. Landry, enamoured by Huff's diverse qualities and athleticism, pulled that man back a couple of yards, thus creating the modern-day middle linebacker and evolving Owen's umbrella into the 4-3. 'Landry built the 4-3 defense around me,' remembered Huff. 'It revolutionised defense and opened the door for all the variations of zone and man-to-man coverage which are used in conjunction with it today.'

Validation of Landry's 4-3 came during the game that earned Big Blue's place in the season showpiece. After Summerall forced a standings tie with the Browns by booting the unlikeliest of 49-yard field goals through a snowstorm – having missed from 31 only minutes earlier – to seal a 13–10 win, the teams did battle once again in an unplanned, hastily arranged Eastern Conference playoff one week later.

Believing his men couldn't rely on another fourth-quarter comeback to triumph, Landry constructed a plan to achieve one goal: stop Jim Brown, the brilliant running back who would cap his sophomore year by winning a second straight MVP award. It worked: Brown managed just eight yards on seven carries. 'We had a defense that could take a ballplayer and shut him down,' said Huff. 'We shut Jim Brown down. No other defense has ever done that.'

On the other side of the ball, the Giants rushed for 211 yards on 53 attempts, an offensive line led by tackle Roosevelt Brown perfectly executing the blocking scheme Lombardi introduced to football as Gifford ran to daylight to the tune of 95 yards. The only touchdown was orchestrated by Lombardi. Conerly handed the ball to Alex Webster, who tossed to Gifford on a reverse. The 'back got eight yards downfield when a sea of white jerseys descended upon him, at which point he lateralled to Conerly and the signal-caller waltzed home untouched.

That the game was won on the genius of the Giants' coordinators was undeniable. 'Jim Lee never had anything to do with the game,' revealed Gifford. 'Lombardi coached the offense and Landry the defense.'

Certainly, Howell was a pale imitation of his predecessor, whose thirst for victory was summed up in the 1934 title game. With his players slipping on an icy Polo Grounds surface, Owens instructed guard Abe Cohen to grab some different cleats from the Manhattan College athletic-supply room that he supervised so they could change at halftime, and their 10–3 deficit at the interval turned into a 30–13 victory over the Bears.

Twenty-four years later – after a different, shorter, interval – the Giants were seeking inspiration once more in an arena just a stone's throw away. For one of the NFL's blueblood franchises, history was on the line.

Even though disaster was avoided on the ensuing kickoff – Hall-of-Famer Don Maynard recovered his own fumble – the

Giants couldn't move the ball in the evening dusk. They were met by an impenetrable wall on a first-down sweep, before Conerly threw incomplete and then came up short of the sticks* on a designed run. Unitas began loosening up on the sideline – he was ready to re-enter the fray.

'When we got that ball,' said Berry, 'we knew – without a doubt in our minds – we were going to win that game.' As he stepped onto the field, the ice-cool Unitas was greeted by the muffled cheers of some 15,000 Baltimore fans who had made the trip, a figure that – while mightily impressive – paled in comparison to the 30,000 that delivered a hero's reception at the airport upon the Colts' return home.

This contest meant everything to the residents of a city locked in an identity crisis as the forgotten place between New York and Washington. Their football team, a perennial loser, could deliver a blow for Baltimore's entire population and repay the fervent fandom that was so crucial to their place in big-time professional football.

The Colts being one of three teams folded into the NFL upon the 'merger' with the AAFC had originally been thanks to their supporters, who delivered an average attendance of 23,000 during the final campaign despite a shocking 1-11 team. Yet they lasted just one year amid crippling financial issues and another miserable 1-11 season.

Baltimore were saved by their fans in 1953 when commissioner Bert Bell told officials – perhaps owing to an impending lawsuit from a city still furious at the Colts' disappearance – 'Sell 15,000 season tickets and you can have your team back.' By hook or by crook, they offloaded 15,755 by January's end and, with Bell persuading old friend Carroll Rosenbloom to purchase the team, the Colts returned.

Renewed energy among the fanbase – their return season in 1953 brought average attendances of just over 28,000, a figure that topped 45,000 four years later – combined with the addition of Paul Brown disciple Ewbank as head coach to transform the Colts fortunes. They entered the 1958 campaign with a growing fanbase who believed in the team, a feeling only enhanced by the Week 1 triumph over a defending NFL champion who had won three titles across the previous six campaigns.

The 1950s Detroit Lions were a collection of mavericks and magicians, led by a man who blurred the lines. Hot-headed and pudgy with a southern drawl, Bobby Layne shirked neither at the thought of a halftime beer or the sight of a pass-rusher. He was both maddening and masterful, a coach's dream and nightmare who Paul Brown declared the best third-down quarterback in football history. Together, he and college teammate Doak Walker perfected the two-minute drill behind an offensive line led by exceptional guard Dick Stanfel, executing it to inflict a second successive Championship Game defeat on Cleveland in 1953, their 17–16 win following up a 17–7 scoreline the year previous.

Detroit's 1957 ilk were no match for the 1952 and '53 versions but still won it all – even after head coach Buddy Parker departed on the eve of their opening preseason game. 'The basic reason for my decision to quit,' the coach told a stunned crowd at Detroit's annual 'Meet The Lions' banquet, 'is that I can't handle this squad. It is the worst team I've had from the standpoint of working on the field, getting the job done and its actions off the field.' The Lions still boasted defensive heartbeat, linebacker Joe Schmidt, while Parker unknowingly helped earn the title by acquiring quarter-back Tobin Rote, who – filling in for the injured Layne – delivered a brilliant title-game performance to topple the Browns 59–14, completing 12-of-19 passes for 280 yards and four touchdowns.

Come 1958, however, the game was up, emphasised by a changing-of-the-guard 28–15 Colts win over the Lions to open the campaign. Baltimore, by that stage, were a fine team who had captured the public's imagination, built around the mastery of Unitas, Berry and running back–flanker Lenny Moore, all of whom profited on the steady base formed by star tackle Jim Parker. On defense, Marchetti and Art Donovan were exceptional players who encapsulated the essence of a blue-collar fanbase. Nearly 50,000 of those supporters packed Memorial Stadium, whose average attendance that season would hit almost 54,000, to watch Baltimore overcome Detroit and Unitas continue a streak of throwing at least one touchdown pass that eventually reached 47 games – the record, remarkably, wasn't broken until 2012.

A practice Unitas made routine was desperately desired by Baltimore's fans as overtime continued in Yankee Stadium, with The Golden Arm facing third-and-15 from his own 36. Sporting signature black high-top cleats, he dropped back from under centre, looked right, pump faked – but, with Giants defenders converging upon him, sprinted left to evade the rush. At the point Unitas began gesticulating, everybody knew what was coming next. Berry sprung open down the left sideline and worked his way back to the ball, collecting Unitas' throw and gaining an extra yard.

'Time and time again, he instinctively came up with the right call,' said Berry. On the ensuing play, sensing the desperation of Giants pass-rushers, Unitas handed off to Alan Ameche on a draw and the fullback raced through the gap vacated by Huff, who had been tasked with stopping Berry. Twenty-five yards later, the Colts were at the Big Blue 20.

An L.G. Dupre small gainer meant, suddenly, it was second-and-seven from the 17-yard line. As the delirious Colts fans inside Yankee Stadium began rocking the bleachers back and forth, millions around the country shuffled forward in their seats.

Then, suddenly, everybody's screen went fuzzy, followed by a simple note:

Please Stand By
PICTURE TRANSMISSION HAS BEEN
TEMPORARILY INTERRUPTED

*

In 1945, an estimated 10,000 US homes had televisions, a figure that rose to 6 million by 1950 and 60 million 10 years later. To say TV changed the world wouldn't be an exaggeration, nor would suggesting it altered the course of sports for ever. Its greatest impact on the latter was undoubtedly in pro football, which rode the wave better than any rival and boasted an ideal product for the medium. Were it not for its near-century-long existence, it would be easy to believe football, shot from high vantage points offering a full view of the field, was a made-for-TV product, an all-action game that demanded absolute focus. But it came with a caveat: putting games on the box removed the necessity to attend stadiums or ballparks, a fact borne out across multiple failed, and in some cases ruinous, experiments by Major League Baseball clubs.

The first to raise their heads above the parapet in the NFL were Reeves' Rams in 1950, albeit having heeded lessons from other sports' failures. Los Angeles predicted a 10 per cent uptick on attendances from 1949, so their deal with TV station Admiral stipulated anything below that mark would be reimbursed. In actuality, punters through the turnstile dropped by half in a year where the Rams boasted the NFL's most exciting squad, and Admiral were billed $307,000. If TV was to be the future, a solution had to be found.

The NFL's Championship Game was on the airwaves on the East Coast in 1948 and 1950, skipping the year in between as the Eagles–Rams tilt took place in Los Angeles and the signal couldn't be transmitted back across the country. From 1951 this issue was fixed, meaning the whole nation saw Los Angeles exact revenge on Cleveland in the first of a four-year run for the DuMont Television Network, which preceded NBC as the league's Championship Game broadcaster.

But Bell wanted more. He knew his weekly product was perfectly suited for TV, both in terms of individual game action and the wider context of an organisation increasingly attaining parity.

'On any given Sunday,' said Bell famously, 'any team can beat any other team.'

'He would say television is going to make the game, that it was perfect for television,' reveals Upton Bell. 'The first-ever television game was in 1939 between the Eagles and Brooklyn Dodgers when he owned Philadelphia. He also was the first man to bring football to primetime, holding Saturday-night games before agreeing to stop due to college football. That was long before *Monday Night Football*.'

His solution was ingenious. Bell blacked out games within a 75-mile radius of venues where games took place. The commissioner was forced to beat the Supreme Court on the matter but won the day. His rule lasted until 1973, when a crucial extra piece was added: blackouts would be lifted if the local game sold out 72 hours before kickoff. In 2015, it was lifted altogether. The NFL was too dominant to worry about gate receipts by that stage.

In its day, the directive created a significant new revenue stream without impacting the most important existing one, and everybody took advantage. Come 1956, all 12 clubs had individual arrangements with CBS – franchises negotiated for themselves, but Bell ratified deals – and the contracts were worth millions of dollars.

TV's most significant impact on the NFL was fresh eyes, captivated by the pulsating drama of its games. There was never a greater example than the day the Colts and Giants did battle in a dizzying affair at baseball's most illustrious stadium. Including Big Blue owner Tim Mara and his son Wellington, the contest – astonishingly – featured 17 future Hall-of-Fame players, coaches and administrators. The show those legends put on was so remarkable that it held the attention of millions around the country. At least, that was, until Baltimore's fans knocked a plug from its socket as they began to celebrate a seemingly certain victory powered by Johnny U.

*

The watching public missed one play during the technical difficulties, Unitas hitting a diving Berry between two defenders for his 12th and final reception of the day, totalling 178 yards. It might have been more but for an act of apparent divine intervention. A seemingly drunk fan picked the very moment nobody at home knew what was happening to storm the field. It only emerged later the man was actually NBC producer Ted Smith.

His interruption allowed enough time for the telecast to return and, when it did, Ameche dived into the line for two yards, leaving the Colts six from glory. A field goal would suffice, but Unitas had little intention of leaving the result down to Myhra's unpredictable boot. Defying convention, he dropped back and hit Jim Mutscheller, who slipped on the ice and was ruled out at the one. 'When you know what you're doing, they don't get intercepted,' said Unitas when quizzed on his decision to throw.

On third-and-one, Unitas called '16 power' in the huddle, went under centre, took the snap and offloaded to Ameche, who powered through a gaping hole opened by perfectly executed crack blocks* from the right side of Baltimore's line. The Colts were world champions, a status backed up by beating the Giants again, 31–16, in the following year's title game. 'I miscalculated,' said winning coach Ewbank. 'I predicted it would take five years to build a winner. It took me an extra quarter.' Berry, having ascended to superstardom alongside his friend and passer, described the day as 'the greatest thing to ever happen'.

And not just for the Colts. The NFL was the real winner.

In the press box, Bell – with tears of joy rolling down his cheek – encountered the *Baltimore Sun*'s John Steadman. 'Bert, it's been a tremendous day for the league, hasn't it?' asked the scribe.

Bell jokingly replied: 'John, old boy, I never thought I'd live long enough to see sudden death.'

The comment proved tragically prescient. The following season, on an unseasonably balmy October day at Philadelphia's Franklin Field – the venue at which he had played quarterback for

Penn – Bell sat in the stands for a game between his two teams: the Eagles and Steelers. There, the 64-year-old, who unbeknown to most had agreed a deal to rebuy the Eagles after the campaign and end his run as commissioner, suffered a heart attack during the fourth quarter. He was pronounced dead a few hours later at University Hospital. 'There was a lot of pressure in his life,' says Upton Bell. 'He died young because of the pressure of trying to lift a sport on his shoulders. If the phone rang in our house, he insisted we woke him up, regardless of the time. He can't have ever had more than three hours' sleep per night. He just loved football.'

Bell left behind a gaping hole at the summit of the NFL, but also a game unrecognisable from what he'd inherited. 'Bert Bell lifted the league to a new level,' remembered Dan Rooney. 'He knew the fans were not going to stand for one team dominating for years and recognised America's growing love affair with television. Not only would teams earn record profits thanks to television rights, but the game's live audience would be bigger than ever thanks to his astute management of the blackout rule.'

With those key factors in place, Bell's NFL was ready – on the heels of what became known as the 'Greatest Game Ever Played' – to be shepherded into a new era by the next wave of football men.

7

World Series of Football

AFL–NFL World Championship Game

KANSAS CITY CHIEFS 10
GREEN BAY PACKERS 35

---

15 January 1967

Los Angeles Memorial Coliseum, Los Angeles

The opening instalment of what would become not only an unofficial American national holiday but the world's biggest annual sporting event was most unbecoming of its rich future. Only the stage, Los Angeles' iconic Coliseum, seems suitable in hindsight – and one-third of its seats sat empty.

If the first edition illustrated anything, it was how much power brokers and fans would learn about the showpiece. Which is what the embryo that was the National Football League Green Bay Packers' clash with the American Football League Kansas City Chiefs grew into – an all-encompassing, week-long bonanza that marries sports, entertainment and everything in between. It is now a stage-managed seven-day show, beginning with an opening-night spectacular in which thousands descend upon an arena to watch their heroes being interviewed by hordes of media, and culminating in 'Super Sunday', when the action fits either side of a 15-minute concert and average ticket prices are around $5,000. But it began as just a game, hurriedly put together after two leagues that had spent more than five years locked in a bitter war agreed to merge. There were no precedents or customs. The two offenses used different types of ball and the game was broadcast to the nation on rival TV networks, except within a 75-mile radius of the stadium.

'It was chaos,' remembers organiser Mickey Herskowitz. 'They agreed to the merger in June, had it approved by Congress in August, but preparations didn't start until December. I went out a month before the game with a 22-page list of instructions, including getting tickets printed and organising hotels and practice facilities. There was no tradition. It was like a brand new baby left on a doorstep.'

A tough sell in every sense, taking place miles from the home of its Midwest competitors. The only part that fit, ironically, was the Coliseum's proximity to Disneyland, what with the AFL having been written off as a 'Mickey Mouse League' for so long. That its representative was competing against the crème de la crème of NFL football, the nine-time champion Green Bay Packers coming off their fourth crown in six years under the magnificent Vince Lombardi, compounded a sense of anti-climax borne from many expecting a one-sided affair.

At $12, tickets were $2 more than the Packers' NFL Championship win over the Dallas Cowboys, and double the cost of Rose Bowl admission. Who would pay that to watch a massacre aired by two channels? Even the decision to enforce the NFL's blackout policy for non-sell-outs backfired, with many people following local-media advice on how to fashion an aerial from broomsticks and coat hangers. Those not willing to go that far were nonplussed. The majority didn't even know the game was happening until weeks before, so it certainly wasn't worth getting worked up over. 'We looked up and there were 35,000 empty seats,' says Hall-of-Fame linebacker Bobby Bell. 'I remember saying to Buck Buchanan: "Who in the world is going to pay $12 for this?" Now it costs more for a ticket than we were paid for that game.'

When a safe holding 2,000 Chiefs tickets was broken into, the thieves only took the money. The burglars were clearly savvy – those vacant seats on gameday confirmed the tickets weren't worth taking. What had been billed as Football's World Series – one of the many names floated before the hardly awe-inspiring AFL–NFL World Championship Game was settled upon – was a damp squib.

At least in the eyes of the public.

The indifference of supporters contrasted sharply with the apprehension and anticipation felt by the competitors. On the NFL side, 47 years' pride was at stake, accentuated by bitter memories of the Philadelphia Eagles' loss to the Cleveland Browns in a similar contest more than 15 years earlier. When Lombardi touched down in California one week before gameday to the unwelcome sight of 1,000 cheering fans – one holding the 'Green Bay: Titletown, USA, population 50,000' sign brought from home – he felt the weight of the world on his broad shoulders.

From the runway, Green Bay hastily boarded a bus bound for the outskirts of Santa Barbara, a two-hour drive from the league's preferred headquarters for the teams. 'I tried to book the Packers and Chiefs into downtown hotels,' adds Herskowitz, 'but Lombardi wanted every edge and to stay as far from the media and distractions as he could.' Even Santa Barbara was a compromise. Lombardi hoped his troops would be stationed in Palo Alto, 350 miles from Tinseltown, after his initial request to arrive the day before gameday was denied.

The Santa Barbara Inn, backdropped by gorgeous mountain views and built around a swimming pool quickly deemed off-limits by Lombardi, provided an unfitting location for several days of endurance facing Packers players. 'I secured a lovely UCLA practice field, but he picked one that would provide as few amenities as possible,' reveals Herskowitz. 'He wanted them as captive as could be.' The paranoid coach also wanted somewhere free of spies.

'The pressure on him was tremendous,' remembers Hall-of-Fame linebacker Dave Robinson. 'The NFL's whole prestige was on the line. We couldn't just win; we had to win by three touchdowns. Vince said: "I don't think you could beat anybody by three touchdowns, including the little sisters of the poor." I remember us going up by seven and Lee Roy Caffey coming over and saying: "Well fellas, we're down 14 points. Let's get it together." When you put pressure on Coach Lombardi, you put pressure on us. We loved him.'

As intense as Lombardi always was, the scrutiny ratcheted everything up a notch. Yet the occasion was low-key compared to nowadays. 'There were probably 12 guys with cameras,' says former Packers tight end Marv Fleming. 'These days, it's madness.'

Much of the pressure on Lombardi was internal. When not demanding more from players, threatening that even the smallest transgression would bring bigger fines than ever, he was answering calls from around the NFL. 'He said he'd heard from the league office and some other coaches around the league,' reveals wide receiver Boyd Dowler, 'and told us that – and I don't know if it was [George] Halas or [Don] Shula – they said there wasn't another team they'd have picked to represent them other than the Packers.'

Lombardi – who once appeared in a TV commercial ridiculing the AFL – projected an outward confidence, pointing to deficiencies in Kansas City's techniques he felt could be exploited. Privately, it was a different story. 'After Lombardi watched Kansas City on tape,' said Frank Gifford, a sideline reporter for CBS, 'he confided he thought the Chiefs were really good and there was a chance his team could lose. He was scared.'

When Green Bay landed, Kansas City had been in town four days. 'We knew we had come too early,' said head coach Hank Stram. Even so, Stram cut a relaxed figure in contrast to his opposite number. One day, star flanker Otis Taylor missed the team bus and rode a scooter to practice, arriving 30 minutes later. Stram, chatting to reporters, simply looked up and said: 'That's Otis for you.'

His attitude permeated a team happy not only to stay downtown, but also promote the game. 'Coach Stram took the game very seriously,' says Chiefs linebacker Stewart 'Smokey' Stover, 'but it was a carnival atmosphere.' Bell remembers similar: 'Most of the press was done the day before and we were all in swimming costumes. We'd do an interview then dive into the pool.'

There is such a thing as too loose, and that certainly applied to star cornerback Fred Williamson. 'They're overrated,' Williamson said of the Packers, before suggesting he wouldn't be shy in introducing their wideouts to his signature 'hammer', an infamous forearm smash often delivered in the AFL. 'We knew he could overload his mouth,' admits Stover. 'We didn't pay too much attention, but he ticked off the Packers.'

For all he went about it the wrong way – Stram nearly sent him home – Williamson summed up AFL emotions ahead of the contest. It was, in essence, a shot fired back, having spent years hearing criticism of the league, its teams, its players, its coaches. The organisation sat in the seat once occupied by those from the All-American Football Conference, determined to uphold the virtues of its existence and shut down the naysayers.

The parallels between the birth of the AFL – some might say rebirth, given it was the fourth iteration of a rival under that name – and that of the AAFC almost 15 years earlier are striking. The NFL hadn't learnt its lesson. Just as the AAFC was created by rebuffed rich men enraged at being denied access to the increasingly insular NFL establishment, so too was the AFL. Similarly, the new enterprise wasn't short of backers with extremely deep pockets, a description that most certainly applied to creator Lamar Hunt.

Lafayette Hunt had long since parlayed poker winnings into oil rights to amass a fortune that made him one of the world's richest men by the time his son Lamar decided against life as an oil tycoon. For all his black horn-rimmed spectacles and unassuming manner gave off the air of a Sunday-school teacher, Hunt Jr's true passion was sports. He set about trying to buy a franchise and was torn between baseball and football until witnessing, from a Houston hotel, his college teammate Raymond Berry and Johnny Unitas lead the Colts to their dramatic 1958 Championship Game victory. Having spent his college career in Dallas' Cotton Bowl, and grown up on the metropolis' outskirts, he intended to place an NFL franchise in the area.

The league was far from excited by the possibility, following its failed previous attempt in the city. The 1952 Dallas Texans opened their only campaign in the 75,000-seat Cotton Bowl – hosting its third game in as many days after SMU and Texas A&M contests – in front of a little more than 17,000 fans. And that was the best crowd of a campaign that brought one victory, $225,000 losses and earned the Texans the dubious honour of being the last NFL club to fold.

Although that led many people to believe, remarkably given the modern-day outlook, that pro football in Dallas would never work, Hunt was resolute. 'My dad was an enthusiast all the way back to his playing days,' says Clark Hunt. 'But that 1958 NFL Championship Game really swung the decision. The problem was that the NFL kept telling him Dallas was a horrible market that would never support pro football. It's amazing to think of that today.'

Hunt initially hoped to buy and move the Chicago Cardinals, for whom the glory days of their second championship in 1947 preceded a return to the doldrums. They were now under the ownership of Charles Bidwill's widow Violet and her new husband Walter Wolfner, a pugnacious St. Louis coffee broker whose time in league circles was spent ruffling more feathers than a Midwest farmer. The friendship Blue-shirt Bidwill enjoyed with Halas made way for genuine animosity that began with the Chicago Bears' owner being unwilling to trade Violet third-string quarterback Bobby Layne at a time when he was buying back the share in his own club that Bidwill acquired for providing a franchise-saving donation. Wolfner was happy to continue the fight but could never win; the Bears captured the Windy City imagination in a manner the Cardinals never managed to replicate.

It was time to move on, only not in the manner Hunt hoped: 1960 brought what many had long anticipated, with the Cardinals relocating from their home of 40 years – not to Dallas with Hunt, but to St. Louis under an existing ownership group who led interested buyers on a merry dance. The *Chicago Sun-Times* summed up their departure: 'CARD LOSS FAILS TO JOLT CITY'.

It proved a fruitful endeavour for Hunt, though. The indiscreet Wolfner let slip names of other wealthy parties interested in pro football, setting Hunt on a course that saw him unite a group of men who would reshape the game. His first port of call was someone similar in backstory, opposite in personality. Bud Adams was also the son of a Texan oil magnate but, while Hunt spent his life operating as the antithesis of that role's stereotype, his bombastic partner played it to a tee. Together, the duo brought pro football in earnest to the Lone Star State, Adams at the helm of the Houston Oilers while Hunt reformed the Dallas Texans in the newly created AFL.

They could, it turned out, have done so in the NFL. Once it became clear Hunt and Adams were contemplating starting a rival operation, the established league suddenly announced its planned expansion: two teams would most likely be added in Dallas and Houston, announced Art Rooney and Halas. Such was the league's desire to avoid the conflict that Halas offered the addition of four teams: Hunt's Dallas club and another in Minnesota in 1960, followed by Ralph Wilson's Buffalo team and Adams' Houston one the next year.

'Once my dad announced his plans,' adds Clark Hunt, 'the NFL realised how serious he was and said: "Look, we're going to put a team in Dallas and will give you an ownership stake if you abandon your plans for the AFL." But my dad had given the other AFL owners his word. He wasn't willing to break his word, even though he could have had what he wanted the whole time. People don't keep their word like that often. That's the type of man my dad was.'

Which is more than can be said for Minnesota Vikings proprietors Bill Boyer, H.P. Skoglund and Max Winter, who – on the eve of the AFL's inaugural draft – defected to the NFL to be one of two new franchises alongside a Dallas club, eventually named the Cowboys.

Hunt quickly found a replacement, and come its inaugural campaign in 1960, the AFL began with eight teams: Dallas, Houston, the Buffalo Bills, Boston Patriots, Denver Broncos, New York Titans, Oakland Raiders and Los Angeles Chargers. Collectively, the owners called themselves the 'Foolish Club', a name brought about by crippling losses suffered during that opening season, headlined by Hunt's $1 million. When quizzed about his son's failure, Hunt Snr replied: 'At that rate, he can only last another 100 years.'

The same wasn't true of sports announcer Harry Wismer, who stewarded the New York outfit. Towards the end of the Titans' third campaign, his money ran out, meaning the league assumed the costs of operating the team until a five-man ownership syndicate – led by entertainment executive Sonny Werblin – purchased the club and renamed them the Jets. Similar tales were not uncommon: Buffalo supremo Wilson lent Oakland $400,000 to stop the Raiders folding after year one.

Such generosity of spirit among the Foolish Club was central to the AFL's ongoing survival, if not success. That the league continued to be written off by the general public and NFL was understandable. Games were played in stadiums comically unbefitting their professional profile: the Titans operated at a Polo Grounds venue that was a dilapidated shadow of the one where Red Grange transformed pro football's fortunes, while Buffalo's War Memorial Stadium, with its tiny two-players-per-locker dressing rooms and dreadful field, was aptly named.

The arenas served as battlegrounds for an often-ludicrous existence during the AFL's early years. The stories are plentiful: of Wismer refusing to turn on the floodlights during the dying embers of a game because it'd have cost him $8,000; of Buffalo players practising amid men shooting pigeons that were eating grass seeds on a surface with less greenery than Mars; of public try-outs which afforded anybody an opportunity to make the roster. There are too many to tell, but one in particular stands out.

'I remember one game in Boston,' remembers Stover, who earned a place in the league at one of those try-outs, 'where we were down seven and driving down the field. The clock ran out after one play and fans stormed the field, but the referees ruled there was another play remaining. So, they clear them off, Cotton Davidson drops back and the pass falls incomplete after a defender deflected it. When we watched the film, we realised it wasn't a defender, but a fan. We laughed so much watching it.'

At least that abiding memory is one of hilarity, unlike the case of the Texans' flight out of their opening training camp in Rockwell, New Mexico. 'We were all packed on this airplane, sitting on top of each other with all our equipment,' adds Stover. 'You could see the pilot was worried, but our general manager told him to take off. We got on the runway and we went, and went, and went, until we finally got in the air. Afterwards, the pilot came back from the cockpit and was sopping wet with sweat. He said he'd never do it again. We were way overloaded. They wanted to save money, so we took one plane instead of two.'

Amid the shambles, the AFL got one aspect spectacularly right: its wide-open, entertaining brand of football perfectly suited the growing influence of television. From the outset, Hunt implemented the TV model Bell had failed to convince NFL owners the merits of. Deals were done by the league and money split equally between clubs, starting with ABC's $2.125-million-per-year pact. 'At the point my father died,' admits Upton Bell, 'that was the one thing he really wanted but didn't manage to push through.'

For all that contract was impressive, it paled in comparison to the one inked with NBC in 1965. A combination of exciting football and Werblin's connections meant the second agreement totalled an eye-catching $36 million over five years, which was comparable in per-team revenue with the NFL's TV contract.

The AFL's ability to strike the deal was aided by the older league switching all of its games to CBS. Previously, they televised the regular season while NBC had the Championship Game. 'They don't have to call us mister anymore,' said Art Rooney upon hearing of the AFL's agreement.

Inadvertently, a new NFL commissioner who had barely put a foot wrong since his surprising elevation, helped the league's rival to thrive. While certainly not the aim, it would eventually strengthen his own organisation.

The 1960 NFL owners' meetings, held at Miami's plush Kenilworth Hotel, boasted an agenda as significant as any. The items couldn't be addressed, though, until those in attendance completed the first task: replacing Bell.

In the frame were existing employees Austin Gunsel, treasurer and acting commissioner, and Marshall Leahy, chief legal counsel. Both came with insurmountable flaws: Gunsel, formerly of the FBI, was a close aide to Bell but a pale imitation whose likelihood of sticking to the status quo didn't appeal to newer owners; Leahy, a rising star, wanted to move league headquarters to San Francisco, deemed too far west by the old guard. An arduous stalemate prompted new candidates to be sought. Names such as Paul Brown and Lombardi were floated to no avail, until Wellington Mara – now the New York Giants' supremo following his father's death the previous year – suggested the Los Angeles Rams' general manager to Dan Reeves. 'I'd hate to lose him,' admitted Reeves, 'but he'd do a great job.'

It took 11 days and 23 ballots but, finally, on 26 January 1960, the NFL had its new commissioner. 'I can honestly say I come to you with clean hands,' joked Pete Rozelle, who waited in the hotel toilets to avoid the press while owners discussed his candidacy, a process that saw him rewash his hands whenever someone entered.

It speaks volumes of Rozelle's fundamental fairness that he was able to unite an increasingly fractious group, and the belief of some owners that they were getting a puppet to be manipulated was wide of the mark. The graciousness Rozelle showed everybody belied his deft ability as a negotiator – he was the type who could bend someone to his will without them realising – and iron boot where necessary. Some owners, it turned out, knew Rozelle about as well as the *Miami Herald* writer who misspelt his name 'Roselle' in print the previous day.

The archetypal California boy with sun-kissed skin, dark combed-over hair and striking blue eyes, Rozelle grew up in the Los Angeles suburb of Lynwood as the eldest of two boys. He was captivated by the magic of nearby Hollywood, but it wasn't Rozelle's main love. His journey into sports writing came via the realisation that it was the next best thing to playing. For the boy wonder whose teenage weekends were spent at the local sports-desk, it was a seamless transition. After voluntarily serving for a couple of years during the Second World War – he undertook clerical duties aboard USS *Guardoqui* and worked on the ship's newsletter – Rozelle headed to Compton, where the newly moved Rams trained, and interned with the club alongside his studies at community college. He left a lasting impression on everybody, so much so that Tex Schramm hired him after his degree at the University of San Francisco.

That didn't set his course for a permanent place in pro football, though. After three years, Rozelle was headhunted by a former contact in the Bay Area and partnered in a start-up PR firm. He spent just 12 months in the role – gaining marketing experience in the promotion of the 1956 Olympics, while acquiring a range of contacts on frequent trips to New York – before answering an SOS from Bell. The relationship between Schramm and Reeves, whose prescient brilliance in pro football was offset by a less-than-together off-field life, had broken down, and Los Angeles needed a new general manager. He entered a club with divisions everywhere, not least between Reeves and the rest of his owner-ship group, and earned universal praise for deftly dealing with conflicts and showing great attention to detail.

At 33, Rozelle was young enough to provide the NFL a fresh face, yet possessed the maturity and experience of someone double his age. He rose quickly for a multitude of reasons, chiefly the absence of a truly obvious replacement for Bell and an out-standing CV that ticked the requirements of the day. He was in the right place at the right time. The 1958 title game had turned pro football into a fertile ground that was as appealing to those in Madison Avenue as it was the die-hard fans of Green Bay. Rozelle, with his background serving both, was a perfect fit.

Within hours, everybody around the table knew their decision was sound. Rozelle immediately addressed key issues with the calm, professional air he would bring to the Rockefeller Center headquarters in New York that the organisation moved to within months of his appointment. From that nerve centre, Rozelle spent the next four years reshaping the NFL to a fresh vision, befitting a booming American society transformed by the growing influence of advertising, PR and television.

Rozelle showed a firm hand in delivering one-year suspensions to former Green Bay MVP and league poster-boy Paul Hornung, along with Detroit Lions All-Pro Alex Karras, following a betting scandal in 1963. He illustrated a defter touch, meanwhile, when delivering perhaps the most significant moment of his early tenure: persuading owners to follow the AFL's lead by having league-wide TV deals split equally rather than club-controlled contracts that saw bigger-market teams profit more. The commissioner also played a key role in the deal being ratified by Congress after the courts ruled it in breach of antitrust* law.

'That profit share is one of the things that sets the NFL apart and makes it the best business model and strongest league,' says Clark Hunt, now a senior owner himself. 'Every year, all 32 teams have a shot at winning the Super Bowl. In a lot of other sports, that's not the case. From day one in the American Football League, my dad was committed to splitting as much revenue as possible, particularly the TV money. And that was one of the principles that the National Football League adopted.

'From a timing standpoint, it really needed to happen then, because you can't go back and implement something like that today. The TV money was relatively small then. Getting the commitment of the owners in Los Angeles, Chicago and New York to split the money was much easier than it would be now. I think that decision's been critical to the success of the league.'

Similarly significant was Rozelle's decision to turn the organisation into a brand, with the additions of NFL Properties, an in-house merchandise and licensing arm from which all revenues were also equally split, and NFL Films, which would set a gold standard in sports broadcasting for decades to come thanks to father–son team Ed and Steve Sabol. 'He was always thinking: "What is the next step?"' remembers his daughter Anne Marie Bratton. '"How can we grow the league?"'

The analysis of Rozelle's early tenure, though, wouldn't be shaped by any of those matters, no matter how impressive. The key test was his handling of an adversary with whom he was already painfully familiar.

*

In his three-year stint as the Rams' general manager, Rozelle enjoyed many successes. The exception was where it mattered most: on the field. A disappointing 2-10 campaign in 1959 saw Sid Gillman fall on his sword, sent on a transformative path to the AFL, and left Rozelle hatching a plan to reverse the Rams' fortunes by agreeing to make Heisman winner Billy Cannon their first overall pick on a three-year, $30,000 contract.

Cannon was also the name picked out of a hat by Oilers owner Adams during the AFL's inaugural draft, in which teams ripped pages from Street & Smith's *Pro Football Magazine* featuring the top seniors at each position and put them into a draw. While many selected wouldn't ever suit up in the AFL, the ambitious Adams wasn't about to let Cannon slip away.

What followed was a relentless courtship that ended with Cannon becoming pro football's first $100,000 football player, a deal concluded when he signed a contract in the end zone after LSU's Sugar Bowl loss. It capped a remarkable wooing process, in which Cannon – having already inked a deal with the Rams – wouldn't return Adams' call until word reached his representatives that the owner was willing to double Los Angeles' offer.

'I should receive a call from Louisiana,' Adams told his wife in bed after making the overture. Sure enough, the phone rang. 'Did you sign [with the Rams]?' asked Adams. 'Yes,' responded Cannon, 'but how do I get twice that salary?' To which the owner, believing the Rams wouldn't pursue the matter further, responded: 'We'll sign you under the goalpost.' Adams underestimated the NFL, who did take the matter to court, but it mattered little. The ruling came down in favour of the AFL, holding up the first return blow for an operation still smarting from Minnesota's defection.

That the Vikings' move was announced at the last possible moment, apparently at the behest of NFL power brokers desperate to embarrass Hunt and co., immediately put paid to hopes of happy coexistence. As did the older league placing a franchise to rival Hunt's Texans in Dallas.

Just 10 years after the city's first crack at the pro game failed so spectacularly, there were two teams in town: the AFL Texans and NFL Cowboys. The result was predictable: the former lost $2.5 million in their first three years and the latter $2 million. In reality, the Texans did a better job of capturing the local imagination, but the ever-pragmatic Hunt realised that sharing the city wasn't good for business, so the Texans headed to Kansas City and became the Chiefs.

Most ruinous was the battle for players. By 1965, amid both leagues being armed with riches from their TV deals, it had gone too far. 'We were doing all sorts to sign players,' said Adams. 'There was cash involved, houses, swimming pools, cattle. You name it.'

At the height of the Cold War, there were acts of football espionage that wouldn't have looked out of place at the Kremlin. Perhaps the most famous example came in 1965, when the AFL discovered the names of all NFL 'babysitters', a collection of part-time employees tasked with acting as security guards to stop players being courted by their rival in what was known as 'Operation Hand-Holding'. 'We got a load of bankers, lawyers, football fans and assigned each a player,' remembers former Cowboys personnel maven Gil Brandt. Upon learning their identities, the AFL sent each babysitter a note saying they needed to meet in Portland under the ruse it was from their own league. The plan, created by Oakland Raiders executive Ron Wolf to ensure all of that year's draft prospects were available for wooing without their minders present, was foiled by Brandt.

For all the NFL and Cowboys triumphed on that occasion, they suffered their share of defeats. In 1966, Kansas City coveted Taylor, but the Cowboys invited the end to enjoy Thanksgiving in the city and stashed him, with babysitter Wallace Reid outside, at the Holiday Inn off North Central Expressway in suburban

Richardson. After calls to Taylor's dormitory went unanswered, Chiefs general manager Don Klosterman called his home and told Robinson's mother he had been kidnapped. Kansas City scout Lloyd Wells knew the family and discovered Taylor's location. He wasn't granted access to the hotel by staff clearly in on the scheme, but – with Reid asleep after too many drinks – got a crucial message into the room: a red Thunderbird – the type he'd always wanted – awaited Taylor in Kansas City. He packed up his stuff, climbed out of the window and enjoyed a 10-year career with the Chiefs. 'We had Taylor and college teammate Seth Cartwright in the room,' adds Brandt. 'We had no interest in Cartwright at all, but they were best buddies. When Taylor escaped out of the back window, we sent Cartwright home.'

The most damaging blow came when Joe Namath ended the protracted battle for his services following a star-studded career at Alabama and immediately became the face of the AFL by agreeing an eye-watering three-year, $427,000 deal with the Jets.

Although that seemed like a huge victory, this was a war without winners. What should have been pro football's first era of prosperity brought only pain as each league bit sizeable chunks out of the other and TV contracts expected to make clubs solvent served to raise the stakes. 'The bidding wars were ruining us,' remembered Dan Rooney.

Common sense prevailed in the end. Just months after his personnel were sneaking around hotel car parks to woo Taylor, Hunt was in a lot of his own – at Dallas Airport's Love Field Terminal – beginning merger discussions with Cowboys general manager Schramm. Not that their words alone guaranteed unification. Standing in the way of the two former enemies now bound by the same ambition were those in their organisations who continued to fire shots back and forth

From Dallas, Hunt boarded a flight bound for Houston, where he and the rest of the AFL owners appointed a new commissioner after Joe Foss resigned. A Second World War flying ace, Foss had performed solidly in a role for which he was ill-suited but carried the can for failing to secure an expansion franchise in Atlanta – the Falcons joined the NFL in 1966 – and not adequately responding to the babysitter programme.

The new man was a slick-black-haired coach-turned-executive whose often-villainous expression perfectly fitted his combative style. Al Davis' reputation as a wheeler and dealer was already established despite his precocious years, and it was only enhanced in the ensuing months. Davis' immediate task was to respond to the Giants' signing of Buffalo kicker Pete Gogolak – the kicker responsible for introducing the soccer-style technique utilised by everyone today – which broke an unwritten agreement between leagues that they wouldn't sign one another's veterans.

Davis subsequently claimed he had seen the ensuing merger coming, and that his retaliatory move – to begin acquiring NFL talent – was done to force the established league's hands. From Bears tight end Mike Ditka to Rams quarterback Roman Gabriel, the AFL swooped on an array of icons and, while it left the NFL with almost no choice but to negotiate, those partaking in inter-league discussions didn't believe giving Davis a seat at the table was wise.

He was left out of talks that saw Rozelle and owners on both sides eventually formulate a deal in which all players remained with their existing teams. Herskowitz, then Davis' AFL PR man, adds: 'The committee didn't involve Al, because he'd have done everything he could to stop it happening.'

In the end, Davis found out, like the rest of the world, when the press release dropped on 8 June 1967. In it were multiple conditions: all 22 franchises remaining in their current locations, to be joined by four more in time; a common draft beginning immediately; Rozelle remaining commissioner; two-network TV coverage continuing; and a single-league schedule starting from 1970. There was also the small matter of bullet-point two: 'A world championship game this season'.

For those on Davis' staff, anticipating further blows in a bloody war, news of unification was shocking. 'The staff found out about the same time as everybody else,' says Herskowitz. 'We went back to the office, and Al sent out a note saying he was going back to Oakland and resigning [as AFL commissioner]. He showed up at everyone's office and slapped a document on our desk. It was a two-year contract that he told us to sign and turn in. It meant our job was safe for two years.'

With his role suddenly redundant, Davis refocused his energies on the Raiders, one of many teams tasked with proving the AFL could compete on the field as well as it had off it. The first to enjoy a crack at proving the league's worthiness, fittingly, were its founders. 'I think it's very appropriate that my dad and the Chiefs were associated with that first championship game,' says Clark Hunt.

Organisers of the end-of-season showdown did an impressive job. The magical Coliseum, home of the 1932 Olympics and USC Trojans, bathed in an afternoon glow that shone down on a giant football, topped by a crown adorned with the letters AFL and NFL, in the centre of the field. The paint job cost $3,000 of Herskowitz's budget, assigned by Rozelle with the aim of ensuring both leagues enjoyed equal representation and those in attendance, most notably media, came away knowing they had witnessed history. 'Pete's one instruction was that when people left,' says Herskowitz, 'he wanted them saying it was better than the World Series.'

The setting provided a perfect stage for the palpable tension besetting both teams. The few observers who believed a close contest could ensue felt the outcome would be determined by Kansas City's youth against Green Bay's experience. Just how that would manifest itself after a tight opening half in which Lombardi's men led just 14–10 was debatable. While Green Bay's players were confident their savvy would win the day, a young Kansas City crew believed they had an ageing opponent just where they wanted them. 'We felt we were doing the things that we had to do,' admitted Stram. 'We were only four points behind and confident we could get that back and more.'

In the Green Bay locker room, Lombardi calmly reaffirmed the stakes: 'Win, lose or draw, you are my football team,' he told his players. 'You are the Packers. You have your pride. Let's regroup and go back out there. We are representing the entire National Football League.'

That Lombardi was rattled showed itself in the coach's actions. His main takeaway from the first half was the Packers' inability to pressure quarterback Len Dawson, who moved the ball more comfortably than expected as the Chiefs utilised five-man passing patterns. The ploy, in essence, capitalised on Green Bay's unwillingness to blitz,* once termed a 'weapon for the weak' by Lombardi. His view seemingly changed by the conclusion of a halftime show that was impressive yet didn't foreshadow the event's evolution: a mash-up between jazz trumpeter Al Hirt, the University of Arizona's symphonic marching band, Anaheim High School's drill team and Grambling College's Tiger Band, featuring thousands of balloons and men flying with jetpacks.

The second half's opening possession saw Lombardi and the Packers break tendency to devastating effect. By then the stadium and press box were abuzz, albeit following the farcical scene of the kickoff being replayed because TV missed the initial one. When Dawson finally got the ball, he began moving it again and needed to convert on third-and-five to cross midfield for the fifth successive possession. The Packers, though, would unfurl their surprise, calling 'blitz three' and sending every linebacker Dawson's way.

The signal-caller dropped back from under centre, back-pedalling as the Packers' six rushers proved too much for the five Chiefs staying in to block. With a sea of green and yellow flowing towards him, Dawson retreated further onto his back foot. 'I had to chip the tight end,' remembers Robinson, 'so by the time I was bearing down on him, Dawson's eyes were saucers. He saw three guys coming with a clear run. He threw a wounded duck.' Aimed towards Fred Arbanas, the pass landed in the grateful arms of defensive back Willie Wood, who raced to the Chiefs' five-yard line. 'That interception changed the complexion of the game,' said Stram. And the scoreline. Elijah Pitts ran over the left side for a touchdown on the next play.

From there, it was all downhill for a Chiefs team whose main ploy had been rumbled. 'I spoke to Len Dawson afterwards,' says Robinson, 'and he told me that, for two weeks, they worked only on five-man patterns. They lost the timing when our blitzing meant they had to go to three- to four-man patterns. We only blitzed three times per game, so they figured they would just throw away on those occasions. When we started coming every time, they couldn't adapt.'

Excluding penalties, Kansas City's offense totalled less than 20 net yards over the remainder of the game, while an outstanding defense eventually wilted under the weight of the burning sun and relentless physicality of the Packers' sweep.* Softened by Green Bay's continuous physicality, their defense – built around speed rather than bulk – also had little answer for a man they never expected to face.

In fairness, Max McGee himself didn't anticipate seeing much action. The wideout had spent the previous evening partying with two air stewardesses, circumventing Lombardi's army of spies and arriving back in his hotel room at the point roommate Bart Starr was getting up. But an hour's sleep was all McGee needed to put in a legendary performance after replacing the injured Dowler in the opening quarter. Having caught just four balls for 91 yards during the whole season, he delivered seven for 138 and two touchdowns against the Chiefs.

If being beaten by a barely sober second-string receiver wasn't bad enough, Kansas City suffered further ignominy in the fourth quarter when premier mouthpiece, Williamson, was stretchered off the field following a collision with Donny Anderson. He departed dazed and with a broken leg to the sound of Packers guard Fuzzy Thurston humming 'If I Had a Hammer'.

For Lombardi, the experience was cathartic, a validation of himself, his Packers and their league. 'Kansas City has a real top team,' he said, 'but I don't think it compares with the top teams in the National League.' Those who showered the head coach with a standing ovation at league meetings the following day agreed, as did most impartial observers.

Hindsight, though, would tell a different story. Stram's Chiefs were exceptional, a marriage of talent and Hall-of-Fame coaching, as demonstrated by their 66–24 preseason pounding of the Bears the following year (exhibition games carried more weight in those days, particularly interleague ones) and victory over the Minnesota Vikings in Super Bowl IV. Kansas City might not have overcome a veteran Packers team with 12 starters aged over 30 compared to their two, but they certainly earned their respect.

'They were very good players but didn't have our experience,' adds Robinson. 'What Vince said beforehand was right: they didn't have the right techniques. I remember seeing one of their guards on film throw a block leading with the wrong foot. Vince said to Ray Nitschke, "If that guy executes that block on you, I'll put my foot in your rear end." But they eventually became a fine NFL team once they got that experience.'

The Chiefs' defeat in Los Angeles wasn't a reflection of the AFL's status compared to the NFL as much as it was the latest evidence of everybody's inferiority to an all-time great team, shepherded by a coach whose name would eventually be given to the trophy handed to each year's victor.

By then, of course, the title of the game itself had been formalised. In initial meetings, Hunt suggested something derived from the 'Super Ball' toy his kids played with. Rozelle derided it as 'lacking sophistication', but somehow the name grew legs. The day after the Packers' triumph, many major newspapers crowned Lombardi's men 'Super Bowl Champions'.

'Run It, and Let's Get the Hell Outta Here'

NFL Championship Game

DALLAS COWBOYS 17
GREEN BAY PACKERS 21

---

31 December 1967
Lambeau Field, Green Bay

From the moment they were roused by the staff's jovial wake-up call at Appleton's Holiday Inn, the Dallas Cowboys knew what lay in store. 'Good morning, it's seven o'clock and 16 below,' the cheerful operator told quarterback Don Meredith. 'Sixteen below what?' he asked. 'Step outside honey and you'll find out,' came the response.

In his room, star defensive tackle Bob Lilly sat confused. He received the same message but opened his curtains to see sunny skies. Only when roommate George Andrie, having felt the Polar conditions on his trip to early-morning mass, threw some water at the window did realisation hit. The liquid had frozen before it hit the windowsill.

What Tom Landry's team, their Green Bay Packers counterparts and the 50,861 attendees didn't know was, with wind chill factored in, temperatures were actually around minus 38 degrees Celsius. 'We walked the last three blocks to the stadium backwards. You couldn't walk into the wind,' remembers Packers fan Pete Helf.

But walk they did, ready to watch Vince Lombardi's ageing squad attempt to repeat the feat managed only by Curly Lambeau's Packers: winning three NFL titles on the spin. For fans, players and officials, it was the ultimate test of endurance. 'People around us were burning newspapers to keep warm,' says Nancy Brooker, another Packers supporter. 'We bought a hot coffee, and it turned cold before it reached my lips.'

A planned halftime show was cancelled because the instruments froze and 11 band members were hospitalised with hypothermia following pregame practice. But the game went on. Referee Norm Schachter blew his whistle to herald its beginning and ripped part of his lip off in the process. The blood streaming down his chin formed into an icicle. 'It shouldn't have been played,' says Packers great Dave Robinson. 'The refs ran in and said: "Stop," when the play was over. Guys hit a little late when there's a whistle; imagine when there isn't. Rules were out the window.'

As if the inhospitable temperature wasn't bad enough for players, the frozen-solid field made firm footing virtually impossible. This was unforeseen, with Green Bay – at Lombardi's behest– installing an $80,000 underground heating system prior to the campaign. The item meant to rid Lambeau Field of its 'Frozen Tundra' nickname only accentuated it. Unable to handle extremities of weather which pushed the limits of human and mechanical durability, it froze. And when the tarp cover was removed from the field, condensation immediately turned to ice. 'It was like an ice-skating rink,' said Cowboys linebacker Bob Long.

Remarkably, a contest that would have been remembered as one of the greatest in NFL history even if it were played in perfect conditions ensued. Those who believed elderly Green Bay bodies would struggle to come to grips with the interminable Arctic

115

temperatures were proven wrong as the Packers – having limped through the season, figuratively and literally – showed the intestinal fortitude Lombardi emphasised to fly out of the gates. They moved methodically down the field on their opening possession, a nine-minute drive ending when Bart Starr hit Boyd Dowler in the end zone. The pair combined again next time Green Bay had the ball, this time for a 43-yard touchdown.

But Dallas, whose speed advantage was negated by poor footing, were similarly mentally tough. Their defense turned the game towards the end of the half, Willie Townes strip-sacking Starr and watching teammate Andrie rumble in for a touchdown, before Danny Villanueva kicked a 21-yard field goal following another Packers fumble, this time on a punt return. The Cowboys scored 10 second-quarter points without achieving a first down.

Lilly and co. seized the initiative, shutting Green Bay out for much of the second half and setting the stage for a memorable victory when Dan Reeves, having taken a toss from Meredith, threw a 50-yard touchdown to Lance Rentzel on a trick play to open the fourth quarter. By the time they began the final drive from their own 32 with 4:50 remaining, Green Bay had registered just three second-half first downs. But Starr wasn't about to give up. 'We were ready,' he remembered. 'When I looked into the guys' faces, I knew.' The quarterback stepped into the huddle, matter-of-factly stating, 'We're going to put this ball in the end zone,' before going to work. Starr mixed well-timed run calls with methodical throws to 'backs flaring out on passing patterns to move Green Bay down the field and to the Dallas one-yard line. 'No one was scared,' says Dowler. 'Least of all the quarterback. He was unusual, so reliable. We faced some tough situations on the drive – including a second-and-19 – but Bart overcame them.'

The Packers stood on the brink. As it somehow got colder, the icy surface grew worse, and Donny Anderson twice slipped attempting to score the winning touchdown. Facing third down from the one with 13 seconds remaining, Starr called his final timeout and headed to the sidelines. He'd determine the next move only after speaking to the man who'd taken Green Bay from decline to dynasty.

An almost complete understanding of Lombardi can be derived from analysing the play that defined his career: the 'Green Bay Power Sweep' – or 'Lombardi Sweep'.

> *The pulling guards form a convoy, with the lead guard taking out the cornerback and the offside guard picking up the middle linebacker or outside linebacker. The centre executes a block on the defensive tackle, and the onside offensive tackle pops the defensive end and then seals off the middle linebacker. The full-back leads the ball-carrier into the hole with a block on the defensive end, and the tight end drives the outside linebacker in the direction he wants to go. If the linebacker makes an inside move, the tight end rides him in that direction and the runner hits outside; if the linebacker goes outside, the tight end moves with him and the runner cuts inside.*

The sweep was the flagship call of Lombardi's football philosophy – it, like many others he ran, featured minimal deception but maximum effort. What made it the coach's favourite, however, wasn't about results: 'It requires all 11 men to play as one to make it succeed, and that's what "team" means.'

When Lombardi landed in Green Bay following his stint as the New York Giants' offensive coordinator, the Packers were in desperate need of a unifying force. In Lombardi, they found somebody who fit the bill – and not just on the field.

Off it, even during the halcyon days of the late 1920s, their battle for solvency was constant. The decade that preceded Lombardi's arrival in 1959 was the most difficult in franchise history, with dreadful on-field returns meeting off-field turmoil. Curly Lambeau departed in 1950, locked in a bitter dispute with management over his decision to purchase an expensive practice facility, and just as he lost his previous magic – winning only 17 games across four campaigns as head coach of the Chicago Cardinals and Washington Redskins – so did the Pack.

They didn't enjoy a winning campaign from 1948 to '58, a seemingly terminal downturn combining with several home games taking place in Milwaukee as complaints over City Stadium's 25,000 capacity grew audible among NFL owners. By the middle of the decade, the team were issued an ultimatum: build a new stadium or move. Complying meant Green Bay would retain their NFL team. They just needed the right man to reclaim a seat at its top table.

The eldest of five children in an Italian family, Lombardi's football life began in earnest at Fordham University. Diminutive stature didn't stop him starring on their famous 'Seven Blocks of Granite' offensive line, comprising tight ends Leo Paquin and John Druze, tackles Al Babartsky and Natty Pierce, guards Lombardi and Ed Franco, and centre Alex Wojciechowicz. Lombardi, the least talented of the septet, eked every shred of skill and effort from himself while exemplifying the toughness he later demanded from his players. Yet his signature college season ended in disappointment, Fordham suffering a shock 7–6 defeat to New York University that ended their Rose Bowl aspirations and delivered a lesson on never underestimating opponents.

Graduating from university during the Great Depression meant Lombardi struggled for work, trying his hand at semi-professional football and a finance company, before briefly enrolling in law school. In 1939, Vince's father insisted he get a steady job if he wanted to fulfil his wish of marrying girlfriend Marie Planitz – advice that persuaded him to take a position at St. Celia High School offered by their new head coach, former Fordham teammate Andy Palau. Lombardi worked as an assistant football coach, head basketball coach and teacher of Latin, physics and chemistry.

It quickly became apparent he possessed an aptitude for

coaching and leadership, often delivering rousing pregame speeches. Palau left St. Celia in 1942 and, one year after taking the reins, Lombardi had built the nation's best prep team. Their most notable triumph came against a Brooklyn Prep's squad quarterbacked by future Penn State coach Joe Paterno.

After eight seasons, Lombardi took an assistant's job at his alma mater with the understanding the top role was his when they deposed incumbent Ed Danowski. As the months wore on, rumours of a conspiracy grew, and an embarrassed Lombardi left to continue his career with Army. In five years under College Football Hall-of Famer Red Blaik, who described Lombardi as the best assistant he ever had, the budding coach's hallmarks – simplicity and execution – were identified.

The Giants provided Lombardi's first opening in the pros as one-half of the best assistant–coach tandem in history. He and Landry helped Big Blue reach two NFL Championship Games between 1954 and '58, winning it all by defeating the Chicago Bears in '56. While success as an assistant was gratifying, Lombardi was desperate to become the main man – only to be denied on numerous occasions by the kind of discrimination he had fought throughout his career. His Italian Catholic roots didn't sit well with some prospective employers. One story goes that the Wake Forest committee, having ignored his application, said: 'Nobody whose surname ends in a vowel is going to coach Wake Forest.'

Waiting so long for that big break didn't rid Lombardi of a direct, to-the-point approach, as summed up by his words to Green Bay's top brass in interview: 'I want it understood that I am in complete command here.'

For the next decade, nobody doubted that fact.

He arrived like a whirlwind. 'I have never been associated with a loser,' said Lombardi, 'and don't expect to be now.' The Packers he inherited were just that: losers who finished 1-10-1 the previous season.

Everybody was afforded a clean slate, as well as an equal opportunity that didn't always exist at other teams. Lombardi publicly stated his players were 'not black or white, but Packer green', a view proven emphatically when he threatened to release any player or coach who exhibited prejudice.

Lombardi built his programme on accountability, grading every player on every play on a scale from minus-two to two and revealing the marks to the team each week. Robinson says: 'That grade is how he calculated your contract for the next year. Nowadays guys just get huge contracts, but he paid based on performance. It's a big difference.' But the players trusted him implicitly. 'You could take his word to the bank,' adds Robinson.

His approach fostered loyalty and love from the players, who carried Lombardi off the field after he won his first game at the helm, versus the Bears, to begin a 7-5 campaign, their best for 14 years. 'A good teacher puts across what he wants, whether on the field or in the classroom,' said Lombardi. 'It's about the how and the why. If players understand that, they will buy in.'

Lombardi's brilliance wasn't just built around a repetitive mantra and straight-talking. Although his approach harked back to previous eras, centred around toughness, he operated at the cutting edge of film study, utilised to analyse his team and opponents. Lombardi took it to another level during games; with the Giants, he instructed assistants in the press box to take polaroid shots of defensive alignments and lower them down to field level inside a weighted sock attached to string.

His unique blend transformed Packer fortunes. Towards the end of a second season in which their team were crowned western champions, Green Bay's residents began calling him 'the Pope'. But a year of unbridled joy for fans wasn't matched by their new hero after a potential NFL Championship-winning drive was stopped 10 yards short, the Philadelphia Eagles winning 17–13 despite being outgained 401 yards to 296. Philadelphia's triumph owed plenty to Lombardi gambling on multiple fourth downs rather than kicking field goals. 'When you get down there,' he admitted, 'come out with something. I lost the game, not my players.'

A different declaration resonated for years to come. After the loss, Lombardi told his charges: 'This will never happen again. You will never lose another championship game.' How right he was. Lombardi's record in the postseason thereafter was 10-1 – the only blot coming in the 1964 Playoff Bowl, a now-defunct third-place playoff game. 'The "Shit Bowl",' Lombardi once said, scornfully. 'Losers' bowl for losers.'

His men didn't appear in it too often, 1961 and '62 seeing the Packers overcome the Giants 37–0 and 16–7 respectively to win back-to-back titles and seal Lombardi's place at the summit of the NFL's coaching landscape at a time when the previous gold standard had fallen on hard times.

Even after Otto Graham's retirement, Paul Brown's Cleveland Browns trucked on, bouncing back from the first losing season of his tenure in 1956 by reaching the NFL Championship Game the following year. That run was powered by their opening-round selection's first of successive MVP campaigns.

A fullback with halfback speed and agility, Jim Brown glided across the field like a figure skater and hit like a truck. He was truly one of a kind, a peerless mix of pace, size, power, balance, grace and football intelligence. 'In terms of natural ability,' remembers teammate Paul Warfield, himself a Hall of Famer, 'he was given more attributes by the Almighty than anybody. His physical attributes – ability, power, speed, strength – were incredible. But he also had incredible drive to be the best. He understood defenses were built to stop him, but was a mental giant; a genius. Combined with physical ability, that was impossible to stop.'

And his career almost never happened. Brown's start at Syracuse was mired by a familiar story of the era: the uber-talented runner riding the bench while inferior 'backs played. The difference between them? Brown was black. 'I was the only black player on the team,' he said. 'I knew I was the best 'back, and they tried to tell me I wasn't. I was going to leave, but the superintendent of my high school flew over and told me to stick it out.' By his senior year, Brown was a unanimous All-American, scoring a then-NCAA-record 43 points in his final regular-season appearance.

Paul Brown didn't even intend to draft his namesake. The coach had longing eyes for that year's quarterback class but, when the Pittsburgh Steelers nabbed Len Dawson just prior to their selection, Cleveland used the sixth overall pick on Syracuse's star rusher. In his ninth game, Brown set a single-game NFL record with 237 rushing yards against the Los Angeles Rams en route to a league-best tally of 942 for the year, the lowest mark of his career.

Despite the frustration of a crushing 59–14 title-game loss to the Detroit Lions, most considered the Browns poised for another run. But those predictions didn't consider the escalating tension between star player and coach. Even before his friend Muhammad Ali ever stood in front of a camera, Jim Brown was among the first in a new age of black superstars ready to fight back against decades of oppression. 'I was never going to let anybody feel I wasn't top shelf,' said Brown. 'I was born black but didn't want to live black. I wanted to live like everyone else.'

The issue for Paul Brown wasn't that Jim was black, but that his outspokenness ran counter to the coach's programme. For all the keys to Brown's curriculum were teaching and innovation, his excellence was also built upon the discipline instilled in players. From the earliest days, he illustrated a ruthless streak, demanding complete focus on football and punishing indiscretions – sometimes with outright release. In Jim Brown, Paul Brown encountered a player as uncompromising off the field as on it, someone who had too much talent and sway to be frightened. 'I was set in my ways to a certain degree,' said Jim Brown. 'So, we always had a little edge in our relationship.'

It left Coach Brown unfamiliarly impotent, often taking his

frustration out on fellow running back Bobby Mitchell. 'He would scream at me about something, but it was always when Jim was around,' admitted Mitchell. 'He was really talking to Jim.'

Compounding matters was the meddling of Cleveland's new owner, Art Modell. Unlike Arthur McBride, who followed Brown's diktat not to get involved in team matters, advertising executive Modell wanted his voice heard and paid $4.1 million for the privilege. It prompted a tug of war that boiled over prior to the 1962 campaign when Brown traded Mitchell to the Washington Redskins for Ernie Davis, the former Syracuse star who became the first black player to win the Heisman, without consulting Modell. The move tragically backfired. Davis was diagnosed with leukaemia soon after arriving and died the following May without ever playing an NFL down.

Against that backdrop, the mercurial head coach became increasingly detached as the grip on a club he built, operating under his name, loosened. Ahead of the 1962 season finale, while players practised in snow, Brown sat in his car with the quarterback shuttling between it and the field to get play-calls.

Modell's hand was forced. He fired Brown on 9 January 1963, albeit without ever using the word, and elevated long-time assistant Blanton Collier, who sought and believed he had received his mentor's blessing. In actuality, the protégé lost a friendship that would never be recovered but gained the opportunity to win a championship alongside someone still considered one of the greatest players in football history.

With and without Paul Brown as his coach, Jim Brown was unequalled, his famous dawdle to the huddle the most unfitting preamble to the explosiveness he exhibited upon the ball being snapped. When he retired at the peak of his powers, nine seasons had brought Brown eight rushing titles, three MVP awards, zero games missed through injury and 12,312 yards at a scarcely believable 5.2 per carry. And, most importantly, the validation all players crave: a championship, won in 1964 via Cleveland's 27–0 win over the Baltimore Colts, with Brown delivering over 150 total yards.

The Browns' victory came the season after Chicago drew level with Green Bay by claiming a league-best eighth title – and last with George Halas as coach – but it wouldn't be long before Lombardi's Packers responded.

The 1963 and '64 campaigns were frustrating for Green Bay. The former was mired in controversy, the Packers being forced to play without MVP Paul Hornung after he was suspended for his part in a betting scandal, while the latter – with the star halfback returning – proved equally unsatisfying.

Yet they still possessed two key qualities: a brilliant coach and outstanding roster comprised largely of players found by Jack Vainisi, their former scout who died of a heart attack at the age of 33 in 1960 and never saw the many future stars he brought to Green Bay build their legends. A Chicago native who grew up alongside Halas' son as a die-hard Bears fan, Vainisi ended up in Green Bay due to those family connections and contributed more to their sworn enemy than anticipated. With the Packers, he built a one-man scouting network, aided by strong relationships with college coaches, and the results were spectacular. In one decade, Vainisi played a key role in drafting or signing nine future Hall of Famers: centre Jim Ringo, tackle Forrest Gregg, guard Jerry Kramer, quarterback Starr, halfback Hornung, fullback Jim Taylor, linebacker Ray Nitschke, defensive end Willie Davis and defensive tackle Henry Jordan.

Of those success stories, the 17th-round quarterback from Alabama sits top. 'Bart wasn't a verbal leader,' reveals Dowler. 'He didn't leap up and down, and yell or holler. He led by example, was a perfectionist, and it rubbed off. He commanded respect – that's the best word I can use. I don't remember him making a bad call, and we believed in him so much that nobody stepped out of line. In my case, I almost knew the play before he called it.'

Those players were the foundation of Green Bay's reign of terror and, for all they enjoyed outstanding coaching, the contribution of a man who delivered the clay Lombardi moulded shouldn't be forgotten. 'Vainisi was a football man,' remembers Hornung. 'Pure and simple. He brought so much talent to Green Bay, but it took Lombardi to make us champions.'

Their collective excellence delivered Lombardi's third title, sealed with a 23–12 win over Cleveland in 1965. Standing in the way of continued success, however, was a team equally concerned with the growing importance of synergy between coach and front office.

Tex Schramm's mark on pro football was already significant at the point he heard of the NFL's plan to start a franchise in Dallas. Alongside Los Angeles owner Dan Reeves, Schramm was instrumental in formulating the initial Rams scouting network that much of the league attempted to emulate, while also providing Rozelle a first break. Schramm's time at the Rams concluded in enmity as he tired of Reeves' erratic behaviour, but the run brought Los Angeles five NFL Championship Game appearances and one victory over ten years.

The bitter departure didn't alter Schramm's passion for pro football and, having spent the intervening years in charge of CBS' sports programming, his interest was piqued at the prospect of a Dallas club. He wanted back in, and oil-magnate Clint Murchison Jr was only too happy to oblige, taking a hands-off role and allowing Schramm to shape the club in his vision.

Schramm was instrumental in contributing to many league-wide innovations: a critical role in the AFL–NFL merger, powerful championing of instant replay and implementation of the electronic coach–quarterback communication system to name just three. So, it's notable that he is most revered for his exploits with just one team. The journey to creating the world's richest sports club began on modest ground, with three men – Schramm, former Rams understudy Gil Brandt and Landry – undertaking the unenviable task of building their pro franchise in a city that had previously shown its disinterest. Augmenting their challenge was the presence of the AFL Texans.

At least the Texans were beginning on solid footing, operating as a start-up in a league of start-ups. The Cowboys, a name settled on after Steers and Rangers were considered, approached their first season with neither players, nor access to that year's draft. 'Myself and Tex didn't have an application or interview,' remembers Brandt. 'He just hired me and said: "This is what I want you to do." The first thing was sign free agents. We came in after the draft, and I was fortunate to sign a bunch of guys who turned out to be pretty good.'

Their biggest early recruit owed as much to smart PR as football. Texan quarterback Meredith's final year at Dallas college SMU coincided perfectly with the advent of the Cowboys, and Schramm was quick to swoop on a local icon who would put bums on seats. Gritty, tough and outgoing, Meredith perfectly encapsulated the Lone Star State, forging a deep connection with the city's new breed of pro-football fans.

Although that big-name splash paid off, unknown rough diamonds built the Cowboys, procured through the most advanced scouting system ever seen. Together with IBM, who Schramm worked with while at CBS after they utilised a chip to determine how fast skiers were moving in the Winter Olympics, Dallas reshaped the art of talent acquisition by blending old-school scouting with new-age computers. 'The size of the computer was incredible,' remembers Brandt. 'It occupied half a room!'

The expensive venture – costs were split with the San Francisco 49ers and Rams, who weren't in Dallas' division – built the first database of available players, concentrating on five critical categories: strength and explosion, quickness and agility, competitiveness, character and mental alertness. 'Coaches used to say: "I have a gut feeling about this guy,"' says Brandt. 'But we graded on the five characteristics that lead to success. The same five are used today.'

Where the three clubs differed is how they weighted each category, and neither of the system's other users enjoyed as much success as Dallas. The Cowboys' talent acquisition became the envy of football, and not just because of their database. Brandt searched far and wide for athletes capable of converting their skills to the gridiron. 'I remember having a kicking camp in Europe and coming away with Toni Fritsch,' he says. 'His claim to fame was scoring two goals in a [soccer] win against England. We brought him to Dallas when he had been a national hero in Austria.'

Another example came in 1964 when Dallas took a seventh-round flier on Olympic-gold-medal-winning sprinter Bob Hayes from Florida A&M. He made his name in Tokyo, earning the tag 'fastest man alive' for running the final leg of the United States' 4×100 metres relay team and moving from fifth place to first. 'Most don't know he was wearing borrowed sneakers,' reveals Brandt.

Hayes only played two years of high-school football and largely operated as a kick returner in college. In the pros, he projected as a running back – but Brandt thought otherwise. 'I wrote in my report that he might be a better receiver. He caught the ball well.' The mother of all understatements. By the end of his 10-year run in Dallas, Hayes had caught 365 balls, 71 for touchdowns.

That so many of Brandt and Schramm's finds went on to become Pro Bowlers, All-Pros or, like Hayes, Hall of Famers was due to the other member of their trifecta: Landry. 'We were fortunate to have Coach Landry, who was a great developer of young players,' adds Brandt. 'Tom had a great insight into what a player was going to be a year or two down the road. We had basketball players who had never played a game of college football, like Cornell Green. We had Herb Scott, who came from one of the smallest schools you can get in Virginia Union. We had him playing behind John Niland, who was an All-Pro player and then one day Tom said: "We're going to trade John Niland." And I said: "Coach, are you kidding me?" He said: "No, Scott is going to be a really good player. He might not be this year, but he will be over the long haul, so we are going to have to make the move."'

The comparison between Landry and his Giants colleague Lombardi is fascinating. Their sideline appearances were similar, both donning smart suits, with Landry's signature trilby setting him apart. So, too, was their devotion to film study. Yet they were never considered friends. Amusingly, Landry once coined the name 'Mr High-Low' for Lombardi, oblivious to the irony of his own reputation as someone in the middle of those extremes. In dealing with players, Landry was accused of being cold and emotionless; Lombardi, while prone to violent bouts of temper, was charming.

'There were three games that made Coach Lombardi extra intense,' says Robinson. 'The Bears, the Giants – because they never elevated him – and the Cowboys. He hated the thought of losing to Landry.'

The biggest difference between football savants was how they viewed the game. While Lombardi believed the biggest edge could be gained through brilliant execution of existing schemes, Landry was constantly locked away with his projector and chalkboard searching for the next schematic twist, à la Clark Shaughnessy.

His first major one in Dallas, ironically, was created as a counter to old colleague Lombardi's sweep. The flex defense, an evolution of Landry's own 4-3, saw linemen alternately align on and just off the line of scrimmage. The idea was to disguise what gaps each was responsible for and allow players to read and react in an attempt to counter the zone-blocking Lombardi favoured. Like his 4-3, it was built to take advantage of a player's unique talents – for Sam Huff in the 1950s, see Lilly, a defensive tackle with wide receiver agility and linebacker instincts, a decade later. Landry also innovated on offense by having linemen hitch* to confuse defenses, while pulling the shotgun out of hibernation.

It speaks to what makes NFL coaching so fascinating that Landry's approach, although diametrically opposed to Lombardi's, made him the next-best thing to the Green Bay legend in the 1960s. For just as Lombardi – blue-collar, traditional and hard-nosed – perfectly fit Green Bay, Landry's continuous innovation suited the progressive Cowboys. 'I remember in 1964, we took five hours to select Mel Renfro because we had sent a doctor from Oregon to Portland to check him out,' says Brandt. 'Vince came by and said: "Ha, ha, ha, what happened? Did your computer break down? I've never liked those things."'

It all created quite the melting pot at the conclusion of the 1966 campaign, when the teams met in an NFL Championship Game to remember. The contest represented a coming-of-age performance for Landry's Cowboys, who overhauled a 14–0 deficit to end the opening quarter on level terms and then spent the ensuing hours scratching and clawing to stay in touch. When Meredith hit Franklin Clarke perfectly in-stride for a 68-yard touchdown late in the fourth quarter, Dallas trailed 34–27.

The Cowboys quickly drove down the field after regaining possession, with 72,000 people left on the edge of their seats as they faced fourth-and-goal from the Green Bay two-yard line. A tactical error from Landry proved critical, the coach instructing Hayes – who never played goalline* – to head onto the field. The wideout's task was to block Robinson, not that he had any idea what he was doing. Meredith took the ball from under centre, faked a hand-off and rolled to his right. The quarterback's path to the end zone looked clear, but, suddenly, an unimpeded Robinson flew in front of right guard Leon Donohue, straight for Meredith. The signal-caller did well to keep the play alive, throwing a desperation pass while in the Hall-of-Fame linebacker's clutches, only to see it land in the arms of safety Tom Brown.

'In the locker room after the game,' remembers Robinson, 'Lombardi came up to me – in front of reporters – patted me on the back and said: "Great play, Robby . . . but that's not how we drew it up!" I said: "I know, coach, but I thought it was the thing to do." And he replied: "Well, I'm going to have to give you a minus-two," and laughed that big Lombardi laugh.'

Nearly a year to the day later, on Lambeau Field's Frozen Tundra, it'd be determined if he or Landry would have the last laugh in their rivalry.

They say revenge is a dish best served cold, and that was most certainly what the Cowboys had in mind as Starr approached the Green Bay bench with 13 seconds left of the 1967 championship game.

For all the setting differed significantly to the previous year's tilt at Dallas' Cotton Bowl, played under glorious skies, the Cowboys' task was nearly identical: make a play, only this time on defense, to force overtime. Or, as it turned out, win. Lombardi – with the Pack down 17–14 – decided to go for broke and run another rushing play. It was an incredible risk. With no timeouts remaining and just seconds left on the clock, there wouldn't be enough time to run the field-goal unit onto the field for a game-tying kick if Green Bay were stuffed.

On the sideline, Starr – after confirming with Kramer that footing was good enough to run a wedge play – reached Lombardi. 'The wedge play is a good play,' he told his coach. 'But our 'backs can't get to the line of scrimmage, so I could sneak it? I wouldn't have as far to go and could just shuffle my feet and lunge in.'

Lombardi's reply was succinct: 'Well, then, run it, and let's get the hell outta here.'

Starr, who hadn't quarterback sneaked all year, took the snap and – to the surprise of teammates unaware of his plan – bundled behind perfectly executed blocks from Kramer, Gregg and centre Ken Bowman, over the goalline and further into immortality. 'I missed it,' remembers Green Bay fan Mary Speerschneider. 'I was so cold I'd jammed myself into a sleeping bag and was stuck! I didn't see Starr go over.'

'That drive was the highlight of my career,' says Dowler, 'and of our career as a football team.'

Afterwards, the Green Bay players carried their leading man off Lambeau Field for the final time. Two weeks later, Lombardi coached his last game for the Packers, a resounding 33–14 win over the Oakland Raiders in Super Bowl II that ensured they emulated Curly Lambeau by winning three championships in a row. 'That was something he talked about from 1965,' says Dowler. 'It was never far from the surface of what we were doing. Coach was on a crusade.'

With that achievement ticked off, Lombardi spent one year as the club's general manager and another as Washington's head coach, only for his career to be ended by colon cancer. He died, aged 57, on 3 September 1970, 17 days before the Packers opened their third season under replacement Phil Bengtson with a 40–0 home defeat against the Lions.

Without Lombardi on the sidelines, Packer Nation could only cling to memories. And none are as vivid as the day everybody froze and heroes arose. Between the astonishing cold, infamous sideline exchange and iconic finish, the game still serves as a touchstone for the wonderment and mythology that surrounds the 1960s Packers and their coach.

Two of Lombardi's teenage years were spent studying for the priesthood at the Cathedral College of Immaculate Conception. It proved apt, for the role that defined his life saw Lombardi lead a congregation, and the experience was certainly religious. To the people of Green Bay, that is what the Packers became during his tenure: religion. Even today, the Pope's aura remains on every street corner around 'Titletown', in the 25 stops along the Packers Heritage Trail and, most importantly, on each pilgrimage to Lambeau Field, undertaken come sleet or shine by virtually the whole town's residents. When the Packers are playing, there is simply no reason not to watch. Anybody attempting to make excuses will be reminded of New Year's Eve 1967 – of the Ice Bowl.

9

'I Guarantee It'

Super Bowl III

NEW YORK JETS 16
BALTIMORE COLTS 7

---

12 January 1969

Orange Bowl, Miami

By the swimming pool at Fort Lauderdale's Galt Ocean Mile Hotel, Joe Namath looked every bit the cool playboy, further emphasising his infamous reputation and enduring nickname. 'Broadway' lay topless, reclining on a deck chair, signature golden smile glistening as brightly as the small beads of sweat on his bronzed skin, surrounded by hordes of reporters on one side and fans desperate to grab autographs, or even just a glance, on the other. They stood, ears poised, waiting to discover whether Namath would back off or double down on his proclamation.

The previous evening, the New York Jets' starting quarterback had been whisked to Miami's Touchdown Club to become the first AFL player awarded Outstanding Professional Football Player of the Year. The subsequent speech perfectly captured the essence of Broadway Joe, part raconteur, part athlete. Lips freed by his old friend Johnny Walker, Namath joked: 'I'd like to personally thank all the single girls in New York for their contribution.' He then turned his attention to the weekend's Super Bowl III match-up with the Baltimore Colts: 'We are going to win Sunday. I guarantee you.'

Ironically, given the historical significance of Namath's guarantee, it didn't cause an immediate splash. Of the press attending, only the *Miami Herald* ran the headline 'Namath Guarantees Jet Victory', and the initial response certainly didn't match the expectations of the signal-caller, who immediately called teammate Johnny Sample upon returning to his hotel. 'We are going to win,' replied Sample, 'but you shouldn't have said that.'

Word had spread by the time Namath was poolside, and he was caught between a rock and a hard place. Coach Weeb Ewbank was livid, not least because the proclamation betrayed the confidence permeating the locker room, and made his feelings clear to the hungover quarterback at breakfast. Namath knew Pandora's Box was already open and taking a backwards step would, if anything, look worse.

So, as reporters stood hoping for more material to fill their column inches, Namath dutifully delivered. 'We're a better team than Baltimore,' he continued. 'Earl Morrall would be the third-string quarterback on the Jets. There are maybe five or six better in the AFL.'

Namath's claims contrasted sharply with media opinions. *Detroit Free Press* columnist Joe Falls predicted a 270–0 Baltimore win and, while written with tongue firmly in cheek, it summed up the mood. The Colts, having ridden through the NFL boasting a near-perfect record under young head coach Don Shula, were 18-point favourites and considered maybe the greatest pro team in history. So, the prevailing feeling was a club from the modest AFL, whose inability to compete with NFL powers was long since proven, had little chance at the Orange Bowl.

*

'We were told for 10 straight days,' remembered Namath, 'how badly we were going to get whipped against the best team ever.' He might as well have said 10 straight years – the American Football League had been written off by purists for nearly a decade.

The signings of stars such as Namath were coups for a league filled with players and coaches who, in the eyes of many, just didn't cut the mustard at the highest level. Ironically, many AFL legends – those enshrined in the Hall of Fame – were just that: men cast aside by the established league who walked straight into the welcoming arms of what was then a bold, new venture: George Blanda spent years alternating at quarterback and linebacker for the Chicago Bears and being utilised as a kicker but enjoyed a second wind as a star signal-caller for the Houston Oilers; wide receiver Don Maynard was jettisoned by the New York Giants due to fumbling issues yet established his legend across town with the Titans/Jets; Len Dawson didn't catch on with the Pittsburgh Steelers or Cleveland Browns but looked perfectly at home piloting the Dallas Texans/Kansas City Chiefs to three AFL titles and one Super Bowl. It extended to coaching, too, Ewbank having turned to the AFL after being unceremoniously dismissed from the Colts having won two NFL titles.

The AFL boasted outstanding players and coaches, operating fine teams who played an exciting game that captured the imagination. As early as 1962, 56 million people tuned in for the Oilers' three-peat attempt in the AFL Championship Game against the Texans, played in front of a packed Jeppesen Stadium in Houston. The Oilers were dethroned as Lamar Hunt scored victory over the AFL's other most influential owner, Bud Adams.

If Houston, powered by Blanda, were the team of the early AFL, the crown was most definitely passed to the Buffalo Bills, who claimed back-to-back titles from 1964 by riding – in spite of the league's reputation – a well-coordinated, rough-and-ready defense to glory. They, too, were thwarted in a quest for three AFL championships in a row by Hunt's team, at that stage in Kansas City.

Although the Chiefs would come unstuck in the inaugural Super Bowl, overwhelmed by the brilliance of the Green Bay Packers, they were exceptional nonetheless. Their offense was marshalled superbly by Dawson, while the defense boasted Hall of Famers at all three levels: Buck Buchanan set the tone up front, linebacker Bobby Bell was the unit's signal-caller and interception-hungry safety Johnny Robinson, as well as cornerback Emmitt Thomas, patrolled the back end. 'We had such a great blend of players,' says Bell. 'Fast, big, small. Coach [Hank] Stram didn't care what you looked like, or what colour you were. He just wanted great players.'

Perhaps no team, however, were as good in any single season as the one most responsible for the AFL's reputation as an exciting, all-passing show that contrasted greatly with the in-vogue power approach favoured by most of the NFL: Sid Gillman's 1963 San Diego Chargers.

The most impressive tribute to Gillman wasn't how greatly he impacted the AFL but his influence on football overall. That the passing game of the 1980s was unrecognisable from the 1970s, which was equally unrecognisable from the early 1960s, can be traced back to Gillman. His fingerprints are also on many parts of the modern-day spread formation,* from wide receivers motioning pre-snap to help quarterbacks determine if the defense is in man or zone to the increased prevalence of the slot receiver downfield, tight ends being split out from the line of scrimmage and the precise squaring of routes.

There are too many small innovations to mention, but all were part of Gillman's wider philosophy. 'The field is 100 yards long and 53 wide,' he once said. 'We're going to use every inch of it to force the other guy to defend it.' It could just as easily have been Bill Walsh talking. The legendary San Francisco 49ers coach who pioneered the West Coast Offense was, like Al Davis, a by-product of Gillman. Davis was more closely associated, serving as the Chargers' wide receivers coach for three seasons from their inception in 1960. 'Sid Gillman was the father of modern-day passing,' said Davis. As for Walsh, his link was indirect. He spent one season alongside Davis with the Oakland Raiders, but the impact of Gillman was significant. 'Much of what I did I got from Sid Gillman,' revealed Walsh.

The pair took Gillman's teachings forward in different ways. Both utilised complex route concepts that were designed to work in conjunction with one another, but Davis focused on the deeper-passing elements, while Walsh became enamoured with the geometric specificity of his horizontal attack.

Gillman's own career was largely nomadic. His 20 years in the college ranks were spent mostly as an assistant, with the most notable stop from a historical context coming at West Point. It was there he began a trend of greatly influencing future all-time coaches by taking under his wing a young operator from the nearby high school, whom he eventually recommended as his successor. Together, Gillman and Vince Lombardi often discussed the zone-blocking schemes on which the latter built his offense.

His apprentice was already a rising assistant in the pro ranks by the time Gillman made the jump, leading the Los Angeles Rams to the NFL Championship Game in his first year (1955) and still fielding the league's second-best offense in a final campaign (1959) that brought just two wins. From there, Gillman enjoyed his longest tenure, with the Chargers, before becoming a human sticking plaster. He would be brought on board by a team in need, transform the offense and depart just as quickly. One of those jobs was a two-year run as the Philadelphia Eagles' offensive coordinator under Dick Vermeil. 'We never would have made it to the Super Bowl if not for Sid Gillman,' admits Vermeil. 'When we hired him, we hired an encyclopaedia.'

The highlight of Gillman's career undoubtedly came in San Diego. The 1963 Chargers were, like many great teams, a timely meeting of innovation and talent. The best of the latter was wide receiver Lance Alworth, for whom the nickname 'Bambi' perfectly encapsulated the grace, quickness and leap that turned him into a Hall of Famer.

Alworth teamed up with Paul Lowe and Keith Lincoln, the halfbacks accruing nearly 2,000 combined rushing yards behind All-Pro tackle Ron Mix, whose technical excellence was summed up by being called for just two holding penalties in his entire career. Alworth's most significant relationships were with quarterback Tobin Rote, enjoying a renaissance of his own six years after leading the Detroit Lions to their fourth NFL title, and John Hadl, a halfback Gillman helped develop into one of the game's great touch passers. Together, they formed a diverse attack – utilising Gillman's numerical verbiage for play-calls, another oft-followed first – that dominated the AFL to the tune of 399 points.

Just as destructive as Alworth and the offense was a defense led by pro football's original 'Fearsome Foursome', the most feared of whom was giant tackle Ernie Ladd. The unit was shepherded by another future Hall-of-Fame head coach in the Gillman tree: Chuck Noll. Like Lombardi, Walsh and Davis before him, Noll learnt from Gillman the importance of film study, leadership and obsession. From a childhood job at the movie theatre until the day he died, Gillman was doing the same thing: cutting up game tape and analysing it. 'The real treasure I got from Sid was learning how to be a winner,' remarked Davis. 'It takes commitment, love of football, excellence, work ethic. No one could ever outwork Sid. He taught me how an organisation should be run.'

Gillman was the ultimate weapon on the sideline, a man utilising his astonishing memory bank to spot and counter opposition tactics in real time. Even now, in the age of bloated staffs and live analytics, there are few head coaches capable of impacting a game as it unfolds quite like Gillman could.

There was no greater example than the contest that crowned his team 1963 AFL champions, a 51–10 destruction of the Boston

Patriots that was Gillman's genius condensed into 60 minutes. The master strategist spent the game moving his offensive players around like pieces on a chessboard, countering each Patriots move to rack up 610 yards of offense. So dominant was their showing that many people suggested San Diego could have beaten that year's NFL champion, the Bears – although such claims endured a posthumous hit when the AFL Chiefs and Raiders were soundly beaten by Green Bay in the opening two Super Bowls. By 1969, the '63 Chargers – like the remainder of the AFL – needed a hero to catapult their past and present into the realms of respectability.

They needed Broadway.

Come 1965, Sonny Werblin was transforming the AFL's New York franchise, eradicating any doubts of whether another pro-football team in the Big Apple was viable. A Titans club on life support during Harry Wismer's disastrous tenure was now thriving as the Jets, having capitalised on the showmanship of Werblin, a veteran entertainment impresario. The Jets were crafted in his imagination, sporting the favourite colour of a man born on St Patrick's Day and operating in a stadium more befitting of professional sports, the decrepit Polo Grounds making way for Shea Stadium. They just needed somebody to put bums on seats.

Namath arrived for a record sum of $427,000 as the centrepiece of a draft class worth $1.1 million. He followed in the footsteps of the previous year's first-round pick, running back Matt Snell, by rejecting NFL advances and the two would pair memorably years later. At the time, though, Werblin's primary concern was capturing the attention of New York's public: 35,000 season-ticket sales by July told their own story.

Namath arrived with two briefs: produce on the gridiron and get to know New York. In his good-looking, smooth-talking recruit, the owner recognised someone with transcendent appeal who could adorn front and back pages. 'When Joe Namath walks into a room,' said Werblin, 'you know he's there. When any other high-priced rookie walks in, he's just a nice-looking young man. With Namath, it's like Babe Ruth and Lou Gehrig or Mickey Mantle and Roger Maris.'

The role seemed an unlikely one for the son of Hungarian immigrants who shined shoes as a child to contribute to the family coffers, but it suited Namath perfectly. He blended movie-star looks with charm and no shortage of wisecracks. 'I can't wait until tomorrow,' he once said, 'because I get better lookin' every day.'

'I've been married for a million years,' says former Jets centre John Schmitt, 'so I couldn't hang with Joe a lot in New York City. If I told my wife I was going to be with Joe, she knew I wasn't going to a library. He's known and loved by everybody. There are very few athletes like that. There's Muhammed Ali, Joe DiMaggio, Michael Jordan and Joe.'

Namath was also a brilliant quarterback who won a National Championship at Alabama under Bear Bryant, the legendary coach declaring him 'the greatest athlete I ever coached'. His acclimatisation to professional football was seamless, Rookie-of-the-Year honours followed by All-Pro nods. By the time Werblin exited stage left in 1968, bought out by fellow owners who had tired of his lust for the limelight, his creation touched superstar-dom because Namath's exploits on the field – he became the first player in pro history to have 4,000 single-season passing yards in 1967 – were matched only by those off it.

Despite their problems with Werblin himself, the remaining owners had no issue with the quarterback reared in his image. If there was one thing they knew about Broadway Joe, it was that he shone brightest on the big stage. And they didn't come any bigger than Super Bowl III against the Colts.

After Baltimore followed up their epic 1958 victory over the Giants in the 'Greatest Game Ever Played' with a comprehensive triumph in the following year's rematch, it seemed like the club had the makings of a dynasty and Ewbank a job for life. But the Colts descended into mediocrity thereafter, hovering at .500 despite the exploits of Johnny Unitas, Raymond Berry and others.

Owner Carroll Rosenbloom had seen enough following their 7-7 campaign in 1962 and fired Ewbank, who was immediately snapped up by the Jets. Rosenbloom sought advice from defensive stalwart Gino Marchetti in his search for a replacement. 'There is only one guy,' replied Marchetti. 'Shula.'

Rosenbloom was stunned. 'Do you mean the guy who used to play here?' he replied. 'Yeah,' said Marchetti. 'He's a better coach than he was a player.'

Memories of Shula's playing days were vivid – he was just 33. 'I was coaching guys I played with and against that were much better than I ever was,' he said. 'Now I'm their head coach. I had to prove in every meeting, practice and game that I knew what I was talking about and could help [us] win.'

Shula quickly set about attaining respect with the uncompromising style that hallmarked his career. 'He would put pressure on you,' says Marv Fleming, who played under Shula in Miami. 'But he was a great coach.' And an instantly successful one, too, going 8-6 in his first year and leading Baltimore back to the title game the next.

But the pounding Baltimore suffered at the hands of Jim Brown and Cleveland earned Shula the unfair reputation of being unable to win the big one. In reality, his Colts' revival coincided with Lombardi's brilliant Green Bay team and endured some rotten luck. They lost the Western Conference playoff to Green Bay – played due to teams tying atop the standings – on a controversial field goal that replays showed missed wide right in 1965 and suffered at the hands of the same team late in the following year's regular season when, with Baltimore down 14–10 as the clock ticked towards zero, Johnny Unitas fumbled at the 15-yard line and the Packers recovered. Even the 'Million-Dollar Fumble' paled in comparison to a 1967 campaign where they were arguably the best team in football but missed the playoffs despite an 11-1-2 record – superior to the Packers and Dallas Cowboys, who would eventually contest the NFL Championship Game.

That year was the NFL's first under a new division and playoff structure in which the Eastern and Western conferences were split further into two divisions within each. In the Eastern sat the Capitol and Century divisions; in the Western were the Coastal and Central. This proved detrimental to Baltimore, who finished the campaign with an identical record to the Rams in the Coastal, but missed out on a playoff spot as Los Angeles had a better point differential in head-to-head meetings. Insult was added to injury when the Rams subsequently lost 28-7 to Green Bay in the Eastern Conference Championship Game.

Invigorated by the sense of injustice, an extremely talented roster set about the following year with added determination. They were without their iconic leader for most of the campaign, a preseason arm injury ensuring Unitas threw just 32 passes – but Morrall excelled. He capitalised on the brilliance of superstar tight end John Mackey to amass 3,000 passing yards and win MVP as Baltimore went 13-1.

That they didn't enter the Super Bowl on the brink of an achievement Shula would become synonymous with – the unbeaten campaign – was due to his coaching error. In Week 6, he tried to bring back Unitas, but the passer wasn't ready. 'Johnny's arm wasn't right,' remembers former Colts executive Upton Bell, 'and he threw three interceptions.'

Baltimore's place as pro football's premier team was undisputed as the Jets contest approached, however. They avenged their sole defeat by pummelling the Browns 34–0 in the NFL Championship Game to leave confidence at an all-time high. 'After watching Jets film, we thought it would be a walkover,' admits Bell. 'People will deny it now, but that was the mood.'

A walkover it was. Only Baltimore, and everybody else, had the wrong winner.

*

There were warning signs throughout the 'Season of Namath', in which Broadway found himself at the centre of multiple contests that would go down in NFL folklore. Most notable, outside of Super Bowl III, was the 'Heidi Game', in which the TV movie of that name interrupted a thrilling Jets–Raiders game with just over one minute left. The broadcast ended with New York leading 32–29, meaning everybody in the Eastern half of the U.S. missed the Raiders' stirring comeback in a 42–32 thriller.

For all that day ended miserably for Namath, it only served to enhance the legend that arose from his performance in the AFL Championship Game between the sides, a three-touchdown masterpiece in which he drove the Jets 68 yards in the face of icy winds for the game-winning score. Combined with his pregame declaration, it created a sense of expectation ahead of the Baltimore showdown that meant the Jets' subsequent shock victory is remembered largely for Namath, even though his individual impact was fairly minimal. Bell adds: 'Namath did a lot of boasting and was good, but the key was Snell and their offensive line. Nobody realised our weakness was running straight at us. Weeb Ewbank did.'

Ewbank also calculated, correctly, the Colts would double-cover star wideout Manyard if he illustrated no ill-effects from an ongoing hamstring injury. As such, the coach instructed his pass-catcher to run a go route against veteran cornerback Bobby Boyd, who Ewbank felt had lost a step, early in the game. Maynard burned the defensive back and, while Namath's ensuing pass was overthrown, the subsequent attention afforded to New York's star receiver allowed number-two George Sauer to collect eight passes for 131 yards.

On the ground, Snell – operating behind a fine line starring Hall-of-Fame tackle Winston Hill – racked up 121 yards with one touchdown on 30 carries. Namath called the correct run plays and delivered a clean 206-yard passing game, while the Jets' turnover-hungry defense combined with several Colts miscues to contribute to a dominant performance. Gang Green gathered four interceptions – the first via Tom Mitchell's shoulder pad as he shelled an easy touchdown to put Baltimore 7–0 up – while the Colts missed an early field goal and Morrall failed to see a wide-open Jimmy Orr on a flea flicker* and instead threw his second pick.

For Shula, the encounter added further weight to suggestions he always fell at the final hurdle. Most damning was not utilising Unitas until the fourth quarter, with criticism amplified by his ability to move the ball on all three possessions. 'Unitas told me Shula said he would put him in at halftime if Morrall was struggling,' adds Bell. 'Shula denied that, but he definitely put him in too late. Even with his bad arm, we would have won the game had he put him in at halftime.'

The game sullied Shula's rapport with Rosenbloom and, following an 8-5-1 1969 campaign, he departed into the grateful arms of Miami (Baltimore subsequently secured a first-round pick after the Dolphins were charged with tampering). 'Rosenbloom spent a lot of time in New York and his friends, or what he thought were his friends, let him know about Super Bowl III continually,' said Shula. 'He would pick up the phone and pass his feelings on to me. It caused our relationship to come apart.'

The Baltimore squad he left behind would go on to win Super Bowl V, a game of redemption for Morrall – who entered in the second quarter following another Unitas injury and guided his team to a 16–13 victory over Dallas. Even so, there remains a sense of regret surrounding that era's Colts. 'If the result of Super Bowl III was different, the Colts would have been remembered as one of the great teams of their time,' says Bell. 'Our players agreed the win two years later was anti-climactic. It never made up for that loss.'

While never the same player after Super Bowl III – knee injuries dating back to his Alabama days were so debilitating he sometimes had to have one of them drained at halftime – Namath was no less controversial. He briefly retired following the Super Bowl campaign having been told to sell his stake in a bar on New York's East Side frequented by gamblers but eventually relented. There were plenty of other income sources once that venture was offloaded. Namath famously promoted male pantyhose among other products.

His legend, though, was built around the game that secured a bust in Canton and legitimised the AFL. 'Are you one of those NFL writers?' Namath asked reporters in the locker room afterwards. Those who said 'yes' were met with the same line: 'Well, listen, the AFL is here to stay, and you'd better believe it. I guarantee it.'

'It was great to feel part of a league that was scoffed at,' added Namath. 'Not so much for me, as I only arrived in 1965, but everyone. When I got back to the hotel, I saw Emmitt Thomas, Buck Buchanan and Willie Lanier from the Chiefs. They met us off the bus, and we hugged. We felt good about that.'

Twelve months later, those same Chiefs players would strike another blow for the league to finally, once and for all, end suggestions they couldn't compete with the NFL.

Even after the Jets' victory, many people continued to write off the AFL. 'We were still 17-point underdogs in Super Bowl IV,' reveals Kansas City linebacker Bell.

Those who called Namath, Snell and Ewbank's exploits a fluke were silenced when Stram's Chiefs dominated the Vikings 23–7. In many ways, the script was similar to the Jets' day in the sun: a victory for schematic diversity over stubbornness that illustrated the differences between two leagues with vastly contrasting styles of play. In the AFL, the key approach was innovation, with most teams utilising modern offensive concepts – such as shifting – that the Lombardis of the world considered smoke and mirrors. NFL clubs, meanwhile, were delivering a more traditional approach by following Lombardi's own recipe for success.

Where the Colts and Vikings came unstuck is that their execution couldn't match Lombardi's Packers, whose roster was drilled on the minutiae of each call in a small playbook. Furthermore, for all the Green Bay coach's approach appeared simple, it was actually considerably more complex. A small call sheet belied Lombardi's intensive scouting, which aided opponent-specific gameplans in which minuscule technical changes performed at the highest level could make significant differences to the outcome.

Stram spent years after the opening Super Bowl stewing over both Lombardi's postgame comments and an inability to adjust to his opposite number's blitzes. By the fourth edition, he was a better operator, overseeing a team showing key upgrades, including Hall-of-Famers Lanier, Curley Culp and Jan Stenerud. His stack defense* shut down opposing running games, while the offense was incredibly diverse. Stram used 20 different formations in Super Bowl IV, including multiple plays with a moving pocket that gave Minnesota fits – no mean feat given the talent of Bud Grant's team. He, like Stram, was a Hall of Famer, directing a defensive line – comprising tackles Gary Larsen and Alan Page as well as ends Carl Eller and Jim Marshall – immortalised as the 'Purple People Eaters'. They provided bite up front that married perfectly with their ball-hawking secondary. The offense, marshalled by veteran signal-caller Joe Kapp, led the NFL in points scored, just as the defense did in those allowed. But Minnesota were no match for the Chiefs' multiplicity; the Vikings didn't feature a motion or pre-snap shift all game.

The ultimate validation of Stram's career was captured beautifully by NFL Films, Steve Sabol persuading him to become the first mic'd-up coach during a game in league history. The resulting footage offered a superb insight into the highs and lows of operating on the sidelines as Stram, dressed in a sharp suit, lived and breathed every moment intently. 'Everybody would say: "Is he really like that?"' adds Bell. 'And he was. He loved to win.'

And win they did, banishing the bitter memories of Super Bowl I at the conclusion of a difficult campaign that summed up their championship mentality. 'Len Dawson was injured most of the year,' says Bell, 'so we had to beat the Jets and Raiders on the road. By the time we played the Vikings, we knew we would dominate.'

Most importantly, Kansas City struck another blow for the league founded by their beloved owner. 'It was important for the Chiefs and AFL to come out on top of Super Bowl IV,' says Clark Hunt. 'My dad looked back with a lot of appreciation because it concluded that era of the AFL, with the series tied 2-2, validating that AFL teams were just as good as NFL, which, of course, was proved over the next several decades.

'It was also reward for lots of hard work. My dad looked back on the AFL with fond memories, but also a full appreciation for how difficult it was. My mother remembers how bitter the battle was and how precarious the AFL was for much of its first five or six years.'

The Jets' and Chiefs' wins also helped confirm the structure once the long-agreed merger finally concluded. As per the initial announcement, the two leagues operated with entirely separate regular-season schedules from 1966 through 1969 but would come together as one from 1970. Following the opening two lopsided Super Bowls, Pete Rozelle had contemplated altering the unification by creating a league championship featuring the teams with the best record, only for back-to-back AFL successes in the third and fourth showpieces to change everything.

Subsequent meetings saw the NFL follow the AFL's lead by adding names to the backs of jerseys and making in-stadium clocks the game clock so that everybody knew the time situation. Most importantly, following lengthy discussions, the Colts, Browns and Steelers joined the 10 AFL clubs to create the American Football Conference (they were compensated $3 million apiece), while the 13 remaining NFL franchises would become the National Football Conference.

Settling the exact alignment wasn't easy, with Rozelle growing so tired of politicking on each side that he placed five different possibilities inside a glass vase and had long-time secretary Thelma Elkjer choose one. It created the ensuing structure:

AFC Central

Cincinnati Bengals
Cleveland Browns
Houston Oilers
Pittsburgh Steelers

AFC East

Baltimore Colts
Boston Patriots
Buffalo Bills
Miami Dolphins
New York Jets

AFC West

Denver Broncos
Kansas City Chiefs
Oakland Raiders
San Diego Chargers

NFC Central

Chicago Bears
Detroit Lions
Green Bay Packers
Minnesota Vikings

NFC East

Dallas Cowboys
New York Giants
Philadelphia Eagles
St. Louis Cardinals
Washington Redskins

NFC West

Atlanta Falcons
Los Angeles Rams
New Orleans Saints
San Francisco 49ers

The make-up was finalised, fittingly, in 1970. Fifty years after its initial formation, the National Football League was reborn.

10

Same Old Steelers

AFC Divisional Round

OAKLAND RAIDERS 7
PITTSBURGH STEELERS 13

---

23 December 1972

Three Rivers Stadium, Pittsburgh

For the Pittsburgh Steelers, the territory was most unfamiliar. It was late December and the Rooney family were watching their men, sporting iconic black and gold, playing meaningful action.

At least some were.

Pittsburgh trailed the Oakland Raiders 7–6 and were on their own 40-yard line, facing fourth-and-10 with 22 seconds remaining. As the Steelers attempted to flip the script on their whole existence by snatching victory from the jaws of defeat, Art Rooney – who had formed the team almost 40 years earlier and coined the phrase 'same old Steelers' that acted as a motto for four decades of futility – stood in an elevator, ready to greet his disconsolate players in the locker room and head home. All things considered, the game had gone considerably better than Pittsburgh's only other postseason outing: a 21–0 loss to the Philadelphia Eagles 25 years previously.

A contest in which the Steelers' Iron Curtain defense dominated, shutting out Oakland until the final two minutes, turned on the intervention of Raiders backup quarterback Ken Stabler. Dropping back to pass and – like twice-intercepted starter Daryle Lamonica – immediately being moved off his spot, 'the Snake' found an alley down the left sideline when Craig Hanneman took a fatal step inside. Stabler, flowing black locks peeking out the back of his helmet, took off, gathering speed like a thoroughbred, cutting back inside and diving for glory. 'Touchdown, Oakland,' screamed the commentators. 'Same old Steelers,' muttered the fans.

Yet these Steelers – assembled and coached by Chuck Noll – were not their predecessors. 'They didn't look a beaten team,' remembered Dan Rooney, Art's son, and an increasingly powerful figure in the club's management. 'Terry Bradshaw still had his swagger and seemed fearless as ever.'

Bradshaw needed all the magic that highlighted his career when the play rolled around. On the sideline, Oakland running back Pete Banaszak put hand to forehead and delivered the sign of the cross. It wasn't the Raiders requiring divine intervention but their opponents.

Bradshaw stood in the huddle and called 'bull right split 66 circle post'. The signal-caller took the ball from under centre, dropped back and surveyed the field, enjoying a clean pocket until Horace Jones sprung inside left tackle Jon Kolb amid Tony Cline bull-rushing Gerry Mullins on the other side. They converged upon the quarterback, ready to seal glorious victory, but Bradshaw had other ideas. 'I got forced out of the pocket,' he remembers. 'I had to move right and was lucky not to have the ball stripped.'

Bradshaw somehow pulled back and escaped their despairing attempts, moved right then cut back as Jones caught him, before unfurling a desperate heave downfield towards John Fuqua. 'It was all a haze,' adds Bradshaw. 'I saw a black jersey flash across my eyes and threw up a prayer.'

It would be answered.

As Fuqua turned, he was met by the stubborn force of safety Jack Tatum, who timed the collision perfectly to arrive just as the ball did. From there, the pigskin flew backwards and out of shot until, suddenly, Franco Harris moved purposefully onto the screen.

'The ball is pulled in by Franco Harris!' screamed Jack Fleming on the Steelers' radio broadcast. 'Harris is going for a touchdown for Pittsburgh! Harris is going! Five seconds left on the clock! Franco Harris pulled in the football. I don't even know where he came from! Fuqua was in a collision. There are people in the end zone. Where did he come from? Absolutely unbelievable! Holy moly!'

'I'm lying on the ground,' says Bradshaw, 'and suddenly hear this huge roar. As a player, you know how to distinguish roars. I said: "Son of gun. Touchdown." I jump up thinking: "I'm a hero to millions. I somehow threw a touchdown pass." So, I start jogging down the field and notice Franco has the ball. I'm totally confused. It was chaos.'

The press box was similarly hysterical. Most thought the play illegal, what with the since-extinguished rule the ball couldn't go from one offensive player to another following a forward pass, but it was unclear whether it touched Fuqua at all or just Tatum. Those who saw Harris collect it, meanwhile, debated whether the pigskin hit the ground. As the arguments grew more audible, the phone rang and Dan Rooney, having made his way downstairs, answered.

'It was Jim Boston, our man on the field,' said Rooney. 'He tells me he's got Fred Swearingen, the referee in charge of the officiating crew standing next to him and he wants to talk to Art McNally, the supervisor of the officials.' Rooney handed over the phone and listened intently while craning his neck to see a replay as McNally – pinning the phone to his ear amid the screams of reporters – told the referee: 'You have to call what you saw. You have to make the call. Talk to your people and make the call!'

It took 10 minutes, by which point Bradshaw's teammates explained to him what'd happened. 'I went from thinking I was a hero to millions to pissed off because it was a deflection!' he jokes. The whole team became heroes when Swearingen returned to the field and raised his arms in the air, heralding a roar from Franco's Italian Army, and the thousands in Three Rivers Stadium parking lots who had been unable to get tickets, that could be heard for miles down Monongahela River.

Pittsburgh emerged triumphant in a playoff game for the first time and did so, ironically, by following the mantra of their colourful opponents: 'Just Win, Baby'.

*

The Autumn Wind is a pirate
Blustering in from sea,
With a rollicking song, he sweeps along,
Swaggering boisterously.
His face is weather beaten.
He wears a hooded sash,
With a silver hat about his head,
And a bristling black mustache.
He growls as he storms the country,
A villain big and bold.
And the trees all shake and quiver and quake,
As he robs them of their gold.
The Autumn Wind is a Raider,
Pillaging just for fun.
He'll knock you 'round and upside down,
And laugh when he's conquered and won.

When he heard 'Autumn Wind', written by NFL Films' Steve

Sabol and narrated by John Facenda, Al Davis would surely have afforded himself a smile. 'If there is anything we've ever done that I'm particularly proud of,' he said, 'I'd say the perpetuation of the greatness of the Raiders. To take a professional football team and give it a distinct characteristic that's different from all others.'

It's an old adage that NFL teams take on the personality of their coach. In the case of Davis' Raiders, it wasn't so much taking their architect's nature as it was his whole being. Every element of the foundations upon which one of pro football's most recognisable brands was built retains Davis' fingerprints. From the silver-and-black colours chosen to resemble the great 'Black Knights of the Hudson' Army teams he grew up idolising to the pirate's-face logo with an eye patch he redesigned and on-field persona that perfectly mirrored the off-field brand.

Straddling the on- and off-field products was Davis, part football genius, part marketing guru. 'Al's legacy,' says former Raiders executive Ron Wolf, 'is that when you think of the Raiders, you think of him. That's a tremendous legacy. There's only one other team you can say that about: the Chicago Bears and George Halas.'

For Davis, the formulation of 'Da Raidahhhhhs', as he bellowed in that signature Brooklyn accent, was a life's work. His footballing childhood might have been spent admiring Army, but the Raiders' roots actually lay in two contrasting baseball clubs: the New York Yankees, to Davis, represented power and intimidation, famously known as the 'Bronx Bombers' due to mammoth home runs that could change the course of a game at any moment; and the Los Angeles Dodgers, who personified speed and player development.

Those contrasting-but-complementary facets left an indelible mark on the teenager already dreaming of 'building the finest organisation in professional sports'. 'I thought someone intelligent could take the qualities of both and put them together,' Davis admitted.

Although inspiration for his creation was formed on the

diamond, it came to pass on the gridiron. Davis headed to Oak-land in 1964, the boy wonder whose shotgun journey to the top of pro football was a by-product of his best and worst qualities, depending on your perspective: half hustle, half excellence. Upon determining that coaching football was his chosen path, he intro-duced himself as 'Davis from Syracuse', hoping administrators mistook him for Orange legend George Davis. Yet his unconven-tional methods worked, and Davis rose quickly – not least because of skill.

His commitment to the craft was undeniable. Sid Gillman recalled giving clinics in which Davis, early in his career as a college assistant, would sit in the front row firing off pertinent questions. It was no surprise, therefore, that Gillman provided Davis' big break. The young coach shone overseeing the Los Angeles/San Diego Chargers' wide receivers over a three-year stint, the highlight of which was spotting something in Arkansas star Lance Alworth and racing onto the field to secure his services after the pass-catcher's final collegiate game.

Davis joined the Raiders as head coach and general manager, remarkably, aged just 33, becoming the youngest person to hold both positions at the same time in pro football. He immediate-ly made his mark. Oakland's colour scheme was altered from black and gold, while the original logo – a pirate face with a black helmet atop a yellow football – became what we know today. Most transformative was the playing product, the Raiders immediately going from 1-13 to 10-4.

Critical to this success were the principles that would become cornerstones of 'Raider Football'. On offense, a deep passing attack. 'It's like having the bomb and being willing to drop it,' said Davis. 'I always hear everyone say: "Take what they give you." I went the other way: we're going to take what we want.'

Defensively, the Raiders were built around relentless pressure up front, while cornerbacks played aggressive bump-and-run cov-erage.* 'Somewhere within the first five or 10 plays,' Davis said, 'the other team's quarterback must go down, and hard. That sets the tempo.'

Davis' fledgling coaching career ended because of his calling in a bigger fight. He became AFL commissioner and struck crucial blows that helped foster the merger most believe Davis never truly wanted. 'Al was bitterly opposed to it,' remembers Mickey Herskowitz. 'He wanted to take down the NFL.'

Unsurprisingly, he scoffed at the idea of remaining in the role as Pete Rozelle's deputy. 'I always say,' said Davis, 'generals win the wars, politicians make the peace.'

Davis returned to his roots in Oakland, only not in his previous role. It was time to begin properly building the franchise of his dreams. Davis set up the holding company A.D. Football, Inc. that assumed a 10 per cent stake in the Raiders, for whom he served as head of football operations.

By 1972, Davis – once described by the mild-mannered Dan Rooney as a 'lying creep' – had staged an extraordinary coup to take full control of the club. He persuaded managing general partner F. Wayne Valley, in Munich for the Olympic Games, to agree to an alteration of their ownership agreement that amounted to giving Davis near full control of team affairs. Valley realised his mistake upon returning to the USA, attempting to sue, but the damage was done. He sold his stake four years later.

Davis didn't assume majority control until 2005 but acted with complete autonomy for the three preceding decades. The run would be filled with bumps and bruises, inflicted and taken, yet it was never dull. Davis waged war with the NFL, on and off the field, assembling a squad that fulfilled his wish of 'not being the most respected team, but most feared', and altering the landscape by moving his Raiders from Oakland to Los Angeles and back again.

That his club garnered such notoriety was thanks to Davis' true skill: as the architect of a team who embarked upon a three-title run during the 1970s and early '80s spanning two cities, two head coaches and two starting quarterbacks.

*

Although he no longer carried the coach's whistle, Davis' presence was felt every day upon his return to Oakland in 1966. He would stand in the accustomed garments – either an all-white or all-black sweat-suit – as the scent of his cologne wafted around the field.

'You could feel his presence,' remembers former safety George Atkinson. 'Al wasn't just a businessman who owned the team. He was a football person. He loved the game, knew the game and understood personnel. He was a one-man show.'

The 'Davis Factor' went beyond just aura. It was reinforced by each of his handpicked head coaches, all of whom executed Davis' unique brand of football. In the case of Johnny Rauch, a former Raiders assistant who ascended to the top job during his boss' AFL commissionership, the necessity to follow Davis' blueprint became an insurmountable issue. After three highly successful years in which he enjoyed winning records and reached Super Bowl II, Rauch sought the opportunity to build his own programme with the Buffalo Bills.

While the coach struggled to scale the same heights in upstate New York, Davis replaced him with a true partner in crime. Offensive lineman John Madden was forced into coaching due to an awful knee injury suffered at his first training camp with the Philadelphia Eagles. He spent the remainder of that year in the film room with Hall-of-Fame quarterback Norm Van Brocklin, honing a passion for schematics that burned even deeper after Madden attended a Vince Lombardi seminar. 'He spoke on one play [the power sweep] for eight hours,' revealed Madden. 'I realised I didn't know a damn thing.'

The learning curve was steep, not least at San Diego State, where Madden prospered under the stewardship of another obsessive genius: Don Coryell. His work aiding the Aztecs' defense caught the eye of Davis, who appointed him linebackers coach at Oakland in 1967. Two years later, the Raiders supremo – looking for a new leading man to replace Rauch – gathered his staff and, with typical forthrightness, said: 'I'll talk to any one of you after the draft about being the head coach.'

In reality, Davis had longing eyes for Baltimore Colts assistant Noll. But the plan was foiled by Noll heading to Pittsburgh, leaving an opening for the ambitious 32-year-old Madden. 'Anything that I ever wanted to do with football, he supported me,' said the coach. 'It was a perfect situation. There was nobody between me and Al.'

'He was tough to work for,' adds Wolf. 'What he put coaches through, it's like 10 additional years each year because he was so knowledgeable and wanted every avenue explored. It was not easy being head coach of the Raiders.'

Davis and Madden melded perfectly, their relationship exemplified by each providing the other's introductory Hall-of-Fame speech. That they have busts in Canton is thanks, in no small part, to their 10 years spent together, during which time Madden moulded the group of outlaws brought together by Davis into a championship squad. His greatest skill was quickly reading the room and letting the guys be the guys. Madden coached with the relaxed air and warmth betrayed by his John Candy-like appearance – the burly frame, curly hair and 1970s hipster dress sense.

'He understood the players, and they understood him,' adds Atkinson. 'He trusted us, and we trusted him. He was our leader, the head coach who set the standard.'

Arbitrary rules – such as players wearing suits on gameday and not being allowed to sit on their helmets – were discarded. Yet the easy-going side of Madden belied the steely edge that exists in all great coaches, which Raiders players would be on the sharp end of if they broke any of his three regulations: be on time, pay attention, play like hell when I tell you to.

'Hell' was the operative word . . . for opponents. 'They were bad to the bone,' remembers Bradshaw. It wasn't just quarterbacks scrambling in the face of fearsome pass-rushers that endured their fury. It was wide receivers unable to break free from man-to-man coverage, a task made harder by outstanding defensive backs such as 'Soul Patrol' Willie Brown and 'Dr Death' Skip Thomas, often wearing Stickum,* which had the secondary benefit of aiding interceptions. Pass-catchers acing that test were met with vicious clotheslines from the likes of 'The Mad Stork' Ted Hendricks and 'the Assassin' Tatum, who once broke New England Patriots wide receiver Darryl Stingley's neck. The impact of blows was often heightened by Raiders defenders wearing casts that masqueraded as protecting injuries but actually inflicted them.

'We were overly aggressive,' says Atkinson, another famed for his tough style. '"Hey, take no prisoners," we used to say – and we didn't. On gameday, we delivered. That's what it was about.'

Opposing defenses didn't have it any easier. Cornerbacks faced the unenviable task of permanently trying to protect the deep part of the field, where the exceptional, also-Stickum-obsessed, Cliff Branch and Fred Biletnikoff raced onto passes tossed by 'Mad Bomber' Lamonica and the 'Snake' Stabler. Linemen went up against Hall of Famers at centre (Jim Otto), left guard (Gene Upshaw) and left tackle (Art Shell).

The combination was irresistible. Madden became the fastest coach to 100 victories and posted a better winning percentage than Lombardi. His short-but-memorable coaching career also featured some of the most remarkable 'games with names' in football history. The 1974 playoffs brought the 'Sea of Hands' game, in which Stabler threw a game-winning eight-yard touchdown against the two-time defending champion Dolphins, Clarence Davis somehow holding onto the ball while wrestling three Miami defenders. In the 1977 playoffs, Stabler delivered the 'Ghost to the Post', a 42-yard pass to Dave Casper that set up Oakland's game-tying field goal in double-overtime and led to Raider victory. Next came the 'Holy Roller' 1978 regular-season game, in which Stabler fumbled on the final play against the San Diego Chargers. In attempting a recovery, Banaszak stumbled over the ball and kicked it towards the end zone, where Casper eventually fell on it after tripping himself.

The contests' notoriety illustrated Oakland so often at the centre of NFL supporters' focus, but it wasn't until Madden's eighth year that their big breakthrough came. In Super Bowl XI, the club captured a first championship by inflicting the fourth 'Big Dance' defeat on the Minnesota Vikings' Purple People Eaters. Their 32–14 victory – concluding a campaign in which the Raiders lost just once – allowed Madden to surprisingly retire two years later with a pristine reputation. 'We won every game that there is,' he said. 'All we could do was do it again, and that didn't excite me.'

For both Madden and Davis, the arrow remained up. While Madden somehow became more noteworthy after his coaching days, spending three decades as pro football's pre-eminent colour analyst and becoming the face of the EA Sports video-game series that retains his name, Davis found a perfect replacement with whom he enjoyed a similarly fruitful partnership.

Davis again looked within to recruit. The next cab off the rank was Tom Flores, the original starting quarterback in Raiders history and an assistant under Madden. When appointed the club's fifth leading man, he became the first minority to hold the position in modern NFL history. Davis would become a long-time champion of equal opportunities, employing Shell as the NFL's first black coach in 1989.

Few were more acutely aware of Davis' philosophy than Amy Trask, who worked alongside him for three decades and rose all the way to chief executive of the organisation. 'He hired Tom Flores,' says Trask, 'then me, then Art Shell. He hired a young woman in the mid-1980s, and not only afforded me the opportunity to advance, but, in his own unique way, encouraged me. That deserves more attention than it gets.'

It wasn't charity. Davis appointed the best person for every job – black, white, male or female. Trask adds: 'This is a gentleman

159

who – whether you love the Raiders or hate them; liked Al Davis or disliked him – hired without regard to race, gender, ethnicity or any other chracteristic which has no bearing on whether someone can do a job, well before anyone else did.'

A long history with Davis and the organisation made Flores the perfect fit, as did a laidback style akin to Madden's. For all the man at the helm might have changed, key tenets of Davis' programme did not. Oakland remained, as Upshaw put it, 'pro football's halfway house', a place with more misfits than nearby Alcatraz. 'We may sign a player who doesn't have good social habits or has been a failure somewhere else,' said Davis, 'but it's predicated on bringing them into an environment that can inspire the will to do great.'

In return for embodying the oft-repeated mantras close to Davis's heart – 'commitment to excellence' and 'Just Win, Baby' – the Raiders' reclamation projects were given a true home. The most obvious early success story was Brown, whose pick-six over the Vikings provided the signature moment of a Hall-of-Fame career.

Even his rejuvenation didn't match that of quarterback Jim Plunkett, the Heisman-winning New England Patriots first over-all pick who failed to hit the heights anticipated upon his lofty selection in 1971. Entering the 1980 campaign, Plunkett had spent five uninspiring years in New England and two with the San Francisco 49ers, and was entering his third year as Oakland's backup quarterback – the ultimate ignominy being that Dan Pastorini, picked two selections after Plunkett, was the starter.

In Week 5, Pastorini broke his leg against the Kansas City Chiefs and Plunkett was given the opportunity to quarterback a team in transition. The Raiders still boasted some stars from their previous title, including Branch, Hendricks, Upshaw, Shell and exceptional punter Ray Guy – but plentiful new faces as well.

Playing meaningful action for the first time in two and a half years, Plunkett tossed two touchdowns and five interceptions as the Raiders slipped to 2-3. Their task appeared hopeless. 'After I was let go by San Francisco,' he admits, 'I very seriously thought about retiring. Maybe I didn't have it any more. I was very down. If I didn't do well with Oakland, I knew it was over.'

Aided by softly spoken Flores' calming influence, Plunkett led the Raiders to nine wins over the next 11 games and a first playoff berth since 1977. Fittingly, the ultimate underdog story would have the perfect ending. Oakland became the first wild-card* team to win the Lombardi Trophy, overcoming the Houston Oilers, Cleveland Browns and Chargers en route to the Louisiana Superdome. There, the Philadelphia Eagles proved no match for Flores' men, who eased to Super Bowl XV glory (27–10) behind Plunkett's MVP performance. He threw for 261 yards and three touchdowns.

While the Raiders were the toast of football on the field, Davis was at loggerheads with the NFL off it, setting the stage for a dynasty-sealing third title secured once the team had rocked the footballing world by relocating.

The roots of the Raiders' eventual move to Los Angeles, concluded after a bitter dispute between club and league headed by Davis and Rozelle, were a by-product of decisions made by the commissioner's good friend Carroll Rosenbloom. Now in command of the Los Angeles Rams, having purchased the franchise in 1972 following Dan Reeves' death and sold his Baltimore Colts to the unpredictable Robert Irsay, former clothing magnate Rosenbloom sparked a relocation domino effect by taking his Rams from the Coliseum to Anaheim and leaving their previous venue open. This piqued the interest of an emboldened Davis, who was locked in a row with the power brokers of Oakland. He, naturally, would take things further by not only pushing for relocation against the wishes of the other owners who voted his initial request down, 22-0 with five abstentions, but by engaging in a battle through court to make it happen.

Davis, the war obsessive, believed he was following the strategy of history's great generals and delivering a pre-emptive strike, convinced the NFL's socialist values when it came to revenue sharing would eventually make way for a survival-of-the-fittest operation. In this, he underestimated the ongoing commitment to clubs operating on an equal footing, a factor confirmed by the Raiders' run in Hollywood lasting 12 years prior to their relocation back to Oakland in 1995.

By that stage, Davis had built a team that would deliver the *coup de grâce* of his tenure. If the 1980 Oakland Raiders were Cinderella-like, riding unlikely momentum to glory, the '83 Los Angeles Raiders were the playground bully. The team was a culmination of Davis' best qualities and Hollywood provided the fitting final stage for the coronoation of a dynasty.

In Marcus Allen, Davis recruited the centrepiece. It's unlikely somebody as obsessed with winning as the Raider supremo utilised the 1982 draft's 10th overall pick for any reason other than believing him to be the best player available. Yet it provided the Raiders a double boost: the team began their run in Tinseltown fielding a handsome California-born running back who won the Heisman Trophy for the city's USC Trojans.

Upon donning the silver and black, Allen impressed not just the star-hungry locals, but pro football's ultimate alpha dogs. On one occasion during his rookie campaign, the Raiders' offense was sputtering and linebacker Hendricks headed to the sideline to deliver a message: 'Just give the ball to Marcus!'

The Raiders weren't afraid of that. Allen claimed the NFL's rushing title and crossed pay-dirt* 14 times across a Rookie-of-the-Year campaign, leading his team to a league-best 8-1 record after player strikes shortened the regular season. But a year that seemed destined to conclude in further silverware came to a shuddering halt, Flores' men falling at home to the New York Jets in the divisional round. 'We were practising in Oakland and playing in Los Angeles,' said Howie Long. 'I think that took its toll.'

Their roster was too good to be denied for ever. On defense, Davis seemingly completed his jigsaw with a pair of ends opposite in age but similar in spirit. Lyle Alzado was a fearsome veteran who took on the mantle of outlaw-in-chief, his reputation fostered by stories of sparring with Muhammad Ali and not going down. 'He was a tortured soul,' said Long. 'We called him "Three Mile Lyle" because he was like the Three Mile Island Nuclear Plant – you weren't sure when he was going to blow.'

Alongside Long, who overcame a robust upbringing on Massachusetts' toughest streets to establish himself early in his career as one of football's best defensive ends, Alzado formed a deadly pass-rushing partnership. In the 1983 campaign, Los Angeles delivered 47 sacks and knocked multiple quarterbacks out of games.

Together, they played in the manner filtered down from their ever-intense leader. Davis' entertaining way of sharpening his players' edge was illustrated early in Long's professional life. Seeing the 1981 second-round pick snarling in practice, Davis remarked: 'Hey, 75, you think you're pretty tough? I'd have taken your lunch money.'

Putting the defense over the top took one of Davis' other qualities, as football's ultimate wheeler and dealer. In Lester Hayes, who took the Raiders' Stickum obsession further than anybody else by coating the majority of his uniform, the club already possessed one of football's finest cornerbacks – a status emphasised by him falling one shy of Dick 'Night Train' Lane's single-season interception record in 1980 with 13. Yet opposing teams' fear of Hayes made life difficult for Ted Watts on the other side, prompting Davis to upgrade by bringing in Mike Haynes, whose career was already on a Hall-of-Fame trajectory following seven seasons with New England. Haynes was locked in a contract quarrel and jumped at the chance to return to his hometown, the Raiders giving up first- and second-round picks to make the move despite sitting pretty at 8-3. 'It was a new team,

163

a new city and a new culture,' says Haynes. 'I was going home.' It was win–win.

Haynes and Hayes comprised one of the best cornerback tandems ever fielded, further enhancing the skills of the Raiders' pass-rushing menaces by affording them more time. 'We could cover anybody one-on-one,' adds Haynes. 'We loved those bump-and-run situations when the game was on the line. When I was able to go in there, everything changed. The team was even better. We were shutting people out left and right.'

The switch provided Haynes the opportunity to enjoy a winning culture. 'Mr Davis was one of the greatest owners and minds ever,' he adds. 'He used to tell us we had the highest winning percentage in pro sports, and you could see why. The Raiders knew what pressure was all about and played great in the big games. I learned winning starts at the top.'

New blood complemented Plunkett's band of renaissance men, overseen by Flores' studious man-management, to comprise Davis' finest team, as evidenced by a dominant playoff run during which Allen – following an average sophomore campaign – rediscovered his spark to the tune of 584 total yards and five touchdowns across three games. The defense, meanwhile, allowed only 33 combined points. 'It was the most talented team I ever played on,' enthuses Plunkett. 'Without question.'

The club's third Lombardi Trophy was sealed against the defending champion Washington Redskins, who succumbed 38–9 in a game symbolised by one exceptional moment from Allen. Late in the third quarter, Oakland called '17 Bob Trey 0', and Allen, as the play demanded, began to run left. Met by a barrier of white, gold and maroon, he turned around completely, evaded Ken Coffey's despairing dive, cut upfield between two defenders and powered towards the end zone like a race-car approaching the finishing line. The 74-yard touchdown was a fitting monument to a team and its owner, the renegades who didn't just jump over walls but knocked them down to gatecrash the NFL's dynasty club.

For all their excellence, the Raiders were neither the NFL's, nor even the AFC's, finest franchise over the golden period. That honour belonged to a team with whom they shared an epic rivalry, kickstarted in 1972 by the play that turned the league's laughing stock into its ultimate superpower.

In 1940, Art Rooney – having rebranded his Pittsburgh Pirates the 'Steelers' – left a training-camp session that he'd arrived at full of hope and uttered the infamous words. 'They look like the same old Pirates to me,' said Rooney after watching a session highlighted by missed assignments and dropped passes.

The comment encapsulated the next three decades and was uttered by fans every time Pittsburgh found another way to lose. There were good times and great characters in the intervening years: Johnny Blood captured hearts as a player and coach following his time with the Green Bay Packers, while fellow Hall-of-Famer Bill 'Bullet' Dudley – who holds the distinction of scoring nine different ways (rushing, passing, receiving, kickoff return, punt return, fumble recovery, interception, field goal and P.A.T.) – began his storied career in Pittsburgh.

Even when the Steelers should have triumphed, they didn't. The club spent the late 1950s and early '60s with serial winners Buddy Parker and Bobby Layne as head coach and quarterback respectively but couldn't find the right formula. Instead, supporters were left wondering what might have been as Johnny Unitas, who the Steelers drafted, dominated football with the Colts.

Throughout it all, Pittsburgh enjoyed the reputation of being as good off the field as they were bad on it. One example was that of Rocky Bleier, their 16th-round draft choice from 1968 who went to the Vietnam War after his rookie season and returned a year later having been shot in the leg. His football future appeared non-existent, but Art Rooney gave him a contract. 'They bought me two years,' he remembers. 'I was on Injured Reserve the first year and the development squad the next.' The move reaped rewards on the field. Bleier, who returned to the USA barely able to walk, rehabilitated and amassed nearly 4,000 rushing yards in a decade-long career.

On another occasion, during contract negotiations with Layne, the quarterback didn't even name his price to Art Rooney, instead telling the owner to write down whatever number he deemed right and saying: 'I trust you.' But that tale perhaps summed up Rooney's fatal flaw. His eventual writing of a bigger cheque than Layne warranted was akin to the practice of hiring friends or recommendations of friends as coach. Rooney's football team was almost a lifestyle business, because it simply wasn't his game. 'The Chief' was a baseball man at heart. 'He only bought it so Pittsburgh would have a major-league football franchise – something he thought important for a first-class city,' remembered Dan Rooney. 'Nobody loved Pittsburgh more than my father.'

In many ways, Dan was his father's son – a good-natured, fair man who immediately commanded respect – but it was where they diverged that proved critical. He possessed a ruthless streak and, while Art Rooney always favoured baseball over football, Dan was reared on the pigskin, entering the world more or less at the same time as the Pirates did. 'When I was a one-year-old, the Steelers were too,' he said. 'I would go to the facility with my mother when I was five through to when I was 10. I started to work as one of the water boys when I was 14, then did everything through the years: scouting, PR, coaching.'

By the late 1960s, Dan had assumed day-to-day control of Steeler operations. The failed tenure of Bill Austin – hired at the behest of Art against his son's wishes after Vince Lombardi's glowing recommendation – illustrated the need for a grander vision, one in which everybody was on the same page.

Austin had replaced Parker, whose tenure as Pittsburgh's winningest coach with a record just better than .500 ended following a dispute with Rooney Jr about team philosophy. Parker, a two-time NFL champion with the Detroit Lions, hated younger players, while Rooney saw the draft as a means to usher in a new, booming era. The owner returned to that vision upon Austin's firing and, within moments of sitting across from the 37-year-old Noll, knew he had found a likeminded partner.

By that stage, Noll enjoyed an impressive reputation as a detail-orientated, brilliant teacher who didn't mince his words. Reared at the school of Paul Brown as one of the messenger guards respon-sible for running on plays for Otto Graham, then under Gillman with the AFL's Chargers, before reaching the Baltimore Colts as Don Shula's defensive coordinator, he boasted an unquestionable track record.

Although so, too, had Parker and many other Steelers appoint-ments. This was about blend as much as past performance. 'We met the day after Super Bowl III, which was embarrassing for him and the Colts,' remembered Rooney. 'His specific knowledge of the Steelers' strengths, weaknesses and potential was extraor-dinary. He also pointed out we had traded away our future. He thought the way to build a championship team was through the draft.'

Noll wasn't an immediate success. The Steelers went 1-13 in his opening campaign, but Rooney showed unwavering support by giving Noll a bonus cheque that the coach left uncashed in his draw. Upon discovering this, Rooney was insistent, so Noll gave it to his wife Marianne, telling her: 'Put it in a separate account. We're not going to touch it until we've earned it.'

Rooney saw Noll changing the culture of his club. 'We had confidence in him,' he said. 'It wasn't like we were going to run him off. We knew he was the man we wanted. He did things the way we wanted.'

In his opening training camp, Noll scolded Pro Bowl lineback-er Andy Russell – a rare bright spot during the previous season – and turned his attention to the rest of the team. 'The reason you've been losing is not your attitude,' he said. 'It's that you're not good enough. You can't run fast enough, jump high enough.

You're not quick enough. Your techniques are abysmal, and I'm probably going to have to get rid of you. We're going to move on.'

Of those in that initial assembly, only five – including Russell – remained by 1974. Noll's second offseason saw him ship Roy Jefferson, who reached the Pro Bowl in 1969 with a 1,000-yard season featuring nine touchdowns, to Baltimore for a fourth-round pick due to off-field indiscretions.

The coach's opening words and actions served to put the players on notice. Noll's were not the 'same old Steelers'.

Joe Greene's introduction to Pittsburgh was fraught. The local press ran with the headline 'Joe Who?' following Noll's opening draft selection of the 6ft 4in, 217lb defensive tackle from North Texas State. The response only served to irk a player less than happy to land in Pittsburgh. 'I was depressed,' he says. 'I didn't want to be a Pittsburgh Steeler. They'd won two games in each of the previous two years.'

His rocky opening didn't stop there. Greene reported late to training camp due to a contract dispute and arrived in Pittsburgh with a group of offensive linemen determined to give the rookie a quick lesson. The Oklahoma drill, in which offensive and defensive players battle mano-a-mano in an attempt to grapple one another to the ground, provided the perfect opportunity. The only lesson heeded by menacing centre Ray Mansfield and his mates was that which so many other O-linemen discovered the hard way: Greene was simply too big, quick and strong to be beaten one-on-one. 'Ray was first,' remembered Russell, 'and Joe threw him away like a paper doll. I was standing there with some other guys, and we just looked at each other. This kid was backing up his mouth. From that day, Joe set a tone on the practice field and in games that losing is completely unacceptable.'

'They were trying to kill me,' adds Greene. 'It was just me and the O-line practising. They were a little upset because it should have been a rest day, but they had to work due to me arriving. I wasn't aware of that, so I worked my way down the line. I guess you could say I had a little bit of success.'

During his opening campaign, Greene reacted to Dick Butkus standing over fellow defensive-line rookie L.C. Greenwood after an egregious hit by spitting in the Hall-of-Fame linebacker's face. The torch had been passed: Greene was now pro football's baddest man. 'I like to think I played with rocket fuel not diesel,' he says. 'Diesel is slow and methodical. I wanted to be fast, quick, relentless.'

Butkus wasn't the only person Greene grappled with. A campaign in which he was voted NFL Defensive Rookie of the Year despite Pittsburgh winning just one game saw the defensive tackle fall foul of the officials on multiple occasions. Were it any other player, Noll would have delivered a firm hand – yet the man he personally spent years scouting was providing the attitude the head coach had anticipated.

Greene remembers: 'I had some pretty bad actions on the field and remember getting tossed out of three or four games in my rookie year – but I think Coach Noll and the Rooney family realised it was all about my desire to win. They didn't quash my actions and, I guess, signalled their approval by not reprimanding me.

'There were some guys who probably realised my attitude and the way I played was what they needed to bring. I don't know that for sure, but I'd like to think the club thought my actions – good and bad – were all about winning. I didn't like losing and wanted to do something about it.'

With it came the enduring nickname that lives to this day: 'Mean' Joe Greene. 'I wasn't real fond of it,' he admits. 'I'd see these grotesque-looking figures being held up in the stands with my name on. The name was also a mistake. My school, North Texas State, were known as the Mean Green. Then, when I went to Pittsburgh, they started calling me Mean Greene. I was never comfortable taking the name. The college nickname wasn't about just Joe Greene; it was about the whole group.'

Greene's impact was a feather in the cap for Noll, whose insistence persuaded Pittsburgh to draft the lineman. It also provided an insight into the Steelers' scouting system, which married Noll's keen eye with computerised data popularised by the Dallas Cowboys. Those factors created the most astonishing six-year run of drafting in football history. Between 1969 and 1974, the Steelers selected nine Hall of Famers: Greene, Bradshaw, Harris and Lynn Swann in the first round; Jack Ham and Jack Lambert in the second; Mel Blount in the third; and John Stallworth and Mike Webster in the fourth. A 10th, meanwhile, joined as an undrafted free agent, safety Donnie Shell completing a 1974 rookie class that remarkably features five players who have busts in Canton.

Their process was helped by the club's involvement in creating the original Scouting Combine, devised by Parker. The idea was progressed by former Steelers cornerback Jack Butler, who established a multi-team operation known as LESTO (Lions, Eagles, Steelers Talent Organisation) that charted measurables on every player and shared it among the clubs involved. Eventually, it expanded with the addition of the Bears (BLESTO), before the Bills, Colts and Dolphins joined to spark further name changes. Other systems were utilised by different clubs, all of which eventually led to Tex Schramm formulating the league-wide NFL Scouting Combine, which still exists today, in 1982.

The combination of Noll, LESTO and brilliant scout Bill Nunn, a former sportswriter who called on links forged during his days putting together the *Pittsburgh Courier*'s Black College All-America Team, gave the Steelers a leg-up on the competition – and it paid huge dividends.

From the moment he arrived in 1969, Noll – whose coaching mantra was 'In order to win, you have to first not lose' – had one immediate ambition: to build a championship defense. Together with coordinator Bud Carson, he constructed not only that, but one that would go down in history.

By the conclusion of the 1977 campaign, the points-per-game average among teams had slipped to 17.2, nearly six fewer than the then-high mark of 23.1 set in 1965. But numbers that appealed to football purists weren't welcomed by the league office. Increasingly, the NFL's business model was centred around TV. In 1977, the contracts penned totalled an eye-watering $576 million over four years, earning clubs a cool $5.2 million annually (more than double the previous figure). For the first time, even during a decade in which clubs moved into new state-of-the-art stadiums, television rights trumped ticket sales.

By then, the contracts were split between three broadcasters: CBS showed the NFC, NBC the AFC and, most significantly of all, ABC held the rights to its groundbreaking *Monday Night Football* (MNF) production that debuted in 1970.

MNF's arrival immediately captivated football fans, collecting a 33 per cent share of the TV viewership when the Jets took on the Browns in Week 1 and changing the way people watched sports for ever. The output was crisp, the slick banter between the ostentatious Howard Cosell and easy-going 'Dandy' Meredith and Frank Gifford, who replaced Keith Jackson after the opening year, providing the soundtrack for producer Roone Arledge's game-changing innovations: instant replay and overlaying graphics were aided by shots collected from double the number of cameras other stations used.

'I don't know if anyone knew the importance of it,' concedes former Jets PR man Frank Ramos. 'It picked up momentum throughout the season, and it was amazing how people took to watching *Monday Night Football*. They started going to bars to watch games, which didn't happen then. The two guys who might have foreseen its popularity were Rozelle, who engineered the contract signing, and Arledge.'

Over the early part of the 1970s, it also helped solidify the NFL's status as America's most popular sport. Yet that position came under threat as a decade dominated by defense wore on and, in 1977, pollster Louis Harris suggested baseball had overtaken football for the first time in nine years.

The NFL's reaction was swift and decisive, introducing a range of measures suggested by its Competition Committee, a group of coaches and executives – comprising Schramm, Shula, Brown and, for a time, Davis – tasked with providing recommendations to improve the game.

Such was the committee's stature, 95 per cent of its suggestions were implemented as part of the ever-changing league. Alterations in the 1970s were plentiful: more central hashmarks, overtime in the regular season, goalposts moved to the back of the end zone, playoff seedings determined by record and a play clock behind each end zone to name just a few. The league also switched to a 16-game schedule, added two expansion teams – the Seattle Seahawks and Tampa Bay Buccaneers – and created a second playoff wildcard in each conference.

For all those modifications were significant, nothing had an on-field impact as wide-ranging or long-lasting as the 'Mel Blount Rule', named after Pittsburgh's star cornerback, that forbade defensive players contacting pass-catchers beyond five yards from the line of scrimmage. That his name was chosen for the title is telling, for it indicates, in an era dominated by defense, Pittsburgh's 'Steel Curtain' stood above the rest.

Offenses enduring such struggle wasn't just because of unfavourable rules as much as it was a series of brilliant coaches coming along at the same time. Like Pittsburgh's Steel Curtain, Shula and Bill Arnsparger's 'No-Name Defense' in Miami, Tom Landry's 'Doomsday Defense' in Dallas, Minnesota's Purple People Eaters and the Denver Broncos' 'Orange Crush' were given enduring monikers. Just as important were teams who didn't contest the era's Super Bowls but made a mark nonetheless. The Baltimore Colts' 'Sack Pack' and Atlanta Falcons' 'Gritz

Blitz' also wreaked havoc while, in New England and Houston respectively, Chuck Fairbanks and Bum Phillips began following college football's lead by introducing the 3-4* into pro football, and the formation would become the NFL's principal scheme in the ensuing decade as teams struggled to find the players to fit a 4-3.

That issue didn't afflict Pittsburgh. The beauty of their system lay in the players executing it, starting with the Steel Curtain defensive line of Greene, Greenwood, Ernie Holmes and Dwight White. The quartet were so dominant Carson rarely needed to blitz. 'I really enjoyed being part of that group,' says Greene. 'I came in with L.C., Ernie was mean and Dwight was the mad dawg who talked the entire ballgame.'

Behind the Curtain, Russell was joined by Hall-of-Fame linebackers Lambert and Ham – the former, who redefined the position with incredible athleticism and coverage ability, was particularly important. Finally, wide receivers weren't given an inch of breathing room by cornerbacks Blount and J.T. Thomas, whose jobs were to get their hands on wideouts and funnel them towards the middle of the field.

The talent was backed up by Noll's obsession with fundamentals and Carson's schematic and play-calling wizardry. Their basic 4-3 alignment belied a complexity illustrated by his system featuring 30 different situations in which a linebacker could operate in coverage. The mix was devastating.

Schematic innovations didn't just come from coaches, either. For all his physical capabilities and success, Greene was still searching for the key intervention that would turn Pittsburgh from a good to championship squad in 1974. Infuriated by uncalled holds stopping his path to the backfield, and noticing the gap between centre and guard, he devised a new stance, tilting his body to the side and exploding into the space off the snap. Greene calculated the natural by-product of his success would be teams being forced to double-team him, paving the way for his Steel Curtain teammates to dominate.

173

'I lined up that way in practice, and our D-line coach George Perles noticed and allowed us to practise it,' he says. 'During the 1974 season, we never used it in a game but practised it during a special period every day. He instructed our offensive coaches to run what they wanted to test it properly and refine it. Everybody had an input so that, when we unleashed it, it was much better. It was special to have coaches buy into it.'

The results were spectacular.

The stunt 4-3 was first unfurled against the O.J. Simpson-powered Bills. The best running back in football starred as part of the 'Electric Company' offensive line, a nickname indicating their responsibility to turn on 'the Juice', which was Simpson's own moniker. Come 1974, Simpson was in the prime of a Hall-of-Fame career, having delivered the first 2,000-yard rushing campaign in NFL history – and only one over 14 games – the previous year.

His sole playoff appearance was a miserable experience. 'O.J. put 189 yards on us the last time we played them,' remembers Greene. 'When we used the stunt 4-3, he managed 50. It was the same story against the Raiders in the AFC Championship Game, and then the Vikings in the Super Bowl. For the next two years, nobody could run inside on us.'

That Vikings victory – 16–6 with Minnesota managing 17 rushing yards on 21 attempts and legendary quarterback Fran Tarkenton throwing three picks – proved a fitting finale for Pittsburgh's first championship campaign, crowning not just the Steelers but the unit that defined the first part of their dynasty. 'Joe Greene is the greatest Steeler of all-time,' says Harris. 'And watching our defense during the game was inspiring. I'd feel bad for the other running back. They set the tone, and we knew we had to follow it.'

Harris certainly played inspired. He crossed 1,000 rushing yards in six of his first seven seasons and, two years after their first playoff win, Pittsburgh rode the formula of outstanding defense, brilliant running game and timely magic from Bradshaw to back-to-back Super Bowls. After their defense dominated Minnesota in IX, the Steelers overcame the 1970s' other best team, Dallas, 21–17 in X. In a game remembered for Swann's incredible diving catch over cornerback Mark Washington, the Steelers triumphed despite missing Greene, who had been sidelined for long stretches of the contest with a pinched nerve in his neck.

Perhaps the greatest example of their excellence, though, came in 1976 when the Steelers overcame a 1-4 start to reel off nine straight wins, including five shutouts, and reached the AFC Championship Game. Bradshaw missed the first month of the campaign, while Harris and Bleier – who became the second tandem in league history to each accrue more than 1,000 rushing yards in a campaign – were sidelined for the season-ending loss to the Raiders. 'It showed the true character of the team,' adds Harris. 'Our backs were against the wall, and we had to find ways to win.'

With Oakland finally getting the better of their rivals, and Pittsburgh losing to Denver in the divisional round the following year, most felt their edge would be nullified by the Mel Blount Rule. In actuality, it underlined their brilliance. Pittsburgh were talented enough to prosper in an immediately more open game, offering men on the other side of the ball the opportunity to craft their own Hall-of-Fame legacies.

Bradshaw's early years in Pittsburgh didn't go as expected after being chosen first overall out of Louisiana Tech in 1970. 'When I got drafted, I didn't know anything about Pittsburgh or their football team,' he admits. 'You know as the first pick that you'll go to the worst team, and that was certainly the case. They had a great owner, but a history of losing, and I naively thought I'd ride in and solve the issues.'

He completed just 38 per cent of his passes as a rookie, improved in the two subsequent years and then saw progress hampered by a separated shoulder that cut his playing time in 1973. The following campaign, Bradshaw was riding the pine behind Joe Gilliam. 'I wasn't prepared for pro football,' he adds.

Despite a gunslinger style that ran counter to what Noll demanded, the head coach knew Bradshaw possessed more talent than Gilliam and inserted him back into the line-up with Pittsburgh 4-1-1. He never looked back. 'When I got the confidence from that man, I became a pro quarterback,' says Bradshaw. 'Prior to that, I wasn't making progress. I knew mistakes would mean being benched. But when he said: "Go make your mistakes. We're going to win with you," was when I became a quarterback.'

Bradshaw's relationship with Noll was never warm but mightily effective. 'He was one of those guys that was so smart,' reveals the quarterback, 'but really lacked common sense. I never, not once in 14 years, was comfortable in his presence. He was often frustrated with me. He'd call me in and say I wasn't studying enough, that I had to be like Johnny Unitas or Brian Griese. To which I'd say: "But I'm not those guys. I'm Terry Bradshaw." I always felt he preferred the defensive guys.' An idea backed up by Greene's experience: 'Our relationship was so special.'

Yet Noll needed more than just defense. Even during the first two Super Bowls, Pittsburgh relied on big plays from their signal-caller, who threw a fourth-quarter touchdown to clinch victory over Minnesota and hit Swann for the memorable 64-yard score the following year, a feat made even more impressive by the looming presence of Larry Cole, who knocked Bradshaw out cold as he released the ball.

After 1978, Bradshaw and his passing potential was truly unlocked. 'The excellence of Bradshaw, Swann and Stallworth really came out,' remembers Harris. Pittsburgh possessed the perfect mix to unfurl a deep passing game, their fine offensive line marrying with Bradshaw's cannon arm, as well as the complementary qualities of Swann and Stallworth. 'We had all bases covered,' enthuses Bradshaw. 'Lynn's ability to leap and make great catches was incredible, and Stallworth was a great route-runner, a real technician.'

The Steelers showcased all of their skills to devastating effect, flying in the face of those writing their squad off as over the hill by transforming into a team built on offense. Individual accolades followed as Bradshaw was named league MVP in 1978, and so did further titles: Pittsburgh overcame Dallas 35–31 on the back of their signal-caller's greatest-ever day – he threw for 318 yards and four touchdowns to almost single-handedly earn victory – in Super Bowl XIII, before taking down the Los Angeles Rams 31–19 the following year.

'The defense in the XIII and XIV Super Bowls wasn't nearly as good as the one in IX and X,' adds Bradshaw. 'Being able to win all those different ways is validation of what Chuck Noll built and that group's obsession with winning.'

It was also validation of whole careers for those on offense who were previously overshadowed by the majesty of Greene and the Steel Curtain. 'I called my own plays, or actually the offense did,' adds Bradshaw. 'I loved it. It's a great feeling to be in that huddle and look over the marker and decide on the play. But it wasn't just me. I'd discuss it with the guys and Stallworth might say: "I'm getting open on the out and up," and we'd adjust. My job was to get information and make a decision with the rest of the guys. It wasn't just me. It was everybody contributing.'

Those contributions delivered the perfect mirror image in Pittsburgh's two-part dynasty – two Super Bowls won on defense, two on offense, separated by two years – while cementing the 1970s Pittsburgh Steelers' place among the greatest teams in NFL history, one every bit as dominant as Lombardi's Packers.

That decade saw the Rooneys appoint the man who would act as their head coach for nearly a quarter of a century, win four Super Bowls in six years, recruit 10 Hall of Famers and create the formula that remains to this day. Upon his appointment, Noll was the 14th head coach in the Steelers' 36-year history. In the 50 years since, they have had just three, all of whom boast titles. 'The coach knows if he has a bad game, we're not going to fire him,' said Dan Rooney in 2014. 'It's worked very well for us as far as consistency. We've won more games in the last 40 years than any team.'

The formulation of an ethos now envied around the league, according to Rooney, started with one man and one play. 'It's so meaningful to have had so many great players,' he added. 'But, interestingly, before Franco came, we were an ordinary team. He came in '72, and then there was that play, and we moved on. After he came, we never lost.'

'The play began at Penn State,' says Harris. 'My coach was Joe Paterno, and he'd always yell: "Go to the ball," and it resonated. When it came to that play, which I was sure would be our last offensive play of the season, I was determined to follow that and fight to the end. It was a 66 play, which meant I wasn't part of the pattern. I was blocking.

'As it developed and Bradshaw was scrambling, I released to be an outlet. He threw the ball, and I turned and went to it. I remember leaving the backfield, and the ball being released, but then my mind is completely blank after that. I remember nothing until I'm stiff-arming Jimmy Warren to get into the end zone.'

The play defined a career that ended with Harris second only to Jim Brown on the NFL's all-time rushing-yardage list and the team on which he starred. 'We were not tied up into the team's history,' says Harris. 'We were making new history, our history. Like that play, it was a special combination of factors that came together. We had every base covered, winning two Super Bowls before the 1978 rule change and two after with the same people. That's what made us a great team.

'Chuck Noll's first three seasons were poor, but once we started having a winning attitude, everything changed. Even our last Super Bowl win in 1979, when we were behind, we weren't scared.

I think it all started with that play in 1972. It summed up how we always found a way to win. We knew if there was still one second on the clock, it wasn't over. You never give up.'

That moment, so significant for the Steelers, will for ever be shrouded by profound mystique. There remains no definitive answer as to whether Fuqua touched the ball and, even at the time, the play carried an almost Biblical air. 'Well, if Frenchy didn't touch the ball,' said Noll, 'and Tatum didn't touch the ball . . . the rulebook doesn't cover the hand of the Lord.'

When watching footage of actions he has never remembered – plucking the ball inches from the ground and never breaking stride – Harris is similarly philosophical. 'What strikes me as quite odd is the position of the ball,' he concludes. 'It's strange that the catch was in-stride. I've never seen someone catch a ball in that kind of position, with the ball that low, but not break stride. How did all that come together?'

Regardless of whether you believe in higher powers impacting a football game in Pittsburgh, it's undeniable that the dynastic aftershock, controversy and remarkable convergence of unlikely circumstances – Bradshaw somehow escaping pressure, Tatum arriving at just the right moment, the ball ricocheting so far backwards and Harris emerging from nowhere – make it the greatest play in NFL history. One immortalised by the name suggested to team broadcaster Myron Cope by a Pittsburgh lady called Sharon Levosky later that evening: 'The Immaculate Reception'.

11

Perfection

MIAMI DOLPHINS 14

WASHINGTON REDSKINS 7

---

14 January 1973

Los Angeles Memorial Coliseum, Los Angeles

Garo Yepremian lined up just behind the Washington Redskins' 45-yard line, the fading Los Angeles sun glistening off his white helmet as he awaited his moment of destiny. Hollywood looked set to provide the setting for an ending the city's finest script writers couldn't have fashioned, with the perfect symmetry to cap the perfect season lying at a left boot that was one of the NFL's most reliable weapons.

The tantalising possibility wasn't lost on anybody inside the iconic Coliseum. With the 16–0 Miami Dolphins leading Super Bowl VII 14–0 in the fourth quarter, Yepremian had the opportunity to complete a moment of impeccable symbolism by capping a 17–0 campaign with a 17–0 scoreline in the ultimate game. Miami's owner Joe Robbie, grinning ear to ear on the sideline,

180

recognised the marketing potential: 'A field goal makes it 17–0 and 17–0,' he enthused as Yepremian lined up.

Even among the many players who trod unlikely paths to Miami, the Cypriot's route via a warehouse job in London stood out. Yepremian's journey across the pond was a result of continuous cheerleading from brother Krikor, the captain of Indiana University's soccer team who urged the Atlanta Falcons and Detroit Lions to give his sibling – playing the round-ball game at semi-pro level in England – a shot. In 1966, the latter team relented. Little did Krikor know that it would lead, nearly seven years later, to his younger brother having the eyes of the United States trained on him.

Yepremian had come a long way from not knowing how to put on pads ahead of his first game, or being chewed out by Detroit's indomitable defensive tackle Alex Karras for celebrating kicking an extra point in a forgettable debut the Lions were losing heavily. 'Because I just keeked a touchdown,' replied Yepremian after Karras asked: 'Why the fuck are you celebrating?'

No matter the stakes, Yepremian usually came through. His 51-yarder to help the Dolphins rally against Bud Grant's fierce Minnesota Vikings in Week 3 acted as one of many lightning rods for Miami's unbeaten charge through the 1972 campaign. And now he stood ready to cap it all majestically, by booting over from 42 yards.

The grin would soon be wiped from his face. 'I don't think we should have gone for the field goal,' remembered bruising halfback Larry Csonka with the value of hindsight. 'The minute you start going for destiny, destiny kicks you right in the ass.'

The snap was perfect, as was the hold by the backup quarterback so influential in helping Miami reach the showpiece, Earl Morrall. But the kick was just low enough to hit Bill Brundige's outstretched hand, and the subsequent seconds resembled a Benny Hill sketch. With the ball bouncing backwards towards the sideline, Yepremian stumbled over and gathered impressively amid the sea of maroon flowing in his direction, yet the pigskin slipped out of his hand on an attempted pass, prompting the instinct to palm it upwards and into the grateful hands of Mike Bass, who raced for a touchdown.

'Garo wasn't a football player. He was a kicker,' says safety Dick Anderson. 'He couldn't throw the ball because he was a soccer player. We were yelling: "Fall on it! Fall on it!" I remember next year at practice, Earl purposely dropped the ball and the whole team was shouting: "FALL ON IT!"'

For the first time since Jim Kiick blasted in behind Larry Little and Csonka for Miami's second score in the opening half, there was a slight question mark over who would emerge triumphant. Don Shula, the man who had fiercely articulated the plan to earn his and Miami's first championship from the opening of training camp, was somehow more intense than usual.

The head coach arrived at Miami Gardens' St. Thomas University for his third campaign as he always did, carrying the air of a schoolteacher laying down his marker at the beginning of term. 'Gentlemen,' Shula told his players, 'just remember one thing from last year: nobody remembers who was number two in the Super Bowl. You go through a season, and the only ones they talk about years later are the winners.'

For Anderson and the rest of a Miami team who most people felt had punched above their weight by even reaching Super Bowl VI, the words were impactful. 'That resonated with us the whole year,' says the member of the NFL's All-Decade Team.

The 1971 campaign saw Miami, in just their sixth campaign, come of age. 'They were 3-10-1 the year before I got there,' remembered Shula. 'They were not a good football team, so I worked them hard and demanded a lot. They did not like it at first but bought in when results changed. Hard work brings success. They started to win and believed in everything I was teaching.'

Shula's players quickly discovered no detail was too small, a fact proven by wins often being made to feel like defeats. 'He treated a close victory as a loss,' admitted Csonka. And he was equally exacting on the practice field. 'If you let up a little in a drill 100 yards from where he was,' added star defensive tackle Manny Fernandez, 'you'd hear him yell and wonder: "How the hell did he see that?"'

Shula didn't inherit a bare cupboard. Joe Thomas, the club's director of player personnel from 1966 to '71, had begun building a talented squad when the coach arrived. Bob Griese was an emerging star at quarterback, Csonka, Kiick and Mercury Morris were a trio of versatile 'backs who could each fill specific roles, while the defense featured strength at every level in Fernandez, linebacker Nick Buoniconti and Anderson.

The team needed direction, from the sidelines and in the locker room. 'The Dolphins were a loser, a ragtag operation,' remembers Paul Warfield, who arrived via trade from the Cleveland Browns. 'They were seeking to find their place in the world. I arrived at the same time as Don Shula, as did Marv Fleming, a big part of the Green Bay Packers' great team. We mixed with a core of good young players who were misfits previously. In their four previous years, the Dolphins – as an expansion team – had never won more than five games.

'I was accustomed to winning and knew what it was about. You had a group of young men there who didn't have that. There wasn't discipline and commitment. They had to embrace the new culture. But a transformation occurred. In Shula's first year, they won 10 games. To more than double the effort so quickly was remarkable.'

The turnaround didn't feel quick to the players. Miami's success was driven by the unremitting nature of their leading man, whose relentless focus on fundamentals hark back to Vince Lombardi more than his earliest coaching inspiration, Paul Brown. Shula the player, like Lombardi, eked every scrap from himself on the field and was uncompromising even in his earliest days. Once praised by Brown for a crunching hit on star fullback Marion Motley – but called the wrong name – the ninth-round defensive back replied: 'The name is Shula. S-H-U-L-A.'

Twenty years later, Miami's players were under no illusions about his name, or that he was in complete charge. 'He was literally the most intense man I've ever been around,' said centre Jim Langer. 'But he worked as hard as we did.' Some achievement given the Dolphins were forced to endure four-a-day practices under the glare of Miami's merciless heat. 'In the Orange Bowl, with the poly-turf field, it could be 140 degrees if it was a day game,' remembered Langer. 'You'd lose 25lb in a game! But we were ready for it because of those practice days. Our opponents weren't.'

Other teams' inability to deal with Miami's demanding formula – a strong, bruising running game, mistake-free defense and quarterback capable of converting third downs – was illustrated by the immediacy of their turnaround. The Dolphins reached the playoffs in Shula's first campaign and went to the Super Bowl, where an uncharacteristically error-strewn performance betrayed a team not quite ready for the big stage, in his second. 'We were young and inexperienced in Super Bowl VI,' admits Warfield. 'We were happy to be there but failed to understand the only thing that matters is winning.'

Following their 24–3 loss to the Dallas Cowboys, Shula caught wind of city plans to hold a parade for the Dolphins upon their return to Miami and immediately called it off. 'I don't believe in a parade for losers,' he told officials. 'Hopefully soon there'll be a parade recognising us as winners. We'll be there for that.' The tone was set – even for a team in its infancy, finishing second wasn't acceptable.

There were few differences between the 1971 and '72 Miami Dolphins. Perhaps the only tangible changes were the increased use of Morris to turn a two-headed-monster backfield into a three and, most pertinently, the desire sparked by the previous campaign's ending. 'The goal, as Shula outlined in that training-camp speech, was to win the Super Bowl,' remembers Anderson. 'But we really took it one game at a time. In each game, different players stepped up and made a difference.'

Perhaps most impressive was that you couldn't attribute success to any one element of play. Their bruising running game, in which Csonka was the enforcer, Morris the speedster and Kiick the pass-catcher, operated behind a brilliant offensive line, while quarterback Griese missing much of the campaign through injury illustrated that position's complementary, rather than crucial, status. The No-Name Defense, called as such because Tom Landry couldn't remember the names of their front four ahead of Super Bowl VI, boasts just one player in the Hall of Fame, Buoniconti, despite being one of the finest in league history.

'It was a very special team in how we melded together,' added Langer. 'You can't plan that. If you find success in life together, you form a bond. It was a very unique bunch of people. We were a team, not individuals. You get a team like that by chance. It comes together day by day, piece by piece. If you could put that formula together on purpose, you'd make a fortune.'

No group epitomised the team's ethos more than the offensive line on which Langer starred. Each member of the starting five – left tackle Wayne Moore, left guard Bob Kuechenberg, centre Langer, right guard Little and right tackle Norm Evans – were cut or traded from other clubs. But the quintet came together to form a historically impressive group. 'We were a bunch of castoffs,' said Langer. 'Our coach Monte Clark told us before every drill we would be "the best in the business". We became it. I don't know if we were the best ever – there have been some great ones – but they say you're only as good as your offensive line. Having a bad O-line is like having a car without a motor.'

There was no doubting the motor of that year's Miami team, who set an NFL season rushing record with 2,960 yards that made up the majority of their league-leading offensive total of 5,036. The Dolphins also featured a fine group of contrasting pass-catchers in deep threat Warfield and possession-receiver Howard Twilley, as well as similar balance at tight end, where Fleming blocked and Jim Mandich primarily ran patterns.

So completely did they cover all bases that even when Griese suffered a broken ankle in Week 5, there was no let-up as Shula's old favourite from Baltimore, Morrall, took the wheel. 'When Bob went down, it shook everybody up,' remembers Shula. 'Earl calmly gave us great leadership.' He piloted an offense that scored 385 points in the regular season at 27.5 per game, three more than the next-best team. Combined with Bill Arnsparger's defense also being best in football by allowing a ludicrous 12.2 per contest, the Dolphins were impossible to beat.

'Coach Shula was the leader, the boss, the screamer, while Coach Arnsparger was very calm,' says Anderson. 'I always remember one day when Shula yelled at Arnsparger, and Bill just walked over, handed him the clipboard and said: "Here you are. You coach the defense."'

Arnsparger's excellence lay in a combination of his and Shula's emphasis on sound team defense and a sprinkling of innovation. The latter was shown best in the creation of the 53 Defense, named after the jersey number of linebacker Bob Matheson, who Arnsparger stood up at the line of scrimmage as a moveable chess piece that blitzed from multiple spots or dropped into coverage. The defense looked like a 4-3 but actually was a precursor to the proliferation of the 3-4.

'We lined up the same on every defensive play,' adds Anderson, 'so the quarterback had to take an extra second reading our first moves. Joe Namath still comes up to me and says: "You SOBs were never where you were supposed to be." We'd take a false step, knowing he was reading that, so there was some disguise. We had some coverages that were man but looked like zone, and vice versa.'

186

That they were able to achieve such successful disguises was down to coaching and execution. 'Our coaches recognised what was needed in that era,' says Anderson. 'We were very physical, particularly our brilliant defensive line, and that married with great communication. We didn't make mistakes. The opposing team are always looking for weaknesses, but our coaches ensured we didn't have any. They drilled in on execution and not making mental errors. We always had everybody in the right place.'

One of the most well-balanced teams in NFL history would enjoy a season for the ages – something the roster became acutely aware of as the calendar continued to turn. En route to the Week 13 game with the New York Giants, Kuechenberg turned to O-line mate Langer and said: 'You know we haven't lost yet? Maybe it wouldn't be such a bad thing if we did so we don't have that jinx on us.'

Langer remembered: 'As soon as we crossed the line, it was a different story. We won that game handily, just as we did so many. We had some games where, if the other team took advantage of certain things, we would have lost. But we'd always make a play that swung it. The other teams shot themselves in the foot – champions don't beat themselves.'

Unsurprisingly, as the number in the W column continued to change, the outside world began chattering about the prospect of Miami winning every game. Internally, though, it was a different story. 'It was all about winning the Super Bowl,' says Anderson, 'but it just so happens we had to win a lot of games to get that done.'

Even having to play the AFC Championship Game in Pittsburgh despite Miami's better record – a factor that led to the NFL shunning its policy of rotating the homefield honour by division each year and adopting seedings – couldn't derail the charge. Pittsburgh were coming off the high of Franco Harris' Immaculate Reception the previous week, but the Dolphins had an answer.

Down 7–0 in the opening half, Miami relied upon a moment

of inspiration from punter Larry Seiple, who gained 37 yards on a fake. 'We saw on a certain return that they peeled to the outside and turned their back,' says Shula, 'so Larry just followed them.' That set up the Dolphins' first touchdown, a toss from Morrall to Csonka, but it proved the quarterback's only real impact on the game.

At halftime, knowing the offense needed a spark, Shula approached Morrall in the locker room and told him he planned to put the fit-again Griese in. 'Coach, I don't agree with you,' replied Morrall, 'but I respect your decision.' Griese's first throw split two defenders and hit Warfield across the middle, with the wideout gaining 52 yards, and Miami didn't look back. They triumphed 21–17 to reach the Big Dance for the second year running.

Yet doubts still existed. Maybe it was the lack of stardust but, despite boasting the NFL's best offense and defense, the unbeaten Dolphins entered Super Bowl VII as three-point underdogs. Most people felt Shula would come up empty-handed again on the biggest stage, this time against another all-time great coach desperate to get the monkey off his back.

George Allen might not have literally eaten, drunk and slept football, but it is true that he rarely ate anything except peanut butter and ice cream, or drank something other than milk, such was his focus on the game. The two tasks were impositions, as was sleeping: time spent away from where he wanted to be, at the foot of his projector, on the chalkboard or patrolling a practice field.

For Allen, football was a way of life. On a family holiday in the Bahamas, he spotted a group of athletic youngsters running around, pulled out a pigskin and stopwatch, and coached 'em up – one flew to Washington for a try-out with the Redskins. For wife Etty, proposed to in 1951 with the message, 'AS THE 1951 SEASON APPROACHES, I WOULD LIKE TO HAVE YOU AS MY TEAMMATE', it was just George being George, living by an old adage that he'd flipped around: football, family and God . . . in that order.

Allen took everything to the next level, setting a new standard by undertaking 16-hour work days and sleeping at the facility. Greater levels of commitment in decades that emphasised the growing importance of coaching weren't unconventional. But Allen's methods were. While contemporaries such as Lombardi and Shula were intimidating embodiments of the classic football coach, Allen showed genuine love for players, motivating with an arm over the shoulder while utilising psychology and study instead of fear and discipline.

On one occasion, ahead of a Redskins game against bitter rivals Dallas, he walked into a team meeting with some karate fighters holding a board. 'I've always told you I'd fight Tom Landry at the 50-yard line,' he told his players. 'Well, if I did, this is what I'd do . . .' Allen unleashed a perfect kick and shattered the board, prompting euphoria from his troops. He'd probably spent months mastering the technique.

Moreover, his approach to team building ran counter to prevailing wisdom in an era where most franchises focused on the draft. To Allen, living by the ethos 'the future is now', draft picks were merely something to be traded for veterans, whom he believed were less mistake-prone and more desperate to achieve the one goal that unified him and the coaches with whom he differed so greatly: winning. Just as Lombardi delivered enduring quotes related to that quest – from 'show me a good loser and I'll show you a loser' to 'winning isn't everything; it's the only thing' – so too did Allen: 'Winning is living, and losing is dying.'

From the moment he made his name at the Chicago Bears, Allen didn't do much dying.

After Chicago's 1963 NFL Championship Game triumph – the 14–10 win over the Giants that brought George Halas' last championship – it was their defensive coordinator whom players carried off the field rather than Papa Bear. Reared at the bosom of a likeminded obsessive, Clark Shaughnessy, Allen stepped out from the shadows following his mentor's departure and coordinated his own unit for the first time. The results were spectacular as the Bears invoked memories of their original Monsters of the Midway to ride Allen's zone system, featuring blitz concepts, to an incredible campaign. They allowed just 10.3 points per game and capped their run with a memorable title-game performance, intercepting the exceptional Y.A. Tittle five times to take their season tally to a scarcely believable 41 in 15 games.

For Tittle and the Giants, defeat represented the continuation of a dispiriting run in the ultimate game amid a truly remarkable story. Considered washed-up when he joined Big Blue in 1961, Tittle enjoyed a remarkable swansong to cap his Hall-of-Fame career, leading the club to three successive NFL Championship Games and breaking the single-season passing-touchdown record in back-to-back seasons (33 in 1962 and 37 in '63); the latter mark wouldn't be broken for 22 years. Unfortunately, successive defeats to the Green Bay Packers were followed by another reverse against the Bears, and Tittle – who retired after a 1964 campaign in which he and the Giants failed to scale similar heights – is still considered one of the greatest-ever players to never win a title.

It's a dubious honour with which Allen became only too familiar: he, too, would never win the NFL's ultimate prize during a decorated head-coaching career that began three years after announcing himself to the world as the Bears' coordinator. Having gone behind Halas' back to take the reins of a Los Angeles Rams squad who went 4-10 in 1965, he immediately transformed their fortunes, producing winning records in all five subsequent campaigns and building such a bond with his players that they forced his reinstatement after rows with Dan Reeves saw their beloved coach fired following the 1968 season. Among those championing his cause were the infamous Fearsome Foursome defensive line led by Deacon Jones, who invented the term 'sack', but it proved a stay of execution.

Allen's programme ran counter to the beliefs of Reeves, the original NFL owner to take advantage of the draft, and his excellent Rams team's biggest failing was perhaps coinciding with Lombardi's great Packers squad. That sent Allen into the grateful arms of Washington and his impact on the Redskins, who had managed one winning campaign in their previous 15, was immediate. Having gone 9-4-1 in his first year, Allen fielded a presumed champion in 1972, Billy Kilmer and Sonny Jurgensen, 33 and 38 respectively, throwing the ball to 31-year-old wide receiver Charley Taylor on offense when Larry Brown – a rare 20-something on the roster – wasn't running it. Linebacker Chris Hanburger, 31, led the way on defense. Collectively, they were known as the 'Over the Hill Gang'.

The Redskins looked anything but that in rolling through the campaign at 11-3. Following their 26–3 crushing of the defending-champion Cowboys in the NFC Championship Game, it appeared the grizzled veterans would enjoy their moment in the sun as the Super Bowl returned to its illustrious original setting.

Venue was the only real common denominator between Super Bowls I and VII. By the time Miami and Washington arrived in Los Angeles, the occasion had become one of the most significant dates in the US calendar, enhanced by interventions from the league office.

Cornerstones of a week that helped grow the game's popularity were on Tuesday, when thousands of journalists would interview players during a 'Media Day' event that four decades later became a primetime show known as *Opening Night*, and Friday, when commissioner Pete Rozelle gave a presidential-style 'State-of-the-League' press conference.

Both achieved different but crucial goals. Media Day, or *Opening Night*, transcends sports and culture with an unabashed light-heartedness that moves so far beyond the border of ridiculousness that the line is no longer visible – it's not unknown for players to be interviewed by people dressed in wedding dresses or as clowns, nor does a query like: 'If you met Big Foot, what would you tell him?' raise any real eyebrows. As for the commissioner's press conference, it adds a State Visit-style seriousness to the show, a counter to Media Day that gives news hacks their angles. Together, they ensure the NFL spots on CNN and TMZ simultaneously.

In and around those, much of the action takes place on 'Radio Row', an ever-growing space in which stations from around the USA and other parts of the world broadcast their programming live from the game's host city, ensuring the Super Bowl dominates every conversation regardless of competitors and location.

As for those representing the AFC and NFC, they arrive seven days prior to the contest, mandated to take part in media availability daily, a stark contrast from Lombardi's Santa Barbara boot camp. The final piece of the NFL's jigsaw is the city itself, selected years in advance and increasingly rotating around stadiums in warm-weather areas or in the modern-day domed arenas.

All of this can be traced back to the 1970s when Super Sunday became a unifying national holiday. The great paradox was that the popularity grew so greatly at a time when the games were often dull, uninspired, one-sided affairs. A description true of the seventh edition, when a Miami team with a chip on their shoulders thoroughly outclassed Washington. 'We were underdogs, and we took offence to it,' admitted Langer.

'They had a masterful coach and veteran players who'd seen everything,' remembers Warfield. 'He felt they wouldn't be rattled, but the fact remains they couldn't beat us on that day. We'd been planning for it from the moment we lost the previous Super Bowl.'

Not since the day he turned up at Albert Einstein's house on the Princeton campus and persuaded the world-renowned genius to play a game of checkers only for the ploy to come unstuck by not bringing a board had one of Allen's plans failed so spectacularly. His big miscalculation was considering star centre Len Hauss capable of handling Dolphins brute Fernandez one-on-one. 'I hadn't been blocked one-on-one really much in my career,' said Fernandez. 'It was like a vacation.'

Fernandez spent more time in the Redskins backfield than Allen had behind his projector screen leading up to the game. 'Manny just manhandled him, and they never really adjusted,' says Anderson. 'Brown was hit so many times, he didn't know what to do.'

Allen underestimating Fernandez summed up the magic of Miami's defense, which belied its unflattering nickname to so thoroughly dominate Washington that the game ceased to be a contest. The Redskins crossed midfield once in the opening half, reaching the dizzying heights of the Dolphins' 48 and, by the time Kiick barrelled in for his second score, few believed a comeback possible. 'For a bunch of no names, we did OK,' said Fernandez.

The only moment of tension was in the immediate aftermath of Yepremian's infamous faux pas, but Washington couldn't mount any sort of fightback. Following Allen's surprising choice to kick deep at the restart, rather than go for an onside kick, the Redskins eventually received the ball at their own 36. Kilmer threw two incompletions, hit Brown on a swing pass for a four-yard loss and was sacked by Vern Den Herder on fourth down to all but end the game. 'I remember being in the huddle,' adds Warfield, 'on that Coliseum field, watching the clock winding down, knowing we weren't running another play. The scoreboard flashed: "The Dolphins are Super". I'll never forget it.'

For Shula, the relief was palpable. 'If we were 16-1, the season would have been a failure,' he remembered. 'I'm sitting with a reputation as a coach who can win – but not the big game. You never want to have that said in this profession.'

As his opposite number knew only too well.

*

In the run-up to Super Bowl VII, Allen was asked by sportswriter Paul Zimmerman to capsulise himself in one paragraph. The Washington coach responded: 'I want to be remembered as a guy who wanted to win so badly that he'd give a year of his life to be a winner.'

Nobody could deny that, nor Allen's place in NFL history following zero losing campaigns in 12 as a head coach, sitting fourth on the all-time career winning percentage standings and eventual enshrinement in the Hall of Fame. Yet Allen's legacy is shrouded in a sense of 'what if'. He spent another five years in Washington without returning to the Big Dance before being fired and heading back to the Rams, where, ridiculously, he was let go after two preseason games. For the rest of his life, Allen was *persona non grata* in league circles, having been written off as too much of a control freak with an overly liberal spending policy.

In most ways, his 12 years stack up impressively well, even against Lombardi's 10 – a winning percentage of .712 compared to .738, for example – except when it comes to one key stat: Green Bay's great delivered five championships to Allen's none. 'Coach Allen got the team up so high ahead of every game,' says Packers legend Dave Robinson, a cornerstone of Lombardi's great squads who finished his career under Allen in Washington. 'But it was exhausting. With Coach Lombardi, there was a balance. Against lesser opponents, he wouldn't take it quite as far. George Allen was a great coach. I loved him. But you were burnt out by the end of the season. We had nothing left for the playoffs.'

After a brief spell in the USFL – the latest challenger to the NFL – in the mid-1980s, the 71-year-old Allen took over lowly college Long Beach State, who won 11 of 35 games in their previous three campaigns, in 1990. Under his stewardship, they went a mightily impressive 6-5. To most it seemed like an undignified ending, but Allen felt otherwise. 'He said it was the most satisfying season of his career,' said wife Etty.

Allen died of a heart attack months later, leaving behind a football programme that disbanded following one more season and hordes of people regretful that his brilliant career never earned the ultimate validation. 'He was maybe the greatest to never win a championship,' admits Robinson.

Super Bowl VII was Allen's only championship game, ensuring he goes down alongside Minnesota's Grant – a four-time Grey Cup winner (the Canadian Football League's Lombardi Trophy equivalent) who reached the Super Bowl on four occasions and lost them all – as the greatest coach not to win an NFL crown.

As for the victorious Dolphins and their leading man, the future was mixed. They immediately went on to repeat as champions, utilising the same method to lose just two games the following campaign and overcome Grant's Vikings 24–7 in Super Bowl VIII, but the next year saw the decade's true power, the Steelers, emerge. 'In 1972, we had 165 points scored against our defense,' says Anderson. 'The next year, it was only 150 and five touchdown passes. That was probably an even better team.'

Miami lost Arnsparger to the Giants after triumphing in 1973 and were never the same. 'Bill leaving was a major change,' admits Anderson, 'even though we had the same players. Vince Costello came in and wanted to blitz on third-and-long. We'd change the play in the huddle. Our thing was always let them catch the ball, tackle them short of the sticks and get the ball back. We never missed tackles. It was stupid.'

Soon after, the heart of the two-time champions was ripped out. Unrest among players had become rife in the NFL, a by-product of spiralling revenues failing to make their way back to the heroes attracting the fans to create a fertile ground for opportunists. Furthermore, the NFL Players Association – established in 1954 – was growing in stature, epitomised by the 1974 preseason beginning amid the first of several players' strikes that blighted coming years, while the campaign itself rolled around with multiple stars – including Kiick, Csonka and Warfield – accepting the overtures of the newly formed World Football League (WFL).

The WFL, on the whole, failed to gain traction, going the way of so many other breakout organisations and lasting little more than a season and a half. Yet its impact on the Dolphins was significant, breaking up a championship squad that might have ridden Shula's blueprint to further Lombardi Trophies.

As for Shula, he continued in Miami for another two decades, eventually retiring as the winningest head coach in NFL history. Yet those 22 years were eerily similar to his first nine, with the coach – who endured just two losing campaigns in 33 – failing to lift another Lombardi Trophy despite drafting exceptional passer Dan Marino in 1983.

Unlike Marino – who sits alongside Allen and Tittle among the most significant NFL figures never to win a championship – Shula's place in history is unquestioned. 'I don't have any regrets,' he said. 'When you look back and your team has accomplished something nobody else has, that is what you're proud of. The baseball player Joe DiMaggio had a 56-game hitting streak, and our record is similar.'

A decade previous, Lombardi famously stated: 'Perfection is not attainable but, if we chase perfection, we can catch excellence.' The irony of the 1972 Dolphins is that they chased excellence and found perfection along the way. That they achieved it only sank in upon the players' return to the Coliseum locker room, when all saw the eternal words written on the chalkboard: 'Perfect Season. 17-0'.

12

America's Team v. American Dream

NFC Championship Game

DALLAS COWBOYS 27
SAN FRANCISCO 49ERS 28

---

10 January 1982

Candlestick Park, San Francisco

The youthful features and curly blond locks draped underneath his helmet, fluttering in the customary Candlestick Park wind, as he turned to join the rest of San Francisco's offense belied the steely confidence emanating from the 49ers' quarterback. Fresh-faced at just 21 years old, Joe Montana stood under centre, inches from the menacing presence of Ed 'Too Tall' Jones, the formidable Dallas Cowboys defensive tackle who had sparked controversy earlier in the week by claiming he didn't respect San Francisco's players. In truth, Jones was merely saying what the rest of the footballing world was thinking.

The 49ers were a feelgood story in 1981, young players coming together under an innovative coach to go from 6-10 to 13-3. But they lacked, in the eyes of Jones and others, the mentality to really challenge the NFL's elite. Their finesse game might have racked up wins in the regular season but wouldn't cut the mustard at the business end of the postseason – especially when meeting Dallas' Doomsday defense and Tony Dorsett-led running game.

Pregame predictions were both proven and disproven over the throes of a dizzying contest. The 49ers had threatened to unravel numerous times, turning the ball over six times compared to just 25 in 16 regular-season contests. And yet, somehow, despite all the errors and some questionable pass-interference calls against star rookie Ronnie Lott, their offense took to the field down just six points with five minutes to go. Hope sprang eternal.

As Montana returned to the fray, he did so carrying the hopes of 60,000 fans filling the stands, donning red and gold while baying for Cowboy blood. But they roared more in hope than expectation, unaware that, in the man who would become known as 'Joe Cool' for his calm in just this type of situation, the 49ers possessed a true believer. In his mind at least, Montana was ready to enact a changing-of-the-guard moment and usher in the next NFL dynasty by doing the unthinkable: conquering 'America's Team'.

While the Pittsburgh Steelers were the franchise of the 1970s on the field, they couldn't come close to matching the Dallas Cowboys off it. That decade saw Tex Schramm's creation move beyond the realms of pro-football club, developing into a cultural phenomenon, bequeathed with an enduring moniker that perfectly encapsulates their mystique.

The Cowboys became America's Team because NFL Films producer Bob Ryan noted Dallas were often better supported on the road than home sides when cutting together a highlights package from the 1978 season and coined the term. But that is an oversimplification.

Their popularity wasn't just a result of five Super Bowl appearances and two victories in the 1970s; the relentless excellence of their head coach; a scouting system that continued to restock the pipeline with players blending skill and character; iconic white-and-silver uniforms; or the cheerleaders introduced by Schramm whose presence added a sexiness that contrasted with the buttoned-up, born-again-Christian, face-of-the-franchise quarter-back Roger Staubach. It was down to a confluence of all these factors, coming together in harmony. 'There was great stability within the organisation, and we were fortunate in many ways,' says Gil Brandt. 'We were fortunate to be in Dallas, too, because it was a football town.'

A football town, in pro terms, built by the Cowboys; Staubach, Jones, Bob Lilly, Bob Hayes, Mel Renfro, Rayfield Wright and Cliff Harris, all of whom were outstanding talents discovered by Dallas' scouting system and reared on equally impressive coaching. 'They were pioneers,' says Jones. 'The scouting system was the first of its kind, and Coach Landry was a genius – the best coach in the league. He ran the offense, defense and special teams. He programmed his assistants, and they programmed us. Several of his assistants went on to be great head coaches themselves, and there's a reason for that.

'As a player, you want to walk onto the field and know that you're prepared. With Landry, we were sure of it. We were never going to be outcoached. You might beat us, but it wasn't because we weren't mentally and physically prepared.'

Come 1971, those Hall of Famers were complemented by title-winning veterans who would also be enshrined in Canton: Green Bay Packers legends Forrest Gregg and Herb Adderley, as well as Chicago Bears great Mike Ditka. Their task was to help Dallas shed a reputation of not being able to win it all, cultivated by back-to-back NFL Championship Game defeats to Vince Lombardi's Packers and a Super Bowl V reverse versus the Baltimore Colts.

The Cowboys managed just that, overcoming a 4-3 start that saw Landry rotate between Staubach and Craig Morton before eventually settling on the former and watching his club rattle off seven straight victories to end the campaign. Setting the stage for that success was their defense, who gave up one touchdown in the 14 quarters preceding Super Bowl VI and then allowed just three points to the Miami Dolphins.

The turning point was placing full faith in Staubach, whose selection as a 1964 10th-round pick represented another feather in the cap of Dallas' scouting department. 'It was made around 2 a.m. in Chicago's Sheraton Hotel,' remembers Brandt. 'It was on Monday during the season, so Landry and the other coaches were only there for a portion of the day. They left, and we looked around the room, and all you saw were empty coffee cups and two guys at each table waiting for a phone call to say who they should select. Tex and I were there, and he asked: "Who's the biggest sleeper and risk-taker we can get?" I said: "Roger Staubach."'

The risk on their part was in selecting a 1964 Heisman winner who was bound by the duty to partake in service following his career with the Naval Academy for an unspecified period. 'He was over in the warzone in Vietnam, and I'd get a letter every once in a while asking for a football and game tapes,' says Brandt. 'Even in service, he was a Cowboy. Then he'd have his leave time. Most guys would enjoy their month off, but he came to camp. We let his wife and him stay in the team hotel.'

The work paid off. In 1969, Staubach was eligible for action, which coincided nicely with Don Meredith's retirement. 'He came in at the perfect time and was prepared to play,' says Brandt.

A summary of Staubach's legend can be derived from the three nicknames – 'Rodger the Dodger', 'Captain America' and 'Captain Comeback' – that illustrate the qualities which turned him into a touchstone. Rodger the Dodger and Captain Comeback conveyed the on-field maestro, who boasted a flair for escapology that would make Houdini blush, both during individual plays and in the wider context of games that were never over if he could get the ball back. Captain America, meanwhile, spoke as much to his off-field qualities. Staubach, in an era when football was thought to appeal only to men, transcended the stereotype as someone fathers screamed for and mothers wanted their daughters to marry. As he said himself: 'I enjoy sex as a much as Joe Namath, only I do it with one girl.'

'He is an incredible individual,' adds Brandt. 'The kind of person where, if you searched for something he did wrong, you'd have a hard time. He was the All-American boy turned man. He was a man of his word. He wanted desperately to go to Ohio State in college, but they didn't offer him early. In the state high-school All-Star Game, he was MVP, and Woody Hayes started to press him to change his commitment to Ohio State, but he went to Navy, even though he had to go to junior college in Roswell, New Mexico, first.'

It's been said that if the southwest is the Bible belt, then Dallas is the buckle. Which explains why the quarterback's attitude played so well in the metropolis, helping to create an aura that began to encapsulate the Cowboys – one compounded by incidents such as Staubach revealing he said a Hail Mary when sending a last-gasp heave downfield against Minnesota that Drew Pearson caught for the winning touchdown in the 1975 NFC divisional round. Not only did Staubach's revelation create the name for which that play would for ever be known, it added to the Biblical air shrouding Dallas, whose Cowboys Stadium was claimed to have a giant hole at the top so God could watch his favourite football team.

Staubach was more than just a cultural centrepiece; he was a footballing one too – the rare blend of athleticism and arm talent that not only made the offense better but improved the whole team. 'We made each other better,' says Jones. 'Going up against Rodger the Dodger made any other quarterbacks seem a breeze.'

Throughout the decade, Dallas were there or thereabouts, posting double-digit wins every year barring 1973 (which still brought eight), and capturing a second title when overcoming the Denver Broncos' Orange Crush 27–10 in Super Bowl XII. 'I wish every player who ever meant something to the game could experience winning the Super Bowl,' adds Jones. 'It's phenomenal to wake up as a champion.'

The Cowboys didn't experience it more often due to the era's dominant team, the Steelers, overcoming Landry's men in tight encounters to win two of their crowns. Yet, even so, Dallas were a great, balanced squad who grew stronger through additions such as electrifying running back Dorsett and defensive-line stud Randy White by the point of their second crown. 'We were, and still are, a very close team,' reveals Jones. 'It was a special group and bond.'

By the early 1980s, America's Team stood as the shimmering standout on the NFL's Mount Rushmore, the previous decade having been spent establishing a hold on the public's imagination that remains to this day, with a blend of timing, execution and innovation. Which, ironically, is exactly the combination championed by the mastermind behind their defeat at Candlestick Park.

In 1968, six years removed from his Cleveland Browns departure, Paul Brown headed a consortium to set up a rival team in Ohio. His creation was a reboot of the Cincinnati Bengals, who played in the second and third editions of the AFL prior to Lamar Hunt's game-changing iteration and were named due to the famous local zoo housing a Bengal tiger. Brown immediately took the coaching reins, enhancing his outstanding record by leading Cincinnati to the playoffs within three years, the quickest period for an expansion team in US sports history to that point.

Upon returning to the sideline, he also furnished his staff by plucking from obscurity an unknown assistant in the Continental Football League who had spent a sole campaign alongside Al Davis at the Oakland Raiders two years previously. Bill Walsh was tasked with overseeing the offense and delivered outstanding returns, deploying a mix of Brown's deep-passing concepts with those learnt indirectly from Sid Gillman to immediately turn 1969 first-round pick Greg Cook into a star. By Week 2 of his rookie season, the 6ft 4in quarterback dubbed a 'blond-haired football God' by *Sports Illustrated*'s Paul Zimmerman demonstrated exactly why he had won the starting job, throwing for 327 yards and three touchdowns on 14 completions against the San Diego Chargers as Cincinnati started 2-0.

'He had great size and a Terry Bradshaw release, just a snap of the wrist,' remembered Cook's former backup Sam Wyche. 'Most of it came from the elbow to the hand to the release. He was extremely accurate, a good runner and displayed amazing judgement for a rookie. He didn't force the ball. His transition was immediate.'

Disaster struck the following week when linebacker Jim Lynch sacked Cook and landed on the passer's throwing shoulder. Cook played through a torn rotator cuff for much of an Offensive-Rookie-of-the-Year campaign in which he accrued 1,854 yards at a scarcely believable 17.5 per completion, but medical deficiencies meant he started just one game over the remainder of his career. 'I still remember the day of practice when he took his helmet off,' added Wyche, 'and just threw it on the ground. He said: "I can't do it any more. I can't take the pain." He was ripping tissue in his shoulder every time he rotated to throw the ball.'

His became the great lost career. 'I believe he was the greatest talent to ever play the position,' said Walsh. 'While he played, he was the best there was: an outstanding athlete with a very quick delivery. The ultimate quarterback.'

Although injury-induced loss of a generational talent can be put down to bad luck, the decision that came to define Brown's legacy in Cincinnati wasn't. Walsh's ability to so quickly help someone possessing all the physical tools might have been impressive, yet it was his response to Cook's injury – at least in the offensive coordinator's own mind – that made him Cincinnati's head-coach-in-waiting. Cook's backup Virgil Carter boasted nothing like the same traits, a Rover compared to Cook's Rolls Royce, but delivered short passes with unerring accuracy and displayed the mental capacity to comprehend Walsh's concepts. What Walsh did next was the hallmark of great coaching. Rather than fit a square peg into a round hole and have Carter run Cook's offense, Walsh adapted it to fit the new man, building a scheme that emphasised short passes and utilised Gillman's horizontal ideas to put receivers into positions where they could accrue yards after the catch. It was the beginning of Walsh's legacy: the 'West Coast Offense'.

Initially, the concepts formed the Ohio River offense, which was among the league's best under the stewardship of Carter and improved further once Walsh developed Cook's true heir apparent, Ken Anderson, a third-round selection in the 1971 NFL Draft.

'I played Division III football in Rock Island, Illinois,' says Anderson. 'I remember Bill coming to our facility, and the weather was terrible. We went into the gym and worked on things, and he began to show me some of the footwork parts. I think he became comfortable that I could do what he wanted. I had scouts come to see me, but a coach doing it was special.'

Anderson didn't realise how that initial session, focused on his feet rather than arm, would become a precursor for many that followed. While predicated on throwing, the most important element of Walsh's offense was footwork. His routes were so complex, weaving together with such precision, that – when a quarterback hit the top of his drop – the first read* would just be coming out of his break.* 'It was so detail-orientated,' adds Anderson. 'When I learnt it, I'd stand on the spot, over and over, doing the footwork. One, two, three, drop. The next week I'd walk through my drop, then jog, then full speed.

'But the receivers had to do their part. The depth was critical, as were the steps they took. Everything was about the receiver being at the right depth on time so I could deliver the ball to the right place on time. The final element was the progressions: those first, second, third, fourth reads were built in, and it was about getting through them on time too. The attention to detail was incredible.'

Through it all, Walsh and Brown were seemingly forging a strong bond. The head coach allowed his protégé to send plays down from the booth for Brown to pass along to the messenger guard, and the results were impressive as the Bengals bucked a run-dominated era's trend by throwing the ball often and enjoying great success. With a young signal-caller and brilliant next leading man seemingly in place, the Bengals should have been bound for greatness.

Yet to the surprise of Walsh, if not his most important player, Brown retired in 1975 and installed another assistant, Bill 'Tiger' Johnson, as his replacement. 'I wasn't surprised,' remembers Anderson. 'In hindsight, we look back based on what Bill [Walsh] would go on to do, but I thought Bill Johnson was more ready. History shows that wasn't the case, but I agreed with the decision. It hurt Bill tremendously that he wasn't the guy.'

Heightening Walsh's disillusionment was his path to other NFL jobs being blocked, Brown illustrating a vindictive streak by giving other teams poor reviews. 'All the way through I had opportunities and never knew about them,' said Walsh. 'When I left him, he called whoever he thought was necessary to keep me out of the NFL.'

After spending one successful year as the offensive coordinator of San Diego and another two as Stanford's head coach, Walsh finally earned the chance he craved when being handed the reins of a San Francisco team that flattered to deceive from the moment they began in the All-America Football Conference. To capture a first title in the franchise's near-35-year history, Walsh knew it was imperative to find the right players, particularly on offense. The task was aided by two concurrent moments of serendipity that changed the face of the NFL for ever.

With the 1979 draft – his first as 49ers head coach – just over a week away, San Francisco's board* was close to being set. For Walsh and his new band of lieutenants, the final job was to cross the i's and dot the t's, ensuring no stone was left unturned ahead of their first opportunity to enact meaningful change in the Bay Area.

As part of that process, Walsh headed to Clemson University to check on their draft-eligible passer Steve Fuller, whom he contacted beforehand. 'Steve, will you find a wide receiver to catch the passes?' Walsh asked. 'I don't want to catch the ball. I want to closely see what you're doing.' Knowing the stakes, Fuller obliged and enlisted the help of a college teammate who looked set to be an undrafted free agent that same year.

Concurrently, Wyche – recruited by Walsh as quarterbacks coach and passing-game coordinator – was on the West Coast facing similar issues. He was in town on a typically balmy day to work out wideout James Owens, who projected as a multi-faceted threat in the pros, capable of rushing, receiving and returning. Wyche's issue? 'I needed a quarterback to throw some passes,' he said. 'Thankfully, there was a kid down there from Notre Dame spending time with his future wife by Manhattan Beach, right near the campus.'

Wyche phoned the former Fighting Irish quarterback, himself projected as a mid-round selection, and asked: 'Can you come over and we'll work out?' He agreed and at 3 p.m. walked onto UCLA's practice field number two to put Owens through his paces.

For Wyche and Walsh, both trips proved extremely fruitful – just not in the anticipated manner. Upon returning to San Francisco, the head coach assembled the staff and detailed his findings. Fuller was a good quarterback, he revealed, but not sufficiently impressive to unseat some other highly rated prospects at the top of their board. The good news? Walsh had unearthed a potential wide receiver. 'We are going to take this kid he was throwing to, Dwight Clark,' said Walsh. 'He's got some potential. We will take him late in the draft or maybe as a free agent.'

En route back from Clemson, Walsh considered the club's quarterback rankings set. Morehead State passer Phil Simms had piqued his interest but would likely go in the first round, and the 49ers had previously traded away their selection for O.J. Simpson. As such, the feeling was Steve Dils, whom Walsh coached at Stanford, would be the choice. At least until Wyche filed his report from Los Angeles, which stated: 'Owens is as a good receiver; I'm not sure he's a great one. But Joe Montana has got something special.'

Wyche followed up his profile by telling Walsh: 'You and I need to go back again before the draft. I want you to see this kid work out and see what he's able to do when you give him some instructions, because he doesn't take any time to put them into practice. He is quick to get adjusted.'

Which is exactly what they did. 'Joe had an even better workout,' remembered Wyche, 'and Owens wasn't quite as good.' Walsh had seen enough. 'Tell the staff when we get back that we will take Owens in the second round and Montana in the third,' he said.

Wyche implored Walsh to reconsider, suggesting the risk of losing Montana by waiting until round three was too grave. But the head coach was unmoved and ultimately proven right . . . just. 'It's hard to forget that 1979 draft,' remembers former Cowboys personnel guru Brandt. 'We never deviated from our draft board. We would establish an order from one to 200 and take the best player available. Always. Montana was our 44th-ranked player and should have been the pick. But we had three quarterbacks and Coach Landry felt we would cut him. We jumped him for tight end Doug Cosbie. He was a good player, but certainly not Montana . . .'

And so it came to pass that, with the 82nd pick of the 1979 draft, the 49ers selected a Notre Dame quarterback they stumbled upon accidentally, then, with their 10th-round selection and 249th overall, a Clemson wide receiver also discovered by chance. Together, Montana and Clark would help transform the 49ers' fortunes and link up for one of the most significant moments in league history.

*

In Walsh's opening campaign, San Francisco won two games and carried their head coach off the field after one. A moment that spoke of the great affinity between commander and battalion also seemed to capture the mentality of a club that had only known mediocrity since entering pro football as part of the AAFC in 1946.

That they were one of three teams from the rival organisation absorbed into the NFL back in 1950 owed much to an offensive flair that typified their early existence, beginning in those AAFC days and continuing through to Red Hickey's brief success with a shotgun attack later that decade. Yet fleeting stints as entertainers who never threatened to win were rare highlights in a dire opening quarter-century.

The commencement of the 1970s brought change, with Dick Nolan leading the 49ers to the playoffs on the back of gritty MVP quarterback John Brodie. But San Francisco continuously saw their progress halted by a Dallas team they simply couldn't pass.

Both clubs were microcosms of their cities: the Cowboys big, brash and bold in a manner befitting a metropolis leaving behind a chequered history, highlighted by the assassination of John F. Kennedy, to become a place of business, God and football; the 49ers, in the era before Silicon Valley, a free-spirited team capable of providing the odd fun night but never caring to offer something more substantive.

Yet the early days of a 25-year rivalry weren't much of a rivalry at all. Dallas simply beat the 49ers every time. Having overcome Nolan's crew in back-to-back NFC Championship Games in 1970 and '71, they provided the ultimate ignominy in the '72 divisional round, Captain Comeback Staubach – having missed much of the year with a shoulder injury – helping turn around a 28–13 deficit late in the fourth quarter to lead the Cowboys to victory.

The consequences of that fixture, in which Dallas recovered an onside kick with less than two minutes left to set up the game-winning score, were far-reaching. While the Cowboys' surge towards America's Team continued apace, the 49ers became a laughing stock. They managed just one winning campaign in the next six and went through five head coaches.

Walsh, appointed by new owner Eddie DeBartolo Jr, inherited a 2-14 mess for which there was no quick fix. Montana required time to develop on the bench, and the opening two years were tough on their perfectionist head coach. 'He would call me,' says former Philadelphia Eagles coach Dick Vermeil. 'I was trying to convince him he might win next Sunday and not to jump off the bridge.'

The lowest point of those opening years came, unsurprisingly, against the Cowboys. Despite not having Staubach, who surprisingly retired prior to the year, Dallas humiliated the 49ers during a 1980 regular-season tilt, running up the score in a 59–14 beatdown. Yet the game proved a turning point. The following week, San Francisco moved their slow-burning plan for Montana to the next stage and made him their starter. 'He was a great kid to work with,' revealed Wyche. 'We drafted Joe and had Steve DeBerg, who was perfect for the situation: a veteran towards the end of his career who was another coach.

'Montana was going to be our quarterback, but we wanted to bring him along slowly. We'd give him series here and there, and up the ante each week. The danger you have with a new quarterback is trying to rush it. The quarterback becomes indecisive and maybe throws an interception or gets sacked when he shouldn't have, and his confidence level goes down. Joe was handled the right way. We went 2-14 the first year, then 6-10 the next. In that second year, Joe became our starter and began to show glimpses of what was to come.'

Montana's potential was best illustrated with three weeks of 1980 remaining, when leading San Francisco back from a 28-point deficit to secure victory over the New Orleans Saints. From there, the 49ers never looked back.

The following offseason brought key additions – not least

first-round pick Lott. Mixed with Montana's growing understanding of Walsh's game-changing offensive system, it turned the tide. The 49ers reversed a 1-2 start to win 12 of their next 13 – the sweetest of all coming when Montana tossed for 279 yards in a 45–14 win over the Cowboys – and brushed aside the New York Giants in the divisional round to set up yet another playoff match-up with Dallas.

This time, claimed the indomitable Jones, San Francisco would tackle the real Cowboys.

The task appeared hopeless. When Montana returned to the field, the 89 yards of grass separating him from the end zone was over-run by a sea of white and sliver. The giant scoreboard, meanwhile, illustrated the scale of the challenge: Cowboys 27–21 49ers, 4:54 remaining.

Dallas' defense was formidable on its own, without the weight of history, or memories of those three previous playoff tilts. Yet Montana – unlike fans watching through their fingers – was unburdened by the past. When his first pass, a dump-off to Lenvil Elliott flaring out of the backfield, fell incomplete, he simply awaited his running back's return to the huddle and called a draw play. Six yards.

The moment before the next play brought with it the nervous hushed murmur familiar to any football fan, signalling a key third down for the home offense and overshadowing quieted calls of 'Go Niners Go'. Trepidation of those in the stands belied the cool emanating from San Francisco's conductor on the sideline and his principal on the field. Montana, taking the call relayed from Walsh, kneeled at the feet of his orchestra, each man waiting for instruction. Freddie Solomon listened intently, broke into his out route perfectly seven yards down the field and came back slightly to the ball to snaffle Montana's wobbly pass, delivered with rush-ers bearing down on him. The Niners were suddenly making sweet music.

With the Cowboys' defense on its heels, it was time for Walsh – advised by eye-in-the-sky Wyche from the press box – to go to work. After Elliott gained 11 yards on a sweep to the right, Wyche messaged down: 'Let's run it the other way.' 'You got it,' replied Walsh, changing the call from 'Bob-18' to 'Bob-19'. Another seven.

Suddenly, Dallas looked tired. White, a first-team All-Pro every year since 1977, was forced off the field with cramps, paving the way for Bruce Thornton to give San Francisco a crucial first down by jumping offside following Montana's incompletion. Even White's reappearance couldn't halt the momentum, Montana hitting fullback Earl Cooper for five yards on a curl pattern. The Cowboys were experiencing what so many 49ers opponents would thereafter: death by a thousand paper cuts.

During the two-minute warning,* Walsh called over his quarterback. 'What do you think of the reverse to Solomon?' he asked. Montana was unsure but delivered the key block on White. Fourteen yards closer.

Next up, Montana returned to territory more comfortable for him, if not those in attendance, by threading the ball through a tiny window over the outstretched hand of Barnes, just out of the reach of Everson Walls – who had two interceptions on the day – and into the chest of Clark. With 10 more yards chalked up, San Francisco stood on the Dallas 25 as the clock ticked towards 1:30.

Those with hearts in mouths on the previous play were left in the same state when Montana, shuffling left, broke one of quarterbacking's oldest rules by delivering a pass back across his body. But he hit the keyhole between Barnes and Walls for 12 more. The same accuracy wasn't displayed after the ensuing timeout. 'I should have hit Solomon in the end zone,' remembered Montana. 'He ran a little shallow cross and would have walked into the end zone, but I threw the football about two feet over his head. I remember Coach Walsh's reaction. He looked pretty disgusted. I was looking for another opportunity.'

After Elliott gained seven on another sweep left to reach the 49ers' six, Montana's wish would be granted. Line coach Bobb McKittrick suggested San Francisco run again versus Landry's nickel package – but Walsh, gazing intently at Montana through his glasses while speaking with eerie calm, had another play in mind.

The previous night, San Francisco's coach was in his happy place, at the foot of a projector screen, finger hovering over perfectly drawn X's and O's as his players watched. 'Dwight is in here sliding back out,' Walsh explained, moving his hand to the right sideline to indicate wide receiver Clark's route. 'This is great for when they're tired, confused and want to get back to Dallas. This is when you knock their asses off.'

The play on the diagram, 'sprint right option', worked to perfection for San Francisco's opening touchdown when, making use of the space created by Clark clearing out the underneath on a semi-pick* play, Solomon found the end zone. In failing to stop the call's initial intention, Dallas hadn't even seen part two. But, with 58 seconds remaining and his 49ers stationed on the Cowboy six facing third-and-three, Walsh was betting they would this time around.

'We're going to call a sprint right option,' he told Montana. 'Dwight will be clear. He's going to break up then into the corner. If you don't get what you want, simply throw the ball away. You got it? Dwight will clear. As soon as you see the angle he's breaking, just drop the ball in there. If you don't get what you want, simply throw the ball away. You know what I mean? Hold it, hold it, hold it, [if it's] not there, away it goes. Be ready to go to Dwight.'

If Solomon was covered, Montana's second read – while moving quickly back and towards the right sideline – was Clark. 'He had to run down to the end line,' said Wyche, 'cut left until he reached under the goalpost – and not before! Then he'd turn back the other way and go back along the backline. But the key was waiting until he was right at the goalpost. It was timed that way.' The timing was such that, once Montana began to head towards the sideline, Clark would be running along the backline in the same direction.

'We practised that play all summer during training camp,' said Montana. 'And Dwight Clark would go crazy because we never threw the ball to him. It was always thrown underneath to Freddie, because Dwight would come in and set a little pick for him. We scored earlier in the game on the same play, but this time Freddie fell down, so I had to keep rolling, and Dwight was shocked that Freddie didn't get the ball. It took him a little longer to get along the back line and, when I let it go, I didn't think it was as high as it was, but Dwight made a great catch.'

In reality, the ball – delivered with Montana back-pedalling and on the verge of going out of bounds – was in the perfect spot. It was, as Wyche had demanded, an 'arching throw', high enough for the outstretched arm of Walls not to reach it, but not so high that Clark couldn't leap into the air, extend his body and come down perfectly straight for his toes to drop into the end zone. 'The Dallas Cowboys swear he threw it away,' said Wyche, 'but we worked on that play as hard as any other, and Joe threw a perfect pass.'

After rising to his feet, Montana picked out the unmistakeable figure of Jones, raced over and screamed: 'Respect that!' The 49ers had clearly earned Dallas' admiration, but the Cowboys weren't finished. There were 58 seconds remaining, and Landry's men boasted the best kicker in football, Rafael Septién.

They also possessed an X-factor speed threat in Pearson, who nearly broke 49er hearts again immediately – only for Eric Wright to somehow drag him down with the wideout gazing at open field having caught a deep post between three defenders. Even so, Dallas still had a great opportunity, having crossed midfield with 38 seconds and one timeout remaining. But Lawrence Pillers sacked Danny White on the ensuing play, forced a fumble and Jim

Stuckey jumped on the ball. 'I saw Lawrence knock the ball out,' he says. 'I knew I could get it, jumped on it and laid like a little baby in the foetal position, cradling it. Lawrence came off, and I screamed: "We're going to the fucking Super Bowl."'

In Super Bowl XVI, Walsh enjoyed the ultimate vindication as San Francisco took down the Bengals 26–21. Although his revenge represented a personal victory, the head coach and his 49ers would forever point to events in the Bay Area a fortnight prior as being the franchise's turning point. 'Looking back on it, that was Camelot,' said Walsh. 'That was the origin of a dynasty.'

'The funny part,' added Wyche, 'is that Bill went to Clemson to grade a quarterback and discovered Dwight Clark. I went down to UCLA to work with a wide receiver and found the quarterback. And then the two of them make the play that changes everything for the 49ers.'

Almost a decade to the day since the Immaculate Reception helped catapult Pittsburgh towards their dynastic run, San Francisco enjoyed lift-off via a memorable play of their own . . . with eerie similarities. Just like Art Rooney 10 years previously, 49ers owner DeBartolo missed the crucial moment as he headed for the locker room to console his troops. When he finally spoke to the players, DeBartolo was regaled with tales of Montana and Clark – and of a signature moment that would define his team's greatness and be immortalised by two simple words: 'The Catch'.

13

Bear Up

Week 6

CHICAGO BEARS 26
SAN FRANCISCO 49ERS 10

---

13 October 1985
Candlestick Park, San Francisco

The passing of nine months hadn't dampened Chicago's thirst for revenge, heightened by memories of bruising guard Guy McIntyre powering his way through weary Bears bodies and words boastfully spoken by victorious San Francisco 49ers at the 1984 NFC Championship Game's conclusion: 'Next time bring an offense.'

Chicago hadn't just been beaten at Candlestick Park the previous year. With a Super Bowl berth on the line, they were humiliated 23–0, in the bitterest of conclusions to a campaign that had seen the team roar back to relevance following two decades in the doldrums. To add insult to injury, with the Niners leading 6–0 in the third quarter, 270lb lineman McIntyre began operating at fullback, powering the 49ers' first touchdown on a

35-yard drive in which every play was a run, leaving the Bears in the dust.

Despite claims that the decision had been Bill Walsh's way of rubbing Chicago's noses in the dirt, it was actually quite the compliment. So concerned was Walsh – the preeminent offensive mind in an era of game-changers – with coordinator Buddy Ryan's 46 Defense that he installed multiple new wrinkles, from McIntyre's package to Freddie Solomon spending one play as option quarterback with Joe Montana split out wide.

'We'd gotten to the NFC Championship and beaten some good teams,' remembers Chicago's Hall-of-Fame defensive lineman Dan Hampton. 'We proved we were legitimate, but realised we weren't good enough. The 49ers mocked us, though we were playing with a backup quarterback.'

The closest Chicago had come to scoring was Bob Thomas' missed 41-yard field goal on the opening possession. With Jim McMahon out due to a lacerated kidney, Steve Fuller was a rabbit in headlights, overmatched against the 49ers' talented defense.

Chicago's equally impressive group on that side of the ball played extraordinary, allowing San Francisco just six points on three drives that reached inside their five-yard line. But, in the end, they spent too much time on the field and were undermined by an offense which managed 16 yards on seven first-half passing plays.

For all their skill – and they certainly had an abundance – the Bears just couldn't get the job done. As defensive heartbeat Mike Singletary stood on the sidelines towards the conclusion of the game, unable to ignore goading 49ers fans, he turned around to return fire: 'We'll be back!'

'It put a chip on our shoulder,' reveals Hampton. 'We came to the door and knocked but were now going to kick it in. I made it my special mission to go to each player, look them in the eye and say: "We need to prove we're good enough to be world champions." We circled the next 49ers game when the schedule came out. It was the moment of truth. Everything was geared to it.'

Chicago's chance to prove themselves came in Week 6 of the 1985 campaign, when the 5-0 Bears descended upon Candlestick Park again to battle the defending champion 49ers. Just as significant as the Bears' animosity for their opponents were the stakes, for head coach Mike Ditka and co. knew victory would not only propel Chicago towards their first championship in more than 20 years – and a maiden Super Bowl – but also validate one of the final decisions made by their tireless founder.

The end of another lacklustre campaign in 1981 brought an increasingly familiar feeling of change to Halas Hall. The firing of Neill Armstrong represented Chicago's fourth coaching switch in 14 years, a run that couldn't have been further removed from the 47 that preceded it.

George Halas had acted as leading man for 39 full seasons (plus one half campaign in 1942 before the Second World War intervened) and, although there were brief interludes in which Papa Bear handed over the reins for various reasons, none lasted more than three years and he always returned. At least until 1967, when – aged 72 – Halas hung up his whistle for good.

He did so amid a period of incredible frustration in which the Bears played second fiddle to their bitterest rivals. Entering the 1960s, Chicago boasted one more NFL championship than the Green Bay Packers; leaving the decade, they lagged three behind despite having added an eighth of their own.

The great paradox was that the beginning of the leanest spell in club history coincided with some of the greatest players to ever don the Bears' famous colours. In the case of Ditka, the all-world tight end who changed the face of his position by being so effective as an in-line blocker and pass-catching weapon, satisfaction came from forming a key part of Halas' last title-winning squad in 1963 and bolstering his ring collection with another at the Dallas Cowboys.

The same couldn't be said for two exceptional draftees from 1965. Linebacker Dick Butkus and running back Gale Sayers arrived one pick apart, the former selected third overall and the latter fourth, with the job of brightening up a team engulfed by tragedy. The previous year, while preparing to defend their championship, Chicago suffered the devastation of popular running back Willie Galimore and wide receiver John 'Bo' Farrington dying in a car accident. Hope sprung eternal in 1965, however, thanks to their historic draft haul.

Local boy Butkus was so good he quickly replaced Hall-of-Famer Bill George, leading the Bears in tackles, interceptions, forced fumbles and fumble recoveries, yet didn't earn Rookie-of-the-Year honours. That gong went to Sayers, whose 22 touchdowns are still the most for any first-year player, while his mark of six in one game versus the 49ers ties Ernie Nevers and former Cleveland Brown Dub Jones' record. 'What got me,' said Butkus, 'is the offense got to the two-yard line, and they pulled Gale. It should have been seven.'

Butkus wouldn't be shy of individual honours either. He ended his career as an eight-time Pro Bowler, six-time first-team All-Pro and two-time Defensive Player of the Year. Sayers parlayed excellence as a runner, receiver and, at times, willing thrower to earn first-team All-Pro honours in each of his first five campaigns and was twice the NFL's rushing champion. He holds the highest average-yards-per-game mark (138.8) in league history, boasts the most consecutive contests with at least 100 yards (23), remains the fastest player to reach 1,000, 2,000, 3,000, 4,000, 5,000, 6,000, 7,000, 8,000 and 9,000 rushing yards, and has the greatest return-yardage average of those with at least 75 attempts (30.56).

More significant than the similarities between two legends were their perceived differences. Butkus, arguably the greatest linebacker of all-time, was a fearsome competitor who played every snap like it was his last and spent a decade as pro football's ultimate alpha dog. Such brutality contrasted sharply with the quick-twitch, stop-start guile of his draft mate, Sayers' beautiful feet and majesty the antithesis of Butkus' unbridled physicality. Yet such descriptions did each a disservice. Just as Sayers wasn't a finesse player who shirked contact, there was more to Butkus than met the eye: the speed and power of his collisions disguised perfect tackling technique that dislodged balls and coverage ability which ensured he was often step to step with pass-catchers.

Most pertinent for the Bears was how each brought the best from one another, their juxtaposing skillsets providing a fascinating subplot to practices in which they went against one another and fostering a friendship that remains to this day. The rigours of those sessions catapulted both to the Hall of Fame, Sayers becoming the youngest inductee at 34, following a seven-year career, and Butkus also enshrined in his first year of eligibility.

Yet their tenures – both shortened by knee injuries – had a missing piece: neither played in the postseason. 'I loved the game,' said Butkus, whose quality was best summed up by winning his second Defensive Player of the Year title when the Bears finished 1-13 in 1969. 'I was all about playing football. I always thought we were going to win – even the year we went 1-13 – but we just didn't.'

The misfortune endured by Sayers and Butkus, who retired in 1971 and '73 respectively, was a familiar story: their prime coincided with a great Packers team. Had Halas' succession plan of elevating George Allen materialised prior to the former Bears defensive coordinator becoming impatient and joining the Los Angeles Rams, things might have been different. Instead, their careers were played out under a fading Halas, as well as Jim Dooley and Abe Gibron – whose combined NFL coaching records were 31-66-1 with zero playoff appearances.

Four years after Sayers' exit, Chicago selected yet another all-time great who not only played the same position but was taken with the identical draft choice. And by 1981, when Halas sent Armstrong packing, there was a sense of déjà vu.

*

A decade after choosing Sayers fourth overall, the Bears used the 1975 fourth overall pick on a 20-year-old from Jackson State called Walter Payton. As running backs, the two were yin and yang: where Sayers claimed he required '18 inches of daylight' to break clear, Payton might have needed just eight. For the latter's primary skill wasn't the elusiveness so often illustrated by his predecessor, but a combination of agility and devastating power which belied a 200lb frame. His art was in the ferocity of stiff arms and high steps that resembled a thoroughbred gathering speed along the final furlong.

Payton endured a most unbefitting start in the NFL – managing zero yards on eight carries in his debut – but the malaise didn't last. In his third year, 'Sweetness' followed up campaigns of 679 and 1,390 yards by racking up 1,852 and 14 touchdowns to be voted NFL MVP as Chicago returned to the postseason for the first time in 14 years. That brought the second of five successive first-team All-Pro berths – he had seven overall – as Payton, blending continuous improvement as a pass-catcher with peerless mastery in the running game and exceptional pass-blocking, became the best and most complete 'back in football.

Yet even somebody with such talent, like Butkus and Sayers before him, couldn't break the Bears' wider malaise. 'Imagine a wannabe actress wanting to go to Hollywood and landing in Montana,' adds Hampton. 'I wanted to play for the Dolphins or the Rams – anybody on the coast. But I was sent to Siberia. Chicago was one of the dregs of the NFL, and their only salvation was having the league's best player, Walter Payton.'

After going 6-10 in 1981, the ship again appeared rudderless and Halas, nearly two decades removed from his last crown, sought inspiration. It came via two surprising letters. The first was from a group of Bears defenders led by star safety Gary Fencik. Sensing a potential coaching change, the unit implored Halas to keep Ryan and his assistants in place. 'Buddy Ryan was a sergeant in the Korean War at 19,' says Hampton. 'He was in charge of 20 guys and got them all out safely. He was a born leader who didn't play favourites. He loved certain guys but treated everybody equally and had an amazing rapport. We would have jumped in front of a bus to save him. I have been coached by Jimmy Johnson, Monte Kiffin, Lou Holtz and Mike Ditka – there was nobody like Buddy.'

So impressed was the frail and diminutive Halas that he threw on an overcoat and woolly hat, braved the snowstorms and headed to the Great Lakes Naval Training Center. 'Without wanting to be insulting,' adds Hampton, 'he was as involved as the Queen is in running the UK at that time. He was the figurehead and ultimate icon – but would just show up on a golf cart for a couple of hours of training camp. The door opened, and it was like being in church and the Pope walks in. Everyone is like: "Holy shit."'

Halas, exhibiting an aura established across more than half a century as the face of the NFL, told his coaches to 'hit the bricks' and addressed the players. 'Sixty-one years,' he said, 'I've run this organisation. Nobody has ever thought enough about their team to do this. I'm overwhelmed. I'll renew Buddy Ryan and his coaches' contracts immediately.'

'It's unbelievable the impact it had on an 86-year-old icon who started the league,' adds Hampton. 'Even then, he still cared. He realised that he needed to make a statement. It was the beginning of making the Bears the envy of every team in football.'

The other letter came from an unlikelier source. For all 'Iron Mike' Ditka had established himself among the most illustrious Bears during six years at the franchise, he and Halas didn't part on good terms. Contract arguments saw the star tight end claim his thrifty boss 'threw nickels around like manhole covers' and led to Ditka's 1967 trade to the Philadelphia Eagles.

Yet Ditka was a Bear at heart and, having spent his most recent years learning the coaching trade on Tom Landry's staff, felt he had something to offer. Ditka implored Halas to give him an opportunity as head coach and, to everyone's surprise, the NFL's elder statesmen agreed, albeit with the caveat that he become the lowest-paid leading man in football.

In the early years of Ditka and Ryan's union, Halas might have been forgiven for thinking he was getting what he paid for. The former appeared as out of his depth as other previous Bears players, such as Gibron and Dooley, who had failed in the hotseat. 'It was adversarial,' says Hampton. 'Neither Ditka nor Buddy backed down. Not just the coaches, but us too. It was like any band where the singer thinks he's the star, as does the drummer and lead guitarist. We all wanted to be stars. We were not going to let the offense block us in practice. The hell with that. We would get into fist fights – it [was] acrimonious.'

Ditka would turn it around spectacularly, only the man who employed him wasn't around to see it. On Halloween 1983, with the Bears a lowly 3-6 following a suitably horrifying 38–17 hammering at the hands of the 3-5 Detroit Lions the day before, Halas died of pancreatic cancer aged 88. He was the last surviving member of the group who had met at Ralph Hay's showroom sixty-three years earlier.

His death came at a time of great uncertainty not only for his football team, but also the organisation in which it sat. For all the internal conflict within the Windy City was significant, it had nothing on the greater storm brewing at NFL headquarters, where two other strong-willed men were engaging in a battle that endangered the future of the league Halas had spent every ounce of his being building from ground zero.

From the moment he ascended for his brief run as AFL commissioner, Al Davis proved a thorn in the side of Pete Rozelle. Their relationship wasn't so much frosty as permanently frozen, animosity stemming from their days at the helm of warring leagues and continuing after Davis retreated back into team ranks.

The hope of Davis edging back into the pack as the Oakland Raiders' supremo proved misguided. His iconoclastic edge, it quickly emerged, was as sharp as ever. When owners began finalising the league's restructure, Davis was among the biggest obstacles – to such an extent that Vince Lombardi physically collared him and declared: 'If you're going to cause trouble, you'll be run out of here.'

Lombardi's intervention worked on that occasion, but there was no stopping future battles between Davis and Rozelle. There were many blows struck on either side. Davis, for example, supported George Atkinson in suing Chuck Noll for suggesting he represented a 'criminal element' of the NFL following a cheap shot on Lynn Swann, although the safety lost a $2 million defamation suit. Meanwhile, Rozelle – usually the conciliator – famously removed the Oakland supremo from the NFL's Competition Committee in 1977. But things reached breaking point at the turn of the 1980s and beyond, when the pair battled through the courts, with Davis eventually succeeding in moving his Raiders to Los Angeles.

Not only did the move represent a rare failure for Rozelle, it opened a can of worms that allowed other owners to follow Davis' lead. Most famously, the volatile Robert Irsay brutally took his Colts from Baltimore to Indianapolis in the dead of night on 29 March 1984, with 15 Mayflower removal trucks shipping everything to Indianapolis. That the city's residents, whose support of the team was central to the Colts' recreation in 1953 and a driving force behind the 20 years of sustained success that followed, went to sleep with a team and awoke without one stands among the most ruthless moments in league history. Three years later, meanwhile, Bill Bidwill took his St. Louis Cardinals to Arizona.

Those episodes presented the NFL's owners and commissioner as a broken group at a time when the importance of solidarity – at least publicly – was crucial. As Rozelle battled relocation, he was also tasked with countering a players' union growing in stature, as well as the advent of the United States Football League, an organisation playing in the spring who were the first true rival since the AFL.

Every issue would take chunks from the commissioner's resolve. 'It caused my dad stress,' remembers Rozelle's daughter Anne Marie Bratton. 'Instead of working towards strengthening the future of the NFL, everything became litigation. He traded his office for a courtroom. Those were difficult times.'

Up until the 1980s, the league had endured three players' strikes – lasting 12 days before the 1968 campaign, a few days prior to 1970 and two months ahead of the 1974 term – without any impact on the schedule. Yet the same wasn't true of those that followed. In 1982, a three-month walkout brought a curtailed nine-game campaign with 16 of 28 teams making the playoffs, while those in '87 reduced the action by one game and saw three weeks take place with replacement players. They eventually found common ground to the point that it'd be nearly 25 years until action was again taken by the players, but not before two under-mined campaigns.

As for the USFL, it began operations in 1985 and succeeded in luring future Hall-of-Famers Jim Kelly, Steve Young and Reggie White into the fold, as well as – most famously of all – 1982 Heisman winner Herschel Walker. They operated with relative success for three campaigns, delivering a solid product that was particularly successful in Denver and Tampa Bay, only to ditch their USP – of playing in the spring – to wage war with the NFL in the attempt to force a merger. A move not supported by many owners was pushed through with typical bombast by New Jersey Generals supremo, and future US president, Donald Trump but proved the league's death knell. It sued the NFL as being in breach of antitrust law but gained a measly $1 settlement – which was tripled to $3 – and folded soon after.

If that could be viewed as another victory for the NFL, diffi-culties in the 1980s took their toll – no more so than in the case of capricious relocations. Even though it was not a new phenom-enon, most previous examples had been collectively approved and necessary. The cases of Baltimore and Oakland, in particular, struck a nerve, robbing impassioned fanbases of franchises their communities were built around while illustrating the collective NFL's powerlessness to stop owners minded to move.

The great irony was that, as the status and location of clubs was coming under question for the first time in years, one of two remaining founding teams, who had played in the same city every season except their first, were enjoying a renaissance.

From their earliest days, the Bears' excellence was predicated on defense, highlighted by men whose play embodied the hard-nosed, blue-collar edge of Chicago and names fittingly symbolised toughness: from George 'Brute' Trafton to Butkus. Collectively, all fell under the iconic 'Monsters of the Midway' moniker.

In the early 1980s, Ryan was tasked with developing a new breed of Monsters, yet it wasn't easy. In Week 7 of the game-changing 1981 campaign, Chicago's defense reached a nadir, surrendering 48 points against the Lions, whose quarterback Eric Hipple amassed a scarcely believable 336 yards and four touchdowns on 14 completions.

Ryan, proving the old adage that desperate times call for desperate measures, ripped up the book and started again. Remembering from his time as the New York Jets' defensive line coach the effort Weeb Ewbank spent on protecting oft-injured signal-caller Joe Namath, his idea was to attack linemen with organised chaos. The first iteration of what became known as the '46' – named after safety Doug Plank's jersey number due to him being brought into the box – was deployed the week after that Lions loss. Chicago were facing the San Diego Chargers' league-best offense, boasting genius coach Don Coryell, sublime quarterback Dan Fouts and electrifying receiving threats Kellen Winslow and Charlie Joiner.

The Chargers – whose deep-passing attack had destroyed all-comers – were bamboozled by Ryan's 5-1-5 alignment and, more importantly, the continuous blitzing from different angles. Fouts completed 13-of-43 passes as Chicago pulled off the upset in overtime, while the Bears' defense improved dramatically by the season's end – hence the players' eventual plea to Halas. 'The 46 was created because Buddy didn't have enough rushers who could win one-on-one,' says Hampton.

Those seeds would grow into something considerably greater, Chicago's five-man front becoming a six with interchangeable pieces. The line was comprised of a standard four, with two line-backers alongside one another on the strong side of the formation (where the opposing tight end stood). From the snap, it was a jailbreak, except when it wasn't. The six wouldn't always rush, but the strong safety – closer to the line of scrimmage – might, or maybe it'd be Singletary.

'It's all about pressure,' said the linebacker. 'We're going to come at you and hit your quarterback until you get another one in. It was a nightmare for quarterbacks. We kept people guessing. It was physical and nasty.'

The centrepiece – ironically given Ryan benched him against San Diego for calling an unnecessary timeout – was Singletary, a Bears linebacker following in the tradition of George and Butkus. His undersized frame camouflaged exceptional speed, athleticism and the smarts to make on-field adjustments that ensured the 46 became so difficult to counter.

As the years wore on, the 46's unique challenge extend-ed beyond X's and O's. Thanks to shrewd additions made by Chicago's general manager Jim Finks, Ryan's cupboard began to be stocked. Joining do-it-all-linebacker Singletary and outstand-ing lineman Hampton were 1983 eighth-round menace Richard Dent, who led the NFL with 17.5 sacks in his second season to begin a run of eight double-digit-takedown campaigns over the next 10, and Steve McMichael, a New England Patriots cast-off capable of penetrating offensive lines from inside.

'When you put three world-class pass-rushers with the scheme, it was impossible to stop,' adds Hampton. 'Nobody could double all three of us, so we'd get one-on-one. Quarterbacks had two

226

seconds to get rid of the ball. Nobody could handle it. We used to make Three Stooges noises. Not only were we sending different guys from outside, we were running stunts inside. There was no way anyone could prepare for us. Maybe you could get acclimatised playing us every week, but it was tough for those teams seeing us for the first time. When you strip it away, even if you had a helmet on everyone, you still had seven All-Pros coming for the quarterback. It was a perfect blend of scheme and skill that created a monster.'

By 1985, the Stooges were complemented by man mountain William 'the Fridge' Perry, with Otis Wilson and Wilber Marshall operating as the linebackers tasked with either rushing or dropping into coverage from their unique position on the line. Singletary and strong safety Dave Duerson patrolled the middle of the field, Fencik covered the back end impeccably, while cornerbacks Leslie Frazier and Mike Richardson played man-to-man coverage. Collectively, they created the greatest defensive unit of all-time, one as adept against the run as the pass and capable of not only limiting opposing offensive output but generating turnovers.

Chicago entered the campaign having fielded a top-five defense in each of the previous two years. Now, as San Francisco told the Bears' players the year before, it was time to bring an offense.

The task of sparking Chicago's overdue offensive revival fell to a combination of Ditka and walking contradiction quarterback McMahon.

His introduction was a blur of what would become typical controversy. The Californian signal-caller from Mormon school BYU blurred the lines as a Christian party boy playing as hard off the field as on it, setting 32 NCAA records and being a three-time Heisman finalist. The only thing sure when McMahon rocked up as the 1982 fifth overall pick in a limousine, swigging beer during his introductory press conference, was he would provide a helluva ride. 'McMahon was an idiot,' remembers Hampton.

'That's not fair,' counters Hall-of-Fame offensive lineman Jimbo Covert. 'He wasn't an idiot. He was the smartest, I think, player I ever played with.'

Whether an idiot or not, McMahon fit the Bears perfectly. 'He resented authority a little bit,' remembered Ditka. 'But there's nobody else I'd have wanted at quarterback. Joe Montana was perfect for the 49ers; McMahon was perfect for us.'

McMahon encapsulated the outlaw spirit that drove the Bears and possessed the ideal on-field skillset. He might not have managed the down-to-down consistency of Montana, but the signal-caller was a playmaker capable of scoring from anywhere on the field, which limited opponents' ability to load the box and stop Payton – who, for the first time in his career, had room to operate.

McMahon's value was never more evident than in Week 3 at the 2-0 Minnesota Vikings. In what would prove a career theme, he was sidelined for the Thursday Night Football contest. 'I'd screwed up my neck and back,' remembered McMahon. 'But once you get to the stadium, with the adrenalin, and I don't know how many muscle relaxers I'd had, I was feeling pretty good. I was throwing the shit out of the ball in pregame, and Ditka looks at me and says: "You're not playing tonight."' But the Bears, also 2-0, were down 17–9 in the third quarter, and 'Mad Mac' was imploring his coach. 'He was badgering me,' added Ditka. 'Finally, I put him in.'

First snap, McMahon called the instructed play – which wasn't always the case. Having informed his offensive teammates of the intended screen pass, he took the ball from under centre and, woozy from painkillers, almost fell down. 'As I regained my balance,' he remembered, 'Willie [Gault] was 10 yards behind his man.' With Payton affording him the necessary time by throwing the perfect block, the result was inevitable: touchdown, 67 yards. As he returned to the sideline, McMahon encountered a furious Ditka. 'What damn play did you call?' enquired the coach. 'I called the screen,' said McMahon. Ditka, still livid, continued: 'So why did you pass it to Willie?' To which McMahon delivered the ideal response: 'Because he was open, Mike!'

Following a Minnesota interception, McMahon's second play was also a touchdown, thrown back across his body to Dennis McKinnon. The Bears won 33–24 with their quarterback completing 8-of-15 passes for 236 yards and three scores. 'He was a genius,' said Dent.

A genius leading an offense that no longer acted as a ball and chain around the Bears' necks. Alongside McMahon and the unequalled Payton, Chicago boasted explosive wideouts in Gault and McKinnon, as well as a fine offensive line led by left tackle Covert and All-Pro centre Jay Hilgenberg.

'The quarterback was ahead of his time,' says left guard Tom Thayer, who played 130 of 134 games in his eight-year Bears career. 'He was built for today's offenses. When Jim came out of college, he had 32 NCAA passing records, and had to make concessions because we had a great offensive line and were going to run more than throw. Jim's creativity would be inserted at different times, with Gault and McKinnon getting downfield. What made Jim special was his ability at the line of scrimmage. He understood and got us into the right plays. And then, of course, you had Walter.

'It was a dream to be part of his greatness. Even if the team was bad, Walter was great. He stood head and shoulders above everybody else. Not only on our team – but other 'backs in the league, be it Earl Campbell, Tony Dorsett, Eric Dickerson or whoever. He was in great shape, never needed a personal trainer and had everything. There was nothing like standing in the huddle with Walter. They'd call a play where my block was going to be instrumental in his success and failure. It creates the type of pressure that every football player craves, the opportunity to do something for the greatest, toughest and one of the most inspirational guys in football history.'

Three years on from his hiring, Ditka had all of the pieces in place. To truly deliver upon the promise he made Halas, however, the head coach would first have to overcome the opponent who so mercilessly beat his Bears in the previous year's NFC Championship Game.

Come 1985, San Francisco were unrecognisable from the team Walsh had inherited. A plucky underdog had become the NFL's latest powerhouse, overseen by a leading man so often overlooked early in his coaching career, forced to wait until he was 47 years old to earn the big break, now known simply as 'the Genius'. Walsh deserving the title was as indisputable as him being the perfect fit for San Francisco.

The city was undergoing the cultural revolution that would see it become the world's technological hub, a place of creativity and freedom.

In its 49ers, San Francisco boasted a team mirroring that rise with a CEO every bit as innovative and brilliant as those building Silicon Valley. 'He could have done anything,' says Brian Bilick, a Super Bowl-winning head coach who began his career as a PR intern in San Francisco. 'He was a true leader, who would have been just as successful running a Fortune 500 company.' Walsh's chosen vocation was football and, like his mentor Paul Brown so many decades previously, he approached its most important role with a new method, evident in both the minutiae – referring to playbooks as 'inventories of plays' – and the bigger picture. 'Coach Walsh had it down to science,' remembers star running back Roger Craig. 'He was a genius, the ultimate perfectionist.'

One of Walsh's most famous innovations owed much to Brown. In Cincinnati, the Bengals' leading man would often collar his assistant and ask: 'What are your openers?' meaning the opening offensive plays. The enquiry set Walsh on a course for scripting his first 15, a methodical task that would be copied by every offensive coach in football. However, imitators' packages couldn't claim to have been put together with the same attention to detail, painstakingly gleaned over hours of study by Walsh and his staff.

'He did analytics before they were talked about,' adds Craig. 'His film breakdowns were insane. He knew every opponent inside out, and that's why he wouldn't deviate from those 15 plays. They had been so meticulously planned. He knew how often teams ran each defense in the red zone, and all things like that. It's common now but wasn't then.'

For coaches such as Landry, equally obsessed in the compilation of opponents' tendencies, that opening script provided a unique challenge. With the plays preordained, and not determined by down and distance, it was tricky to get a beat on what San Francisco would run.

Yet the brilliance of Walsh went beyond just invention. Unlike similar X's and O's obsessives who struggled with man-management, he married creativity with an ability to draw the best from a group of alphas. 'He knew how to play players,' reveals Craig. He did so with a unique mix, the blunt honesty and relentless pursuit of perfection offset by lighter moments, such as going into the wide receiver meeting room dressed in full kit and pads, and the day, ahead of a Super Bowl, Walsh walked off the bus dressed as a porter and began to unload the bags.

'Bill set the tone,' adds Ronnie Lott. 'We wanted to please him. It's like with your dad – you feel like you want to please him. We all ask ourselves now why that was – why we wanted to please him so much. A lot of it was the way he was always so consistent with his message. Coaching is not about wanting you to be your best. It's getting you there.'

Walsh paired those traits with an exceptional scouting eye to create the crucial synergy which rarely exists in the modern NFL. As both the head coach and leading decision-maker when it came to personnel, he was able and allowed to fulfil one of the signature lines uttered by his great coaching rival Bill Parcells: buying the groceries *and* cooking the dinner.

By 1984, a campaign in which the 49ers went 15-1 en route to their second Super Bowl in four years, Walsh had further added to his first championship team of Lott and Montana, trading for veterans such as defensive end Fred Dean and talented draft picks.

On the latter front, Walsh used a second-round pick on Craig, who would change the face of his position by playing both fullback and running back – becoming the only player in league history to earn Pro Bowl honours at both. Most importantly, he was equally adept blocking, running and catching. In 1985, Craig became the first person to hit 1,000 rushing and 1,000 receiving yards in the same campaign.

'I don't think we'd have had the success we did without me,' says Craig. 'I'm not trying to be arrogant, but I was the first player in history to rush and receive for 1,000 yards in a season. Marshall Faulk did it 14 years after I did it, but he was a running back. I was a fullback as well. I changed the game for everybody. Now, running backs have to do what I did: run, catch and block.' He would also become the first player to score three touchdowns in a Super Bowl as the 49ers crushed Don Shula and Dan Marino's Miami Dolphins 38–16 in XIX. To outside observers, it seemed Walsh had found the final piece of his jigsaw in Craig. But the coach knew otherwise.

In Week 13 of that campaign, the head coach sat in his New Orleans hotel room the night before meeting the Saints, perusing local TV channels until he spotted some local college highlights. Within seconds, Walsh sat captivated by a wide receiver who flashed across the screen. Within weeks, he was drawing up plays specifically for that player and, within months, executing a trade with the Patriots in the 1985 draft, jumping ahead of the Cowboys and using the 16th overall pick to select a kid from little-known Mississippi Valley State University who had expected to go undrafted.

'Being born in Mississippi, everything is a little more difficult. I had five brothers and two sisters. I was born in Starkville and then moved to Crawford. It's a very small town, and there's not much to do. I could have gotten into a lot of bad things, but I had great parents who taught me the value of hard work.'

That value was ingrained in Jerry Rice every summer he spent working alongside brother Jimmy with their father Joe. The task was as gruelling as it was hypnotic, young Jerry stationed atop scaffolding, sweat pouring from every orifice on account of Mississippi's unrelenting sticky heat, catching bricks thrown up by his sibling. There was no room for mistakes. Joe, a bricklayer, needed to operate fast, for that would mean more work and money. 'They would sometimes come up three and four at a time,' says Rice. 'My brother would toss them about twenty feet in the air, and they'd separate. My job was to pluck them out of the air one by one. I prided myself on catching everything and, if I didn't do it the way he wanted, I'd be disciplined.'

When Rice wasn't catching bricks, he could usually be found running. For miles and miles, either alone in the wilderness or chasing horses around Crawford's rural lands. 'If I caught one, I was allowed to ride it for the rest of the day. My favourite was Pete, the fastest in the community. It'd take me 45 minutes to an hour to run him down. Once I caught him, he was mine the rest of the day – and nobody wanted to race me.'

Little did Rice know that he was honing his body for a future career, ironically in neither bricklaying nor the Rodeo, that would lead him to become one of the most recognisable faces in America – a career, much like the skills that forged his greatness, he stumbled upon by accident. 'I had no interest in football,' Rice remembers. 'I was playing hooky from school one day in my sophomore year, and the principal walked up behind me and scared me. He noticed I could run really fast and suggested I play football. Of course, I was disciplined first. Back in the South in those days, you got disciplined differently too.'

In the game he never wanted to play, Rice found his true calling, an outlet for relentlessness, restlessness and thirst for victory. First, he starred in high school and then the envelopes started dropping through his door. 'I got an offer from USC,' says Rice, 'but Mississippi Valley State sent a coach out. I was able to shake his hand, and to me a handshake goes a long way.'

It'd become the handshake heard across the state, bringing a Division II programme the biggest recruit in their history, while providing Rice a platform to star in coach Archie Cooley's no-huddle, Air Raid offense that became known as the 'Satellite Express'. 'We threw the ball almost 90 per cent of the time,' says Rice. 'It was perfect. I had chances to catch the ball, and we gained notoriety, with scouts coming from different NFL teams.'

Despite an outstanding career that hit its crescendo with 28 touchdown receptions as a senior, most NFL scouts doubted Rice due to his small-school pedigree and 4.71-second 40-yard-dash time at the Scouting Combine.

Most, but not all.

'I didn't even think I was going to get drafted,' reveals Rice. 'I expected to be a walk-on. Most players have draft parties and things like that. I was in Jackson, Mississippi, with my brother in a two-bedroom apartment with one television. We had one TV station that came out to cover me on draft day, and then my dream came true. I got the call from the greatest coach of all-time.'

'We're going to make you the 16th player taken in the first round,' Walsh told Rice, his voice belying the excitement at select-ing a player for whom he already had specific plans. Not only did Walsh get his man, he beat San Francisco's biggest rivals to the punch. 'Jerry would have been our pick,' says former Cowboys personnel man Gil Brandt. 'We thought we were home safe. Sam Jankovich was the Patriots' GM [general manager], and we knew him well. He came to our training camp as a guest every year! But he made the trade with San Francisco and didn't call us . . . We were lazy and thought we would have Rice, but they jumped ahead of us.'

The boy who'd never known anything but Mississippi's green fields was teleported into the burgeoning eye of technological

America, sharing a city with Steve Jobs, who had launched his first Macintosh computer the previous year. As if that wasn't enough, his first-round status would bring added scrutiny from a fanbase forgetting its lowly past to demand constant success.

'Everything was different,' Rice admits. 'Going to the big city, having the big fanbase and the media – it was all an adjustment. And then there was the team. When you are drafted to an elite team like the 49ers, who had just won the Super Bowl, and you're from a small town in Mississippi, it's tough. It was like: "Oh my God, I am in a locker room with Joe Montana." I had to find my place.

'That took away from my football at the start. I was dropping balls during preseason – and I'd never done that. I was distracted, and there was way too much going on. It took me a little time. But that adversity was good for me. People could see my skills in practice.'

Not just people – future Hall of Famers. 'The first time I covered him, I got beat by him,' admits Lott, considered the best cornerback in football at that time. 'Nobody wanted to get beat by Jerry, but everybody did.'

Entering Week 14, a *Monday Night Football* contest with the Rams, Rice had produced a solid rookie campaign. But Walsh expected more and told his young receiver: 'Look, Jerry, you're going to be the greatest football player to ever play the game.'

'When he told me that,' admits Rice, 'there was no way I was going to let him down.' The wideout caught 10 passes for 241 yards and a touchdown in primetime. 'It was my coming-out game,' he enthuses. 'The penny had dropped. I went into that week, knew I was going to be the starter and exactly what to do in the system once Joe called the play. It was just a case of making plays. That game showed that I belonged, and everything else is history.'

For the next decade, nobody would wonder who the best wide receiver in football was, just as nobody now wonders who the greatest to lace up cleats is. The answer to both is the boy from Mississippi who began crafting his legend during the 1985 campaign.

For all the excellence he would go on to enjoy, that season wasn't about Rice – nor the incredible team on which he starred – but an eclectic mix of characters coming together to pen the latest chapter in the NFL's oldest storybook.

The reckoning, as Hampton reminded his teammates all year, came in Week 6. Chicago could get even with San Francisco at the scene of their haunting: in the 49ers' backyard.

The Bears illustrated the differences between this game and the previous season's from the opening drive. McMahon hit Payton and Tim Wrightman to move the chains,* before unfurling a signature deep ball to Gault. Having moved inside the opposing five-yard line, Payton – enjoying another All-Pro campaign – finished the job. How about that for an offense?

The next drive brought three more points, but the game's bigger story was the offensive scheme of its day – Walsh's West Coast variety – being unable to come to grips with its defensive equivalent in the 46. San Francisco were in touch at the half thanks to McMahon's pick-six, but Montana only managed 45 yards and three first downs after the interval and was sacked seven times.

'Bill Walsh was special,' says Hampton. 'Fundamentally, he gets an awful lot of credit – but he had some really good players. There was something about Joe. He couldn't throw it like Dan Marino or John Elway, but he could make plays. Their receivers and line were great, and Roger Craig was a terrific 'back. That was the ultimate match-up. Everyone had to be accounted for and covered. Buddy Ryan devised a masterful game plan, with aggressive bump-and-run coverage that bought the pass-rushers time. When they kept people in to block, he brought more rushers. Most would be content to just play coverage, but Buddy said: "To hell with that. We're going to keep coming."'

With an offense that, having created the lanes for Payton with splash plays, was now moving down the field methodical-ly, Chicago's combination proved irresistible. Payton prospered behind exceptional fullback Matt Suhey, and the Bears kicked a crucial fourth-quarter field goal to make it 19–10 before their star running back sealed the deal from 17 yards out.

When the score read 26–10 with under two minutes left, Ditka provided the finishing touch as Perry played the McIntyre role with some late offensive action. 'What goes around comes around,' said Ditka when discussing his introduction of Perry on offense. 'It was calculated. It was payback time and I'll never apologise for it.'

'When we were getting ready to play in San Francisco,' says Thayer, 'knowing what happened the year before, Ditka got Perry ready to play in the backfield. We knew what we had to do. We couldn't prepare that and then lose! Going out to San Francisco, facing a team as great as the 49ers, beating them on their own field convincingly and Walter Payton having a huge game was one of the turning points. It took us from a contending team to a Super Bowl team.'

Chicago made their statement.

Ironically, that moment inadvertently added another weapon to Chicago's arsenal, for Ditka realised Perry's marriage of quick feet and 340lb frame was effective. The following week, the Fridge turned folk hero by lead-blocking for a Payton touchdown and then adding one of his own on *Monday Night Football* against arch-rival Packers. 'I had the same agent,' says Hampton. 'He fielded 375 calls from people wanting him for commercials. This is before the internet and cell phones! It was incredible.'

And symbolic of a team capturing attention like few ever have. The '85 Bears – with personalities to match their on-field physi-cality – became the only show in town. 'We were bigger than life,' adds Hampton. 'If we went to Cleveland, there'd be 3,000 people at the hotel waiting to see us. It was like a rock show.'

'There was something for everybody,' adds Thayer. 'There was the super-good-looking businessman Fencik, who contrasted with the overweight, fun-loving Perry. There was the committed tough John Wayne people, McMichael and Hampton. There was the three linebackers – Wilson, Wilber and Singletary – considered the best in the league. There was the five offensive linemen that stuck together like glue, did everything together and had a close association with a quarterback who was the wildest of the wild. Jim is also someone who, whether he's getting a deal from Honda scooters, promoting Revolt sunglasses or doing his Adidas shoe contract, he was all for one and one for all. Jim took care of all of us, gave us sunglasses, scooters, shoes, all of that stuff.'

Behind the superficial fleeting fame was true brilliance on the field. Come Week 13, entering a *Monday Night Football* matchup, the Bears were 12-0 and beginning to dream of an unbeaten season. But, in a moment of true symbolism, they were denied by the one franchise and coach to accomplish that feat in the NFL, on a night where everything that could go wrong did. For all the Dolphins' 38–24 victory owed plenty to a signature display from Marino, it also featured some moments of fortune – not least a pass hitting Hampton's helmet and landing in the arms of Mark Clayton for a touchdown.

Yet that shouldn't detract from the Dolphins, who spread the Chicago defense out and utilised a quick-passing game to neutralise the 46 and score 31 first-half points. 'We thought we were going to kick the hell out of them,' says Hampton. 'But that coach and quarterback are in the Hall of Fame for a reason.'

'Everything we did was right,' said Shula. 'Marino got rid of the ball before they got to him. We had all the answers and made all the plays. I always refer to it as the best first half of football I have ever been around. It was magical because the Bears were very good, and we wanted to keep our streak alive. The fans got there early and the '72 players showed up on the sideline and really got into it. It was a game that I will always remember.'

The '85 Bears were not about to be denied their own place in history. They recorded their song 'The Super Bowl Shuffle' the next day and continued to march towards New Orleans, brushing aside the Colts, Jets and Lions before delivering truly historic efforts in the playoffs. Chicago shut out the New York Giants – coached by Parcells – in the divisional round before doing likewise in the NFC Championship Game against the Rams, for whom Eric Dickerson – who became the second man to post a 2,000-yard rushing campaign in 1984 when setting a single-season record of 2,105, which still stands – fumbled twice.

'Coach Ditka set the tone,' says Thayer. 'Ahead of the Giants game, he walked in and said: "I'm not going to let Lawrence Taylor beat us. We are going to attack him – going to be vicious; going to beat him in every way possible." For our head coach to tell us we were going after one of the most dominant players in NFL history filled us with confidence. L.T. was the type of guy you'd want an autograph from after the game, but all you saw that day was him being attacked and hit from all angles.'

Super Bowl XX, meanwhile, wasn't so much a contest as it was a coronation. The Bears enjoyed every trapping of the Big Easy in a manner only they could – 'They say don't leave any stones unturned; we didn't leave any beer bottles unturned either,' admits Hampton – while McMahon delivered his own unique moment. With questions abounding regarding his health after a heavy hit against the Rams, the quarterback mooned reporters to show a bruise on his rear end.

By Saturday, though, game faces were on.

For the unit that defined Chicago, inspiration came from realisation that their mentor was about to coach his last game for the club. Ryan, bound for the Eagles, stood in front of his troops and simply said: 'I want you all to know that you will always be my heroes.' McMichael responded to the coach leaving the room by throwing his chair at the blackboard, and the rest of his teammates followed suit. Hampton, who put his fist through a projector, remembers: 'I knew he was leaving. He told Fencik on Thursday. Me and him got together and agreed we needed to do something to divert everyone's attention from Buddy. I told Mongo to follow my lead. He threw a chair and it spiked into the chalkboard. I punched the projector and it flew across the room.'

Moments before the game, Coach Ditka invited the captains to speak. Stepping up first was the brilliant Payton, already the NFL's all-time rushing-yardage leader by this point. 'Guys, I never thought I'd be here,' he told his teammates. 'Finally, I have a chance to be a winner.'

His words resonated. The loveable running back's reputation across the footballing world was exemplary, subsequently illustrated by the NFL's annual Man-of-the-Year award – honouring a player's volunteer and charity work – being named in honour of its 1977 winner after Payton's death in 1999. In the Bears' locker room, meanwhile, he was a God-like figure. 'He was the glue that held that whole thing together,' says Covert. 'People don't really think about that from a character perspective because it's like, well, you know, he was kind of quiet. But he was the best teammate, and the greatest football player I ever saw. He played 13 years and never missed a game. I mean, that's a pretty special guy.'

His words were the final emotional fuel needed for the Class of '85. Which spelled terrible news for the Patriots, who were held to seven yards rushing, the same number of times their two quarterbacks – Tony Eason and Steve Grogan – were sacked. The final score (46–10) was, at the time, the largest margin of victory in Super Bowl history. Perhaps the only missing piece was a touchdown for Payton, used as a decoy for most of the contest, when McMahon twice crossed paydirt* with his legs, and Perry did too.

Yet Payton walked off the field a champion, part of a scrum responsible for creating the iconic image of the offense carrying Ditka off, while the defense did likewise with Ryan. It's a shot that encapsulates the most unique group in NFL history, led by two men who barely spoke – but were never the same without one another. 'We wouldn't have won without Coach Ditka,' adds Hampton. 'Buddy was here nine years before we went to the Super Bowl. It was a complementary situation. It was oil and vinegar, yes, but man it made a great dressing.'

Neither Ryan, as head coach of the Eagles and Cardinals, nor Ditka, who remained in Chicago another seven seasons and later spent three in New Orleans, would scale the same heights. As for the Bears, McMahon's continued injury problems coinciding with Ryan's departure restricted their excellence to a single title.

But the legacy is indisputable. That incredible season saw the Bears go 14-0 in games McMahon started and 16-1 overall, win the club's first Lombardi Trophy behind one of the NFL's three greatest-ever running backs – who accrued more than 1,500 rushing yards – and a defense still considered the best ever. They overcame one of the league's finest dynasties in their own back-yard and won three playoff games by a combined score of 91–10.

The '85 Bears were perhaps the most deserving recipient yet of the moniker Monsters of the Midway – as demonstrated by allowing just 7.4 points per game on home soil – and arguably worthy of an even more significant title. 'I don't think there's any question that the 1985 Bears are the greatest team ever,' says Hampton.

'There's nobody that has ever been better than we were,' concludes Covert. 'I don't care who it is. You can stack them up, the '72 Dolphins, the 49ers, whoever. There is nobody. Nobody!'

14

'Black Doug'

WASHINGTON REDSKINS 42
DENVER BRONCOS 10

---

31 January 1988

Jack Murphy Stadium, San Diego

'Would it be easier if you were the second black quarterback to play in the Super Bowl?'

Never in its 23-year history had the Super Bowl's build-up been so spectacularly dominated by one storyline. Such was the level of hysteria surrounding Doug Williams becoming the first black quarterback in the showpiece's history that one reporter addressed him simply as 'Black Doug'. The Washington Redskins quarterback did his best to alter the narrative: '[Coach] Joe Gibbs and [general manager] Bobby Beathard didn't bring me in to be the first black quarterback in the Super Bowl. They brought me in to be the quarterback of the Washington Redskins.'

Yet the topic wasn't going away. For this was a seminal moment, transcending sporting and cultural lines, as well as racial, and

242

Williams stood in the eye of the storm. It would have been easy in such circumstances to agree with the enquirer who queried whether his week might have been more comfortable were he not such a trailblazer, especially in light of one media member prefacing a question with: 'Obviously, you've been a black quarterback all your life.'

Williams, unflinching and statesmanlike in the face of rapid-fire repetitive questions, struck a conflicted tone. 'If young people want to use me as a role model, that's fine,' he added. 'But I'm not going on tour saying: "I'm Doug Williams, the first black quarterback to play in the Super Bowl." Jackie Robinson was the first black to play baseball; I'm not the first black to play football.'

Although he played the connection down, Williams was one of the era's Jackie Robinsons. His breakthrough would be the latest in a long line delivered by people spanning all walks of life: from Rosa Parks in Montgomery to those who marched alongside Martin Luther King in Birmingham, to Tommie Smith and John Carlos in Mexico City. Their connection? Breaking down barriers when being black in the United States often meant facing extreme prejudice and having doors and paths blocked at every turn. 'Back in 1966,' remembers Williams, who was raised in segregated Zachary, Louisiana, 'all the black folks lived down the same highway. Every Friday night, there was a cross burned at either end of the highway, surrounding where we were. You understood the divide. We are all human beings, but some people thought they were better than others.'

A reminder of this discrimination wasn't just provided in the outright threats. It was reinforced by every bus that forced black people to sit at the rear, every shop which refused service, every decrepit building of segregated shanty towns. 'I was 14 before I had running water,' Williams – who honed his throwing technique throwing a plastic Clorox jug – remembers.

Through it all, the easy-going Williams found sanctuary in sports. He excelled on the playing fields of Louisiana for

Chaneyville High School, under the guidance of the legendary Eddie Robinson at Grambling State University and, finally, in the pros. Even after becoming the maiden quarterback taken with a first-round NFL Draft pick, though, Williams encountered bigoted stereotypes.

Because, although the shackles of slavery had been lifted a century ago, metaphorical chains continued to constrain America's black community. Williams turned the Tampa Bay Buccaneers, two years removed from creation upon his arrival, into playoff contenders. Yet after complaining at being not only the lowest-paid starting passer in the league, but earning less than 12 backups, he became embroiled in a bitter dispute with owner Hugh Culverhouse. Their disagreement coincided with the tragic death of Williams' wife to a brain tumour, prompting him to take a year off from football to look after his baby daughter Ashley. He returned in 1984, spending two seasons entertaining the masses in the United States Football League with his helter-skelter brand of quarterbacking before accepting his lot as the Redskins' backup upon the organisation folding.

Yet there was another magical chapter to be written. Williams would eventually battle his way to the starting job in Washington and dare to tread another path never before taken. And the great paradox was that, when his Super Bowl bow came, he walked onto Jack Murphy Stadium's field donning the uniform of the team who best symbolised the struggle of all black NFL players before him.

The impact of pro football's earliest club owners was fundamental to the early survival and eventual success of the NFL. Their innovations and willingness to scrap for survival amid multiple impediments was laudable, as was the foresight that helped transform the face of the game over those initial decades. But amid a tale of remarkable persistence yielding unforeseen riches, there is an obvious stain.

It occurred in 1933, when the league where Fritz Pollard crafted

Above: An overhead shot of Triangle Park from 1920, showing the football field where the Dayton Triangles and Columbus Panhandles played the first APFA/NFL contest.

Left: Red Grange sits alongside George Halas. Together, the two men transformed professional football when Grange played for Halas' Chicago Bears following his collegiate career in the mid-1920s.

The Chicago Bears and New York Giants battle out the first planned NFL Championship Game at Wrigley Field. The contest, which began being scheduled due to the success of the hastily arranged indoor playoff that settled the 1932 season, was won 23-21 by the Bears to earn George Halas' team a second successive title.

The Washington Redskins' Jimmy Johnston is tackled by Sid Luckman, remembered best as the NFL's first true quarterback, during their 73–0 loss to the Chicago Bears in the 1940 NFL Championship Game.

Paul Brown and Otto Graham, the double act behind incredible success for the early Cleveland Browns. Graham is holding the MVP trophy from the Browns' significant 1950 Week 1 tilt with the Philadelphia Eagles. Cleveland, having just joined the NFL from the AAFC, beat their new league's best 35–10.

Above: Alan Ameche rumbles over from one yard to settle The Greatest Game Ever Played. The Baltimore Colts' overtime 1958 NFL Championship Game victory over the New York Giants captivated the nation and made Johnny Unitas an icon.

Left above: A modest crowd at the Los Angeles Memorial Coliseum witnesses the Green Bay Packers and Kansas City Chiefs doing battle in the first AFL-NFL World Championship Game. The contest, later renamed Super Bowl I, didn't boast the same interest and pageantry of future editions.

Left: Vince Lombardi on the sidelines during Super Bowl I, which his Green Bay Packers won 35–10 against the Kansas City Chiefs.

Left: The referee raises his hands after Bart Starr goes over on a quarterback sneak to seal a 21–17 Green Bay Packers' victory over the Dallas Cowboys in the 1967 NFL Championship Game, better known as The Ice Bowl.

Left below: Joe Namath speaks to reporters after backing up his pregame guarantee by leading the New York Jets to victory over the Baltimore Colts in Super Bowl III. It remains arguably the most significant single win in NFL history.

Below: Franco Harris evades one final despairing attempted tackle after completing 'the Immaculate Reception'. His play not only sealed a divisional-round victory for Pittsburgh over the Oakland Raiders, but heralded the beginning of the Steelers' 1970s dynasty.

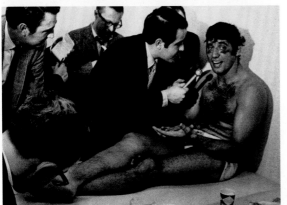

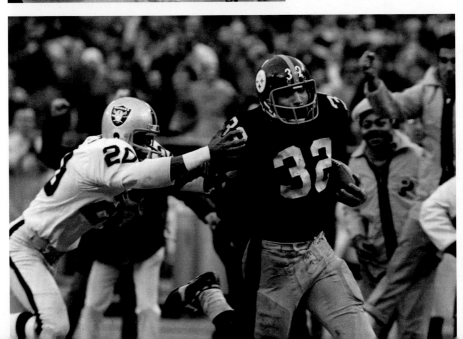

Right: Head coach Don Shula is carried from the Los Angeles Coliseum field after the Miami Dolphins complete the perfect season with a 14–7 Super Bowl VII victory over the Washington Redskins.

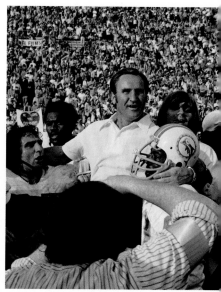

Left: Dwight Clark rises high above Everson Walls at Candlestick Park to complete 'The Catch'. His touchdown proved the winning score as the San Francisco 49ers edged out the Dallas Cowboys in the 1981 NFC Championship Game. They would go on to win the first of five Super Bowls in 14 years.

Buddy Ryan and Mike Ditka, the two architects behind the infamous 1985 Chicago Bears, are carried from the field after sealing a Super Bowl victory courtesy of their dominant 46–10 win over the New England Patriots.

Right: Doug Williams is mobbed by photographers after becoming the first black quarterback to win the Super Bowl in the 22nd edition. Williams delivered a then-showpiece-record 340 passing yards as the Washington Redskins beat the Denver Broncos 42–10.

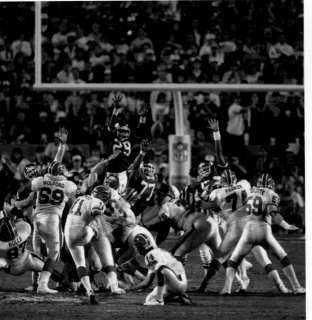

Left: Scott Norwood sends a potential game-winning field goal skywards at Tampa Stadium. His effort would famously go wide right as the Buffalo Bills lost Super Bowl XXV to the New York Giants 20–19, due largely to Big Blue defensive coordinator Bill Belichick's gameplan, which is now displayed in the Hall of Fame.

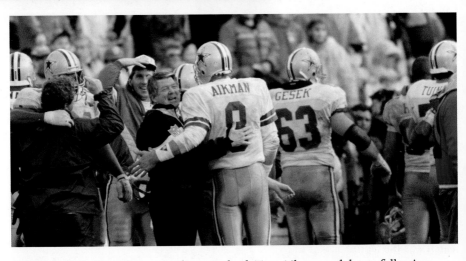

Head coach Jimmy Johnson and quarterback Troy Aikman celebrate following the Dallas Cowboys' 30–20 win at the San Francisco 49ers in the 1992 NFC Championship Game. Victory helped propel Dallas to the first of three Super Bowl wins in four years.

Right: John Elway completes his 'Helicopter Run', the iconic play of a Hall-of-Fame career and the Denver Broncos' Super Bowl XXXII win over the Green Bay Packers. After multiple unsuccessful brushes with the big game, Elway signed off his career with two Super Bowl titles.

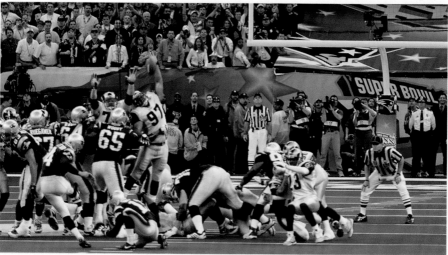

Above: Adam Vinatieri sends his game-winner skyward, helping the New England Patriots shock the world by overcoming the Greatest Show On Turf St. Louis Rams to win Super Bowl XXXVI 20–17 in New Orleans.

Right: Little-known wide receiver David Tyree pins the ball to his helmet to stop New England Patriots safety Rodney Harrison forcing Eli Manning's pass to fall incomplete. Tyree's catch was the iconic play of the Giants' game-winning drive in Super Bowl XLII that ended New England's hopes of a perfect 19–0 season.

Bill Belichick and Tom Brady bask in the afterglow of their remarkable Super Bowl LI victory over the Atlanta Falcons. The New England Patriots rallied back from 28–3 down in the third quarter to win in overtime, sealing the fifth of six titles won by their dynamic head coach/quarterback duo.

his legacy became segregated. While the blame cannot be laid entirely at his door, it wasn't a coincidence the move synchronised with the arrival of George Preston Marshall, the Redskins founder once quoted as saying: 'We'll start signing Negroes when the Harlem Globetrotters start signing whites.'

The NFL weren't the only ones enacting such a policy, but its commitment to the practice was best summed up during the Second World War when teams were stretched beyond their limits due to the unavailability of many stars, but olive branches still weren't extended to black athletes. The folly of its inability to act then, a decision that could easily have threatened the league's future, was illustrated just after the war, when the unwritten policy departed because of the Coliseum Commission's insistence upon Dan Reeves moving his defending champion Cleveland Rams to Los Angeles.

There was a cruel irony to the first black player brought into the fold being Kenny Washington. The former UCLA star – a brilliant halfback as adept at throwing as rushing, who many believed was also a better baseball prospect than Bruins teammate Jackie Robinson – illustrated what the game missed out on. In college, he made up an all-black backfield alongside Ray Bartlett, Robinson and Woody Strode. The trio would join Washington in making momentous contributions to differing fields, Bartlett as a decorated police officer, Strode by playing in the NFL before enjoying an acting career and Robinson breaking Major League Baseball's colour line in a Hall-of-Fame career.

Yet, in the case of Washington, there will always be an unmistakeable, resounding 'what if?' surrounding him. After signing off college at an All-Star Game in Chicago, George Halas asked the halfback to stay in the hopes of making Washington a Bear. But he couldn't convince the other owners, and the man described by Hall-of-Famer Bob Waterfield as 'the best football player I ever saw' spent his prime years in the lesser Pacific Coast League, winning yearly All-Star honours with the cocktail of skills Robinson

so perfectly summarised: 'He had everything needed for greatness – size, speed and tremendous strength. Kenny was probably
the greatest long passer ever.'

Such was the outrage after the 1940 draft that NBC's Sam
Balter used the airwaves to publicly deride the owners' failure to
select 'not only the best football player on the Pacific Coast this
season, but the best of the last 10 years and perhaps the best in all
the sport's glorious football history – a player who had reduced to
absurdity the All-American teams selected this year because they
did not include him – and all know why'.

When finally offered a place in the NFL, Washington was a
shadow of his former self, with barely any cartilage remaining in
either of his knees. Even so, he led the league's per-carry average
among those with more than 200 yards in the second of three
seasons and was afforded a rapturous reception by 80,000 fans in
the Coliseum at his curtain call. Perhaps the ovation would have
been even greater – if possible – had those upstanding realised
the on-field struggle. Following one clash with the Pittsburgh
Steelers in which Washington overcame the usual dirty tactics
to score two touchdowns, he confided in teammate Jim Hardy:
'Sometimes it's hell to be a Negro, Jim.'

Washington's struggle in the face of prejudice exemplified that
of many black people around America, particularly those who
fought alongside white compatriots during the Korean War. The
idea of returning to segregation was understandably unpalatable,
offering a shot in the arm for a Civil Rights Movement beginning
to deliver results, albeit slowly.

The same painstaking pace was true in the NFL, where Los
Angeles' signings of Washington and Strode didn't quite signal
the anticipated rush. It wasn't until 1948 that the Detroit Lions
joined the Rams in ending segregation by adding ends Mel
Groomes and Bob Mann. In the same year, the Giants signed
defensive back Emlen Tunnell, who would be the first black player
inducted into the Hall of Fame.

Progress eventually ensued, the Bears becoming the first team to draft a black player in 1949 – although 13th-round pick George Taliaferro opted to play in the All-America Football Conference. In the 19th round, the Lions chose Penn State halfback Wallace Triplett, who became the first black draftee to play in the NFL. Perhaps most important that year was Los Angeles' unprecedented decision to sign someone from a Historically Black College and University (HBCU) in Paul 'Tank' Younger. The linebacker shone under the tutelage of Grambling coach Eddie Robinson, who saw many stars pass through his doors across 56 years at the helm – including, two decades later, Williams.

'He was so underrated,' says Williams. 'He's had some attention, but not the fame he rightly deserves. The product he put on the field, at Grambling and putting players into the league, is unmatched by a lot of people when you consider what he had to work with. He used to say: "We have done so much with so little that we can almost do anything without nothing," and we used to live by that. He was more than a coach; he was the parent away from home. If he said jump off a bridge, you'd do it because you'd survive.'

Among Robinson's first protégés was the hulking Younger, leading a slowly growing number of black players starring on NFL fields across a career that brought four Pro Bowl and three All-Pro berths. Early in that run, he was joined by Marion Motley and Bill Willis, who shone in the AAFC for the Cleveland Browns and further bolstered the established league's pool.

By 1952, every NFL team featured at least one black player . . . except one: Marshall's Redskins. Conventional wisdom suggests this provides evidence of Marshall being racist. At the very least, he was opportunistic. The owner cultivated the Redskins as the team of the South, an area without an NFL club, where segregation remained prevalent. Marshall's all-white Washington team barnstormed there in the offseason and broadcast in-season games on the owner's profitable Southern radio network.

Such was his desperation to maintain monopoly on the

territory that Marshall strongly opposed Clint Murchison's plan to put a new NFL team in Dallas, his disapproval only overcome via a moment of true ingenuity on the future Cowboys owner's part. Capitalising on the Redskins proprietor's falling out with Barnee Breeskin – composer of the club's fight song that Marshall's wife wrote – Murchison purchased the track's rights and made it clear they would only be signed over with a 'yes' vote.

At the point of the Cowboys' entry to the NFL in 1960, the Redskins somehow remained segregated and critics began to swarm. The most vocal was *Washington Post* columnist Shirley Povich, whose condemnation reached something of a crescendo following that year's clash with Cleveland: 'For 18 minutes the Redskins were enjoying equal rights with the Cleveland Browns yesterday,' she wrote, 'in the sense that there was no score in the contest. Then it suddenly became unequal in favour of the Browns, who brought along Jim Brown, their rugged coloured fullback from Syracuse.

'From 25 yards out, Brown was served the ball by Milt Plum on a pitch-out and he integrated the Redskins' goalline with more than deliberate speed, perhaps exceeding the famous Supreme Court decree. Brown fled the 25 yards like a man in an uncommon hurry and the Redskins' goalline, at least, became interracial.'

It would take intervention from President John F. Kennedy's administration to actually force Marshall's hand. Its threat to refuse the Redskins a lease at the city's new DC Stadium, built on federal land, brought change, albeit after the owner attempted to fight his corner. But Kennedy was an adversary Marshall couldn't bend to his will.

In 1962, Washington drafted Syracuse's Ernie Davis, who refused to play for the club and was traded to the Browns. Bobby Mitchell and Leroy Jackson, received in the deal, became the club's first black players and completed NFL clubs' integration. A momentous step? Certainly. But the battle had only just begun.

*

Attitudes permeating NFL locker rooms underwent significant change in the 1960s. 'I was shocked to see how many people from the South played on the Packers, from Texas especially,' admits 1963 Green Bay Packers first-round pick Dave Robinson. 'I thought I was on the wrong team because in college when I went south of the Mason–Dixon Line for a football game, I got trouble – big trouble. Now I was going to be playing with these guys and didn't know if I could do it or not. But when I got here, the guys in Green Bay, under the tutelage of Vince Lombardi, knew not to care what colour a guy is.'

That mentality dripped down to every player, black or white. 'We had a great bunch of African-Americans on our team,' adds former Packers wide receiver Boyd Dowler. 'We'd go out for dinner. They'd come over to my house after games. We'd hang out with each other and had a wonderful time together.'

For all the nature of the NFL was changing, the older organisation fell some way short of matching the American Football League's impact on integration. The most significant example, symbolically, came amid the AFL's All-Star Game following the 1964 campaign, when black players were refused services by numerous New Orleans hotels and businesses, prompting a boycott from all players that meant the event was moved to Houston. The NFL also lagged behind in purely statistical terms and the precocious league was richer for their willingness to use more black players. Where the new operation diverged was in its willingness to tap into the rich resources available at HBCUs, which – despite Younger's success – were underutilised in NFL circles. The AFL homed in on those programmes immediately, Elbert Dubenion (Bluffton) joining the Buffalo Bills, Lionel Taylor (New Mexico Highlands) the Denver Broncos and Abner Haynes (North Texas State) the Dallas Texans/Kansas City Chiefs.

Broadest in scope were Lamar Hunt's Chiefs, who employed pro football's first black scout, Lloyd Wells, and made Buck Buchanan the game's maiden black first overall pick in 1963.

Between 1960 and '62, the AFL averaged 17 per cent more black players than the NFL – and its founder, Hunt, played a key role. 'Lamar starting the AFL gave black players an opportunity to play,' reveals Hall-of-Fame linebacker Bobby Bell. 'The league recruited a lot of players who would never have played.'

'It's not something I had an in-depth conversation with him about,' adds Clark Hunt, 'but his friends told me he was colour blind. He saw everybody as equal, which was just the kind of person he was. He wasn't trying to make a statement. To him, it didn't matter where you came from, or what colour your skin was. If you were the best player, coach or scout, you would be part of the Chiefs. He was ahead of his time. It speaks to his underlying character.'

It felt like all those efforts climaxed at the turn of the decade. Of the 22 starters in the Chiefs' victorious Super Bowl IV team against the Minnesota Vikings, 13 were black – making Kansas City the first championship club with more than half of their first-string players being non-white.

'It was groundbreaking,' adds Hunt. 'I think the Chiefs and AFL played a big role in integrating the NFL. Here we are 50 years later, and the greatness of the game has grown on many fronts, including the prevalence of people from different backgrounds in all facets of the business.'

The timing was perfect, extra poignancy created by the ensuing campaign heralding the start of the NFL's new, merged structure after four years in a holding pattern. Pro football was changing, not just structurally – but in its diversity.

With NFL and AFL unified, and the Chiefs' Super Bowl victory forcing teams to accept black players were becoming crucial in the battle to win championships, a near-30-year journey looked to have finally unearthed light at the end of the tunnel. Yet there were other frontiers to conquer, not least black players' ability to profit from pro football's burgeoning commercial sphere.

'I'm a premier receiver, they say, or a premier this or that,' said Chiefs wideout Otis Taylor, a member of that championship team, in 1972. 'But I'm a black man. I can't express myself. I can't do anything. People always ask me what I've endorsed. I haven't even done a dog-food commercial, and that's pretty sorry for a guy who would be so happy to do one he'd eat the dog food.'

Even Jim Brown, whose playing career was followed by Hollywood's bright lights, was unable to break down that barrier. His issue was an outspoken unwillingness to fit into white America's profile of how a black person should act that ran counter to another outstanding running back who broke out in the 1970s. O.J. Simpson, at least in those days, was seen as everything Brown wasn't: an unthreatening conformist. His easy assimilation with rich whites made Simpson the ideal person to become the first black celebrity to feature in a national corporate ad campaign, running through airports and advertising Hertz rental cars from 1978.

'O.J. Simpson, if you could put away what happened later, was one of the big commercial stars in America whose endorsements were ubiquitous,' says super-agent Leigh Steinberg, the inspiration for Tom Cruise's character in the film *Jerry Maguire*. 'He broke the ground because he was a handsome, charming personality with a big smile – and that really broke the barrier. It became clear white audiences would respond to black superstars, to the point some of the biggest commercial stars, whether it's Michael Jordan or Tiger Woods, in the athletic sphere are black.'

For all Simpson lacked the uninhibited black consciousness of Brown, he aided the cause of his contemporaries. One year after the running back's first Hertz spot, 'Mean' Joe Greene won hearts and minds by starring in an advert still fondly remembered today. During a 60-second clip, an injured Greene limps through the tunnel and is offered a Coca-Cola by a white child. The defensive lineman – football's ultimate tough guy – initially scowls before accepting the drink, smiling widely and tossing the kid a jersey with the famous line: 'Hey, kid, catch.'

'Before that commercial,' remembers Greene, 'I was Mean Joe, the unapproachable guy. The way that took some of the mystique away was special. Coca-Cola is one of the most recognisable brands in the world. When they buy an ad spot, it's the best one. First time I saw it was during the MLB playoffs, then the Super Bowl. A lot of people had an opportunity to see it. Fortunately, the little kid and giant football player captured the imagination of fans. The relationship between the two was special and something that tugged at the heart strings of the millions who saw it.'

It also illustrated fertile ground for black athletes to begin defining their image beyond just colour. 'That commercial was a turning point, because it featured an empathetic and sympathetic black athlete that was appealing to all audiences,' adds Steinberg. 'The fact the Pittsburgh Steelers were repetitive Super Bowl winners also helped. That gave an amazing opportunity to elevate the profile of the athlete. But, most importantly, the commercial was against type. Greene was someone noted for ferocity; emphasising the gentleness and empathy was clever.'

Despite it offering evidence of the broadening horizons for black players, stereotypes remained prevalent. In 1973, when almost 50 per cent of NFL players were black, no African Americans played centre, while Kansas City's Willie Lanier and Washington's Harold McLinton were the only middle linebackers. 'When I came out of high school,' remembers Bell, 'I was a quarterback. There was no way I could have played that in the pros. Back then they didn't have black quarterbacks, middle linebackers, safeties or centres.'

To counter the issue, it'd take two factors: outstanding players who disproved the stereotypes and open-minded coaches. In the case of the Giants' 1976 fifth-round pick Harry Carson, Marty Schottenheimer – a defensive assistant who became an exceptional head coach – provided the opportunity.

'The Giants gave Marty one pick, 105, and he used it to select me for a position I had never played,' remembers Carson. 'I was a defensive lineman and thought I'd play there in the pros. That move was bold because there hadn't been a black middle linebacker in New York. And I was the third in the NFL.'

Schottenheimer's instincts proved correct. Carson spent his entire career with the Giants and now has a bust in Canton. 'I'm very much aware that I was asked to play a position that white guys played,' he admits. 'I feel very good about helping blaze that trail.'

But the same trail blazed by Lanier and Carson was most needed at what had become the game's pre-eminent position. 'The position with the most name recognition is quarterback,' says Steinberg, 'and there was a generalisation in certain circles that African Americans weren't the best candidates for the so-called "thinking" positions, particularly quarterback.'

The prejudice afflicted passers for decades, with rare opportunities proving fleeting. Utilised as a passer in the AAFC, Taliaferro became a utility man for the NFL's New York Yanks, Dallas Texans, Baltimore Colts and Philadelphia Eagles. He featured a little at quarterback – becoming the second in league history after Pollard – yet also played running back, wide receiver, punter, kick returner, punt returner and defensive back.

It'd be an oft-repeated tale: the aptly named, cannon-armed Willie Thrower threw just eight passes for the Bears, although that's five more than the Packers' Charlie 'Choo Choo' Brackins, who was the first quarterback from a HBCU. After Brackins' only outing, in 1955, the league didn't see another black quarterback for 12 seasons, with star college passers told switching position was their only option. Sandy Stephens, a 1962 AFL first-round pick and second-rounder in the NFL, won the Rose Bowl with Minnesota – but opted to play in the Canadian Football League.

The impasse finally ended in 1968. A draft in which the Oakland Raiders selected Tennessee State's Eldridge Dickey, who threw for more than 6,500 yards during a stellar college career, in the opening round to use him as an offensive chess piece and kick returner saw Denver choose Marlin Briscoe with pick 357. He immediately won the starting quarterback job and ranked sixth in the AFL for passing yards, touchdowns and quarterback rating, while leading the way in yards per completion. The start of a stellar career? Unfortunately not. Briscoe lost his job after the season and signed for the Bills to play wide receiver.

Joe Gilliam was next to try in Pittsburgh, having been drafted in 1972, and he briefly unseated Terry Bradshaw as starter for the '74 campaign. 'Joe Gilliam had a phenomenal preseason,' remembers Bradshaw. 'He won the starting job and I lost it.' Although the Steelers started 4-1-1, Bradshaw reclaimed the role midseason and led Pittsburgh to their first of four Super Bowls, making Gilliam a footnote in club history.

Around the same time, James Harris was enjoying a second coming with the Rams. Selected alongside Simpson in the Bills' draft class of 1969, eighth-rounder Harris endured a chastening debut after being named opening-day starter, then was scarcely used over the campaign's remainder and ensuing two years. He spent 1972 out of football but returned with aplomb as the Rams' signal-caller to become the first black Pro Bowl passer. Shoulder issues would derail a promising career and, despite spending 11 seasons in the league, Harris managed just 8,136 total passing yards and didn't have the transformative effect he might have.

By the conclusion of the 1977 campaign, it seemed as though a meaningful breakthrough might never come. Until everything was tipped on its head by two passers who took different routes to stardom after leaving college that year.

Approaching the 1978 season, one of the NFL's youngest clubs needed a spark. The expansion Buccaneers' first two terms brought a combined two victories, and John McKay, the coach who created his legend on the back of winning four National Championships for USC, was looking to initiate change. He called new offensive coordinator Gibbs into his office and gave him clear instructions: 'We need to find out everything about this quarterback from Grambling.'

Gibbs was sent on assignment, spending three days in Louisiana and testing Williams on everything from physical skills to X's and O's. The visit backed up the tape and statistical evidence that made Williams a household name. In four years as starter, he set an NCAA record for touchdown passes and led the Tigers to three conference titles. 'I got real comfortable with him,' said Gibbs. 'He got it.'

So comfortable that the Buccaneers utilised the 17th pick to procure his services. Momentous? Absolutely. But also an exception: Williams was the first black signal-caller selected above the sixth round, a fact that prompted another prospect to choose an alternative path.

Warren Moon was similar to Williams in stature – both were 6ft 3in, thick set and capable of delivering a spiral tight enough to make Unitas blush – but hadn't featured in a pro-style system during his nomadic college career. He initially planned to go to Arizona State, only for the offer to be rescinded when they recruited two other – white – quarterbacks. 'They wanted to move me to defensive back,' he says. 'I wasn't going to have any part of that. I knew I was good enough to play quarterback.'

Moon was forced to attend junior college, starring at West Los Angeles and utilising access to the film library there to send clips to major programmes. He caught the eye of the University of Washington but endured typical hostility from the fanbase upon being named starter at his new school. 'There was name-calling,' he remembers, 'and people trying to get me replaced. They didn't want me as their quarterback.'

Approval eventually came. Moon's three seasons were hallmarked by yearly improvement and culminated in him being voted Rose Bowl MVP following a 27–20 upset of Michigan. Even so, Steinberg knew his client's professional prospects were bleak.

He enquired as to whether Moon would be willing to consider a position change and received short shrift in return. His charge fixed a steely glare on Steinberg and insisted: 'Never. I was born to play quarterback.'

'Warren didn't have real experience as a drop-back passer,' remembers Steinberg. 'He didn't play in an offense that was relatable to the NFL. It wasn't a pro-set, three-, five-, seven-step offense. He hadn't played major college football for long enough and never really hit his peak in college, even though he was MVP of the Pac-8. He was still getting better but didn't have Doug Williams' experience. We were pretty sure Warren would have been drafted, but not as high as his talent dictated. Because he wasn't going to be selected as a franchise quarterback in the first round, he wouldn't be a starter. And for all there weren't many black starting quarterbacks, there were even fewer backups.'

Steinberg and Moon delivered a pre-emptive strike. Six weeks prior to the selection weekend, the passer penned a contract with the CFL's Edmonton Eskimos. Just as importantly, he went undrafted in what most perceived as a slight – but Steinberg knew otherwise. 'It was a Godsend,' adds Steinberg. 'We knew what was coming.'

What came was an unparalleled career north of the border. Moon helped the Eskimos to five successive Grey Cups and became Canada's biggest football star. 'It was a very refreshing place to play,' admits Moon. 'When you went onto the field, you weren't cringing waiting to see what the reaction was going to be. You just played.'

Moon was also richly rewarded. 'It wasn't the NFL,' says Steinberg, 'but the CFL, at that time, was competitive financially. They couldn't compete over a whole roster but could for a super-star, and Warren was the highest-paid player in the league.'

Such was the financial competitiveness that Steinberg and Moon initially refused NFL overtures, despite the passer's desperation to eventually challenge himself at the very top. 'I'd take him to Super Bowls, and he looked like a young kid at home sick, pressed against the window watching his friends out playing,' reveals Steinberg. 'You could see the yearning.'

Timing, though, is everything – and Steinberg could see a unique window on the horizon. Not only did being undrafted mean no NFL teams held Moon's rights, the advent of the USFL would drive the price up even further. Following a 1983 campaign in which Moon was voted the CFL's Most Outstanding Player, the signal-caller headed south and, in the process, became football's first free agent at a time when the system's advent was a decade away. 'It was a complete novelty,' says Steinberg. 'Warren held all the aces. He was in his prime, at the most critical position, and all teams had to do was sign him. They didn't have to give up draft picks or trade. They could simply enhance their roster at the most critical position. It set off this massive competition, where 12 different teams were interested, in Canada, the USFL and the NFL. So, we undertook tours of several teams, and there was a highly publicised battle for his services.' Steinberg parlayed that battle into rich returns; Moon headed to the Houston Oilers as the NFL's highest-paid player ever.

His story couldn't have contrasted more with that of the illustrious prospect who entered professional football the same time as him. At the point of Moon gearing up to display his talents in the NFL, Williams sought salvation in the USFL following years of frustration and personal tragedy. Having missed much of his rookie year with a broken jaw, Williams led the talent-deficient Buccaneers to the brink of the Super Bowl in his second – they lost the NFC Championship Game to the Rams – and won plenty of admirers. 'I'll never forget his first practice,' said Gibbs. 'He fired a couple of balls that were 45 yards on a line. It was the only time I saw players look and say: "Did you see that?"'

'Most quarterbacks were around 6ft,' remembers the Rams' Hall-of-Fame defensive end Jack Youngblood. 'Doug was as big as

I was and a tremendous athlete. It put defensive guys on alert: it's not going to be easy to bring this guy down.'

The Buccaneers returned to the postseason twice in the ensuing three campaigns, but Williams wasn't happy. An annual salary of $120,000 was unbefitting of his status, and he wanted that figure upped to around $600,000. Culverhouse – who some felt was uncomfortable having a black face of the franchise – wouldn't go beyond $400,000 despite protests from McKay.

After taking a season-long break due to his wife's death, Williams' two years with the Oklahoma/Arizona Outlaws were a continuation of his career story, in which outrageous arm talent created big plays, incompletions and interceptions in equal measure. Certainly, he wasn't sufficiently good to have NFL teams knocking his door down. The only call came from a familiar name: Gibbs, now Washington's head coach, needed a backup.

While Williams rode the pine, Moon had a transformative effect in Houston. The signal-caller threw for a club-record 3,338 yards in his first campaign, during which the Oilers' most famous son – all-time great running back Earl Campbell – was traded to the New Orleans Saints. That paved the way for Moon to become Houston's biggest star, especially following the arrival of Jerry Glanville as head coach in 1986. Piloting the Oilers' innovative run-and-shoot attack,* Moon used athleticism, arm talent and smarts to lead an offensive explosion and establish himself on football's top table of quarterbacks. 'Warren Moon, black quarterback' became 'Warren Moon, great quarterback'.

'The greatest thing that happened,' says Glanville, 'is somebody in the press conference asked: "How does it feel to be coaching the only black quarterback in the league?" And I said: "Who you talking about?" When they said Warren Moon, I said: "I had no idea he was black." That was how our team was. Warren did something most quarterbacks couldn't do. If we got a holding penalty or did something illegal, he had the arm to overcome it. You get three holding penalties, it's supposed to stop your drive.

With Warren Moon, we'd gun it 27 yards downfield on a dig.'

The team's mentality contrasted sharply with some of Moon's initial moments in Houston. His ex-wife, Felicia, remembered a fan once shouting: 'Warren, throw that ball like you would a watermelon.' To his family, it was shocking; for Moon, it was a continuation of his life story. 'I'd gone through it all my life,' he concedes. 'The big difference was I now had a family. My son would come into the locker room in tears.'

Like Huskies fans before them, the Oilers' faithful would be transformed by his sheer excellence. Those years under Glanville became the high watermark of an outstanding, lengthy career that saw Moon, remarkably, play until the age of 44. At the point of his retirement, he sat in the top five of the NFL's passing-yards, passing-touchdowns, pass-attempts and pass-completions categories and, including his CFL numbers, racked up 70,553 yards and 435 touchdowns. In 2006, Moon was inducted into the Hall of Fame, becoming the first black quarterback and undrafted player to achieve the feat. He changed the game.

Steinberg says: 'He is a Yoda-like figure. He crisscrossed the country in the offseason doing speaking events, banquets and endorsements, and was everywhere. He continuously went out of his way to mentor other young black quarterbacks. He became a symbol. During recruiting visits of prospective black quarterbacks, I'd go into houses and see a poster of Martin Luther King and one of Warren Moon next to it.'

The only missing piece? A Super Bowl berth. That mountain would be scaled by the signal-caller with whom he was inextricably linked.

Upon arriving in the nation's capital in 1986, Williams' playing prospects appeared limited. The Redskins were established as one of the NFL's finest teams, with Gibbs sitting in the esteemed company of Bill Walsh and Bill Parcells as the game's most exceptional coaches. His reputation was fostered by an exemplary second year

that brought the club's maiden Super Bowl and first championship since 1942 – a drought that owed much to Marshall's refusal
to sign black players.

Their return to glory came during the strike-shortened 1982
campaign, behind the bruising running of exceptional halfback
John Riggins, who shone alongside an equally rough-and-ready
offensive line nicknamed 'the Hogs'. If they didn't dominate
opposing defenses, a wide-receiving corps whose penchant for
wild celebrations earned an equally legendary moniker would.
'The Fun Bunch' prospered on the end of throws from Joe
Theismann, whose year ended with a memorable display in the
27–17 Super Bowl XVII win over the Miami Dolphins. As well as
throwing two touchdown passes, Theismann made a key tackle
on Dolphins lineman Kim Bokamper that stopped a sure interception and likely pick-six after a pass deflected into his arms.

Yet a very different tackle would become the symbol of his
career. It came in the 1985 campaign, two years after the Redskins
failed to repeat as champions when losing to the Los Angeles
Raiders in Tampa. With their Week 11 game against the Giants
tied at 7–7, Washington called a flea flicker. Theismann began to
be engulfed by blue-shirted bodies and attempted to step up in
the pocket – only to be twisted down by the exceptional Lawrence
Taylor. The fall was such that he shattered his fibula and tibia. 'It
just went so suddenly,' he remembered. 'It snapped like a bread-
stick. It sounded like two muzzled gunshots off my left shoulder.'
Theismann never played football again.

But Washington bounced back impressively, triumphing
23–21 and going on to win four of their next five to finish 10-6.
Even though they missed the playoffs on account of their inferior divisional record, having ended with the same overall
mark as the Cowboys and Giants, optimism was high given the
manner in which 1984 third-round pick Jay Schroeder deputised
for Theismann. They just needed a backup – and that's where
Williams came in. When asked if he would undertake the role, the

passer told Gibbs: 'I don't have a job at this time and can play any "up" you want me to play.'

Any aspirations of winning the job looked remote after the ensuing campaign, in which Schroeder earned Pro Bowl honours by throwing for a franchise-high 4,109 yards as Washington went 12-4 before coming unstuck against the Giants in the NFC Championship Game. Along with being shut out in that 17–0 loss, Schroeder also managed to fuel Williams' fire. When the signal-caller went down injured, Gibbs instructed Williams – who threw one ball all year – to enter the fray. But as the backup made his way onto the field, Schroeder – now back on his feet – delivered a dismissive shooing gesture that left an indelible mark. 'It's the most I've ever been embarrassed in football,' he admits. 'That memory stuck.'

There was no brushing his backup off when Schroeder suffered a shoulder injury in the 1987 season opener versus Philadelphia, Williams leading Washington to a 34–24 victory and setting the stage for the back-and-forth quarterback controversy that engulfed the capital all year. Its decisive moment came during the finale of a regular season in which both saw significant action and Gibbs flip-flopped on who was the number one. Williams came off the bench in the third quarter against the Minnesota Vikings, delivered a 46-yard touchdown to Ricky Sanders and made other key plays as the Redskins outlasted their opponents with a 27–24 over-time triumph. The win secured an 11-4 record and Williams' role as starter for the postseason. 'Not only had the city been moving towards me,' he admits, 'the locker room had as well.'

For Williams, the new challenge was to eradicate doubts over his ability to shine in big moments that had engulfed his pro career. Those questions were answered emphatically in the divisional round. With Washington in a 14–0 hole against the still-outstanding Chicago defense at a frigid Soldier Field, Williams dragged his team from the abyss. He stared down the Bears' disguised coverages and overcame Washington's rare running-game deficiencies by embarking upon a pair of seven-play touchdown drives. From there, Washington never looked back and sealed their passage to the NFC Championship Game courtesy of Darrell Green's punt-return touchdown that proved the winning score as the Redskins triumphed 21–17.

'One thing about Doug Williams today,' said CBS announcer Brent Musburger afterwards, 'he fell behind by two touchdowns, and there was a theory he didn't perform too well in the playoffs. As a matter of fact, people were kind of ugly about it and said he choked sometimes. This man did not choke today.'

Following a 17–10 win over Minnesota, in which he threw a game-sealing fourth-quarter touchdown to Gary Clark, Williams would now face the ultimate pressure cauldron. And not just because of the natural anxiety that accompanies Super Bowls. 'That year,' said Gibbs, 'I don't think anybody ever thought of Doug as a black quarterback. He was our quarterback. But then we got to San Diego . . .'

Although Williams projected calm throughout a week of unfathomable intensity, playing down the all-encompassing focus on race, reality was different. 'I was emotional and nobody knew it,' he reveals. 'There would never be a first black quarterback to play in the Super Bowl again. I was it.'

Towards the end of the first quarter, it appeared Williams' fairytale would end miserably. He lay stricken on the ground, face planted into the turf as a panicked silence descended over Washington's fans. Their mood didn't improve when Williams rolled over clutching his right knee, rose to his feet, stumbled around, then retreated back to the ground. As trainers attempted to grab his leg, which had buckled after his cleats failed to indent into the slick field, Williams said: 'Don't touch me! If the good Lord lets me get up today, I'm gonna finish this.'

He obliged. Williams missed two plays before returning to the field facing a not inconsiderable hole. His opponent – the sublime

John Elway – looked as masterful as ever in the opening quarter. The signal-caller earned Denver's place in the contest courtesy of 'The Drive', a memorable 98-yard march down the field on the road against the Browns over the dying embers of the AFC Championship Game, and looked similarly threatening early in San Diego. His first throw was a 56-yard touchdown strike down the right sideline to rookie Ricky Nattiel, hit perfectly in stride, while a clever trick play in which Elway caught a pass set up the Broncos for a field goal on their next drive.

When Williams crossed the white line with 14:17 remaining in the second quarter, Washington trailed 10–0 and needed a spark. 'Let's get this sucker rollin',' he ordered his teammates. Within moments, a runaway train was careering down the tracks.

Unexcited by the idea of easing himself and injured knee back in, Williams dropped back from under centre, faked a hand-off to Timmy Smith and unleashed a dart into the chest of Sanders, who – like Nattiel – was streaking down the right sideline. Touch-down, 80 yards.

The play proved the beginning of Williams' perfect day in the sun, written his way, for the Redskins spent the remainder of the quarter playing to the style of their passer; a team built on the clever running game implemented by Gibbs became an air show. Painstaking, clock-killing drives made way for Williams' passing bombardment in a devastating display of offensive football that turned the game on its head.

He completed 10-of-11 passes for a scarcely believable 228 yards and four touchdowns, two to Sanders complemented by tosses to Clark and Clint Didier. In between the blitz, Smith – a running back fuelled by Williams' pep talk during the week – raced for a 58-yard touchdown. 'I've been trying to get to this shit for 11 years,' the signal-caller had told his young 'back following two fumbles in practice, 'and I'm not going to let you screw it up! If you fumble that shit on Sunday, I'll personally kick you in the ass.'

Smith had initially laughed it off but, seeing the tear in

Williams' eye that betrayed his seriousness, realised the gravity. 'I'll run hard, old man,' he said. 'I'll make you proud of me.'

Pride was the operative word. With Washington's defense tightening up against Elway, the game ceased to be a contest. The Redskins led 35–10 at the interval and eased to victory on a day in which records tumbled as fast as the walls that had previously blocked the path of black quarterbacks. Williams' 340 passing yards were a Super Bowl record, as were Sanders' 193 receiving and Smith's 204 rushing.

As he walked off the field, the quarterback thrust his helmet into the air, the floodlights glistening down on a logo that had previously symbolised the footballing oppression of Williams' people. By the tunnel, he ran into his old Grambling coach Robinson, who declared Williams 'the Jackie Robinson of football'. As the two embraced with tears rolling down their cheeks, his former coach continued: 'It wasn't the four TD passes. It was that you got off the turf.'

That moment, Robinson realised, summed up the very essence of Williams. Throughout his life, from the hate-filled roads of Zachary to the slippery surface at Jack Murphy Stadium, he was knocked down and continued to rise again. He persevered through personal tragedy and racism, all leading to a glorious moment encapsulated perfectly by legendary broadcaster Keith Jackson, who turned an interview into a fitting serenade: 'May I say to you, sir,' he enthused in the locker room afterwards, 'you've handled your personal week of history nobly.'

Not only had a black quarterback won the Super Bowl, he was being addressed as 'sir' by an ageing white broadcaster. The times, they were changing. 'It was perfect timing,' concludes Williams. 'Growing up during the Civil Rights era, we listened to Martin Luther King talk about the mountaintop. When it came to professional football, the Super Bowl was the mountaintop – and I felt like I reached it.'

15

Seeds of Genius

Super Bowl XXV

NEW YORK GIANTS 20
BUFFALO BILLS 19

---

27 January 1991

Tampa Stadium, Tampa Bay

'Mike, can this guy make this?' asked Bill Belichick, the New York Giants defensive coordinator who so masterfully constrained the Buffalo Bills' talk-of-the-NFL offense with a gameplan as ballsy as it was brilliant. The 38-year-old stood with a strained look, anxiety palpable on every line adorning his face as he awaited special-teams coordinator Mike Sweatman's response. The answer came from another assistant coach, Charlie Weis: 'Hey, Bill, Bill, he can make it – but it's not real sure.'

High above Belichick's head, beneath the Apache helicopter hovering ominously, the scoreboard at Tampa Stadium read '0:08'. The Giants' 20–19 lead was suitably precarious on a day in which the tension in the stadium seemed close to boiling over, amplified by every additional search of supporters and the looming presence of security personnel.

'Our press-box spot was really poor, and I couldn't see very well,' remembers former Bills general manager Bill Polian. 'We went up on the roof, but there was no room because of SWAT teams all over the place.'

By kickoff, the atmosphere was ready to burst. Whitney Houston's genre-defining rendition of the national anthem left not a dry eye as she bellowed 'bombs bursting in air'. Amid the burning patriotism echoing around the amphitheatre, present in every defiant wave of the American flag, it was clear bodies stood in Tampa while minds lay in Iraq. The Gulf War, 10 days old, loomed over every element of Super Bowl XXV, from the build-up through to gameday. But the NFL, amid swirling rumours of postponement, remained steadfast in determining the show would go on. With the clock stuck on '0:08', its call had been justified. Minds, as well as bodies, were now very much present.

Following the highly charged opening, a thrilling football game broke out, in which Bill Parcells' Giants flipped the script on a Bills team that were a touchdown favourite. That Big Blue sat in front, having taken the field against Buffalo and their 'K-gun Offense' without starting quarterback Phil Simms due to injury, was as shocking as their brilliant defense allowing 135 yards rushing to Bills 'back Thurman Thomas.

Yet Thomas' dominant day, like everything else, resulted from Belichick and Parcells' brilliant design. The risky strategy they deployed exemplified the difference great coaches can make in football, even though the outcome was now completely out of their control. Hours of painstaking film study, debate over whether such a ploy could be utilised at all, and imprinting it into their players' consciousnesses all came down to the right boot of Bills kicker Scott Norwood and 47 yards separating field-goal holder Frank Reich from the goalposts.

'Now Norwood tries to kick his longest-ever on grass,' said

ABC commentator Al Michaels. 'Forty-seven yards, eight seconds left. Adam Lingner will snap it . . .'

In 1980, Ray Perkins was a year into his quest to rescue the Giants from their near-two-decade decline. Big Blue had managed one winning campaign since 1963, and the low watermark was still seared into the brains of those in the locker room. The moment that heralded Perkins' arrival transpired in Week 12 of the 1978 campaign.

The Giants were up 17–12 in the dying seconds, and the Philadelphia Eagles didn't have any timeouts. A simple kneel-down by quarterback Joe Pisarcik would seal the game, but offensive coordinator Bob Gibson had other ideas. He called 'brown right, near wing, 65 slant', a hand-off to Larry Csonka, to set into motion an embarrassing series of events that saw the pair botch the hand-off and allowed Eagles cornerback Herm Edwards to scoop up the ball and race in for the game-winning score.

Pisarcik says: 'People come up to me and actually say: "Hey, do you remember that play?" I feel like saying: "No, I'm only reminded of it 89 times day." What people don't know is a couple of weeks before, I changed a play and the coach screamed at me: "Don't ever change a play I send in ever again!" The guys in the huddle were like: "Joe, don't do it. Just fall on the ball." I said: "No way. I'm not going to get yelled at again."'

The fateful mistake served as a seminal moment for a once-great, blue-chip franchise who couldn't get out of their own way. On the sideline, brilliant linebacker Harry Carson stood motionless for 15 minutes, unable to comprehend what had occurred. 'It was one of the more devastating moments of my career,' he concedes. 'We were going to win, and everybody thought it was over. Then it happened. It was a shock to everybody's system.'

The 'Miracle of the Meadowlands' might as well have been the 'Massacre at the Meadowlands' given how quickly those of a blue persuasion fell on their swords. Gibson was fired immediately and head coach John McVay departed at the campaign's end, sent on his way towards becoming a key personnel man for Bill Walsh's San Francisco 49ers.

His replacement in the Big Apple was Perkins. 'When I arrived in 1976,' adds Carson, 'we had a lot of heart but no talent. After the fumble, they brought in a new staff and general manager. George Young was the GM, and he hired Perkins. Perkins instilled a sense of purpose and discipline, and that really is where the change in the Giants took place.'

Perkins' biggest impact wasn't the direct culture change – it was hiring two assistants who would alter the face of Big Blue. Of the pair, the most unspectacular was a fresh-faced 27-year-old just four years into his career, having bounced between stops in the league. He spent Perkins' first season as an assistant special-teams coach before being elevated to overseeing Carson and crew.

To a room of domineering alphas who were sceptical, and unacquainted with winning, linebackers coach Belichick's presence was about as intimidating as a house cat in a lion's den. He looked like the geek trying to live a frat-boy's life, sporting shaggy brown hair and an unathletic frame which betrayed a playing career that peaked in high school and never got started at Wesleyan college.

'When he inherited us,' reveals Carson, 'there were things he tried to get us to do that we were resistant to because Bill wasn't a football player. We questioned whether the things he wanted us to do were sound.'

He had to earn their respect. 'When we started incorporating what he wanted us to do, it worked,' adds Carson. 'That won us over. Man for man, we improved, and so did the team. We started gradually believing in him.'

Wherever he landed, no matter the role, Belichick impressed. He took his first job, with the Baltimore Colts, by offering to work for free and impressed so significantly that a franchise notoriously focused on tightening the purse strings quickly offered him a salary of $25 per week that rose to $50 by the season's end. Not only that, but his work expanded. Belichick went from glorified lackey, responsible for shipping game film to and from airports, to integral member of the staff almost immediately.

By the middle of that inaugural campaign, Belichick – despite officially working in special teams – was a key part of the defensive staff, breaking down opposing teams' tendencies to help create gameplans for the Colts' defense. Their system was a simplified version of that created by George Allen, focused upon proactivity over reactivity, which meant having a full picture of the opponents' likely mode of attack. 'It was like having two or three graduate courses in one year,' remembered Belichick.

Yet Belichick's defining early-career moment came on offense. One year with the Colts was all he needed for his legend to grow. Word of the boy wonder reached Detroit, where Lions head coach Rick Forzano – a former colleague of Belichick's father, Steve, who watched film with Bill in his formative years – needed an assistant and was willing to offer $10,000 per year and a car.

Belichick arrived in Detroit with belief in his ideas, yet it took a moment of trademark inspiration – ironically against the team with whom he later built his legacy – to reinforce that confidence. The Lions were 1-3 when they took on the 3-1 New England Patriots, Forzano having just resigned. They needed a win, and Belichick – despite being an assistant special-teams coach – had an idea for the offense. The previous year, while studying film in Baltimore, he noticed how the Los Angeles Rams deploying a two-tight-end set created problems for the kind of 3-4 defense New England utilised. Belichick approached offensive coordinator Ken Shipp and said: 'Look, I know we haven't ever used this formation, but I studied it last year. I think this is going to give the Patriots a problem. Can we take a look?'

The result? A 30–10 upset that had a seismic impact on Belichick and, indirectly, the NFL. 'It was one of those where I'm like: "OK, I can coach in this league,"' revealed Belichick. 'I realised you should never be afraid to use what you think is a good idea, just because it's unconventional and somebody else hasn't done it.'

It provided affirmation that the childhood years Belichick spent obsessing over football at the feet of his dad had formed a knowledge base that belied his inexperience. 'Bill grew up being a ball boy at Navy, grabbing balls for Roger Staubach,' NFL Films' Ken Rodgers, a friend, says. 'His father was close to Paul Brown, so he spent summers at Browns training camps. Just as Mozart was composing music as a child and Pascal was thinking about geometry, Bill Belichick's genius was born from very early work in the only job he's ever had – studying football.'

By the age of nine, Belichick's passion burned strongly. His dad was renowned as a fine coach who literally wrote the book on scouting: *Football Scouting Methods* was the definitive text on the art. He was also a Naval Academy man through and through, comfortable in his role to the point that he refused multiple job opportunities across 33 years as the university's scout from 1956.

In the early days, Belichick Jr's enthusiasm was harnessed watching Navy on TV, but eventually he would join his father on advance scouting trips at the conclusion of a week spent obsessing over the minutiae of the game. 'He was working with his dad as a nine-year-old,' Phil Savage, a personnel man who worked with Belichick later in his career, adds. 'Bill would end up in a room or closet with a projector and stack of film, and it's like: "Son, take these tapes and tell me how many times they ran split back." Bill devoured it.'

Time spent honing his craft not only developed an aptitude for spotting intricacies from film – he was just as adept noticing the coverage as he was a minor tell in an offensive lineman's stance – but developed the foundations of Belichick's programme. 'I learnt coaching at an early age,' he said. 'How they think, what bothers them, different styles. There might have been 10 coaches and you realise they're all good but very different. You figure out what works for you. I took a lot from everybody.'

That process continued through all of his stops, Belichick cherry-picking the best parts to develop a formula, from the original ideology of Brown to the defensive learnings indirectly gleaned from Allen. By the time he reached the Giants, his approach was beginning to take shape. Belichick blended football acumen gleaned from his father with instructional skills learnt from mother Jeannette, a multi-lingual teacher, as well as little snippets from many coaches along the way. But the strategy was undoubtedly his own: the Belichick Way. 'I saw him as a coach who wanted to do things differently,' says Carson. 'He had his way of getting a point across and was a student of the game who understood it differently.'

In New York, however, Belichick was defined not by himself, but by the other Bill that Perkins employed at the time of his arrival. The one who would jokingly call Belichick 'Doom', and with whom he had a fascinating and productive, if not always warm, relationship.

They recognised one another immediately upon boarding a flight at Denver International Airport bound for New York, not least because Belichick had spent the previous weeks leaving Parcells unanswered messages. The younger Bill had been given encouragement regarding a role on the older man's Air Force staff and was surprised by the lack of answers, until he boarded the jet and discovered Parcells was the Giants' new defensive coordinator. Within weeks, they would indeed be colleagues – just not in the fashion Belichick had anticipated.

Nor would their relationship follow the expected pattern. Prior to an opening campaign in which the duo were expected to work with one another – Belichick was a defensive assistant as well as special-teams coach – Parcells returned to Colorado due to his family's displeasure at the idea of moving cross-country again. Belichick drove Parcells to the airport, and the two said their goodbyes.

Parcells spent the ensuing year, in his own words 'miserable', working for a land-development company and scratching his football itch with a Denver Broncos season ticket. So miserable, in fact, that wife Judy decided one more relocation was necessary to bring Bill back. Parcells was the Patriots' linebackers coach in 1980, before returning to the Giants in '81 to undertake the job accepted two years previously, directing a staff that had seen Belichick elevated to sharing the duties of special-teams coordinator with coaching Big Blue's linebackers.

Their connection was an unusual one, the larger-than-life jock Parcells and understated nerd Belichick. But, as is often the case, contrasting skillsets made for a perfect mix, Parcells' Vince Lombardi-esque intensity and ability to draw the best out of players fusing with Belichick's Clark Shaughnessy-like obsessive genius.

'People talk about players' coaches, and Parcells was definitely one,' adds Carson. 'He knew his players and how to motivate: the ones who had a thin skin he couldn't yell at, and those he could really tear into. He really pushed buttons.'

Together, they helped transform a defense that had finished second-last in the previous campaign. The Giants were third and ninth in those standings for 1981 and '82. Under the exacting Perkins – who'd been moulded playing for Alabama's Bear Bryant – a ragtag unit gradually learnt discipline.

Yet discipline alone wasn't enough. Having returned to the postseason for the first time since 1963 in '81, Big Blue went 4-5 in the strike-shortened campaign that followed and their leading man took his dream job by replacing Bryant. Perkins' move to Tuscaloosa paved the way for New Jersey native and Giants fan Parcells' elevation to head coach, a role that – for two years – he carried out while retaining defensive-coordinator duties.

The anticipated promotion of Belichick occurred in 1985 – with emphatic results. Big Blue had reached the divisional round the previous campaign, but it wasn't coincidental that their defense became a top-five unit once Belichick took the reins, and neither was the success being driven by the men their new coordinator had moulded for the previous half-decade.

The early iteration of Belichick's linebacker corps were known as the 'Crunch Bunch', Carson operating at the heart of a four-man unit featuring Brian Kelley, five-time Pro Bowler Brad Van Pelt and young phenom Lawrence Taylor. As the years progressed, the full defense earned its own moniker, the 'Big Blue Wrecking Crew', and the respect of their peers. 'They were a nightmare to play against,' remembers San Francisco 49ers star Roger Craig. 'The Giants and the Bears were the defenses we found it toughest against.'

By 1986, the unit warranted being mentioned in the Chicago Bears' class. They were following the growing trend of operating in a 3-4, with Carson and Taylor the obvious stars. 'Those nick-names were laid on us by fans,' adds Carson, 'but the key was understanding each other. I knew what Lawrence was thinking, and vice versa. We were able to play off one another.'

Carson, described by Belichick as the greatest middle linebacker he has coached, would be enshrined in the Hall of Fame – but even his legacy is nothing compared to Taylor's. 'Taylor's the best player I've ever seen,' added Belichick.

The second overall pick from North Carolina in the 1981 NFL Draft, Taylor wasted little time announcing himself. 'We knew from his first practice,' adds Carson. 'Lawrence is the greatest player I've ever played with . . . easily. I'm very fortunate he was on my team.'

During that opening session, in which Belichick claimed Taylor was immediately the best player on the field, the rookie went from running with the third team to the first inside half an hour. Taylor was a 6ft 3in, 238lb beast who married ferocious speed and power with relentlessness that bordered on recklessness, as well as an incredibly high football IQ. The mix created the most dominant defensive force in the game's history. 'He was so respected for his competitiveness and toughness,' added Belichick. 'All those traits weren't just good; they were rare. He was all about winning. He wasn't about personal stats, even if he appreciated them.'

'He could've made a helluva coach,' adds Carson. 'He's one of the smartest people I know, especially from a football standpoint.'

Taylor was an All-Pro in each of his first nine campaigns and the de-facto answer when people mused on who was the NFL's best defensive player. Yet his impact wasn't just illustrated in individual accolades. Taylor was, in the truest sense, a game-changer, for offenses who would usually block outside linebackers with running backs or tight ends could no longer do so – not even the best tackles could stop him. As such, teams began deploying a one-back offense* in order to double- or triple-team L.T., setting the wheels in motion for 11 personnel to become football's most common package. 'We had to have a special gameplan just for Lawrence Taylor,' said former Washington Redskins coach Joe Gibbs.

In no season was Taylor quite so dominant as 1986. Garlanded with an enviable array of honours over his first half-decade in the NFL, the gong he craved most had proven elusive. Moreover, Taylor entered the campaign with a point to prove having spent a brief spell in rehab prior to the campaign for drug addiction. The outside linebacker produced a league-best 20.5 sacks to earn his third and final career NFL Defensive Player of the Year Award and, most pertinently, became only the second defensive player in history, after Alan Page, to be voted MVP. Those efforts contributed to a unit that allowed just 14.8 points and 80.3 rushing yards per game, while racking up 59 sacks and 24 interceptions. It was the result of excellent players being overseen by a genius.

'Coach Belichick had counter measures for whatever was happening on the field,' says Carson. 'He would see something happening, call everybody over, get on the chalkboard and put in a scheme that we may not have even practised during the week – but still get the point across. That's the sign of an outstanding coach. Being able to make adjustments in the midst of chaos, to stop and analyse the situation, then get everybody on the right page. Not all coaches can do that, but it's the mark of his brilliance.'

With Belichick's defensive mastery sitting comfortably alongside Parcells' impressive ability to fuse all of his units into a wider, complementary strategy, the Giants boasted all the right ingredients. Not only that but the whole squad – like their star player – had an extra incentive. Their 21–0 loss in the previous year's divisional round against Chicago still stung, especially given the Bears' first touchdown came through Sean Landeta barely connecting with a punt that rolled to Shaun Gayle – who eased into the end zone.

'We knew what was coming,' confirms Carson. 'After losing to the Bears in 1985, everybody recommitted to coming back and being in the Super Bowl as our singular goal. For the older guys like myself, the clock was ticking. I already had 10 or so years in the league and didn't know how many more opportunities would come. Everybody got on the same page, and we used the Bears loss as a catalyst for the Super Bowl season.'

The campaign's biggest turning point occurred in Week 11. The Giants were seemingly rolling at 8-2, but pressure was mounting on Simms, who had rebounded from struggles early in his pro career to justify his selection with the 1979 seventh overall pick the previous year – only to return to inconsistent type. Parcells knew it was time to intervene with someone he had benched early during his tenure and with whom he enjoyed, as was his wont, a volatile relationship. He pulled Simms aside and said: 'Look, just go out there, let it go and I'll support you 100 per cent, no matter what.' The words were echoed by Belichick, who made a beeline for Simms and said: 'You're a really good player. I have great faith in you,' before signing off with a line that would become his signature: 'Just do your job.'

Simms not only torched the Minnesota Vikings' secondary to

the tune of 25 completions for more than 300 yards, he helped win the game in spectacular fashion. With the Giants trailing 20–19, 1:12 remaining, facing fourth-and-17, the quarterback stood in the face of the pass-rush and hit wideout Bobby Johnson 22 yards downfield to help set up Raul Allegre's game-winning field goal. 'From that time on,' said Taylor, 'I felt if we were going to win a championship, it was going to be behind the arm of Phil Simms. He became my man right then.'

The win was the Giants' fourth in succession, a run that would stretch to nine by the regular season's conclusion. In the playoffs, Big Blue were, indeed, a Wrecking Crew, knocking Joe Montana out of the divisional round in the second quarter on a play that ended with a Taylor pick-six. If that 49–3 triumph over the 49ers was impressive, it didn't carry as much emotional significance as shutting out bitter rivals Washington in their 17–0 NFC Championship Game win at a blustery Meadowlands.

The Giants had followed in the footsteps of Chicago the previous year by roaring back to relevance to reach their first Super Bowl, although the wait had been even longer. It'd been 30 years since Big Blue were kings of the NFL, so long that even veterans such as Carson were indifferent to the historical significance. 'That history was meaningless and nothing to do with the current team,' adds Carson. 'It meant something for Wellington Mara, the owner, and maybe the fans – but nobody on that team was part of those previous teams. We had no frame of reference.'

Not even the Rose Bowl's 101,063 auditorium, the Broncos' exceptional young quarterback John Elway and a poor opening half could derail the Giants in Super Bowl XXI. Having entered the break 10–9 behind, Big Blue were jumpstarted by Parcells calling a fake punt on fourth-and-one at midfield. Thereafter, Simms took centre stage, completing 22 of his next 25 passes and leading the Giants to scores on each of their next five possessions to secure a 39–20 demolition. The performance would see the signal-caller utter the famous words 'I am going to go to Disneyland', having become the first Super Bowl MVP invited to the theme park in what became an annual tradition.

It wasn't the only first. After their regular season had concluded with a 55–24 thumping of the Green Bay Packers – delivered after a particularly harsh halftime speech from Parcells – Carson gave his head coach a Gatorade shower to begin another ritual.

It proved one of the last significant acts from a pioneer who retired content following the 1988 campaign. 'When you get to the precipice of a Super Bowl, you think of everything that has taken place in your life to put you in that position,' he admits. 'All of your high-school plays, going to college, the down years and everything. I had an appreciation that was greater than other players because of the struggles in the 1970s. Those games gave deeper appreciation for the later achievements.'

For all Carson's journey was coming to an end, the same wasn't true for those instrumental in the Giants' title. Big Blue were back at the NFL's top table – mixing Parcells and Belichick's exceptional coaching with Hall-of-Fame general manager George Young's talent-evaluation prowess – and intended to stay there by utilising an old-school approach that flew in the face of the day's relentless pursuit of innovation.

Wherever you looked on NFL Sundays during the 1980s, from the San Francisco Bay to the outskirts of Capitol Hill, football was undergoing radical change. Most illustrious of the innovators altering the landscape was Walsh, not least because of the Lombardi Trophies he lifted, but others were just as impactful.

With the St. Louis Cardinals between 1973 and '77, Don Coryell successfully translated concepts – such as the I-formation* – which had made his name in high-school and college. Coryell, who starred as an assistant at USC before turning lowly San Diego State into an offensive powerhouse as head coach, was responsible for a thrilling era that spawned the nickname 'Cardiac Cards' but ended following disagreements with Bill Bidwill. The tight-fisted owner was unwilling to cede personnel control and allowed running back Terry Metcalf, having set an NFL single-season all-purpose yardage record of 2,462 two years previously, to leave for the Canadian Football League.

The Cardinals' loss proved San Diego's gain, Coryell transforming the Chargers' talented offense into one of the league's greatest-ever units. Even as Walsh and the 49ers were taking the NFL by storm, their offensive output couldn't match Coryell's playmaking pack.

San Diego were powered by a trio of Hall of Famers – quarterback Dan Fouts, tight end Kellen Winslow and wide receiver Charlie Joiner – but all agree their places in Canton owe everything to the coach and system given his name: 'Air Coryell'. Its philosophy was similar to Walsh's, with pass setting up run. Where Air Coryell diverged from Walsh's West Coast offense was in the nature of its aerial attack, which capitalised on the team's battery of pass-catchers by attacking all portions of the field, deep and short, while moving weapons around like chess pieces to target opposing weaknesses. He did this via numerous pre-snap shifts and motions designed to simultaneously confuse defenses and force them to tip their own hand.

The central piece was Winslow, an X-factor tight end who brought never-before-seen athleticism to the position. He combined superb blocking with the speed and soft hands of a wide receiver, allowing Coryell to create the first 'move' tight end by utilising him in-line and wide. Together with Joiner, who led the all-time receiving-yardage charts at his career's end, he formed one of the deadliest duos in NFL history.

Their efforts might not have brought championships, but the Chargers fundamentally transformed the game. Coryell's numerical play-calling system – refined and simplified from Sid Gillman's – became oft-copied, as did the route concepts and wider focus on passing that saw San Diego lead the NFL in air yardage for six successive years between 1978 and '83. Fouts, who became the league's second 4,000-yard passer in 1979 and repeated the feat in each of the next two campaigns, said: 'Whoever heard of the nickel* or dime* pass defense before Air Coryell forced opponents to come up with strategies to combat the aerial assault?'

The fact that those concepts have now essentially become base personnel* in the NFL has roots in Coryell's creation. 'If you talk about impact on the game, training other coaches – John Madden and Joe Gibbs to name a few – and influencing how things are done,' says Hall-of-Fame coach Tony Dungy, 'Don Coryell is right up there with Paul Brown. He was a genius.'

The likes of Madden and Gibbs, who credit their careers to Coryell, succeeded where he failed, by understanding the bigger picture and fielding complementary teams. San Diego, while entertaining, didn't reach a Super Bowl because the defense never matched the offense. Their best squad – the 1981 edition featuring Fred Dean – was undermined by an AFC Championship Game against the Cincinnati Bengals known as the Freezer Bowl. The weather negated San Diego's offense in a 27–7 loss, contributing to Coryell's 3-6 postseason record that helps explain why, astonishingly, he hasn't yet been inducted into Canton.

Gibbs learnt the coaching trade under Coryell during spells with San Diego State, the Cardinals and Chargers before catching the eye of Washington general manager Bobby Beathard, who shocked the fanbase by naming him the club's new head coach in 1981. At least Redskin supporters unfamiliar with Gibbs' name – and unimpressed by his diminutive stature and whistling voice – could anticipate an entertaining brand of offensive football.

Yet the perceived positive quickly became a negative – it was high wire without the success enjoyed by the Chargers. In Washington's first five games under their new head coach, they turned the ball over 21 times and were 0-5. To add insult to injury, the Redskins weren't utilising to the fullest their best player: bruising halfback John Riggins, who Gibbs had lured back to the field after he sat out the previous campaign due to a contract dispute.

'I thought I was going to be the first guy to coach in the NFL and never win a game,' said Gibbs.

Over the course of that disappointing run, however, Gibbs would illustrate his own quality by altering the landscape of NFL rushing attacks. Against the Giants, Joe Theismann became the latest signal-caller to see a whole game completely undone by a player with whom he would become eerily linked: the incomparable Taylor. Knowing Big Blue were on the schedule twice per year, Gibbs determined that a unique ploy was required. He settled upon a two-tight-end offense, with one always responsible for aiding the tackle in dealing with Taylor. The second tight end's role would eventually evolve into the formation of a different position entirely: the H-back. A hybrid tight end/fullback who lined up just behind either tackle, he became the key piece of a new offense in Washington.

Crucial to the H-back was versatility: depending on the call, he could follow the original intention and help block opposing outside linebackers, take care of a cornerback on outside runs, move inside and wham opposing interior defenders to create inside lanes, deal with opposing defenders blitzing and operate in the passing game. When combined with the pre-snap motions often undertaken, the H-back presented unique challenges for opposing teams. 'He could move all over and create all kinds of formations [with the same personnel],' said Gibbs.

It was also a key piece to the counter-run plays popularised by Gibbs and his team. The most famous of those calls was the 'Counter Trey', which was essentially a sweep with two crucial differences. Unlike Lombardi's iteration, there was just one pulling guard, while the concept focused on misdirection as opposed to execution. Initially, linemen would fake their block to the weak side and the ball-carrier pretended to run that way before both switched course. That split-second of defenders being on their heels was devastating, especially with the likes of Riggins and Timmy Smith running behind Washington's illustrious Hogs.

Counter plays provided the foundation for one of the most balanced offenses ever fielded. With teams so conscious of countering the running game – and, therefore, devoting extra resources to stopping it – Gibbs was able to install a series of devastating play-action passes. By the conclusion of the 1991 regular season, Washington had fielded a top-five scoring offense in six of 11 campaigns. Most importantly, they achieved the feat in each of the previous three years, by which point Washington's offense had evolved further. With Mark Rypien, an excellent deep thrower, now under centre, Gibbs began to call upon elements of the vertical-passing game learnt from Coryell and implemented further tweaks: he was among the first coaches to regularly deploy bunch formations* that are now commonplace. 'He had a great technical mind,' said Walsh. 'His tactics were outstanding, and he could utilise personnel as well or better than any other coach.'

'Not to take away from the Bill Walshes, Mike Ditkas or Tom Landrys,' added Gibbs' great rival Parcells, 'Joe Gibbs is the best coach I ever coached against.'

His place among the elite was sealed that postseason. Having gone 14-2 and won by an average of 16 points per game, the Redskins – still driven by their Hogs, who allowed an incredible nine sacks across 19 games that year – marched to Super Bowl glory once again to earn Gibbs the incredible distinction of being the only coach to win three Lombardi Trophies with three different quarterbacks.

Moreover, the campaign cemented his reputation alongside Walsh and Coryell as one of the most significant offensive visionaries during football's most significant era of tactical change. Not least because the team they overcame in Super Bowl XXVI were at the cutting edge of another schematic advance entertaining the masses by the banks of the Ohio River and Falls of Niagara.

Despite being engulfed by issues ranging from strikes to relocations throughout the 1980s, the NFL's on-field product never looked better. The decade was highlighted by strategic twists that not only had long-term ramifications for the sport but created continuously tantalising match-ups. From Cowboys–49ers and 49ers–Bears to, well, every NFC East divisional game.

Just as intriguing as those bitter rivalries were others that didn't boast the obvious newsworthy appeal but were equally fascinating when you scratched beneath the surface. One such example was the 1988 AFC Championship Game, which pitted Cincinnati against Buffalo and delivered more subplots than the movie *Die Hard*, which premiered that same year.

Most notably, there was the spectre of the ageing Brown, the foundation of NFL coaching whose Bengals team was now overseen by a handpicked, bright-eyed leading man feeling the pressure to win an icon his first Lombardi Trophy. That victory would potentially pit Sam Wyche against mentor Walsh – whose own ties to the Bengals and Brown were significant – in Super Bowl XXIII only added to the delicious prospect. 'I wanted to win it for him [Brown] in the worst way,' remembered Wyche. 'He had the number-one high-school team, [was] national champion at Ohio State and the Cleveland Browns had won seven championships in the AAFC and NFL, but not the Super Bowl.'

For Buffalo, the prospect of a coming-of-age moment akin to that enjoyed by Wyche and Walsh's 49ers against the Dallas Cowboys years earlier was similarly enticing. The Bills were a bright team with young talents on both sides of the ball overseen by a first-time general manager and perky head coach. In long-time associates Polian and Marv Levy, Buffalo appeared to have found their dream ticket: a fine talent evaluator in the former and moulder of men in the latter, unified by the symbiotic relationship necessary to craft championship squads.

'He's the best friend I have in football,' admits Levy. 'We go back quite a way. I was the head coach in the CFL with the Montreal Alouettes, and the man in charge of scouting asked if he could hire a part-time scout. He did, and it was Bill Polian. I kept reading his reports and thinking: "My goodness are these good. I'd like to meet him." We did, and when I coached the Kansas City Chiefs, we hired him as a full-time scout. We went different ways for a while, but once Bill went to Buffalo, he recommended me to Ralph Wilson. He's a brilliant football mind and great guy.'

The fruits of a burgeoning partnership were beginning to show in 1988, a roster meticulously built by Polian being rounded into shape as Levy made his imprint. 'My brain is his brain,' adds Polian. 'He trained me. He's my everything. Everything I know about pro football, I learned from Coach Levy.'

Offensively, a good line marshalled by brilliant centre Kent Hull opened holes for Thomas and provided quarterback Jim Kelly enough protection to hit Hall of Fame wideout Andre Reed. More impressive was the defense, led by an edge defender in Bruce Smith who still tops the NFL's all-time sacks chart, and the league's best special-teams unit.

Yet the Bills' focus in the build-up to the biggest game in team history, much like the rest of the footballing world, wasn't on themselves. It centred around the validity of Cincinnati's unique offense, a Wyche brainchild that, like many evolutions, was stumbled upon accidentally.

The lightbulb went off during a 49ers practice. In 1982, San Francisco signed Renaldo 'Skeets' Nehemiah, a former world-record holder who spent four years as the finest 110m hurdler on the planet. One day during practice, Skeets ran a go route and Wyche noticed how heavily he was breathing on the way back to the huddle. 'Skeets, what you doing, man?' he said. 'I thought you were a world-class sprinter. You're breathing like a racehorse.'

'Coach, I'm breathing heavy,' replied Nehemiah, 'because I just ran 60 yards fast as I can run it. If you give me a few more seconds, I'll be breathing through my nose again.'

'That registered with me,' admitted Wyche. 'He was going to recover from that 60-yard sprint because of conditioning in a short period. What if we could tempo practice to teach the team to recover in 18 to 20 seconds? The defense is used to practising with a lot more time than that because the scout team has to look at a card, then mimic their opponent. So, it's maybe a minute each play. If we could stay fresh because that's the way we practised, it'd give us an advantage.'

From that embryo, Wyche's no-huddle offense was born.

With the information stored away in the recesses of his brain, Wyche returned to it in 1984, his first as the Bengals' leading man following a sole season as Indiana's head coach. Preparing his team for a third-and-long situation, he contemplated the lunacy of offensive players huddling and allowing defenses to send on the requisite counters to the inevitable pass.

Wyche experimented first with a basketball-style huddle, in which 15 or 20 offensive players surrounded the coordinator during timeouts so defenses didn't know which 11 would take the field. Then, there was the 'sugar huddle', named as such because it was short and sweet: five seconds compared to the league average of around 20. And then it hit Wyche: why huddle at all?

'It was never a hurry-up,' revealed Wyche. 'Some people called it that, but it was all about the threat of the hurry-up. We just got up off the ball and into formation. When the team was unpiling, I was giving Boomer Esiason the next play – that's how fast we had to be. Once chronic fatigue sets in, maybe we score four touchdowns and win a game we might not have won.'

By 1988, Wyche had perfected his plan. He entered the campaign under pressure, the Bengals having gone 4-11 the previous year largely due to replacement players not being able to digest the offensive playbook. But Brown's faith was rewarded. Cincinnati were the number-one offense in football – by a wide margin: their 6,057 regular-season yards was a whopping 852 better than the next-best mark. It was unstoppable. 'Fans loved it because they saw more football,' says Wyche. 'We were fun to watch. A team's season-ticket holders want to see more touchdowns.'

Around the league, opinion differed. 'They changed the rules every week for almost four years,' adds Wyche. 'Every week they had a different rule. I'm not exaggerating; it was frustrating. People wanted to throw the no-huddle out. I don't think anybody in the league was on my side. We beat Dallas 50–24 and Houston 61–7 another year. We were scoring 30 and 40 points fairly regularly.'

No NFL intervention was quite as dramatic as the 11th-hour one ahead of the Bengals' meeting with Buffalo. With the Bills threatening to follow the Seattle Seahawks' unsuccessful lead from the divisional round by feigning injuries and Wyche steadfast in his refusal to eliminate a tactic some considered akin to cheating, Pete Rozelle intervened. Two hours prior to the contest, the league office issued a diktat that if the Bengals went no-huddle, the officials would issue a 15-yard penalty. Wyche's response? 'The heck with them,' he said. 'We will play by their rules and still beat them.'

The hoopla was ironic on two fronts: the Bengals won 21–10 not because of their hamstrung offense but due to the zone-blitz defense* overseen by another of the era's great innovators, Dick LeBeau. Buffalo, meanwhile, were forced to adopt the no-huddle offense themselves in the playoffs 12 months later. With Norwood's inability to kick off due to a groin strain playing into the hands of the Browns' exceptional returner Eric Metcalf in the 1989 divisional round, Buffalo found themselves in a shootout. 'Every time we scored, he'd at least bring it back to midfield and he scored on one too,' remembers Polian. 'It was a basketball game.' From early in the second half, therefore, Buffalo went no-huddle, continuing a back-and-forth thriller that featured three lead changes, 64 points and an incredible finale.

Even though the game ended in heartbreak – Kelly was intercepted by Bruce Matthews in the end zone as Cleveland won 34–30 – it inadvertently provided the final building block for Polian and Levy's patient construction. As the head coach headed off the field, he turned to coordinator Ted Marchibroda and offensive-line coach Tom Bresnahan. 'That ought to be our permanent offense,' said Levy.

'There was no talent, but I knew what I was getting into. I was pretty honest with the public when I said we were 2-14 on merit, it wasn't a mirage and there was a lot of work to do.'

At the point of his elevation to Buffalo's general manager, Polian had already begun altering the story of a perennial also-ran in the NFL, whose only days of success were during the early throes of the AFL. He spent the previous two campaigns as director of pro personnel, undertaking the unenviable task of reversing Buffalo's fortunes in the face of considerable challenges from the USFL.

With the drafting of Kelly 14th overall in 1983, the Bills believed they had their key ingredient – a franchise quarterback could fix many ailments. But Kelly, despite being from nearby Pittsburgh, quickly made his displeasure at being drafted by Buffalo known – claiming to be on the verge of tears when the pick was made – and jumped at the chance to back out when the USFL's Houston Gamblers came calling.

The situation illustrated the scale of Polian's task. The NFL was, for the first time in two decades, drafting players with trepidation they might join the rival organisation. 'We lost lynchpins to it,' remembers Polian. 'The USFL eventually failed, but there was a lot of top talent in it. They were beating the NFL to players and driving up salaries. It was tough.'

Tough but not impossible. With the first overall choice in the 1985 selection class, Buffalo chose Virginia Tech defensive end Smith and fought off the challenge of their rival organisation's Baltimore Stars to secure his rights. In the fourth round, meanwhile, the Bills delivered an all-time selection by nabbing Reed.

Buffalo may have finished 2-14 once again that season, but at least the cupboard was no longer bare. With the USFL folding following their ill-fated legal campaign against the NFL, the Bills held Kelly's rights and Polian prepared his sales pitch. 'Jim reiterated immediately he didn't want to play in Buffalo,' admits the executive.

But the young general manager wasn't about to be pushed around. 'You need to understand what my situation is, Jim,' Polian told Kelly. 'I'm a new general manager. This is my first opportunity. I can't possibly let you go to where you want to go, which I suspect is the Raiders.' The Raiders mention drew a smile from Kelly and confirmed Polian's suspicions. 'We can't possibly let you go there,' he continued. 'It would be the end of my career, and I have a family to support. It would be the last nail in the coffin. The Bills would have no credibility whatsoever. So if you're going to adhere to that standard, you're either not going to play football or . . .'

At that point, Kelly intervened: 'I could force a trade.' But Polian made clear the terms: 'Look, I don't disagree with that completely. But we would control where we were going to trade you, and I would trade you to the worst possible team for you. I have to do that. You understand that that's the business part of it.'

'Before we get there,' continued Polian, 'let's talk football. I'm a football guy; you're a football guy. Let me tell you what we're constructing here, with you in mind. We have a great young receiver in Andre who's going to be an All-Pro. We have a great backup in Frank Reich, who's already played a year. We have a tight end we just traded for in Pete Metzelaars who's going to be dynamite for you and a pretty good offensive line. And we're committed to adding people from the USFL, some of whom you played with. We're rebuilding Buffalo, and the object is to win the Super Bowl. Not to be .500.' Kelly sat silently as Polian spoke, paused for what felt like an age, and stated: 'You know, that doesn't sound too bad.'

It was a crucial moment in the Bills' history. Although Polian couldn't have predicted it at the time, Kelly was the perfect triggerman for Buffalo's future offense: the 'K-Gun'.

The opening blasts were fired two-thirds through the 1990

campaign, Philadelphia the unfortunate recipients of the bullets. The first was the ultimate warning shot, a 63-yard strike to free-agent signing James Lofton, who shared a field with Reed in Buffalo and a room in Canton down the line. It was the start of a run that saw Kelly go eight-for-eight for 229 yards and three touchdowns, leaving the Eagles dazed.

Dick Vermeil's crew, however, didn't suffer the same embarrassment as Buffalo's playoff opponents. Following a 13-3 regular season, the Bills went on a tear in the postseason, Kelly out-duelling 1983 draft-mate Dan Marino as the Dolphins fell 44–34 before the Los Angeles Raiders were blown off Rich Stadium's field in a 51–3 beatdown.

Entering Super Bowl XXV, it appeared the Bills were set to fulfil the pledge delivered by Levy when he first entered the building in 1986. 'Fellas, this is going to be a short meeting. Our objective here is to win the Super Bowl, not to play in it. But to win.'

The great irony of those introductory words was that Buffalo would play in lots of Super Bowls without ever managing to win one, a run that began with the occasion that catapulted the greatest coach in NFL history towards superstardom.

In the facility of the Patriots team with which Belichick has become synonymous, a sign displays a famous quote from Sun Tzu's *Art of War*: 'Every battle is won before it is fought'. It's one of the few messages in the facility and important because of its significance to the man who put it there. In many ways, it is a tableau to Belichick's entire coaching career.

The one trait that separates him from his peers is, and always has been, adaptability, a defining attribute that not only hallmarks his career as a head coach but the highly successful run as an assistant that preceded it. The ultimate showcase of his unique qualities came during the Giants' 1990 playoff run in which Big Blue's defensive coordinator met three differing challenges with wildly different approaches.

By that stage, Parcells was already well-versed in Belichick's willingness to shun conventional wisdom. In Week 11, with the Giants sitting pretty at 9–0, the head coach scoffed at his lieutenant's suggestion of playing dime defense on first down to counter the Lions' run-and-shoot offense. Belichick determined his men simply had to match the speed of the Lions' small, fast receivers, but the ploy was risky given Detroit also boasted young phenom running back Barry Sanders. With Belichick steadfast, Parcells slammed down his notepad and said: 'Geez, you got all the answers. Why don't you put [wide receiver] Stephen Baker in there – he's fast.' Baker never did see the field on defense, but Belichick's plan worked a treat: the Giants won 20–0.

Such displays bolstered the unique trust Parcells had in Belichick. 'Bill is quite cerebral,' said Parcells, 'and pays close attention to detail all of the time. I admire that in him. He has the wherewithal to maintain concentration for a long period of time.'

That obsession with the particulars bore fruit over an astonishing playoff run. First up were the Bears, now without Walter Payton but exhibiting the same bruising philosophy under head coach Mike Ditka. To counter that challenge, Belichick shunned the 3-4 defense on which his Giants were built and played a 4-3 for the first time all year. The result? A 31–3 triumph that set up the seemingly annual showdown with San Francisco.

The 49ers, of course, presented the polar opposite challenge to Chicago, so Belichick changed course again. Big Blue played exclusively nickel – a tactic that's common now but wasn't then – to shut down Montana, Jerry Rice and co. The 49ers, attempting to win a third successive Super Bowl, were beaten 15–13.

For all such definitive week-to-week change was radical, it was nothing compared to what Belichick cooked up for the Bills. Six days out from one of the most highly charged Super Bowls in history, Belichick stood in a conference room and unveiled his latest plan: 'We're going to let Thurman Thomas get 100 yards.' The mood became a mixture of bemusement and rage. Belichick's defense prided themselves on stopping the run, a mantra instilled since day one that led to just two rushers managing more than 100 yards in two seasons. But Belichick was insistent: 'I'm telling you, if Thomas runs for 100 yards, we'll win this game.'

'I thought it was a collective brain fart,' said linebacker Carl Banks. 'Like, what the hell are you talking about? I think because we were a team that prided itself defensively on not giving up 100-yard rushers, not even giving up 100-yard games for a total offensive rush stat. But he says it, we are all-in uproar, and we're thinking Bill is just conceding that Thurman is too good and we won't be able to stop him. And then he reeled us back in and kinda gave us a method to the madness.'

While many around the United States spent the previous week overwhelmed by the spectre of the Gulf War, Belichick was locked away in a film room studying Kelly and the K-Gun. His task was thankless: coming up with a strategy to not only shut down one of the most explosive offenses ever unleashed but to fit it into the wider picture of the Giants' plan for all three phases.

Although Thomas had been an MVP candidate, Belichick knew the true threat in Buffalo's new system was aerial. Kelly's ability to put defenses on their heels and deliver the quick strike to Reed or Lofton – who accrued yards after the catch with terrifying ease – was fatal. As such, Belichick concocted a ploy that saw Big Blue put just two men on the line of scrimmage, opening inevitable holes for Thomas. Those immediately behind were tasked with making life miserable for pass-catchers over the middle, hitting them hard as they ran crossing routes and quelling any aspirations of additional gains from Kelly's passes.

'The gameplan was ingenious,' remembers defensive back Everson Walls, who was tasked with providing tight coverage and producing key disguises Belichick felt would confuse Kelly. 'Buffalo always beat people with the quick six, one of those passes to Andre or James, who hauled ass into the end zone. Belichick's genius is to look at an opponent, identify what they do well and shut that down. He makes teams take an alternative route. At times, we only had one D-lineman in the game. Who does that? But he knew his team, that we had great linebackers, and understood the opponent. It took balls. I don't think there's another coach in history who would do it. There are coaches that can match his intellect, but he has the balls.'

Defense was one part of the wider strategy, however. Complicating matters for the Giants was an offense piloted by backup quarterback Jeff Hostetler due to Simms being sidelined. That a number two had never won the Super Bowl illustrated the scale of Big Blue's challenge. Enter Bill and, well, Bill. 'I was a detail person,' said Belichick, 'but Bill saw the big picture in great clarity. I think that's one of the things that made us work so well together.'

Parcells' part was fitting Belichick's unique concept into the overall blueprint. He surmised the best counter to Buffalo's offense was to keep Kelly off the field. To do that, the Giants would have to deliver a methodical offensive gameplan, driven by their running game, that afforded Parcells control of the clock. 'Nobody had ever won with a backup quarterback,' said Parcells. 'So, we wanted to try to shorten the game and minimise their time of possession.'

On an occasion marked by emotion, the Giants were driven by ruthless efficiency. 'We were very aware it was a different occasion,' says Levy, 'especially after that unbelievable rendition of the national anthem, where she sang it like never before or since. Patriotism was in abundance, and it really became more than a game. There were bigger things on the table.'

Not for the Giants. Their only aim was to meticulously carry out the detailed plan devised by the two Bills – and they did it to a tee. Thomas rushed for more than 100 yards, and Buffalo managed just 205 through the air, converting only one-of-eight third downs. There was one big play – a 61-yard play to Lofton on a tipped ball in the opening quarter – but none of Kelly's other 29 passes gained more than 20.

On offense, the Giants set a Super Bowl time-of-possession record with 40:33, driven by MVP Ottis Anderson's 102-yard, one-touchdown day. Hostetler efficiently delivered 222 yards on 20 completions with zero interceptions, although his biggest moment was not fumbling under the weight of a first-quarter sack from Defensive Player of the Year Smith. The play resulted in a safety that gave Buffalo a 12–3 lead but could've been far worse had the signal-caller not somehow retained possession. 'I have no idea how he held onto that ball,' remembered Smith.

Perhaps the greatest indicator of Big Blue's achievement was that despite Belichick's gameplan being so legendary that it's proudly displayed in the Hall of Fame, the outcome of an all-time great Super Bowl still came down to one point and, eventually, one man's right boot.

'No good,' bellowed Michaels from the ABC box as the ball exploded off Norwood's foot with the Bills trailing 20–19. 'Wide right.'

16

The Return of America's Team

NFC Championship Game

DALLAS COWBOYS 30
SAN FRANCISCO 49ERS 20

---

17 January 1993

Candlestick Park, San Francisco

Eleven years after Dwight Clark leapt at the back of a Candlestick Park end zone to complete 'The Catch', the 1992 campaign's NFC Championship Game saw battle lines drawn once more in a situation that was both similar and dissimilar. With the fourth quarter winding down, the San Francisco 49ers trailed the Dallas Cowboys in the same venue, a Super Bowl berth again on the line, when their quarterback returned to the fray. Just as they did the day Joe Montana permanently catapulted himself into the city's sporting folklore, 49er hopes rested on a signal-caller desperate to prove his worth.

That was where the parallels ended. Unlike a little over a decade earlier, the home crowd no longer betrayed nervousness, nor were they simply happy to be there. The feeling emanating from

the stands was one of expectation, built across four championship seasons in the previous 12. Events over the coming minutes
would help determine whether, like Montana before him, Steve
Young warranted a special place in their hearts.

This is what Young had waited for, validation . . . and vindication of all the years spent riding the pine behind Montana after
joining San Francisco in 1987, of the frustration built up by his
interjections into the line-up being as brilliant as they were brief.
That a healthy Montana, whose injury-induced absence for much
of that and the previous season had allowed Young to illustrate his
MVP qualities in 1992, watched from the sidelines only accentuated the pressure.

Montana stood near George Seifert, Bill Walsh's former defensive coordinator who so ably filled his mentor's shoes after being
elevated to the top job. For him, too, the occasion represented an
opportunity to step out from Walsh's shadow, while quieting suggestions the championship won immediately after replacing the
revered head coach wasn't really his. Three years on from their
55–10 destruction of the Denver Broncos in Super Bowl XXIV,
San Francisco's team wasn't too different. Yet Seifert had put his
own stamp on it, jettisoning star defensive end Charles Haley to
the opponents who stood in the 49ers' way and shepherding in
a new era at quarterback, even if Young was ostensibly Walsh's
man.

Taking over at his own seven-yard line with just under seven
minutes left and San Francisco down 24–13, Young went to
work just as Montana had done so often before, spreading the
ball among his pass-catchers – most notably running back Ricky
Watters – to methodically move down the field. Within two minutes, the southpaw passer was shuffling left in the pocket and
sending a dart into Jerry Rice's chest for a five-yard touchdown.

Down just 24–20 after the ensuing point after touchdown
(P.A.T.) and, with their quarterback having authenticated his
MVP credentials, most of the 64,920 in attendance felt they were

bearing witness to another glorious chapter of the 49ers' recent tale, one that would sit comfortably alongside The Catch and their most recent two-word masterpiece, 'The Drive'.

Towards the end of the 1988 regular season, 49ers fans could have been forgiven for thinking their masterful head coach was losing his touch. San Francisco were nearly four years removed from their last championship and in danger, at 6-5 following a dreadful 9–3 loss to the Los Angeles Raiders, of missing the playoffs for the first time in six seasons. All the while, players wrestled with the walking contradiction that was their leading man.

On the one hand, Walsh was someone who showed genuine love for his charges in a manner that contrasts with some other all-time greats. 'The one thing I cherish most,' reveals Roger Craig, 'is he'd invite Stanford professors to talk to us. He was really concerned about our lives after football. Lots of us have been successful since football.' On the other, Walsh was as cut-throat as any team builder in history. 'Bill liked to get rid of players too early rather than too late, regardless of who you were,' admits Rice.

Proof nobody was safe came during the 1988 campaign. By that stage, Montana had begun to suffer with the injury problems that blighted the latter part of his career, enduring lower-back niggles resulting from a spinal-disc issue which forced him to miss a large chunk of the 1986 season. Such was Walsh's concern, he used second- and fourth-round picks to acquire Tampa Bay Buccaneers flop Young prior to the 1987 campaign, a decision the passer immediately justified by throwing 10 touchdowns to zero interceptions in sporadic appearances when the 49ers' eminent starter was unavailable. Rumours subsequently spread of Montana being on the trading block, growing legs when Walsh not only confirmed the pair would battle for the starting job in 1988 but spent much of the campaign rotating between the two.

Against that backdrop, San Francisco were falling short of the expectations Walsh had laid out at the beginning training camp.

'Men, we have one goal and one goal only – and that's to win a championship,' he told his players. 'Nothing less is acceptable. What we do day in and day out throughout this season will determine if we want it bad enough. It's on you.'

Heeding their coach's advice, Walsh's players took action. 'We were 6-5, and people were booing us,' says Craig. 'I remember we, as a team, took ownership and called a players-only meeting. Leaders like myself, Joe, Ronnie [Lott] and Jerry spoke. We needed to win four of the next five games.'

Combined with Walsh stripping away uncertainty at quarterback by confirming the job would henceforth stay with Montana, the 49ers redisplayed their championship quality. 'We kicked ass for those next four games,' adds Craig. 'We lost the last game, against the Rams, but we had already made the playoffs.'

'Coach Walsh was ruthless, and I think Joe felt a little bit of that,' says Rice. 'There was some competition and adversity but, once he decided on Joe as the guy, we rallied around that.'

Even though a players-only meeting can sometimes be seen as a red flag, in San Francisco it actually highlighted the culture fostered by Walsh – of the tone set from the moment players first donned the red and gold. 'It was about being a Super Bowl champion,' says Bill Romanowski. 'I was a rookie in 1988 and never forgot his first speech. You realise immediately the person talking is at the top.'

'Bill was that smart coach where he built the roster with the right group of guys and would let us take over,' adds Rice. 'If players misbehaved off the field, or weren't practising hard, he would leave it up to the players to address. It was like having our own coaches in the locker room.'

The come-to-Jesus moment also helped Walsh's most talented team fulfil their potential. Romanowski was the latest in a long line of outstanding players selected in the 1980s, alongside the likes of '86 draftee Haley and '85 class member Rice, who had yet to reach the pinnacle. 'I remember watching those guys wear their rings,' admits Rice. 'Ronnie and Joe would let me try them on, and it was like: "I want one of those."'

Following a playoff run in which the 49ers belied their underdog status to beat the Minnesota Vikings and then march into Chicago and do likewise versus the Bears in Ice Bowl-like conditions, a familiar face lay in wait: Walsh protégé Sam Wyche and his Cincinnati Bengals. 'We were winning big,' said Wyche. 'We had great players and a great coaching staff. But so did they.'

As for much of their run, San Francisco were every bit as good on defense as offense. They gave up just nine points against Minnesota, triple the number allowed versus the Bears in a game that flew in the face of those who claimed the 49ers were soft and only capable of winning in perfect conditions. 'Our offense defined a new style,' says Lott. 'That innovation and creativity meant the defense was somewhat overshadowed. But we had great players – Charles Haley and those guys. The defense meant Joe, and he would tell you this himself, had two or three more opportunities than most quarterbacks per game. In sports, it's fascinating how things complement each other so directly.'

Complementary football would be needed against a tough Bengals squad. Cincinnati's offense was powered by Wyche's brain and Boomer Esiason's arm but starred arguably the greatest left tackle in football history, Anthony Munoz. The defense, meanwhile, was overseen by exceptional coordinator Dick LeBeau.

So aware was Walsh of their various strengths that he returned to a familiar image in emphasising the tight contest that awaited: imitating one of his great heroes, Muhammad Ali, by dancing and shadow boxing to illustrate the ebbs and flows of a bout. 'He was saying that a boxer can win the first couple of rounds,' says Haley, 'and then get knocked out in the third or fourth.'

Come Super Bowl XXIII, it'd prove prophetic. What ensued was a dogfight in which the teams swapped a pair of field goals prior to Stanford Jennings scoring on a 93-yard kick return that San Francisco immediately answered with an 85-yard touchdown drive capped by Montana hitting Rice. Cincinnati went back ahead via Jim Breech's 40-yard field goal, leaving the 49ers 16–13 behind and, following an illegal-block penalty, on their eight-yard line with 3:10 remaining.

At a time when the stakes couldn't be any higher, San Francisco's players needed to follow the mantra laid out by their coach. 'He would always say: "The Super Bowl is just another game,"' adds Haley. 'And if we played the same way, we wouldn't have any problems.'

That sense of calm transferred to his quarterback. Upon reaching the huddle, Montana – surveying the crowd – spotted a famous face. 'Hey isn't that John Candy?' he asked his teammates before undertaking 'The Drive'. 'It was calming, and we knew if there was any time on the clock,' admits Rice, 'we would move the ball and win.'

What followed was a distillation of Montana and Walsh's greatness, the former hitting passes with the rhythm and tempo demanded by the latter one final time: Craig for eight on an angle route; John Frank for seven on a stick; Rice for seven on an out; Rice for 17 on a corner after two Craig runs gained five; Craig for 13 on an angle; Rice for 27 on a square-in; Craig for eight on an angle; and, finally, John Taylor – unusually lined up at tight end to capitalise on the attention afforded to Rice – for a 10-yard touchdown on a seam.

Amid the repetition of completions, however, there was one moment Wyche would never forget: 'I let Dick handle the defense without interference. But I knew Montana. If you played prevent, he'd pick you apart. Dick decided to go another way, and, to be fair, it worked. Lewis Billups dropped an interception a couple of plays before the touchdown. But that's the way it is. Somebody has to win, and somebody has to lose.'

And that is all history remembers. That 'The Drive' would never have earned its name had Billups held on in the end zone serves as a footnote to the bare facts: Montana completed nine passes for 97 yards and earned San Francisco a 20–16 victory. Fifty-one of those yards were caught by Rice, taking his total to a Super Bowl-record 215 with one touchdown that brought the game's MVP award. In the process, he helped Walsh enjoy the perfect symmetry to a tenure kickstarted by a Super Bowl victory over the Bengals and, unbeknown to the team, ending with another. 'We had no idea he was going to resign,' admits Rice. 'He broke down in tears. I had never thought about football without Bill Walsh.'

Winds of change didn't just pass through San Francisco, however; they engulfed the whole NFL.

By the end of the 1988 campaign, Pete Rozelle's legacy was secure. He had already been inducted into the Hall of Fame as part of the '85 class – an astonishing achievement for somebody still active – and overseen the NFL's incredible growth. Yet the mental exertions of the previous decade were beginning to show – cosmetically in the absence of the signature tan, receding black hairline and increasingly present crow's feet. It was time, with an unmatched legacy that earned him the reputation as the greatest commissioner in sporting history, to step away.

'Pete was a distant icon, if you will – the most successful commissioner in the history of sports in America, maybe the world,' remembers Bill Polian. 'He brought the NFL to its peak as the number-one sport in America and was the beacon of integrity. From his handling of Hall-of-Famers Paul Hornung and Alex Karras at the start, through the AFL and helping effect the merger, he was first-class. At his heart, he was a football guy. I went out to dinner with him one night, and all he wanted to talk about was his time as the Rams' GM! I remember saying to my wife: "He's a real guy, just like us."'

To Anne Marie Bratton, the daughter he raised as a single parent for most of her life, Rozelle was simply 'Dad'. 'It truly amazes me as a single father he never missed any event in my life,' she remembers. 'He came to every father–daughter dance, ballet recital, Christmas pageant and birthday while at the helm of one of the most difficult jobs, working for 28 owners.

'He took so much pride in how the NFL blossomed. Even after a lifetime in the NFL, he would chuckle to see his name as a newspaper crossword puzzle answer. His pride was in the relationships he made and all the people that got together to create something great. He loved team efforts, and that was what the NFL was all about in every way.'

Just as pro football's leading light and exceptional coach exited the stage, revolution also hit its most recognisable franchise. The aftermath of Dwight Clark's infamous grab had seen the Cowboys fall on unfamiliarly hard times. Tom Landry, the only coach the team had ever known, lost the sparkle that hallmarked his Hall-of-Fame career just as the franchise's principal owner was besieged by financial troubles. Such was the scale of money worries brought about by the collapse of his First Republic Bank Corporation engulfing Bum Bright – who had purchased the club from Clint Murchison Jr for $85 million in 1984 – that he sold the team.

New owner Jerry Jones' introduction to Dallas fans didn't go as planned. Theoretically, as a Cowboys supporter fulfilling his lifelong ambition of owning a professional football club, whose understanding of the game dated back to being a co-captain for Arkansas' 1964 National Championship-winning team, the oil magnate's arrival should have been welcomed, not least because his passion was exemplified by spending every penny he had – $140 million – to purchase the club.

Yet Jones' intention was to buck the existing trend of operating a franchise from the shadows. He intended to be front and centre, involved in every aspect of Cowboy business on and off the field. And thus began a purge that would become, in Jones' own words, 'the greatest PR disaster in the history of sport'. It started with Landry's firing, which was prefaced by the new owner being sighted in an Austin restaurant with University of Miami head coach Jimmy Johnson, a former Arkansas teammate of Jones'. It ended with Gil Brandt, the last of the old guard, who stayed on board for the 1989 draft that yielded Hall-of-Fame quarterback Troy Aikman with the first overall pick but departed soon after.

'When he fired me,' says Brandt, 'I told him: "You're in way over your head." And he was. He would admit that himself. It's like kickers – everybody thinks it's easy. We used to have open try-outs for them, tell them what to do and guys would come from all over and weren't able to kick extra points. Jerry's learning curve was similar.'

Five weeks into his first campaign, Jones had an even bigger problem. The Cowboys were winless and seemingly directionless, and whispers that he and the 'college coach' were out of their depth grew more audible by the day. Not that you'd have sensed any anxiety from Johnson. He entered the Cowboys' facility in Irvine, Texas following a 31–13 loss to the Green Bay Packers much the same way as always, wide smile adorning his sun-kissed chubby face, silver hair perfectly coiffed. 'Time for our jog,' Johnson said, motioning his assistants to the door.

They set off as they always did, Johnson leading administrative assistant Bruce Mays, offensive coordinator David Shula, defensive coordinator Dave Wannstedt, trainer Kevin O'Neill and offensive-line coach Tony Wise into the Dallas sunshine and through the 1.5-mile circuit around the Cowboys' unfinished practice facility. Shula, in typical fashion, raced ahead – only this time he missed something. Six blocks from the finish, Johnson shared an idea. 'You know,' he told his coaches, 'to fix this we're going to have to trade Herschel Walker.'

Wannstedt's response best summed up the suggestion: 'After that, do you think you could get the Texas A&M job and take us with you?'

But the ploy wasn't crazy in Johnson's mind, nor Jones' – the owner not only supported but played an integral role in ensuring it went ahead. With Walker threatening retirement upon learning of Dallas' plans, Jones agreed to pay a $1.25-million exit bonus, while persuading the team with whom he was negotiating to give the running back free accommodation and a Mercedes-Benz of his choosing.

The trade occurred with the entire NFL world in the area. Just as Walker was in the Cowboys' facility clearing out his locker, the league's owners were in a small town nearby – ironically named Grapevine – appointing former chief counsel Paul Tagliabue as Rozelle's replacement.

In 1989, Walker was the Dallas Cowboys. The code to enter the club's facility – 3412 – adjoined his jersey number, 34, and Roger Staubach's 12. Not only had the running back been the sole bright spot in Landry's last campaign – 1,514 rushing yards and 505 receiving – he also served as a reminder of the excellence so often delivered by the previous Cowboys regime that supporters increasingly longed for as the days wore on. His capture had been yet another example of the savvy demonstrated by Tex Schramm and Brandt, who selected Walker in the fifth round of the 1985 NFL Draft due to their belief that the USFL – where the 1982 Heisman winner spent the first two years of his pro career with the New Jersey Generals – would eventually fold. 'We're still proud of that one,' reveals Brandt.

They were proven correct. Walker arrived in 1986 and immediately filled the void left by now-departed former greats such as Staubach and Ed Jones. Imagine the reaction, then, when a new management team already accused of ripping the heart from the club offloaded Walker via a convoluted trade for, in the words of *Dallas Times Herald* writer Frank Luksa, 'a bag of beans and a cow to be named later'.

'Many of us were surprised and didn't see the vision behind getting rid of probably the most talented player on the team,' says former Cowboys fullback Daryl Johnston, a rookie at the time. The reaction couldn't have contrasted more starkly with Johnson's, the head coach bragging he had committed 'the Great Train Robbery'. 'We were already 0-5 with him,' remembers Johnson. 'We needed to start the rebuilding process. I had to figure out a way to parlay our best asset into a whole team.'

In the Vikings – a club submerged in desperation fostered by more close shaves than the local barber – Johnson found an ideal trade partner. The club's 28-year history featured 14 playoff berths and four Super Bowl appearances with zero championships, and their executives convinced themselves 1989 would reverse the trend if they could secure that one missing piece: a star running back. The agreement certainly catapulted one of the clubs involved towards the NFL's top table, only not who Minnesota anticipated.

At a basic level, Dallas gave up Walker, third-round picks in 1990 and '91, as well as a 10th in '90, while Minnesota sent line-backers Jesse Solomon and David Howard, defensive end Alex Stewart, running back Darrin Nelson, cornerback Issiac Holt and '90 first-, second- and sixth-rounders. Yet the devil was in the details, because those five Vikings had further conditional draft selections attached to them that Dallas would earn if they were cut.

Stewart immediately refused to report, so the Cowboys traded him to the San Diego Chargers for second- and sixth-round choices, while Johnson's intentions for the other four became clear by his refusal to play them, a situation he leveraged into eventually striking another deal with Minnesota that allowed the Cowboys to keep Solomon, Howard and Holt while lessening the draft impact on the Vikings.

'In canvassing all the teams,' says Brandt, 'the best offer was a first-round pick from Cleveland, until Mike Lynn came along. They thought Herschel could put them over the top. It's some-thing you see a lot. In doing something brilliant, you have to have luck. Dallas had a lot in finding that offer. It might have been a lot different if they only got Cleveland's first overall pick.'

The true genius of the deal lay in what those draft picks

became. 'The advantage we had having come from college is we had seen the players we were drafting,' adds Johnson. 'We had relationships with assistant coaches, so we knew who to call to get an honest assessment.'

Such knowledge was illustrated by the Cowboys' draft haul the year before. A class headlined by the selection of UCLA quarterback Aikman also featured future Pro Bowlers Johnston, defensive end Tony Tolbert and centre Mark Stepnoski. Yet even that group paled in comparison to what Walker was turned into, with All-Pros such as defensive tackle Russell Maryland, cornerback Kevin Smith and safety Darren Woodson joining alongside Hall-of-Fame running back Emmitt Smith. Not only was Smith an ideal replacement for Walker, he completed a terrifying trifecta alongside Aikman and wide receiver Michael Irvin known as 'the Triplets'. Each was selected in the opening round of successive drafts – Irvin with the 11th pick in 1988, Aikman with the first in '89 and Smith with the 17th in '90 – and became cornerstones of an offense that catapulted Dallas back to relevance. 'We are all the best of friends,' says Irvin.

Come 1991, the Cowboys were beginning to click, winning five straight games to reach the playoffs with an 11-5 record before overcoming Chicago in the wildcard round. Yet they came unstuck the following week, losing 38–6 to the Detroit Lions in a divisional-round game best remembered as being the only playoff victory enjoyed by one of the all-time-great running backs. Barry Sanders capped the triumph with a 47-yard touchdown displaying the lightness of foot, shiftiness and excellence that drove his career.

If anything, defeat showed a Cowboys team in the same position as the Vikings had been the previous year: they were a good squad lacking that extra X-factor to put them over the top. Unlike Minnesota, who reached the playoffs with Walker only to lose to San Francisco in the divisional round, their choice of final jigsaw piece was the correct one.

The object of Dallas' affection was Haley, the outstanding

defensive end who married relentlessness and savvy to lead the 49ers in sacks every year after his arrival. Yet the continuous quality of his play ran counter to the headaches headstrong Haley created off the field. Such was the volatile nature of his relationship with Seifert by the conclusion of 1991 that the 49ers were happy to take a 1993 third-round pick and '94 fourth for his services. 'They sent me to Dallas,' admits Haley, 'and it was like: "What have I done?"'

Haley was immediately won over by Jones, who met his troubled star at the airport, introduced himself and said: 'From now on, I'll have your back.'

'He was instrumental in calming me down,' adds Haley. As was the realisation of just how exceptional his teammates were: 'I'd never seen that much talent amassed at any level. It rejuvenated my career.'

With a reinvigorated Haley dominating offensive linemen to lead Dallas' fine young defense and the Triplets wreaking havoc behind one of the best offensive lines in history, the Cowboys had their ideal formula for success. Johnson adds: 'People always talk about those guys on offense – Aikman, Irvin and Smith – and don't realise we led the league in defense and had a great O-line.'

By the time they had beaten their NFC East-rival Philadelphia Eagles in the 1992 divisional round, having gone 13-3, Dallas were scenting a third Super Bowl and first under the new regime. To lift the Lombardi Trophy, though, they would have to topple a dynasty that had continued uninterrupted even amid the absence of its creator.

Although Walsh conceded regret at leaving behind 'the best team in football', he bowed out on top and only saw his legacy enhanced thereafter, not only via San Francisco winning another title in the first campaign following his departure but through the writing of a book that became every coach's bible: *Finding the Winning Edge*. In it, Walsh documented all the lessons learnt over the course of his career, producing the blueprint that subsequent head coaches – including those today – have attempted to emulate. Yet even the various people who successfully heeded the publication's teachings couldn't claim to understand the Walsh doctrine quite like Seifert, the loyal assistant who had spent eight years by his side acting as a sponge. Such was his intimate understanding of the system and players that San Francisco were unperturbed by Walsh's departure, capping a thoroughly dominant 1989 campaign in which they went 14-2 by delivering one of the most destructive Super Bowl performances of all-time against Denver, before reaching another NFC Championship Game appearance in '90. Even the following year, when the 49ers missed the play-offs and Montana was sidelined, Seifert's men won 10 games.

In 1992, with Young retaining the starting job as Montana continued his injury battle, normal service was resumed. The 49ers boasted an MVP quarterback, racked up 14 regular-season victories and reached the cusp of another Super Bowl courtesy of a divisional-round victory over the defending champion Washington Redskins – who had beaten the Buffalo Bills 37–24 in Super Bowl XXVI.

Being behind to Dallas at Candlestick Park hadn't dampened the sense of inevitability, either. With five minutes still remaining and Young having just hit Rice in the end zone, Seifert's outstanding defense needed only one stop to get their quarterback the ball back. Then he, like Montana 11 years previously, would drive the final dagger through Dallas hearts.

Or so everybody thought.

Unfortunately for San Francisco, the Cowboys hadn't read the script. Johnson's team were not about to play second fiddle again, for America's Team had aspirations of reclaiming their own place at the NFL's summit. 'Going into that 49ers game, we sat on the bus and talked about it being our time,' remembers Irvin. 'We were willing to do whatever it took to win. Period.

'On one play, we came into the huddle and Troy called "Bang

Eight", named because he was going to throw it and you were going to collide with the safety. Despite that, I had to catch the ball. Troy looked at me and said: "Go up big." And I said: "I'm willing to trade a concussion for the reception right now," because that was our mentality. Woo . . . I got hit! I span and went right down. I wanted to come back [to the huddle] and say: "Troy, why did you throw that?" but he looked at me, and before I could say anything, he said: "You said you were willing to trade a concussion for the reception, so I threw it in there."'

Leading 24–20 and taking over at their own 20-yard line with just over four minutes remaining, Irvin and Dallas' offense knew this was their chance to finally avenge the teams' last meeting at this stage of the postseason. Irvin adds: 'When I joined Dallas, all everyone was talking about was Dwight Clark and "The Catch", which turned the tide from the Cowboys to the 49ers. They dominated the 1980s, winning championships, beating the Cowboys. When I got there, we were wondering how that turn was going to be made.'

It'd be made, basically, by one play: a singular moment that was the antithesis of Montana's systematic march down the field. Offensive coordinator Norv Turner said to Johnson: 'How do you want to play this? Do you want to take time off the clock or throw the football?' The head coach's reply was succinct: 'I want to score!'

On first down, Turner returned to a call utilised often: '896 F Flat'. The pattern was primarily a two-man route in which Irvin ran the post and Alvin Harper a curl. On this occasion, Irvin took it upon himself to switch the combination because Aikman usually threw curl. 'I'm thinking: "Forget this, Alvin, I'm going to catch the curl,"' remembers Irvin. 'The game's on the line, and I'm the one more ready.'

When Aikman got under centre, he noticed San Francisco were showing blitz, meaning the middle of the field could be clear for Harper. 'I remember running the route, looking for the ball and seeing it go to Alvin,' adds Irvin. It proved wise. Harper caught a perfect ball in-stride and broke away for a huge gain. 'He was streaming up the field with my football,' laughs Irvin. 'I'd dreamed about that moment. I blew it.'

His 70-yard catch left Dallas on the San Francisco 10-yard line and, after Smith's four-yard run preceded an Aikman incompletion, the quarterback hit Kelvin Martin underneath, the wide receiver diving over for the game-sealing touchdown. 'I think that was our best game as a team,' says Johnston. 'The rivalry was the greatest of our time. All the games had so much at stake. For us to go to Candlestick, knock them off and assume the dominant role in the NFC was massive. They were huge games.'

'Everybody said we had a good team but were a little early,' adds Irvin, 'that we didn't have playoff experience and the 49ers would win again because we were on the road. But in Dallas, we were thinking: "We're going to take that mantle back." I had never been more confident in a game in my life. I knew we were going to win, even if nobody else in the world thought we would.'

The victory not only led to Dallas' first Super Bowl under Johnson – won via complete domination of the Bills – but also set the stage for two further NFC Championship meetings that rank alongside the likes of Muhammad Ali-Joe Frazier among the greatest trilogies in sporting history.

The early 1990s saw Dallas' playoff meetings with San Francisco become almost bigger than the NFL's showpiece, the appetiser to each year's Super Bowl actually representing the main course. 'Whoever won the Championship Game went on to win the Super Bowl,' remembers Rice.

Perhaps the best evidence of its importance is provided by the lopsided nature of the subsequent Big Dances, beginning with Dallas' first over the Bills. The game ending 52–17 emphasised that the Cowboys had done the hard part prior to arriving in Pasadena, and it was the same a year later. In the 1993 season's NFC Championship Game, Dallas backed up Johnson's pregame guarantee of victory on the back of another stunning display from Haley. 'We would watch each other every week,' added Young. 'Seeing the standards and where we were to each other. We knew what was coming.' Just as everybody else did in the ensuing Super Bowl, Dallas overcoming the Bills once again in XXVIII, this time 30–13.

By that stage, Buffalo were the butt of everybody's jokes. The loss continued an astonishing run of four successive Super Bowl defeats, two versus Dallas following their reverses against the New York Giants and Redskins. For all the jibes that ensued, the Bills provided no shortage of memorable moments which encapsulated their own excellence. In the 1993 wildcard round, Buffalo produced the biggest comeback in NFL history, overcoming an injury to Kelly and 32-point deficit to beat the Houston Oilers behind the arm of Frank Reich. For head coach Marv Levy, the 41–38 overtime success serves as a true reflection of his club. 'That game remains so prominent in my 47-year memory of coaching,' he says. 'It was a special group of individuals with great resilience.'

Another example came in the third Super Bowl defeat, when the Cowboys' Leon Lett looked bound for the end zone having picked off Reich and begun racing the other way. The score would, theoretically, have been immaterial, giving Dallas a 59–17 lead. But Bills wideout Don Beebe didn't see it that way, racing back more than 50 yards to knock the ball from Lett's hands before he crossed paydirt. 'Those moments show what our team was made of,' says Polian. 'Never-say-die attitude, no matter what. Give 100 per cent all the time.'

That the Bills' brilliance cannot be measured in championships is due to misfortune on multiple levels, from the moments that didn't go in their favour during Super Bowl XXV to the most significant: coinciding with some of the greatest squads ever assembled. For Levy, the overall feeling after a tenure overseeing the finest team never to win a championship is pride. 'It would have been very easy after being defeated in a Super Bowl to just lie there in the foetal position and whimper, but [we] fought back,' he said. 'It's a very difficult road you have to travel to get to the Super Bowl.'

Super Bowls XXVII and XXVIII weren't just illustrative of the chasm separating Dallas and Buffalo; they showed the gulf between the Cowboys, 49ers and everybody else. What made the rivalry so epic wasn't just the obvious political and cultural differences between two cities and teams but the similarities. Like the 49ers a decade earlier, the Cowboys were a team being shepherded into a new era by a bright, young owner and silver-haired coach who displayed great flair for motivation as well as X's and O's acumen.

While Johnson reversed fortunes on the field, so did Jones off it. From losing $1 million per month when he arrived to ascending towards the otherworldly stratosphere in which the Cowboys now exist, as the world's most lucrative and valuable sports franchise. In both achievements, Dallas had their enemies to thank. Just as the 49ers supplied the final brick in Johnson's team by trading Haley, Eddie DeBartolo Jr helped set Jones on his path by ignoring his instinct to hire Johnson as the 49ers' head coach after Walsh retired and allowing the Dallas supremo to spend two weeks at San Francisco's state-of-the-art facility as he formulated his blueprint.

'The rivalry was nasty,' adds Rice. 'I'm serious. There was a lot of respect, but we didn't like each other. There were fireworks. It was like the Boston Celtics against the Los Angeles Lakers, Michael Jordan against the Detroit Pistons. If we had the Cowboys, I couldn't sleep the night before. It was that type of game – exciting – with everyone glued to the television. I loved the rivalry, but there were a lot of sleepless nights.'

The story wasn't complete without a fightback from the 49ers, set in motion by a key departure in Dallas coinciding with a crucial arrival in San Francisco.

*

Outwardly, everything was rosy in the Cowboys' garden after the 1993 campaign. Dallas' revival mirrored that of its metropolis, rising from the ashes of the crippling debts that forced Bright to sell and going on to enjoy an economic boom. At the centre of it were the Cowboys, fronted by two visionaries who appeared in lockstep. 'I didn't see that their relationship was strained,' says Johnston. 'We were so focused on what we had to do as players that I didn't see them parting ways.'

But part Jones and Johnson did, the former giving the latter a $2-million payout as frustration over the owner's lack of final say in personnel became an insurmountable issue. 'It really caught me off-guard,' adds Johnston. 'It was very difficult. Nobody had ever won three Super Bowls in a row, and we stood on the cusp of that history. I really think if he had stayed, we would have won another. It was a bitter pill, because I knew what we were capable of with Jimmy. We were not the same team when he left, and we lost our edge a little. We missed a chance to make history.'

The timing couldn't have been worse, for it coincided with San Francisco welcoming a player who would prove every bit as important to the 49ers as Haley was to the Cowboys, and had rejected the silver and blue for red and gold.

'He was very different but also the missing piece,' adds Rice. 'We needed that shutdown corner to build around. When he first came in, he was flamboyant – but realised how hard we worked. He started doing the same and got better.'

He was known, simply, as 'Primetime'.

Prime's given name was Deion Sanders, and his star shone as brightly as the Cowboys'. He was the brashest in a new breed of athletes beginning to make their mark in the NFL, dominant in sporting and cultural realms. The first true shutdown cornerback, and still widely considered the greatest player in his position's history, he also became one of the few men in the modern era to play professional football and Major League Baseball at the same time. On one day – 11 October 1992 – he attempted to play both,

311

flying from the Atlanta Falcons' Week 6 contest with the Miami Dolphins at Joe Robbie Stadium to the Braves' postseason trip to the Pittsburgh Pirates, where being on the bench robbed him of a unique moment in history.

By 1994, Sanders was solely focused on football and the object of affection for the NFL's best teams. It was San Francisco's desperation that won the day. In an elevator after their second loss to Dallas, DeBartolo told his personnel team: 'This will not happen again.' He was willing to spend whatever it took, adding linebacker Ken Norton Jr from the Cowboys and beating their bitter rivals to the signing of Sanders on a one-year $1.2-million contract.

Not only did Sanders, individually, enjoy the best campaign of his career, recording six interceptions that he returned for then-NFL records of 303 yards and three touchdowns, the cornerback reversed the course of a bitter rivalry. Cowboys and 49ers contests had become as infamous for pregame altercations as the thrilling action on the field, but it was San Francisco who came out on top in 1994. They triumphed 21–14 in the regular season and followed that up with a 38–28 NFC Championship Game victory, the signature play coming in the fourth quarter when Sanders stopped a potential touchdown from Aikman to Irvin that many still feel should have been called for pass interference. 'If they had called that like they should have, we would have won,' says Irvin. 'I don't feel like he interfered. I know he did.'

'It was great execution,' argued Sanders. 'A defensive play, man. That's really what it was.'

The pair would agree in the offseason that followed San Francisco's 49–26 Super Bowl XXIX victory over the Chargers, sharing a three-hour phone call that Sanders revealed was instrumental in his decision to switch San Francisco for Dallas. As well as the five-year $30-million deal offered by Jones to prise him from the 49ers, of course. 'We knew it was us or the 49ers,' said Aikman. 'A lot of the moves we made were not about anyone else but beating the 49ers.'

Just as he had been for San Francisco, Sanders proved to be the last piece for Barry Switzer's Cowboys, the head coach following in the footsteps of Johnson by winning a National Championship (with Oklahoma) and Super Bowl, sealed via a 27–17 win over the Pittsburgh Steelers in XXX and without having to tackle a fading 49ers squad in the postseason. 'You have to give Barry credit,' adds Johnston. 'That was a difficult position for him to be in, because he would not get credit if things went well and, if they never, he would get all the blame. Barry won the Super Bowl and didn't get the credit.'

In the process, the game cemented the Cowboys' dynastic status and the Hall-of-Fame legacies of their stars, not least the Triplets. All three are in Canton, with Smith enjoying the honour of being the league's all-time rushing leader with 18,355 yards. 'In the NFL,' says Irvin, 'it's: "Who are the next Triplets?" – the top wide receiver, running back and quarterback. We always tell people that it's great to have the top players, but the Triplets are not just cemented by the position, but by those three players at those positions bringing you three rings. So, it's "triplets" all the way around. No one else has been able to do that.'

Despite Dallas matching San Francisco's Super Bowl tally, there remains the question of how many more titles could have been won had Johnson stayed. 'He was just an incredible motivator,' adds Irvin. 'It's no coincidence Bill Belichick spends a week with him every year, stealing and gleaning and learning more about how to build and run a team. He and Belichick are great friends, and Belichick reminds me a lot of Coach Johnson.'

Johnson's run in Dallas was as glorious as it was brief and impactful enough that the Cowboys are considered the team of the 1990s, just as the 49ers are of the 1980s. 'I played with the best team in the 1980s and best in the 1990s,' says Haley.

Just as pertinent as which team dominated each decade was the feud which brought out their best, between clubs intrinsically linked, by iconic owners, coaches, players, plays and games.

Together, they turned the NFL, briefly, into a two-team league in which the Cowboys and 49ers ascended to heights of excellence never seen before or since. Johnson adds: 'We hit the ultimate level. If you look at the NFL, that run in Dallas – in terms of being the team of the '90s – is a huge part of the league's history.'

And it was kickstarted one thrilling afternoon by the San Francisco Bay, when Dallas marched into Candlestick Park and emerged triumphant. That same day, Johnson stood aloft in the victorious locker room and screamed four iconic words that served as a mantra for everything which followed: 'How 'bout them Cowboys?'

17

Broncos Buck the Trend

Super Bowl XXXII

DENVER BRONCOS 31
GREEN BAY PACKERS 24

---

25 January 1998

Qualcomm Stadium, San Diego

The wear and tear of every hit from a 15-year career was visible as the 37-year-old John Elway bent in front of his flock. The play-call, 'Point slice', was only just audible amid the noise generated by a crowd unmistakeably favouring the Green Bay Packers at a zealous Qualcomm Stadium. Denver spread out into a four-wide-receiver set, their fabled passer in the shotgun, flanked by the young running back fashioning a similarly illustrious reputation among the Broncos' patient faithful: Terrell Davis.

This particular play was another pre-planned part of vibrant head coach Mike Shanahan's masterful strategy. The offensive-minded leading man spotted some significant tells on Green Bay's defensive film that left him and Elway positively giddy as they finalised their plot the previous evening. Most of the assessments, including one which allowed Elway to predict do-it-all safety LeRoy Butler's responsibilities, proved ingenious. Denver, despite not attempting a second-quarter rush due to Davis briefly suffering a migraine, racked up 179 yards on the ground. Yet the most crucial run wouldn't come from 25-year-old phenom Davis, but the quarterback 12 years his senior. Nor would it owe anything to Shanahan's intellect. It resulted from one of the NFL's icons operating on instinct, a football player making the ultimate got-to-have-it football play.

Although Elway shared his coach's enthusiasm for most of the carefully constructed blueprint, he wasn't sold on all of it. 'Point slice', designed specifically for the red zone based on Shanahan's conviction Green Bay would counter it with a specific defense, wasn't his favourite. Elway approached Shanahan and offensive coordinator Gary Kubiak during the week and said: 'I really don't like that play.' But Shanahan was emphatic: 'In that location on the field, it's 100 per cent that the play will be wide open.'

And so, with two pass-catchers either side of him on third-and-six, Elway waited for centre Tom Nalen's snap. Immediately, he knew there was a problem. 'When I got to the line of scrimmage,' said Elway, 'they weren't in the expected defense. I was going to have to try to make something happen.'

Having surveyed the field to find those in Denver blue blanketed by Packer white, Elway darted into the gap between two defenders, shifted right and began making his way downfield. With Butler, Mike Prior and Brian Williams converging towards the ball, Elway – eyes bulging – glanced at the first-down marker, lowered his head and took off, contact sending him spinning through the air in a manner that earned the play its eventual name: 'the Helicopter Run'.

'John Elway, grizzled 37-year-old quarterback', for a few remarkable seconds, turned back into 'John Elway, fresh-faced 22-year-old thoroughbred'.

*

'Elway was the best player in the draft the year he came out,' says former Oakland Raiders executive Ron Wolf. 'He was as gifted an athlete and performer at his position as I have ever seen. He is certainly, in my scouting time, in the top 10 of all evaluations.'

In 1983, the ace up a once-in-a-generation prospect's sleeve wasn't just his football prowess. Although the blond-haired, blue-eyed boy embodied the archetypal California surfer dude, Elway's true skill lay in his ability to play American's original and new pastimes. When leaving Stanford as a 22-year-old, Elway boasted similarly prodigious talent in baseball and was sought after by the New York Yankees. Their interest would allow Elway to flip the script on the entire history of the NFL Draft.

Unwilling to merely show gratitude for being drafted into the league with the Baltimore Colts – who held the first overall pick – Elway used his leverage. The quarterback made it clear he had no interest in representing Baltimore, publicly citing a desire to play on the West Coast while privately acknowledging his issues with Colts owner Robert Irsay and disciplinarian head coach Frank Kush. It set the stage for the most dramatic selection weekend ever, with Irsay, general manager Ernie Accorsi and Kush seemingly acting independently of one another in negotiating with every team under the shield. The upshot was Baltimore selecting Elway, the player reaffirming his stance and, eventually, Irsay brokering a dreadful deal with the Broncos without consulting Accorsi, who resigned when the terms were announced. In return for a transcendent talent, Denver gave up fourth-overall-pick Chris Hinton, a 1984 first-round selection and backup quarterback Mark Herrmann.

It wasn't even the best offer on the table. 'We offered three starters and a future pick for next year,' says then-Dallas Cowboys personnel man Gil Brandt. 'It was a better offer. We were dealing with Kush instead of Mr Irsay. I think Tex [Schramm] wanted to fire me because I didn't get Elway.'

The Elways' misgivings about those at Baltimore's helm would be proven over the ensuing years, Kush's hot-tempered style failing to translate to pro football and Irsay shipping the club to Indianapolis. Even so, opinion was split on Elway holding the club to ransom given it flew in the face of the spirit of the draft. 'He should play baseball,' said Terry Bradshaw at the time. 'In my opinion, he is not the kind of guy you win championships with.'

Despite Elway's ensuing success, it appeared Bradshaw was being proven right for much of an exceptional career with one missing piece. Theoretically, Elway was an unqualified success who established himself as one of the greatest quarterbacks not just of his era but all-time. He brought rare athleticism to the position, blending exceptional arm talent with speed and grace as a runner, and delivered his share of iconic interventions, including a memorable 98-yard march down the field at the conclusion of the 1986 AFC Championship Game. Yet the key disclaimer to something known, alongside Joe Montana's final act of Super Bowl XXIII, as 'The Drive' is what it preceded: the second of three defeats in the Big Dance over the first seven seasons of Elway's career. After the third, in which he played poorly against Steve Young's San Francisco 49ers, Elway privately confided in a member of Denver's staff: 'The fans will never, ever, forgive me for this.'

Sympathy for Denver supporters was in short supply among those in Baltimore and Indianapolis. While the former were still contemplating being jilted by their team, the latter bore the scars of being jilted by Elway. Not only did the Colts' new supporters endure the dreadful team brought to town, they did so amid the shadow of the entire first round of a draft in which the Colts held all the aces and somehow lost their chips.

The 1983 class' mystique extends beyond Elway to the five other quarterbacks selected in the only first round to feature six, two of whom also have busts in Canton. They were chosen with picks seven (Todd Blackledge by the Kansas City Chiefs), 14 (Jim Kelly by the Buffalo Bills), 15 (Tony Eason by the New England

Patriots), 24 (Ken O'Brien by the New York Jets) and 27 (Dan Marino by the Miami Dolphins).

Of that quintet, Blackledge represented the other meaning of bust, having ended his career with just 5,286 passing yards, while Eason's eight-year run peaked during a 1985 campaign in which he was destroyed by the Chicago Bears in Super Bowl XX. O'Brien ended in the middle of the pack, his 11 years yielding solid output highlighted by famously outduelling Marino in a 51–45 thriller during the 1986 campaign – the 884 passing yards delivered by both set an NFL record that stood for more than 25 yards.

Although O'Brien edged that battle, he couldn't top his draft rival in his wider career arc. Marino, remarkably, was every bit as good as Elway, boasting an effortless natural delivery that saw the ball explode from his hand with a marriage of speed and velocity unmatched before or since. So talented was Marino, fuelled by a desperation to disprove his draft position, the great Don Shula ripped up the formula that had brought Miami two Super Bowls during the 1970s and an appearance in the 1981 campaign's edition.

'Things completely changed when we got Dan,' he said. 'We went the other way. If I had him hand the ball off, every defensive coach in the league would have patted me on the back. I coached Bob Griese and Johnny Unitas, but Marino was the best pure passer I coached. He is maybe the best to ever play in the league. He had that uncanny accuracy, and a great, fast delivery. He could fit that ball into tight places.'

Having led Miami on a playoff run as a rookie after finally being given the starting reins in Week 6, Marino began a remarkable tear in 1984. Tossing to a pair of receivers known as 'the Marks Brothers' – Mark Clayton and Mark Duper – and supported by a fine offensive line, the second-year passer unleashed an astonishing aerial assault. Marino broke almost every single-season passing record, from completions (362) and yards (5,084) to touchdown tosses (48). He was unsurprisingly voted league MVP.

But the year ended in disappointment, Marino on the end of a hammering in Super Bowl XIX as Montana and the 49ers collected their second title. Afterwards, Pepsi ran an advert with the two quarterbacks in which Montana buys Marino a drink and the Dolphins passer says: 'It's the least you can do,' before signing off: 'Joe, next time I'm buying.' The underlying message was clear but, unfortunately for Marino, 'next time' didn't come. The signal-caller ended his career leading the NFL in passing yards (61,361) and touchdowns (420), yet never returned to the ultimate game.

His story was eerily similar to that of the other quarterbacks enshrined in the Hall of Fame from that 1983 opening round: Elway and Kelly. The three were intrinsically linked: by draft year, being the faces of AFC franchises and their failure to win the big one. Each enjoyed outstanding coaching, Kelly and Marino under Hall-of-Famers Marv Levy and Shula respectively and Elway with Dan Reeves, who boasts more than 200 NFL wins. Yet they seemed engulfed by a curse hovering over the whole first-round group, stretching across nine Super Bowls and peaking with Kelly losing four on the spin in Buffalo. By the mid-1990s, with a new wave of stars headed by the Dallas Cowboys' Troy Aikman and Packers' Brett Favre making their marks, it appeared the greatest quarterback draft class in NFL history would for ever be defined by the rings missing from their fingers.

Until, from nowhere, the emergence of an unlikely star running back and innovative coach provided Elway with one final shot.

The feeling of a new dawn was palpable around Denver's facility in 1997. Although Pat Bowlen (the club's principal owner since 1984), Elway and their 'Broncos' moniker remained in place, the club were rebranding, aiming to move beyond the chequered history of zero championships in 37 years and four unsuccessful brushes with the Super Bowl.

The alterations were mainly cosmetic, the Broncos' logo re-designed and signature orange uniforms replaced by a navy-blue variety that Elway showed his distaste for during the unveil. Although minor, the changes delivered a clear message: Denver were moving forward, ready to put one of the worst defeats in franchise history – a 30–27 home divisional-round loss to the Jacksonville Jaguars, a second-year expansion team – in the rear-view mirror.

Although Denver's resurgence would coincide with the alterations, the seeds were planted two years previously when a familiar face walked back through the door at Mile High Stadium. Shanahan's return ended a prolonged courtship. He turned down the opportunity in 1992 due to discomfort with replacing Reeves, who – believing a coup was being staged with Elway's blessing – had fired him as offensive coordinator. Though Shanahan rejecting the role didn't work out for Denver imme-diately – second-choice Wade Phillips went 9-7 then 7-9 in two campaigns and lost his only playoff game – it proved beneficial. He headed back to the Broncos as a shrewder operator, shaped by the experiences of a rocky career and ready for a second crack as a leading man.

His first came with the Los Angeles Raiders, Shanahan having caught Al Davis' eye by rising through the college ranks and then aiding Elway's early development. But the young coach melded with Davis about as well as the Raiders supremo did with the league office and lasted just two campaigns. From there, he returned to Denver for a second stint as OC before enjoying a highly productive three-year run as Young's string-puller with the 49ers.

At the Broncos, Shanahan amalgamated the best qualities of mentors such as Oklahoma's Barry Switzer, George Seifert and even Davis to become more well-rounded. He immediately immersed himself into every area, bringing a keen scouting eye as well as the anticipated X's and O's expertise. Yet the defining characteristic of his early tenure was that little slice of luck seemingly enjoyed by all successful team builders.

It's fair to assume that, when utilising 1995's 196th overall pick on Georgia running back Terrell Davis, Shanahan didn't think he was selecting a future Hall of Famer. Davis' college career, at Long Beach State and with the Bulldogs, was unspectacular. In Athens, the staff's failure to understand a long-running migraine issue that would rear its head in his defining game earned Davis a reputation of being soft and sullied his relationship with Ray Goff. The head coach was far from complimentary about his former charge, but Davis found cheerleaders in Broncos running backs coach Bobby Turner and offensive coordinator Kubiak. The person who impacted Davis' ability to make the team most was himself, in the unlikeliest of settings. Midway through the club's second preseason game – taking place in Tokyo, Japan – Davis still hadn't seen the field and became so disillusioned that he ate a hot dog. Then, suddenly, special-teams coach Richard Smith shouted: 'Hey, 30, we're putting you in.'

It heralded the hit heard from the Japanese Alps to the Rocky Mountains.

With San Francisco's Tyronne Drakeford bringing the ball out towards the 20-yard line, an orange blur exploded across the field and collided with the returner like a homing missile perfectly striking its target. It's unlikely Elway even knew the sixth man in Denver's running back battle, but he made it his business afterwards. The quarterback approached Davis on the sideline and delivered a high-five that heralded the start of a devastating partnership.

On the headset, Shanahan called down to Turner: 'Did you see that? I want him in the game at running back.' Davis, having just thrown up following his fast-food binge, barely knew the playbook but heeded Turner's advice to 'run his tail off'. 'I had a horrible week of practice and wanted to go home,' says Davis. 'I was a sixth-round pick, getting no chances, and I'd tried to go home – but the lady at the hotel desk didn't understand me.'

From that moment, he never looked back. 'To this day,' said Kubiak, 'every year on opening weekend of preseason I show the rookies that hit. I say: "You want to make the team? Don't think you're getting enough reps? Go do this on a kickoff."'

Davis not only won the Broncos starting job but quickly established himself as one of the league's finest runners. Prospering behind Shanahan's zone-blocking system, he boasted outstanding vision and an innate ability to shake free of would-be tacklers. 'We had seen the zone scheme with Jim Kelly and the K-Gun,' says former Jacksonville Jaguars defensive end Jeff Lageman. 'But the way they blocked it was revolutionary. They would set up the run one way and have the lineman cut defensive lineman to the ground in the other direction. And then you add a back like Davis, who could stretch the play, plant his foot and hit the hole so quickly – it was tough to stop.'

In the bigger picture, Davis relieved pressure on a quarterback used to shouldering hopes of a city entirely on his own and teamed up with superstar tight end Shannon Sharpe to complete Denver's diverse offensive weaponry. He racked up more than 1,000 yards as the Broncos fielded a top-10 offense and went 8-8 in his rookie season, but cranked things up a notch alongside the rest of the team in 1996. Davis accrued more than 1,500 yards on the ground, and Sharpe easily topped all tight ends with 1,062 through the air as the Broncos offense rose to fourth in football, leading the charge for a team that secured the AFC's number-one seed by finishing 13-3 – only to run into the upstart Jaguars in a loss described by Elway as 'the most devastating of my career'. 'The expectation was that they were going to win the Super Bowl,' remembers Lageman. 'You could see when the tide started to turn on the field . . . the anxiety and shock on their faces.' It was a continuation of the script that had haunted Denver and the quarterback who was a microcosm of his team.

Yet Shanahan was not about to let the trend continue. Having noticed Davis still ran the ball well against Jacksonville – 14 times for 91 yards and a touchdown – he made a vow to his staff: 'We'll return to the playoffs next year, and T.D. will run at least 25 times per game.'

That they fulfilled the coach's promise was thanks to another exceptional season by Davis, whose year-by-year improvement was shown in a league-best 1,750 rushing yards. In the postseason, following Denver's 12-4 record, he went even further, delivering carries-yards-touchdowns stat-lines of 31-184-2, 25-101-2 and 26-139-1 as the Broncos avenged the previous year by hammering Jacksonville 42–17 before edging out the Chiefs and Pittsburgh Steelers.

Denver reaching Super Bowl XXXII wasn't just driven by Davis, though. Shanahan furnished the roster with smart, yearly additions. Ahead of the 1996 campaign, he recruited two-time Super Bowl-winning San Francisco 49ers linebacker Bill Romanowski. 'They needed a leader on defense, and I provided that,' he reveals. 'I just tried to make people accountable and set the tone in practice. That's what made us special.'

Romanowski wasn't the final piece. The following offseason, with the wounds of that Jacksonville loss still raw, Denver added Kanas City defensive end Neil Smith, while fullback Howard Griffith joined from the recently formed Carolina Panthers to bolster an already-potent offense as a blocker and pass-catching threat. Their additions proved crucial, helping Denver through the playoffs as a wildcard team and setting up the Broncos' date with destiny against Green Bay. 'We had a really great blend,' adds Romanowski. 'Guys who played hard for one another. There was a definite sense that it'd be great to win for John, but he almost thought about it as being great for all of us. It was infectious.'

That Denver were able to assemble those crucial recruits was thanks to a system that changed the face of the NFL and was synonymous with Reggie White, the defensive star of their Super Bowl opponents.

*

When viewed with the benefit of hindsight, there's an inescapable sense that free agency and a salary cap were inevitable in the NFL – but something first mooted during the opening meeting at Ralph Hay's showroom in 1920 wouldn't come to pass, remarkably, until 73 years later. By then, much blood had been drawn across many battles between league and NFL Players' Association (NFLPA).

Even as recently as the late 1980s, many chief power brokers were unwavering in their fight against unrestricted free agency, believing it represented a death knell to the game. During one particularly fraught exchange amid the most damaging players' strike in 1987, Dallas Cowboys executive Tex Schramm burst out: 'Don't you see it? You are the cattle and we're the ranchers!' to NFLPA head Gene Upshaw.

A quote that seems scarcely believable in the modern age was most fitting for its time. Schramm echoed the sentiments of multiple owners and executives – most significantly himself and Tampa Bay Buccaneers owner Hugh Culverhouse – who operated for decades under multiple structures that weighted the power balance heavily in favour of the teams. The original reserve clause was most restrictive of all, affording clubs complete autonomy over their players' rights by having it written into contracts that they could be resigned to one-year deals at the end of each season under the same terms. Simply put, there were only two ways out of bad situations: retire or be traded.

It wasn't until 1947 that players enjoyed a modicum of freedom. Under the one-year option rule, teams could only utilise the reserve clause once per player. It was, in many ways, similar to the eventual system. But, in 1962, when wide receiver R.C. Owens exercised his rights and left San Francisco for the Colts, 49ers managing owner Vic Morabito's complaints prompted further change.

Pete Rozelle instituted the 'Rozelle Rule', giving the commissioner complete discretion to award what he deemed fair compensation – be it players or draft picks – to teams losing a free agent. In essence, signing a player would carry the risk of giving up unforeseen returns to his original club, which understandably cooled the market.

As the 1970s progressed, the mood among players was becoming increasingly militant. The NFL's merger with the American Football League had dented salaries following the inflated payments made during the organisations' war, and new wealth wasn't filtering to those generating it. Combined with the ongoing frustration surrounding the Rozelle Rule, the workforce took part in its most significant action to date when holding out from the start of the 1974 training camp.

Yet the union's mistake was being too ambitious and broad in scope, and their 57-point list of demands – featuring reasonable goals such as abolishing the Rozelle Rule alongside ambitious suggestions like scrapping the NFL Draft – meant inevitable failure. After two months, players returned to work having achieved little.

What the NFLPA came to realise is that their biggest victories would be struck in court. In 1976, *Mackey v. NFL* – brought by the union's leader, Hall-of-Fame former tight end John Mackey – saw the Rozelle Rule overturned. But the players would eventually settle for something frustratingly similar in the 1977 Collective Bargaining Agreement.

The Rozelle Rule became the 'Right of First Refusal and Compensation', in which existing teams had the ability to match the best offer received by a free agent. If they didn't, that club would still be eligible for compensation, which created the same issues as the original regulation, until 1982 when the next CBA outlined specific salary-to-draft-pick recompense. That agreement was signed on the back of a particularly ruinous strike in which there were no winners: the NFL was forced to play an abridged schedule and lost an estimated $450 million, while players revolted against their own union. It did, however, lead to the appointment of their next leader in Upshaw.

Together with Paul Tagliabue, Upshaw would eventually achieve what Schramm famously claimed wasn't possible. But it wasn't without significant wounds being inflicted. In 1987, with the latest CBA negotiations underway, the players hit the picket line again one week into the campaign. On this occasion, the league called their bluff, cancelling the ensuing week and subsequently utilising replacement players.

By persuading networks to broadcast games that still drew crowds, if admittedly smaller, the NFL's hardliners felt they'd achieved a great victory. Especially as several stars crossed the picket line, including the Cowboys' Danny White, Ed 'Too Tall' Jones, Tony Dorsett and Randy White, 49ers' Joe Montana, Seattle Seahawks' Steve Largent and New York Giants' Lawrence Taylor.

Even though the Washington Redskins' replacement players – some of whom would form a key part of that year's Super Bowl-winning squad – provided a great NFL moment when famously beating Schramm's Cowboys team featuring the aforementioned quartet, measured observers considered it harmful. 'If you're going to have a labour disruption every five years, well, "labour disruption" is an industry term,' says Bill Polian. 'When you translate that to the fan, that means that his favourite player is tarnished; his team is disrupted. We're in business to entertain so, if you erode that bond between fans and players, it becomes a disruption.'

Furthermore, the players' return wasn't an end point. When the Court of Appeals rejected another suit aiming to dismantle the existing player-movement rules because restrictions were contained within CBAs, the union disclaimed interest in representing NFL players in collective bargaining and reformed as a professional operation. This step afforded players the opportunity to begin pursuing legal action in various individual antitrust cases. The battle, in other words, still very much raged.

Around that same time, Rozelle brought down the curtain on his illustrious tenure. Tellingly, he did so just two months after attempting to broker a deal between the two sides on an issue in which he hadn't been heavily involved over the years. The NFL's negotiating had been left to its Management Council, a counterpart to the NFLPA, led by Jack Donlan. Rozelle spent much of his final decade privately frustrated at the inability to agree on something he considered an inevitability.

The same wouldn't be true of Tagliabue. Upon his appointment, Rozelle's successor was sought out by Al Davis, who expressed his dissatisfaction at Donlan and the Management Committee's hard-line tactics. 'You're dealing with an educated guy who wants to get something done,' he said of his former Raiders star Upshaw. 'All of you have built up a stereotype. You've painted them as militants, when all they want is equal rights.'

Tagliabue made clear his intentions to lead negotiations and fostered a sound relationship with Upshaw. Crucial to formulating an agreement was the union's structural alteration. On 9 September 1992, Jets running back Freeman McNeil earned a landmark ruling as the lead plaintiff among several players who challenged the league's latest system.

'Plan B' free agency, implemented in the hope it would circumvent antitrust laws, allowed every team protection rights over 37 of their 47 players, which sparked some movement among those 10 unprotected, but still fell considerably short of the players' ambitions. Across three years, Bears linebacker Wilber Marshall was the only restricted player to move teams. In Minneapolis, Judge David Doty determined Plan B in breach of antitrust law by being more restrictive than necessary to achieve competitive balance.

With Upshaw and Tagliabue continuing discussions and further lawsuits – most notably that of superstar Philadelphia Eagles defensive end White – pending, Doty pulled the heavy hitters from each side around his table in December. He showed both a sealed envelope and warned it contained a solution neither side would enjoy.

Further incentivised to end the impasse, the two parties

accelerated discussions and finally, in spring 1993, the first CBA since 1982 was signed. In the seven-year pact, the league agreed to offer unrestricted free agency to all players with five years' experience (eventually reduced to four), in return for a salary cap and the introduction of franchise tags.* Furthermore, players won something long fought for: a percentage of the league's overall gross revenues, which totalled around 60 per cent. 'It gave everybody a chance to win and spread the talent,' says former executive Polian. 'Paul would always say that a rising tide will lift all boats.'

Tagliabue played a significant role in securing peace. After five strikes in 19 years between 1968 and 1987, there wouldn't be another until 2011. 'Getting to free agency was a four-year slog,' adds Polian. 'It was brutal. I was by Paul's side every step of the way, and there were many times that everybody was ready to throw in the towel, but Paul just wouldn't give up.'

Unfortunately for Tagliabue, it was far from the only issue that afflicted his precocious commissionership.

The headaches created for Tagliabue as his tenure hit its first half-decade could best be summed up by two owners who represented the NFL's past and future.

Art Modell and Jerry Jones famously battled in 1992, when the former – in his longstanding role as chairman of the league's Broadcasting Committee – agreed a deal with TV networks in which the NFL would offer a $230-million rebate to CBS in return for a two-year contract extension. Modell, supported by Tagliabue, understood the broadcaster's complaints of losing money amid a gloomy economic landscape and felt the concession necessary. But Jones strongly disagreed and helped ensure the plan was voted down, which prompted Modell's resignation. 'We think there will be an economic uptick down the road,' Jones said at the owners' meeting. 'It's way too early to make a decision on the contract. The NFL holds up well in recession times.'

The move further accelerated Jones' rise in importance, a fact

epitomised by Tagliabue including Dallas' supremo in TV negotiations the following year. Their union was an unbridled success
as a new player in the market, Fox Sports, offered $1.58 billion
across four years, which totalled $395 million per team compared
to CBS's best offer of $290 million, to attain the NFC rights,
ending the latter's 36-year stronghold on the package. Combined
with renewals from ABC, ESPN, NBC and TNT, NFL television
revenues rose above $1 billion annually for the first time, with
$4.39 billion spread across four seasons.

But Tagliabue's admiration for Jones' wheeling and dealing
would turn to frustration. Fox owner Rupert Murdoch's gamble
that he could, essentially, build his entire sports network on the
back of an NFL contract illustrated the scale of its appeal, and
Jones was ready to capitalise on another gap in the market. He
spotted his latest opportunity in Cowboys Stadium. Jones was
one of just three owners who owned his club's arena outright and
was therefore able to negotiate independent stadium-sponsorship
deals with Nike, Dr Pepper, Pepsi and American Express. The
contract signed with Pepsi – in which the company bought the
'pouring rights' at Cowboys Stadium – was a 10-year $40-million
pact.

His moves struck at the heart of the league's revenue-sharing
model, offering the Cowboys an opportunity to generate cash
other clubs couldn't and threatening to supersede national deals
signed with competitors such as Coca-Cola and Adidas. Furthermore, with the new salary cap providing teams the chance to
pro-rate signing bonuses over the length of contracts, such additional revenue presented Dallas an advantage when it came to
luring stars such as Deion Sanders, whose seven-year $35-million
Cowboys pact included a $13-million bonus. Tagliabue declared
Jones' actions 'short-sighted and self-serving'.

It paved the way for a year-long battle through the courts in
which NFL Properties filed a $300-million suit against the Cow-
boys, and Jones responded with a $750-million counter-suit,

asking the court to dismantle the 'unlawful cartel' used by the NFL to market trademarks and logos of league clubs. Eventually, the sides settled. Jones was allowed to continue profiting from existing and new contracts at Cowboys Stadium, and the league's other revenue-sharing principles remained intact.

The disagreement illustrated the unique challenges facing a modern-era commissioner. Unlike his predecessors, whose role was to ensure the organisation's very survival, Tagliabue was at the controls of a behemoth basically holding a license to print money. But that brought its own issues, both in managing the egos of multi-millionaires and billionaires used to getting their own way and the many outside forces determined to secure a slice of the pie.

Nowhere did those factors intersect more dramatically than with relocation. The NFL, as had been proven throughout the previous decade, didn't enjoy the wide-ranging antitrust exemption of Major League Baseball that could be utilised to block franchise moves. With multiple cities clamouring to be part of the league's exclusive club and team owners aiming to outdo one another with new stadiums, it would present the greatest challenge of Tagliabue's tenure.

Setting the stage for the strife that would follow was the NFL's surprise decision, in 1993, to award expansion franchises to Charlotte and Jacksonville at the expense of strong bids from former NFL heartlands in St. Louis and Baltimore. Nowhere was the ire felt more than Baltimore, whose fanbase's ferventness was illustrated by the Colts' former marching band gathering at Memorial Stadium each Sunday Indianapolis had a home game.

The spurned cities, therefore, turned their attentions to existing teams. In January 1995, Georgia Frontiere – Carroll Rosenbloom's widow – announced the Los Angeles Rams would move to St. Louis. Her decision might not have met the criteria, established in 1984, of being necessary to ensure survival, but it didn't matter. After being voted down 23–1, the switch was eventually approved when the Rams threatened to follow Davis' lead from a decade earlier and pursue legal action.

Davis, meanwhile, was engaging in his own negotiations with cities, consummating a return to Oakland just months after the Rams' intentions were announced. In a statement that would prove astonishingly ironic, Modell said: 'We can't hopscotch franchises around the country. We have built this business on the trust of the fans. If we treat that as if it doesn't count, it isn't going to wash.'

For his part, Cleveland's owner seemed consumed in fulfilling an ambition he claimed would be worth 'giving up 10 years of his life for': winning the Browns' only Super Bowl and first championship since 1964. The intervening years had been cosmically heart-breaking for Browns fans, who filled the bleachers at Cleveland Municipal Stadium donning dog masks to earn the nickname 'The Dawg Pound'. Most notable were the 1980s, when Marty Schottenheimer's exceptional team did everything but reach the big game, the low watermark coming during the back-to-back AFC Championship Games against Denver in 1986 and '87. In the former, Elway executed 'The Drive'; in the latter, Earnest Byner delivered 'The Fumble', shelling the ball on the one-yard line in the dying seconds with a game-tying score in his sights.

Entering the 1995 season, however, optimism filled the Pound. Head coach Bill Belichick was seemingly beginning to reach the other side of an arduous rebuild, complicated by the necessary-but-unpopular release of ageing fan-favourite quarterback Bernie Kosar at the conclusion of his first season. Cleveland didn't go better than .500 over Belichick's opening three campaigns but reached the divisional round the following year when the coach overcame mentor Bill Parcells – now with the Patriots – on wild-card weekend. The Browns subsequently entered 1995 among the Super Bowl favourites. The season would indeed be notorious, just not in the anticipated manner.

On 6 November, with the Browns still in contention at 4-5, Modell – completely out of the blue – announced the franchise was uprooting to Baltimore. Cleveland lost six of their remaining seven games, the exception being a home finale played out amid near mutiny at the Dawg Pound, with fans ripping out bleachers and throwing them onto the field. Modell didn't attend any of those contests and never set foot in Cleveland again.

Further horror would be added posthumously for Browns fans, who have spent many of the ensuing years watching Belichick – fired after the season – become the greatest coach in NFL history and his defensive coordinator Nick Saban build a similar legacy in college football.

In the immediate aftermath, the Browns' relocation sent shockwaves through the league office and fanbase. There was an uncomfortable paradox in the fact Baltimore, the previous city on the end of such a shotgun departure, were the beneficiaries on this occasion – but even their case didn't threaten the sanctity of the NFL quite like this one. For it could at least have been predicted that Irsay, considered something of a clown by his contemporaries, might do something so unpredictable. To see Modell – a pillar of the league office and champion of its virtues – do likewise was truly shocking.

With the Houston Oilers announcing their move to Nashville, Tennessee, to eventually form the Titans five days later, the epidemic became a full-blown crisis – from player free agency to franchise free agency. Only the latter was most unwelcome.

Tagliabue responded swiftly. Three months later, the commissioner announced an agreement with the city of Cleveland to place an expansion team there by 1999 that would retain the Browns' name, team colours and heritage. At the ensuing league meetings, he advised all clubs that the NFL would fight any owner wanting to fill the now-vacant territory of Los Angeles.

His wider-ranging solution, ratified in 1999, was the 'G-3 Stadium Programme'. As the fallout over four relocations in a year raged, it was increasingly clear clubs could no longer rely entirely on existing team cities to pay for new arenas. As such, Tagliabue devised G-3, which saw the NFL advance clubs up to 50 per cent (or $150 million) of private funding for joint public–private stadium projects.

By that stage, with the Browns back in Cleveland, shaken public confidence was being restored. Not least because the musical-chairs acts of many NFL clubs coincided with the on-field re-emergence of a team who displayed the sacredness of loyalty to its base like few others.

As calendars flicked through the early 1990s, memories of the great times introduced by Curly Lambeau and continued over Vince Lombardi's glorious run were fading in the halls of Lambeau Field.

The Packers fanbase remained fanatical as ever, America's smallest town with a pro-sports team bleeding green and yellow despite two decades of misery following Lombardi's departure. Those years were spent harking back to former glories, recollections of on-field excellence dooming the tenures of Packer legends who couldn't emulate their playing exploits from the sideline. Among those who tried to fill Lombardi's significant shoes were two of his mainstays: quarterback Bart Starr and tackle Forrest Gregg. But the football overseen by a pair of Hall of Famers wasn't even a pale imitation of that played by the great 1960s squad on which they starred.

From Lombardi's departure up until 1992, Green Bay featured in three playoff games across 25 seasons. Starr and Gregg were given time – nine and four years respectively – without ever fielding the winning teams fans had come to expect, and even those with greater coaching pedigree endured only struggle. Upon the departure of Lindy Infante – the fifth leading man since Lombardi – there was a growing concern the NFL's most successful club would never rediscover their winning aura.

The latest person tasked with initiating a turnaround was Wolf, Davis' long-time right-hand man making a second go at running his own operation having been burned during a brief stint with the expansion Buccaneers in the 1970s. His record there was actually impressive. In those days, expansion teams operated completely from scratch, without the significant player pool to select from enjoyed by the Jaguars and Panthers years later. As such, the speed at which Tampa Bay became competitive – they reached the NFC Championship Game in their fourth season – owed plenty to Wolf's hard yards during the inaugural years. 'To be with an expansion team at that time,' he says, 'you had to crawl before you walked. And I mean crawl.' In Oakland, meanwhile, Wolf was a key architect of three Super Bowl teams.

To craft a similar squad in Green Bay, Wolf set about finding three crucial ingredients across his first two offseasons: a franchise coach, passer and pass-rusher. For the former, Wolf chose very much from right field. Mike Holmgren was the hottest assistant in football, acting as Bill Walsh's quarterback coach and Siefert's offensive coordinator for six campaigns in San Francisco that yielded two championships. His CV was exceptional. 'He was the offensive coordinator for the most successful team of that era,' adds Wolf, 'and he'd won 10 games in 1986 with Mike Moroski and Jeff Kemp at quarterback when Montana was injured. Having seen what he was able to do with players of that ilk, I thought he'd be perfect. The fact they won played a huge role for me. Being around a winner permeates the entire operation.'

At quarterback, Wolf went so left field that grass faded from view. His move was driven by memories of the 1991 draft when, during a brief spell as the Jets' personnel director that intersected tenures with the Raiders and Packers, Wolf spent much of the early throes trying to get into the first round for a quarterback he adored. While most observers wrote off Southern Mississippi's Favre as a risky project following his spotty senior season, Wolf considered him the best player in the class. He was able to look beyond that fifth year, played just a month after Favre had 30 inches of intestine removed following a car accident, and see the diamonds lurking in his junior film. After the ensuing East–West Shrine Game, Wolf and general manager Dick Steinberg were convinced. 'He was outstanding,' remembers Wolf. 'Dick and I turned to each other and said: "This is the best player in the draft."'

Yet the Favre starring on early college film who turned Wolf into a believer was very different to the 1992 version: a third-stringer failing to take his chance having been selected by the Atlanta Falcons with the 33rd pick, one spot ahead of the Jets. Not only had the signal-caller been unable to shine on the field – outside of when coach Jerry Glanville bet opponents he could toss pigskins into the top tier of stadiums prior to games – Favre fell foul of the four golden rules: 1. be on time; 2. prepare all week to play; 3. spill your guts on the field; and 4. only accept victory. Favre's weight of personality would have made three and four simple, but there was a problem. 'To get to three and four, you have to get past one and two,' says Glanville. 'He's the only player I coached in my career that didn't make it for the team picture.'

The mix proved toxic. Favre was selected against the wishes of Glanville, who considered Chris Miller – a Pro Bowler the previous year – his starter. 'Had he come in and won the job,' adds Glanville, 'he might have behaved and paid attention. But he was like a colt who couldn't be tamed.' As Favre himself reveals: 'I tried to drink up Atlanta. I wouldn't be answering these questions had I stayed.'

Favre's way out came via Wolf's unwavering support, backed up when the still-intrigued executive headed to Portland to see the rookie passer during a scrimmage against the Seahawks. 'Favre was the star,' says Wolf. 'He substantiated everything I believed.' Wolf didn't attend the subsequent preseason game against the Rams in which Favre struggled mightily.

What the scrimmage confirmed, in person, was Wolf's man had all of the physical talents illustrated in those precocious college years. From his earliest days in Green Bay, with Favre's situation in Atlanta having unravelled further, Wolf began harassing Falcons counterpart Ken Herock until he got his man.

Seventy-five days into his tenure, Wolf made the decision that would define it by sending the Packers' first-round pick for Favre. To the outside world, it looked like a huge overpay – but Wolf knew otherwise. 'I staked my career on him,' adds Wolf, 'and he didn't let me down. Anytime a franchise gets a player like Brett, it's rare. He changed that organisation from a loser to a winner. In all my years – I spent 38 years in the NFL – I've never been around a player who did for a team what Brett did for the Packers.'

He was the right man, at the right time, in the right place. For all Green Bay was footballing Nirvana, it was Siberia in a social sense. 'We could have traded him to New York,' adds Glanville, 'but I knew nobody would ever have known his name. He would have had the same problems as Atlanta. Neither Atlanta nor New York go to bed – everything's open all night. In Green Bay, everything is closed at 9 p.m. The only thing open after is Chilly John's!'

Favre concurs: 'Playing quarterback in the NFL is special and quite an honour, but doing it in Green Bay is in a class by itself. Walking out the tunnel into Lambeau is like trying to describe to someone how big a redwood tree is. You can't! You have to be there to appreciate it. The key for me was that Green Bay is a small town who love their football. I needed both. It saved my career.'

Not only was Green Bay perfect for Favre; Favre was perfect for Green Bay. At his heart, the quarterback was just a Regular Joe like those roaring from the bleachers, a country boy reared on the hunting terrain of Mississippi that he returned to after retirement. His rough-and-ready toughness evoked memories of Lombardi's golden days, with the ultimate badge of honour earned by not missing a game after becoming the Packers' latest favourite son. It was no mean feat considering Favre's gunslinging style, which attracted adoration and bruises in equal measure. 'I played every game because I loved playing,' he adds, 'but I also took enormous pride in not letting my teammates and fans down.'

In Week 3 of his opening foray in green and yellow, Favre took the field after starter Don Majkowski – a hair-raiser fondly nicknamed 'Majik Man' who was one of the few Packers to sparkle post-Lombardi – went down. For the next 15 years, he would never give up the starting berth. Favre led the Packers to a memorable 24–23 comeback victory over the Cincinnati Bengals and began to cement his place in Green Bay hearts.

It wasn't always straightforward. Teaching the quarterback Walsh's West Coast Offense was akin to him teaching the scheme's originator how to hunt coyotes. 'I remember the coaches would talk about nickel,' says Favre. 'And I'd play along saying: "Yeah, yeah, I understand." I only learnt it meant five defensive backs after asking backup Ty Detmer. People talked about how I ran a lot early in my career. I had no idea where to throw it!'

In Holmgren, Favre found a willing teacher and, even amid the growing pains, produced enough breathtaking moments to reach the Pro Bowl in 1992 and '93. At the end of the latter campaign, Favre's physical capabilities were illustrated in a wildcard playoff game versus the Detroit Lions. With the Pack down 24–21 and 55 seconds remaining, he shuffled left in the pocket and threw a 40-yard dart back across his body to hit Sterling Sharpe in the back-right corner of the end zone for the game-winning score. Green Bay's first playoff appearance for 11 years was victorious.

The club still needed consistency to match the scarcely believable bombs thrown by their quarterback and, by 1995, the hard work was paying off. The Packers' thoroughbred might not have been completely tamed, but he was contained – the perfect mix. In Week 11, Green Bay were 5-4 with their season at a crossroads and arch-rival the Bears up next. Worse yet, Favre hadn't practised all week due to a badly sprained ankle. Come gameday, he told Holmgren: 'Hey, I think I can go,' and proceeded to throw five touchdown passes in a 35–28 win. 'It was a remarkable performance,' says Wolf. 'That's Brett Favre. The game has got to be played, and he wants to play.' That day was the high watermark of a campaign that began a run from Favre that will surely never be matched: winning three successive NFL MVP titles.

For all the personal accolades, what Green Bay and their quarterback really craved was a championship. 'Our fans waited a long time, and I wanted so bad to give them what they wanted,' admits Favre. Aiding his quest was the team constructed by Wolf. One year after luring Favre to town, the general manager pulled off another coup by landing 'the Minister of Defense' White – a pass-rusher every bit as dominant as Lawrence Taylor – in the NFL's first offseason with free agency. 'That was a really difficult sell,' Wolf remembers. 'To be honest, we just paid more money than everybody else.'

Four years and $17 million was a worthwhile investment for somebody who had racked up 124 sacks in 121 games with the Eagles. Not only did White immediately transform their defense with his unmatched combination of quickness and power, he legitimised Green Bay as a destination for other free agents.

In 1996, the Packers were ready to return to their perceived rightful place: on a podium lifting the trophy named after the club's most illustrious icon. They did so at the conclusion of a Super Bowl against New England in which players sported small decals inscribed with the words 'Pete', a tribute to former commissioner Rozelle, who had died two months earlier. The game itself would prove an equally fitting tribute to professional sports' greatest commissioner, won by the team who benefited most significantly from him convincing owners of the game-changing revenue-sharing model.

Nothing sums up the league Rozelle was so instrumental in building quite like the Packers, the team who represent a town of just 100,000 and continue to punch above their weight so spectacularly. 'Winning that Super Bowl was like giving someone a gift in a sense,' says Favre of Green Bay's 35–21 win against New

England in which he threw for 246 yards and two touchdowns, while White delivered a then-Super-Bowl-record three sacks.

The following year, it appeared Favre truly was the gift that would keep on giving. Not only did Green Bay return to the Super Bowl against the Broncos, they did so as 14-point favourites, seemingly poised to spark the next great Packers dynasty.

Following Elway's signature spin through the air, events in San Diego weren't adhering to the forecast. Two plays later, the indomitable Davis crossed paydirt for the second time to give Denver a 24–17 lead and reaffirm the migraine that forced him to miss almost all the second quarter had disappeared. 'By then, I felt like I was seeing things in full HD clarity,' he remembers.

Yet those factors only served to induce a hair-raising conclusion, highlighted equally by magic and mistakes. The first came from Antonio Freeman, who fumbled the ensuing kickoff and set Denver up just outside the Packers 22. That elusive Lombardi Trophy seemingly in his grasp, Elway delivered an all-too-familiar big-game blunder, tossing an interception to Eugene Robinson in the end zone.

Favre's response was devastating. With Broncos supporters perhaps wondering whether time had come to put their thoroughbred out to pasture, Green Bay's young stallion delivered four strikes – three, including a touchdown, to Freeman – without a single incompletion: 24–24.

Both teams punted on their next two possessions, but Denver edged the field-position battle to such an extent that Elway returned with 3:27 left at the Green Bay 48-yard line. If the quarterback was to end the hoodoo, the time was now.

The big difference from Elway's other brushes with this game was that he didn't have to be the Broncos' everything. The offense ran through the zone-blocking, stretch-running scheme created by Shanahan and perfectly executed by Davis' unique vision. Such was the Packers' difficulty stopping the halfback that linebacker

Darius Holland grabbed his facemask on the drive's first play, turning a two-yard gain into 17.

Denver were rolling.

The core tenet of Shanahan's scheme didn't just create yards on the ground. Equally important was what it set up – play-action passes and bootlegs – that often looked identical to rushing plays. Following a small Davis gain, Elway dropped back from under centre again, faked the hand-off to his running back, shuffled left and hit Griffith for 23 yards. Not even a holding penalty on the ensuing play could derail Denver, Davis delivering 17 yards on first-and-goal from the 18 following another dart around the outside. With the Broncos on the brink and seconds ticking down, Holmgren let Denver score: Davis eased in for his third. 31–24.

Holmgren's gamble, of course, was that Favre could bring them back. It looked inspired when the passer connected on a screen with Dorsey Levens, who rumbled over midfield. After failing with a similar play next up, Favre hit Levens on a swing pass and, suddenly, the Packers were 35 yards from a tying touchdown.

Yet Denver were more than just their offense. The defense boasted stars at every level in Smith, linebacking pair John Mobley and Romanowski, as well as Hall-of-Fame safety Steve Atwater. In the moments that defined the game, first-team All-Pro Mobley was to the fore, bringing down Levens on first down and then making the key play on fourth-and-six. The Broncos faced up to that reality, with Favre perched on the 32, without Atwater, forced from the field following a sickening collision with cornerback Randy Hilliard on the previous play.

While Atwater regained consciousness on the sideline, the onus fell on Romanowski to make the call: 'Bomb Blitz'. 'It was an all-out blitz,' he remembers. 'Favre got the ball out pretty quick because he knew we were coming after him. I saw John cut underneath and bat down the ball. And that was it: the most satisfying game, play and high of my career.'

The moment that cemented Romanowski's third ring brought

Elway's first. On the sideline, Denver's legendary quarterback leapt on Ed McCaffrey, then raised his arms aloft as he roared to the crowd. 'After 15 years of work, three Super Bowl losses,' he said, 'to finally reach the pinnacle . . . it still gives me shivers.'

Having waited all that time, two came along in quick succession. Denver – who snapped an NFC Super Bowl winning streak of 13 games by overcoming Green Bay – were back in the big game the following year, and Elway again stood on a podium, this time in Miami, after throwing for 336 yards in their 34–19 victory over the Falcons. Months later, he retired a two-time champion.

Super Bowl XXXIII capped rare feats for the man in Denver's engine room. Having followed Barry Sanders the previous year by becoming the league's fourth 2,000-yard single-season rusher, he completed, versus Atlanta, an achievement nobody else has ever managed: running for at least 100 yards in seven successive playoff games. Davis was never quite the same again thereafter – robbed of the burst of pace that was central to his excellence after suffering a horrific knee injury early the next year – but his legacy remains indisputable. Denver's two Super Bowls were won amid perhaps the most dominant four-year run by a running back in the game's history, one that didn't match the longevity of Elway's but secured his place alongside the quarterback in Canton.

Perhaps Davis' biggest impact, though, was the crucial role he played in validating one of the finest careers in NFL history. For it was only after the arrival of Davis that Bowlen could stand atop a podium, holding aloft the Lombardi Trophy, and utter the words that hit Broncos Nation ears like the sweetest sounds of a symphony: 'This one's for John.'

18

The Brady Bunch

Super Bowl XXXVI

ST. LOUIS RAMS 17
NEW ENGLAND PATRIOTS 20

---

3 February 2002
Louisiana Superdome, New Orleans

Wherever you looked on the New England Patriots' bench, exhausted defensive players gasped for air. To a man, Willie McGinest, Ty Law, Lawyer Malloy, Richard Seymour, Mike Vrabel and Tedy Bruschi had left everything on the field, impeccably executing head coach Bill Belichick and defensive coordinator Romeo Crennel's gameplan to leave New England on the brink of the greatest upset in Super Bowl history.

Yet, as the clock wound tantalisingly towards '0:00', the dam burst. New England finally succumbed under the weight of the indefatigable St. Louis Rams offense, piloted by Kurt Warner. On the play that completed the Rams' fourth-quarter comeback, Tebucky Jones could barely outstretch his arms as Ricky Proehl, wide open following a pick play, took Warner's pass down the left

343

sideline, cut back inside and hit paydirt for a 16-yard touchdown.

'We put so much into the game,' admits McGinest. 'We knew they were a finesse team and, if we played that game, we wouldn't win. We couldn't keep up with the speed and athleticism. They did not like contact – at all – and we were about making it a physical game. Other teams would have been passive. We hit everything moving.'

Entering the final quarter, their efforts left New England with one hand on a first Lombardi Trophy. The Patriots, driven by three defensive turnovers that included Law's pick-six, were up 14–3, having suitably roughed up their opponents – from the cornerbacks' physical man coverage disrupting the timing between Warner and outstanding wideouts Isaac Bruce and Torry Holt to do-it-all running back Marshall Faulk barely being given room to breathe.

'The gameplan was genius,' admits Warner. 'Belichick came out and basically said: "These guys are fast and athletic, and want to win with timing. We gotta beat them up." They were daring the officials to throw flags, and it was ingenious. They pushed the envelope, and it led to us making a lot of uncharacteristic mistakes. It wasn't until at the end we got going.'

Perhaps just as impressive as the Patriots' coming-of-age performance was the Rams' reaction. In a game where much had gone wrong, they levelled with 1:17 remaining as Jeff Wilkins' P.A.T. capped a fine riposte to spark celebratory scenes on the sideline that emphasised the belief St. Louis had finally cracked Belichick's code.

Yet New England's head coach personified calmness as he contemplated the permutations. The Patriots had no timeouts and were playing a quarterback taken with the 199th overall pick of the previous year's NFL Draft. John Madden, the CBS colour commentator who had tackled similar choices over a short-but-illustrious career as the Oakland Raiders' head coach, considered the decision simple: 'You have to just run the clock out and play for overtime,' he said. 'You don't want to force anything or do anything stupid, because you have no timeouts and you're backed up.'

Belichick viewed the situation with similar clarity, only his perspective differed. The head coach knew New England's defense, the cornerstone of their stunning performance, was weary and that his young passer Tom Brady boasted coolness which belied inexperience. As such, Belichick's meeting of minds with Brady, offensive coordinator Charlie Weis and starter-turned-backup-quarterback Drew Bledsoe was brief. 'OK, let's do this,' said Belichick after confirming everyone was on the same page.

'There was absolutely no thought of playing for overtime,' admits Weis. 'The four of us looked at each other on the sideline and had the same thought. The Rams had all the momentum, so we decided to go for it. I remember telling Tommy not to do anything dangerous, and we were pretty conservative.'

In the blink of an eye, Brady took a snap from the shotgun and stepped up in the pocket amid pressure from St. Louis' leading sack artist that year, Leonard Little. J.R. Redmond collected a dump-off and gained just four yards. 'I don't agree with what the Patriots are doing right here,' continued Madden. 'I would play for overtime.'

Undeterred, New England continued to press the accelerator, Brady hitting Redmond over the middle once again, this time for eight yards. With the clock ticking under a minute, the signal-caller ushered his troops quickly to the line of scrimmage and spiked the ball. 'This guy is really cool, though,' added Madden. 'The way he's played today – he's been very, very impressive with his calmness.' Madden didn't know the half of it: Brady spent part of pregame napping in the locker room.

'They need about 40 more yards before they are going to be in field-goal range,' said Madden as Brady stood in the shotgun once more with 41 seconds remaining. After the snap, Redmond leaked out of the backfield to the left of Brady, who surveyed his downfield options then dumped it to the 'back. Redmond cut inside one defender then back outside to the sideline for 11. 'We shouldn't have allowed him to get out of bounds,' remembers star Rams linebacker London Fletcher. 'We didn't tackle well enough, and that created their mindset that they could win.'

The hushed buzz echoing around the stadium was illustrative of a collision between the spectators' tension and excitement. 'He got out of bounds and stopped the clock,' added Madden. 'Now I kind of like what the Patriots are doing.' Something momentous was happening, a shock to rival the one produced by Joe Namath and the New York Jets decades earlier felt possible again. But surely the lowly Patriots – with their written-off head coach, unknown quarterback and collection of cast-offs – couldn't topple the 'Greatest Show on Turf'.

When commissioner Paul Tagliabue stopped by St. Louis' Macomb, Illinois, training camp in July 1999 to discuss the Rams' 'tremendous opportunity' in a league with 'great competitive balance', it rang hollow. The franchise hadn't just been a loser since moving cities in 1995, they were the dud of the decade having managed a league-low 45 wins across nine seasons. The previous year had brought only four and raised questions of whether head coach Dick Vermeil, back on the sideline after a 15-year absence due to burnout, could still cut it. Among many issues, Vermeil was unable to tame controversial running back Lawrence Phillips, whose on-field talent was undermined by a litany of off-field troubles. Midway through the 1997 campaign, Vermeil's first, the sixth overall pick from the previous year was released after trainers smelt alcohol on his breath prior to the Week 10 game versus the Green Bay Packers. 'He was potentially the best running back I ever coached, a wasted, gifted human being,' remembers Vermeil. 'It still haunts me.'

More pertinent to the '99 campaign was the quarterback situation. Vermeil couldn't draw consistency from young gunslinger

Tony Banks, a 1996 second-round selection, and opted to look elsewhere. In came Trent Green, the former San Diego Chargers 1993 eighth-rounder who had so far produced an undistinguished career. He flamed out in San Diego, failed to make the Canadian Football League's BC Lions and spent three seasons riding the pine for the Washington Redskins. But, in 1998, Green started 14 games and seized his chance, throwing for 3,441 yards, with 23 touchdowns and 11 interceptions, to earn a four-year $17.5 million contract in hometown St. Louis.

As such, the preseason began with intrigue. The Rams' new fanbase were rabid, filling the TWA Dome despite a poor on-field product, and it appeared their patience would be rewarded. Not only had St. Louis snaffled Green in the offseason, they had also furnished their roster with shiny new weapons. Faulk, the dual-threat running back who amassed more than 2,000 all-purpose yards in 1998, was stolen from the Indianapolis Colts for second- and fifth-round picks during a draft that also yielded first-round wide receiver Holt.

While in Washington, Green had been groomed by quarter-backs coach Mike Martz. As such, he knew St. Louis' new offensive coordinator's playbook inside out and completed 28 of his opening 32 preseason passes. Anticipation reached fever pitch.

But then, during the third exhibition game, it all came crumbling down as quickly as Green did under the weight of a typically fierce hit by San Diego safety Rodney Harrison. Vermeil wept afterwards as he told reporters about Green's season-ending torn ACL.

Part of that reaction owed to the uninspiring next man up. If the Rams' anointed starter was green in NFL terms, his backup took it to another level. An undrafted free agent for Green Bay in 1994, Warner failed to make the roster and was soon stacking shelves for $5.50 an hour at Cedar Falls' Hy-Vee grocery store. Thereafter, Warner spent three productive years with the Arena Football League's Iowa Barnstormers and a season as the World

League of American Football's Amsterdam Admirals quarterback. He sufficiently impressed at those stops to be the Rams' backup in 1999, but little was expected of him. 'I knew, unlike other guys, I wasn't getting another chance,' admits Warner. 'This was it. My one chance.'

To players and media, Vermeil expressed confidence. 'Listen, this is the team. We have to go out and win with the guys in this locker room. We are going to go with Kurt Warner and be a good football team.' When the ball didn't hit the ground in Warner's first practice as starter, his teammates began to believe. 'We knew he would play well,' admits Fletcher. 'He shredded our defense the year before as scout-team quarterback. But we had no idea he'd become a Hall-of-Fame quarterback.'

Nor did Vermeil. Ahead of their season opener versus Baltimore, the coach privately confided in new Ravens leading man Brian Billick that he merely hoped Warner could tread water until veteran signing Paul Justin got up-to-speed. 'All he had to do was run the offense,' remembers the head coach. 'We had no idea that he would take it to the next level.'

Not only had the struggle to reach the top created the necessary fortitude required of all great quarterbacks, Warner's experiences made him the perfect triggerman for Martz's innovative attack. 'I was going through all these different routes,' he admits, 'and setbacks, and I was just thinking to myself: "Why couldn't I be the one to take that straight path?" Now I can't say thank you enough for the route I took.'

In Arena Football,* the key tenet of quarterbacking was reading defenses quickly and getting the ball into the hands of playmakers. Which is exactly what the Rams' unique scheme called for. Martz's revolutionary ideology was a mix of three strategies that had come to the fore over his life and time: Sid Gillman's vertical passing concepts, Bill Walsh's West Coast Offense and the Run-and-Shoot. A child of San Diego in the 1960s, Martz's obsession stemmed from Gillman's time coaching the Chargers that had altered football tactics, while his coaching career coincided with Walsh's and the proliferation of the Run-and-Shoot. As such, Martz built his own concept from all three, utilising Gillman's oft-copied three-digit-play system, option routes from the run-and-shoot and honing the timing of the West Coast Offense. The most obvious link was philosophical: Martz, like those pioneers, flipped the idea of running to step up the pass. 'Nobody, in the history of the league, made the kind of immediate contribution to a team that he made,' says Vermeil.

Where Martz took everything a step further was in his laissez-faire attitude to protections. He seldom deployed tight ends as blockers, theorising that utilising every weapon as a potential pass-catcher would enable quarterbacks to distribute the ball with enough speed to render it moot. As such, the key piece in his system was a signal-caller capable of making quick, decisive decisions. It helped, too, that Warner had an impressive array of options at his disposal with as many as five pass-catchers available on plays.

Protected by Hall-of-Fame left tackle Orlando Pace, Warner – following a range of pre-snap shifts that bamboozled defenses – would distribute the ball to wideouts Holt and Bruce, as well as exceptional 'back Faulk. The latter was the offense's heartbeat, sublime in the ground game – albeit aided by lighter boxes* provided by the wide assortment of weapons – and capable of running a diverse route tree. That season, he became the second man, after Roger Craig, to deliver 1,000 rushing and receiving yards in a single campaign, just one of many ludicrous accolades the Rams amassed. Over a three-year span from 1999 to 2001, St. Louis became the first team to breach 500 points in three successive years. 'We took the league by storm,' says Holt.

Like the geniuses from whom he built his ideology, Martz would leave an indelible mark on pro football. His 'Show' spawned many copycats and is considered the starting point for the proliferation of spread offenses* seen in professional football today. 'In the moment, you never really understand what you're part of,' says Warner. 'But the way we played shaped the NFL. You look at the game now and say: "We started this." The pass-first, attack, get-the-ball-out-of-your-hand-quick approach. The beginning of that was the Greatest Show On Turf.'

'That name is the ultimate honour,' concludes Vermeil. 'When you're given a title, it stays with you for ever. It's been 20 years since that 1999 season, and people still always ask me about the Greatest Show On Turf.'

More broadly, Martz's group combined with a fine defensive unit in 1999 as St. Louis – 150–1 to win the Super Bowl ahead of the campaign – went 13-3 to claim the NFC's number-one seed. As if Warner's nomadic journey from unknown to NFL Most Valuable Player didn't offer enough subplots to the regular season, the Rams' greatness was truly sealed by emerging triumphant following the most dramatic postseason in league history. Over the course of a scarcely believable fortnight to conclude that campaign, Tennessee Titans wide receiver Kevin Dyson was involved in two remarkable plays. The first came at the conclusion of the AFC Championship Game, when Dyson collected Frank Wycheck's lateral on a kick return and raced 75 yards for a touchdown as the Titans, down 16–15 with 16 seconds remaining, booked their place in Super Bowl XXXIV. 'It was pure elation,' he remembers.

Yet the script would be cruelly flipped against St. Louis, who themselves had overcome the Tampa Bay Buccaneers 11–6 in a similarly tense NFC title game. The anticipated coronation of the Greatest Show On Turf turned into a defensive slug-fest against the Titans until Warner put the Rams 23–16 ahead on a 73-yard touchdown to Bruce with a little under two minutes left. The Titans took over at their own 12-yard line with 1:48 remaining, yet quickly ate up the yardage behind the brilliance of Steve McNair and a pair of Dyson catches, the last bringing them down to the Rams' 10 with five seconds on the clock.

Tennessee got the look they wanted. Key to the play was Rams linebacker Mike Jones, who the Titans calculated would shade towards Wycheck on the right sideline and leave the middle of the field open for Dyson's angle route. Yet the studious Jones had noticed the same formation when preparing for the game. He made an initial move towards Wycheck but kept his left eye on Dyson, who thought another glorious moment was coming after receiving the pass from McNair. 'I could see the yellow paint of the end zone so vividly,' he remembers. 'As I'm trying to score, I remember in my eyes seeing that yellow end zone and thinking it was just right there in my grasp.'

'It seemed like slow motion,' remembers Jones. 'I couldn't see McNair throw the ball, but I could feel it. I knew I was about at the two- or three-yard line, and when [Dyson] caught the ball, I knew he was short of the end zone a couple of yards. I was right on top of him.'

As Dyson prepared to lunge for glory, Jones grasped his right thigh, clung on and pulled the wideout to the ground, 'One Yard Short' – as the play became known – of the goalline. 'Ah, man,' adds Dyson. 'You're talking about the yin and yang of sports.'

'In all honesty, I thought I was going to kill Kevin Dyson,' Jones reveals. 'I'm used to covering the angle route but, when you're covering a running back who usually isn't as quick as a wide receiver, you've got to drop your pads, because they're a little bigger but not as quick. Then I'm thinking this guy's a lot quicker than I thought, so I'll just get him on the ground. It won the Super Bowl, so it's obviously the best tackle of all time . . .'

Remarkably, the ultimate validation of perhaps the outstanding offense in NFL history was delivered by defense. Not that Vermeil minded, for it served as equal endorsement of his own coaching career. Three years after returning from self-imposed exile, the 63-year-old became the oldest coach, at that time, to lift the Lombardi Trophy. 'I had lost one with the Eagles,' says Vermeil, 'and the depression of losing and excitement of winning go to both extremes of the human emotion.'

Remarkably, given the increased coverage and importance placed upon Super Bowls, the Rams' victory was quickly overshadowed in the national media. In the days after Vermeil hoisted the Lombardi Trophy, headlines were dominated not by events from the Georgia Dome, but those that occurred just a few miles away hours later. They surrounded Baltimore linebacker Ray Lewis and would loom over a 2000 NFL season in which the young phenom overcame scandal to star on a defense every bit as good as the Greatest Show On Turf offense.

In the hours after St. Louis' victory, Lewis and a pair of associates became embroiled in an altercation with two men who were subsequently stabbed to death in the parking lot of Cobalt, an Atlanta nightclub. Lewis spent the ensuing offseason facing a double-murder charge until he cut a deal. After testifying for the prosecution, Lewis pleaded guilty to a reduced charge of obstruction of justice, while the other two facing charges were eventually acquitted after the jury ruled it self-defence.

Though no longer contemplating the cold reality of imprisonment, Lewis would still face the fire of both the NFL office and court of public opinion. Tagliabue handed the linebacker an unprecedented fine of $250,000, and the scandal lingered as an uncomfortable shadow on much of the next campaign.

Strong through it all, and supportive of Lewis, was Baltimore's level-headed coach Billick. 'It unfolded on us very rapidly,' he remembers. 'Our support stemmed primarily from our faith in Ray Lewis as a person. We did not have access to all the facts, because it took months and months for that to unfold, [and] to find out that Ray Lewis really wasn't culpable in any of those events. We had to go on, kind of, a leap of faith.'

'Unfortunately, everybody has their journey in life, and we cannot change that,' adds former teammate Rod Woodson. 'It was hard for us too. They said things about Ray, who was our good friend. Before our first preseason game, we told Ray: "Don't react to the fans," but we ended up reacting, wanting to climb over the gates and get into fights. He was pretty level-headed.'

In return for his team's unwavering loyalty, Lewis produced one of the most dominant defensive seasons in history as the fulcrum of a unit that occupies the same rarefied air as the 1985 Chicago Bears. Like Mike Singletary in that group, Lewis was the heartbeat at middle linebacker, playing with a controlled anger that saw him voted Defensive Player of the Year and hallmarked his first-ballot Hall-of-Fame career. As well as Lewis, the defense was anchored by exceptional tackle Tony Siragusa and marshalled by a punishing secondary starring Woodson, a Hall-of-Fame cornerback enjoying a second life at safety. Over the regular season, Baltimore allowed only 970 rushing yards and 165 points, both records for a 16-game season.

Such excellence was necessary, for the offensive side of the ball was a different story. Entering the Week 9 contest against the Pittsburgh Steelers, with whom a rivalry was burgeoning, Baltimore hadn't scored a touchdown for four weeks. 'We struggled on offense a lot,' remembers left tackle Jonathan Ogden. 'Although we still won two of those games!'

The turning point was introducing Trent Dilfer – 'Not the most talented guy in the world,' adds Ogden, 'but he gave it his all and didn't make mistakes' – at quarterback in place of Tony Banks. So good was Baltimore's defense that mistake-free football was all the Ravens required. Dilfer played smart and was complemented by some truly talented offensive players, such as rookie running back Jamal Lewis, as well as Shannon Sharpe and Ogden, both of whom reside in Canton.

That formula took Baltimore all the way through the post-season, where Lewis and co. allowed just three, 10 and three points respectively to the Denver Broncos, Titans and Raiders. 'We had leaders in every spot,' says Woodson, 'and Ray started becoming a playmaker at the end of the year. When you're that good on defense, it is hard to lose. A lot of teams thought they would be able to do things . . . until they started playing us. It was fun to see how good we became.'

The ultimate vindication of the unit and Lewis came via the linebacker's MVP performance in Super Bowl XXXV, when the New York Giants managed a mere seven points, and those on a kick return. The upshot was Baltimore, who became only the second team to score touchdowns on offense, defense and special teams in a Super Bowl, cruising to a 34–7 triumph. 'We wanted a shut-out, and technically we got it,' adds Woodson. 'We just gave back the kick return, which went against us as a defense. But winning was really nice.'

'They beat the crap out of the Giants,' adds Ogden. 'It was physical domination.'

Victory provided yet more evidence of the NFL's growing unpredictability. Amid the unwanted attention of Lewis' off-field troubles, Tagliabue would doubtless have enjoyed seeing a second successive unlikely Super Bowl victor. It offered the ultimate validation of the free-agency system he was so instrumental in bringing about and hinted at the NFL achieving the parity craved throughout its existence.

Suddenly, 'Any Given Sunday' became 'Any Given Season' – and the whole league knew it.

The prospect of fast turnarounds was most welcome in New England, where, entering the new Millennium, familiar antipathy reigned. Their 40 years of existence – first as the Boston Patriots and then New England after their name was changed in 1971 – had been almost entirely miserable, barring two occasions the club flickered into life. They reached the Super Bowl under Raymond Berry before being hammered by the 1985 Bears in a contest only slightly less competitive than their next trip to the Big Dance. That came at the conclusion of the 1996 campaign, when New England proved no match for Brett Favre's Packers.

The Patriots were seemingly bequeathed with the same curse that hovered over the city's famous Boston Red Sox, a Major League Baseball giant, at least in name, who hadn't won a championship since securing their fifth overall – and fourth in seven years – in 1918. The football team couldn't even boast the Red Sox's brand identity. Entering 2000, New England had reached the postseason in just 10 of 40 campaigns without ever winning a championship.

Robert Kraft, the self-made Massachusetts billionaire who had roared the Patriots on from the bleachers of Foxboro Stadium before fulfilling his long-held dream of purchasing the club, stood at a crossroads. The fresh excitement following his purchase of the team in 1994, accentuated by Bill Parcells leading the Patriots to the Super Bowl in his third season, had disappeared.

Much of the reason for this centred around the coach's departure following their showpiece against the Packers, an occasion overshadowed by word leaking in the build-up that it would be Parcells' last game at the club and that he was bound for the division-rival Jets. The situation represented the apex of an ongoing feud with New England's owner, who Parcells accused of meddling. The two-time Super Bowl champion wanted to run the programme his way, or as he put it: 'They want you to cook the dinner; they might as well let you pick some of the groceries.' Kraft, Parcells believed, was too involved in personnel choices, epitomised by New England using a first-round pick on wide receiver Terry Glenn in 1996 when Parcells wanted to select a defensive player.

Yet there was a third man who would become somehow embroiled in the situation – Belichick – setting the scene for a transformative series of events. They began with Parcells heading to New York with Belichick in tow, but only after protracted talks between clubs and mediation from Tagliabue. At one stage, the Jets announced Belichick as their head coach with Parcells acting as consultant until he was freed from his contract in New England the next year. Six days later, a less clandestine solution was reached as the Patriots received first-, second-, third- and fourth-round draft picks across multiple years for Parcells' services.

While the pair began the process of transforming the Patriots' AFC East rivals, New England floundered under Pete Carroll, a defensive-minded disciple of Walsh who went 27-21 overall, but just 8-8 in 1999. After that campaign, Kraft decided to change course once again. The interview process whittled his list down to one man – former Carolina Panthers leading man Dom Capers – but the owner felt a nagging at the back of his mind. There was somebody else he really wanted: the assistant from Parcells' tenure with whom Kraft had built an exceptional rapport as his relationship with the head coach simultaneously deteriorated. Side by side, Kraft and Belichick had often ridden exercise bikes in the facility, discussing everything from X's and O's to the salary cap. For the owner, their connection had represented an opportunity to gain insight into football and his own team.

With Kraft again on the lookout for a head coach, he faxed an interview request for Belichick to the Jets. But, during the wrangling over Parcells, it was written into Belichick's contract that he would succeed his mentor in New York. Upon seeing the request, therefore, Parcells accelerated the plans: he remained as head of football operations, with Belichick becoming the coach. The announcement would be made on 4 January 2000 at the Jets' Long Island facility.

It became arguably the most stunning press conference in league history. Just before heading to the podium, Belichick handed club president Steve Gutman a note with seven words scrawled on it: 'I resign as HC of the NYJ'. At the microphone, he explained the club's uncertain ownership situation – they were about to be sold to an unknown consortium following long-time steward Leon Hess' death the previous May – meant he couldn't take the role. 'I've been in situations, and more importantly my family has been in a situation, where I was the head coach of a team in transition,' he said. 'Frankly, it wasn't a really good experience for me or for them.'

In Jets PR man Frank Ramos' mind, there was another factor at play. 'I think prior to that day,' he says, 'Belichick had already negotiated a contract with Bob Kraft and the Patriots. I think Parcells was aware. I wasn't surprised – disappointed, but not surprised.'

'We had the opportunity to be a great team,' says Hall-of-Famer Curtis Martin, well versed in the Patriots and Jets rivalry having followed Parcells from the former to the latter in a move that infuriated Kraft.

Not only did Belichick's decision create a remarkable situation in which he had two head-coaching stints with 'Gang Green' spanning seven days and zero games, it set the stage for another battle between the clubs. Much like previously, there would be involvement from the league office until, finally, Parcells and Kraft ironed out an agreement.

'My assistant came to me,' remembered Kraft, 'and said: "There's someone saying he's Darth Vader on the phone." I knew that was Bill.' He and Parcells agreed a trade that transferred Belichick's services to New England in return for three draft selections, including that year's first-rounder (16th overall).

After three years, Kraft had finally got his man. 'He was the right man at the right time,' admits McGinest. 'He had a clear blueprint. He wanted tough, physical, smart and versatile guys. He took a nucleus from the team he was an assistant on and added to that.'

The advantage Belichick enjoyed in New England as opposed to Cleveland was intimate knowledge of the squad. On his first day, the head coach was greeted with a black-and-white depth chart on his desk, but it offered few insights. Belichick knew the discombobulated nature of the roster, just as he did the names that would remain as he and handpicked personnel man Scott Pioli reshaped it.

The first order of business was to clear through the rubble of Carroll's dwindling tenure. It wasn't easy. New England were $10 million over the salary cap and a pair of talented players – diminutive wide receiver Troy Brown and linebacker Bruschi – were about to hit the open market. Belichick and Pioli made the necessary adjustments to keep two players who, alongside McGinest, Law, Milloy and kicker Adam Vinatieri, became cornerstone holdovers. New England's changing culture was illustrated by the release of tight end Ben Coates, a five-time Pro Bowler who refused to cut his pay, but it didn't translate to wins. The Patriots finished 5-11 during a campaign that offered few hints of the ensuing turnaround.

Yet the mood inside the the camp differed. When the next free-agency window rolled around, New England were interested in Roman Phifer, a friend of McGinest. He signed following a glowing endorsement. 'You should come here because we've got something special brewing, and you're gonna help this team win,' McGinest told Phifer.

The former Raider formed part of a transformative group of new arrivals during Belichick's second offseason. With existing scouts jettisoned for his own guys, he and Pioli homed in on two goals: find footballing treasure in other people's trash and players with the character profile defined by some of Belichick's mistakes with the Cleveland Browns. Essentially, team-first guys who wanted to win.

Alongside Phifer came Pittsburgh linebacker Vrabel, who didn't fit their scheme but did Belichick's, and underrated wide receiver David Patten. The draft, meanwhile, brought defensive lineman Seymour and offensive tackle Matt Light.

The new pieces left Belichick quietly confident for a 2001 campaign that began under the cloud of heartbreak created by quarterback coach Dick Rehbein's shock death following a heart attack suffered in the facility. Yet at the conclusion of Week 1, a 23–17 loss to the Cincinnati Bengals, the Patriots were back in familiar territory: holding a losing record. Their home opener, pitting Belichick against the Jets team he had jilted at the altar, at least provided ample incentive to refocus. Not that the coach needed any. He attacked the week with the application and determination illustrated throughout his time in the NFL, acutely aware of the forthcoming contest's importance for New England's season and his own flailing head-coaching career.

Come Tuesday, however, football felt utterly irrelevant.

On the morning of 11 September 2001, a despondent Giants team landed at Newark airport following their season-opening 31–20 loss to the Broncos. As they exited the aeroplane, some players noted that a nearby jet – United Airlines Flight 93 – was being readied for its departure to San Francisco just over an hour later.

Four minutes after the Boeing 757's wheels left the tarmac at 8.42 a.m., just across the Hudson River, American Airlines Flight 11 ripped into the North Tower of the World Trade Center to commence one of the most devastating terrorist atrocities in the history of mankind.

As the city in which NFL headquarters were located and the wider USA came under attack, Tagliabue sat only 6.6 miles away from the tragedy in the league's Park Avenue offices. When the scale of what occurred emerged – two aeroplanes hit New York, another struck the Pentagon in Washington, while hijackers on Flight 93 were overthrown by passengers, who ditched in rural Pennsylvania – Tagliabue unsurprisingly cut short a conference call with league charity partner United Way.

'The initial focus was entirely on the people of the city of New York and specifically the people of the NFL and their families,' he remembered. 'Two of our employees lost their spouses. So, we ended up going as a group to St. Patrick's Cathedral at 5.30 p.m. to reflect and pray.'

Such are the demands placed upon those in high-profile roles that the New Jersey native wasn't able to just grieve, however. He quickly donned his commissioner's hat, calling those in the NFL's extended family situated closest to the attacks: the staffs of the Jets, Giants, Redskins and NFLPA, which was headquartered in the capital. Tagliabue's greatest task over the coming days was to determine whether the NFL's schedule would continue as planned that weekend. It was one for which he was uniquely qualified, having worked at the Pentagon in their defense department during the 1960s.

Yet perhaps the greatest influence on the eventual decision was how another incident had been handled: the murder of President John F. Kennedy. Two days after Kennedy was cut down by an assassin's bullet in Dallas, the league opted to play its planned schedule. It did so with the backing of the White House, who declared it was what the former president – such an avid pigskin fan that the Kennedys were sometimes called the 'First Family of Football' – would have wanted. Yet they misread a public simply not ready to return to normality so quickly.

With college and other major sports leagues – including the American Football League – cancelling games, and CBS scrapping all sports programming, the NFL ended up out on an island and Rozelle was criticised. The *New York Herald Tribune*'s Red Smith wrote: 'In the civilised world, it was a day of mourning. In the National Football League, it was the 11th Sunday of the business year, a quarter-million-dollar day in Yankee Stadium.'

'He regretted the reaction he received,' says Rozelle's daughter Anne Marie Bratton, 'but he did what he was told to do by the Kennedy family. And took the fall for it.'

Whatever line of that particular debate the NFL's new commissioner sat on, the hindsight gleaned from the aftermath of Kennedy's assassination was valuable, especially as Tagliabue attempted to find a route through the swirling differences of opinion engulfing his league. For those located near the attacks, the prospect of playing was unpalatable. 'It was devastating, man,' remembers former Jets safety Victor Green. 'The buildings – we were watching it. I was at work. It was a Tuesday, I still remember. You see it on the television, you hear about it, then you see the other one almost live right on television, a building going down. It was a very, very tough time for New Yorkers, for the world.'

The Giants' practices were playing out amid a smoke-filled backdrop sans the iconic two towers that had previously risen above the skyline. Their stadium's parking lot was being used to house excavation equipment, while cars of victims who parked and subsequently commuted across the water remained in place. It was much the same story with the Jets, where the players determined they were willing to forfeit the game against Oakland.

But the feeling wasn't universal. 'Many owners were aware the league played through after Kennedy's assassination,' adds Tagliabue. 'There was a large, though not unanimous consensus, that we shouldn't be playing.'

Bill Polian, then the Indianapolis Colts' general manager, remembers: 'Some of the players, especially those in the middle part of the country who are not emotionally connected to New York, did not necessarily want to cancel the games.'

Eventually, however, the Players' Association voted in favour of cancellation, aided by impassioned words from the commissioner: 'Pete Rozelle said the greatest mistake he ever made was playing during John F. Kennedy's funeral,' Tagliabue said on a conference call. 'I cannot countenance playing when Giants Stadium is being used as a morgue. I give you my word we'll work out the compensation. Nobody's going to be harmed financially because of this. We just have to do the right thing.'

'At that point,' adds Polian, 'Major League Baseball and college football had publicly said they didn't know whether they were going to play or not. The minute he made that decision, everybody else fell in line. That's the persuasive power he had, because of his integrity and vision.'

Sports Illustrated's Peter King described Tagliabue as giving 'a waffling sports world its sense of direction', while the *Washington*

Post's Thomas Boswell was equally effusive: 'The NFL acted first, which is appropriate since it is clearly America's dominant game, as well as a worldwide symbol of the country.'

Looking back, Tagliabue's decision feels like an obvious one. Yet the reality is far from as clear-cut, for there was a persuasive argument it could be viewed as giving in to the terrorists, as well as presenting myriad logistical challenges. The Chargers were due a bye that week, meaning they would have played 16 games to everybody else's 15 were the fixtures scrapped altogether. As such, the games needed to be moved to 5 to 8 January, the weekend after the regular season's scheduled end. However, with just one week between the conference-title games and Super Bowl, such a switch would have required the playoffs to be sped up. The possibilities of staging midweek games or cutting the postseason field from 12 to eight were both considered. Even pushing the Super Bowl back would be tricky. New Orleans, the host, was set to stage the National Automobile Dealers Association (NADA) convention a week later, with hotels already booked.

But the right decision was made. Whereas two days after Kennedy's death football players walked onto NFL fields, two days after 9/11 Tagliabue announced the Week 2 games would be moved to the season's end. 'In my mind, you couldn't continue with business as usual,' says Tagliabue, 'because this was not business as usual. This was a cosmic, unprecedented event, and playing football games that weekend was not appropriate.'

As for the Super Bowl issues, a resolution was reached with NADA that saw the NFL pay them $7.5 million in compensation for moving their event, paving the way for fans to focus again on who would do battle in New Orleans. But not before an emotional 23 September, when the league metaphorically reopened its doors amid scenes of perfectly judged patriotism around the country. The most poignant occurred at Foxborough, Massachusetts, where one of New York's two teams – the Jets – faced the Patriots.

Jimmy Andruzzi, the brother of New England guard Joe, was

one of the brave first responders, making it all the way to the 23rd floor in the midst of the rescue efforts then being forced into a quick retreat as the North Tower came crumbling down. He avoided death, narrowly. The Patriots made Andruzzi's three siblings – all New York City firefighters – and their father – a former NYPD officer – honorary captains. When the football-playing Andruzzi ran onto the field between a guard of honour holding up two United States flags, it served as a symbol for all the similar events taking place around the country.

Just as the Giants did in front of Tagliabue against the Kansas City Chiefs, New York's Jets emerged triumphant. The game was fairly uninspiring – finishing 10–3 to the visitors – yet its place in NFL history is hugely significant. Not only did the contest symbolise a grief-stricken nation turning the page, with weight added by Jets coach Herm Edwards giving the game ball to the city, it delivered a moment in the fourth quarter that remains one of the most notable in league folklore.

With just over five minutes remaining, Patriots quarterback Bledsoe stood under centre facing third-and-10 on a crucial drive with New England down 10–3. The signal-caller took the ball and scurried back for a long drop before spotting an opening down the right side of the field. With nobody free, Bledsoe took off. As he began to veer out of bounds towards the sticks, the man who signed a 10-year $100 million deal six months earlier saw Gang Green linebacker Mo Lewis in the corner of his eye. It was too late. The thud from the ensuing hit could be heard all around the stadium. Green says: 'I remember it, Mo, it was on the Patriots' sideline, and he drilled him, hit him right in the lungs. It was a great hit.'

'I couldn't think straight,' Bledsoe would later say. 'On top of the internal thing, I really got my bell rung pretty good. My insides didn't hurt until after the game, but then it was pretty bad. There were some sequences in the hospital where I was under when they considered opening my chest up.' Unaware he was suffering internal bleeding, Bledsoe played in New England's next series. By the evening, a sheared blood vessel meant he was undergoing life-saving surgery at Massachusetts General Hospital. Such was the severity of his injuries that football, once again, took a backseat, and most Patriots fans thought their season was as good as over without their starting passer. Certainly, Bledsoe's replacement, Brady, did little to inspire confidence against Gang Green, ending the game with four straight incompletions having led the Patriots to the opposing 29-yard line. In fact, the only question around New England surrounding Brady was: 'Tom who?'

Brady arrived in the NFL amid a weekend of embarrassment that would fuel his unique burning desire to succeed. That two-day stretch began on 15 April 2000 when Tagliabue put the Browns on the clock to commence that year's NFL Draft. Including their selection of Penn State defensive end Courtney Brown, a total of 198 choices were made – including six quarterbacks – before Brady heard his name called. The agonising wait, the latter part of which was spent heartbrokenly strolling around the block with his parents, was a fitting end to a collegiate career highlighted by rejection.

The day he arrived on campus at Michigan, Brady faced an uphill battle. He was barely a blot on the radar of most scouts following an unspectacular career at Serra High School in San Mateo, during which he only earned the starting job as a sopho-more after the number-one guy quit the team following a season in which they didn't score an offensive touchdown. Even amid that barren run, Brady hadn't been deemed good enough to see the field.

But the boy who grew up in the Bay Area idolising Joe Montana was hooked on football from the day he stood in the bleachers adjacent to the end zone at Candlestick Park and watched Dwight Clark complete 'The Catch'. He shunned a promising baseball career – Brady was selected in the 18th round of the MLB Draft by the Montreal Expos, but would have gone much higher had he opted against college – to pursue his dream of being an NFL quarterback.

Opportunity was provided by a recruiter called Bill Harris, one of the few men who saw the skinny quarterback's potential. Yet before Brady made it onto campus, Harris departed Michigan for Stanford, leaving the man he vouched for in the hands of a staff who had little use for him. Brady was one of seven quarterbacks on the depth chart in year one, and his prospects only diminished the following season when Michigan won the battle to recruit All-Everything local star Drew Henson.

For Brady, the Wolverine years were frustrating. He consistently outperformed Henson, only for coaches to implement a job share as outside pressures demanded the illustrious recruit was given opportunities. That trend continued until midway through his senior season when Brady entered the contest with fierce rivals Michigan State in the second half. Michigan trailed by 17 at that stage, only for number ten, as he was then, to almost engineer a miraculous comeback as they narrowly lost 34–31.

While he fell short in that outing, better returns were to come when Brady was finally handed the starter's job as he led the Wolverines to wins over Penn State and Ohio State, before signing off with a stunning 35–34 Orange Bowl triumph over Alabama despite Michigan twice trailing by 14 points.

As overdue respect began to come in Ann Arbor, most observers at the next level were unconvinced. Steve Mariucci, then head coach of Brady's beloved San Francisco 49ers, was among those looking for a quarterback. Instead of the hometown boy, he and Walsh – at that stage the team's general manager – opted for Giovanni Carmazzi in the third round.

'I couldn't forget about Brady if I tried,' says a rueful Mariucci. 'What if we drafted Tom Brady? I think about that a lot, but we were looking for a different kind of guy. He ran a 5.2-second 40-yard dash, which I think may be the slowest of all-time for a quarterback. But I think his story has made a lot of people look at how they evaluate quarterbacks. It's not just about the measurables – a big part is what's inside.'

Carmazzi was out of the league in a year, never playing a regular-season game. Yet the great Walsh was far from alone. Brady was passed over 198 times, a continuation of the rejection that still drives a crippling fear his job is always up for grabs. 'You don't take it for granted – you really never know when your last day is going to be,' Brady admitted.

Even with the various bitter moments up to that point, Brady was not lacking the assurance that earned him the moniker the 'Comeback Kid' in college. 'I always had confidence and belief in myself that I could do the job,' he said. So confident that, upon arriving at his first training camp with the Patriots, Brady sought out Kraft to pass on a simple message: 'I'm one of the best decisions this franchise has ever made.'

As the 2001 season unfolded, it became increasingly clear he was right. Brady led the Patriots to a surprisingly lopsided 44–13 win over Indianapolis for his opening act, in what proved to be the first instalment of an epic personal rivalry with Colts quarterback Peyton Manning. From there, the Patriots won four of their next seven games to reach 5-5.

When Bledsoe regained fitness, Belichick had a decision to make. 'Brady didn't establish himself as the leader right off,' remembers McGinest. 'The defense was the foundation of the team, and Brady was finding himself. But he was very consistent, took care of the football and did everything the coaches asked. They had just paid Drew Bledsoe $100 million that year, so we thought they were going to make the switch back. Belichick is the only person who could have made the decision to stay with Brady when Drew was healthy.'

Belichick being Belichick, he zagged when others would have zigged. His faith in Brady – who made the roster the previous year amid the coach's surprising decision to carry four quarterbacks on the 53-man roster – was rewarded. He helped New England conclude the regular season with six straight wins to reach the playoffs.

Once in the postseason, their unlikely journey took on an even greater mythical air. In the divisional round against Oakland, it appeared a game in which the snow was so severe yard lines were impossible to discern would end New England's aspirations with 1:50 left. Brady, who had been about to release the ball before beginning the process of tucking it back in towards his body, was strip-sacked by college teammate Charles Woodson, Greg Biekert recovering the football to seemingly earn Oakland victory.

But referee Walt Coleman dug deep into recesses of his mind and unearthed NFL Rule 3, Section 22, Article 2, Note 2: 'When [an offensive] player is holding the ball to pass it forward, any intentional forward movement of his arm starts a forward pass, even if the player loses possession of the ball as he is attempting to tuck it back toward his body. Also, if the player has tucked the ball into his body and then loses possession, it is a fumble.'

The Tuck Rule dictated that Coleman adjudged it to be an incomplete pass and allowed Brady to march New England to Oakland's 28-yard line. With 27 seconds remaining, Vinatieri made arguably the finest kick in NFL history, driving a 45-yard field goal low against the wind and snow to just clear the uprights. Then, in overtime, Vinatieri repeated the trick, this time from 23, as the Patriots emerged 16–13 victors.

New England's AFC Championship Game win was no less notable. Brady suffered a high-ankle sprain in the second quarter, meaning Bledsoe was called from the bench to see the Patriots to their 24–17 triumph at Pittsburgh that booked the club's third Super Bowl berth.

Team of destiny? Not if the mighty Rams, who raced into the postseason with a 14-2 record and then overcame Green Bay and the Philadelphia Eagles, had anything to do with it. 'You could make an argument that the 2001 team was the best of all that we fielded,' says Warner.

Before they tried to upset the odds, the Patriots first had to determine the answer to the same question that had raged weeks earlier: Bledsoe or Brady? Once again, Belichick opted for the latter and, as the seconds ticked down in the fourth quarter that weekend at the Superdome, a referendum on his choice was in progress.

The situation was most fitting: a Super Bowl to rival the 25th edition for its intemperate patriotism, featuring the aptly named Patriots, a team sporting red, white and blue who, as became the tradition of their season, shunned convention by entering the field together rather than individually. It proved to be a symbolic manifestation of the ties that bound the players and helped them to write the latest chapter in sport's oldest tale: David v. Goliath.

Their excellence in New Orleans went beyond symbolic clichés, though. An astonishing performance owed everything to mantras that define New England head coach Belichick's remarkable career: 'complementary football' and 'do your job', both of which would become their own timeworn definitions of the 'Patriot Way' as introduced to the world that night.

In truth, that 'Way' is simply a refined version of the blueprint adopted by all the NFL's great coaches, of building rosters in which all three units supplement one another and players subjugate their own ambitions for the greater good. The entire 2001 campaign was an introduction to Belichick's mastery of that doctrine, in which some games were won on the relentless excellence of their defense, others on the right arm of Brady and the rest on Vinatieri's right boot.

To overcome the Greatest Show On Turf, the Patriots needed all three to come together in one final performance that would serve as a microcosm of their season. With the defense having done its part by largely shutting down the Rams' incredible offense, all eyes were now trained upon Brady as the Patriots stood at their own 41-yard line with 33 seconds remaining and the scores locked at 17–17.

Sensing they were sitting off too much, St. Louis responded by blitzing. Brady retreated quickly, reaching just outside the pocket, and threw the ball out of bounds. 'I always say that was Tommy's most impressive play of the game,' says Weis. 'An incomplete pass that looks like nothing. But the kid was so smart. It's a blitz from the weak side, and that blitz triggered a sight adjustment. If we'd actually hit the intended receiver, I think that the clock would have run out.'

It also informed Weis' next call: '64 Max All In'. 'It was exactly the same play,' adds the former offensive coordinator. 'I called it again to the opposite side of the field. We changed the personnel from three receivers and a tight end to four receivers to make it look like a new play, but it was exactly the same call. Troy Brown replaced the tight end, and he was the open guy. I knew they'd kick into "Cover 2 Defense", which they did, and we knew they wouldn't blitz again, because they hadn't run back-to-back blitzes all season long.'

It worked to perfection. As Brady reached the top of his drop, Brown – having been lined up in the slot – was beginning his cut left. The quarterback skipped up into the pocket and delivered a dart perfectly in-stride that Brown collected and raced to the left sideline. 'The play was there, just as we drew it up, because of the work we'd done,' reveals Weis. 'Troy makes the catch, and we're in field-goal range.'

'This is amazing,' enthused Madden in the commentary box. 'It's something I'll admit, as a coach and analyst, I don't think they should have done, but they have the guts. They have a young quarterback, and they did it. They were backed up inside their own 20, had no timeouts left and are not only calling these plays but making them. At some point when you're in the Super Bowl, you have to let it all hang out. I'll say this, Charlie Weis and this Patriots team are letting it all hang out.'

With 21 seconds left, New England stood on the Rams' 36-yard line. Brady, in the face of another blitz, dumped the ball down to Jermaine Wiggins – who fell at the 30 – then gathered his troops quickly to the line of scrimmage and spiked the ball as the clock ticked to '00:07'. 'I'll tell you,' added Madden. 'What Tom Brady just did gives me goose bumps.'

'It's funny when you go back to that game, Tom only threw for maybe 150 yards,' says Warner of Brady, voted the game's MVP. 'That's not great by our standards, and you wouldn't say he had an overwhelming game. But to watch him manage that drive was incredible. Nobody knew he was going to be this guy, but it was special. That ability to settle down, be calm in the moment and handle big situations.'

With defense and offense having done their parts, it was time for the third piece of Belichick's complementary machine to seal the deal from 48 yards. 'This has been a year about Vinatieri and making some great kicks against the Raiders,' added Madden. 'He made two of the greatest kicks I've ever seen in my life.'

'This one is of greater importance if he makes it,' added co-commentator Pat Summerall. 'And it's right down the pipe . . . Adam Vinatieri, no time on the clock, and the Patriots have won Super Bowl XXXVI. Unbelievable.'

'That's the way you should win a Super Bowl,' interjected Madden. 'They came in here against all odds.'

On a night of stars and stripes, the Patriots embodied the American Dream. 'We're all patriots,' bellowed Kraft as he clutched the Lombardi Trophy with red, white and blue confetti dotted on his body. 'And, tonight, the Patriots are world champions.'

19

Nineteen and . . . No

Super Bowl XLII

NEW YORK GIANTS 17
NEW ENGLAND PATRIOTS 14

---

3 February 2008
University of Phoenix Stadium, Glendale

As Tom Brady locked eyes with Randy Moss, roaring through gritted teeth amid their helmets colliding, a sense of order being restored descended upon University of Phoenix Stadium.

Super Bowl XLII couldn't have drifted further from the anticipated script. The coronation of 18-0 New England, already considered the finest team ever to grace NFL fields, had turned into an unlikely slugfest as the Patriots and their outstanding quarterback crumpled under the weight of the New York Giants' devastating pass-rush.

'We were built along our defensive line,' remembers Osi Umenyiora, who spent much of his night in New England's backfield alongside Justin Tuck and Michael Strahan. 'They weren't able to block us and, if they couldn't block us, we could get to their

371

quarterback and take him out. That was the gameplan, and we executed it flawlessly.'

The idea of 'taking out' Brady and his record-breaking offense was considered fantastical, epitomised by the quarterback's giddy reaction when told about wideout Plaxico Burress predicting his Giants would win 23–17. 'We're only going to score 17 points?' said Brady, laughing. 'OK . . .'

His confidence was understandable. New England had spent the previous weeks redefining the parameters of offensive football as Brady broke Dan Marino's single-season touchdown record of 48 by tossing 50, 23 of which were collected by Moss to surpass Jerry Rice's NFL-best 22. Their exploits helped the Patriots accrue an unmatched 589 points over the regular season, with 38 coming against the same Giants in Week 17. Even a hard-earned AFC Championship Game win over the San Diego Chargers had brought 21.

Yet Burress, it turned out, underestimated his own team. Over the course of the game, a rejuvenated Strahan – no longer the force that set the NFL's single-season sack record with 22.5 in 2001, but still ferocious – and Big Blue's other quarterback hunters collected Brady's scalp five times. Their efforts not only derailed New England's offense to the point they stood on just seven points as the fourth quarter headed towards a conclusion but left the Giants contemplating arguably the most shocking victory in sporting history.

Until, at least, Brady displayed typical efficiency after regaining possession with 7:54 remaining at his own 20. A 12-play, 5:09 drive ended in much the same way as many others over the preceding months, Brady connecting with Moss on a seven-yard slant to leave the Patriots 14–10 ahead and on the brink of making history.

The only remaining obstacle to sporting immortality was a baby-faced 27-year-old boasting a name with which New England were incredibly familiar: Manning.

*

From the moment Robert Irsay purchased the Baltimore Colts in 1972, just 18 months after their only Super Bowl victory and third NFL championship, the club spiralled downhill. And not only on the field, where the Colts went from yearly contender to also-ran after Irsay touched down. Off it, the embarrassment of the John Elway affair was compounded a year later by Irsay's contentious decision to rip the club from its ever-loyal Baltimore fanbase. Come 1998, Indianapolis' Colts stood where Baltimore's did in '83, holding the first overall pick of a draft most felt featured multiple stellar quarterbacks. That, however, is where the similarities ended.

Irsay's death in 1997 ensured the reins were passed to son Jim, a respected figure in league circles who illustrated his pull by recruiting Bill Polian as general manager. Polian was the best team builder in football, his fine Buffalo Bills tenure followed by constructing an expansion Carolina Panthers club that reached the NFC Championship Game in just their second season. The move to Indianapolis, which brought Carolina a third-round pick, was too good to refuse. 'Jim Irsay was the reason,' Polian remembers. 'We served together on a couple of league committees, including the Management Council. I knew he was committed to winning and understood football.'

Polian's first decision would headline his career. Their opening selection was as inevitable as it was unpredictable, for everybody knew the choice lay between Tennessee's Peyton Manning or Washington State's Ryan Leaf. The question was which one Polian would choose. Most considered Manning, steeped in the game's minutiae as the son of former NFL signal-caller Archie Manning, to be a safer bet whose lack of X-factor arm talent was offset by a deep understanding of what it took to be a pro, both in terms of X's and O's and work ethic. Leaf, on the other hand, was a young gunslinger with questionable temperament but outstanding physical gifts, coming off a memorable junior campaign with the Cougars.

'The scouting staff was split right down the middle,' remembers Polian. 'People that liked Leaf intensely disliked Manning. To this day, I don't know why. People that liked Manning didn't intensely dislike Leaf. That's just a quirk of personality I guess.'

Polian sought outside counsel from the football cognoscenti's most distinguished quarterback whisperer – 'Manning by a wide margin,' said Bill Walsh – but the decision was informed as much by off-field traits as on-field. 'We'd started to dramatically change the level of background work done in Indianapolis,' remembers Polian. 'We did more in terms of investigating players' background, personality and character. It became clear Peyton was the right guy.'

Leaf ballooned by 20lb in the pre-draft process and, according to legendary ESPN draft analyst Mel Kiper, was 'self-confident to the point where some people view him as being arrogant and almost obnoxious'. Manning, on the other hand, displayed greater arm strength than anticipated in workouts and illustrated his desire by turning up to the Colts' facility to study the day after being the first overall pick. 'The work habits, intellect, desire to be the best and willingness to leave no stone unturned were always there,' says Polian.

While Leaf floundered with San Diego at the beginning of a career that marked him as one of the greatest busts in NFL history, Manning excelled. The Colts went 3-13 in his rookie campaign but reached the playoffs in each of his next two on the back of exceptional displays from their three star offensive pieces: Manning, running back Edgerrin James and wide receiver Marvin Harrison.

However, the ensuing season – in which their talented squad went 6-10 – hinted at a missing piece. After head coach Jim Mora carried the can, Polian and Irsay huddled to discuss their options. When the general manager provided his list of six interviewees, his owner threw a spanner in the works. 'What if Tony Dungy becomes available?' Irsay asked. 'I'm hearing Tampa Bay might do the unthinkable and let him go.'

'If that's the case,' replied Polian, 'just gas up the plane, let me fly straight down there and bring him back. All bets are off.'

Dungy had already built a championship Tampa Bay Buccaneers squad, only he wouldn't enjoy the credit. Following a 9-7 campaign in which Tampa Bay lost to the Philadelphia Eagles in the wildcard round, he was – as Irsay predicted – fired. Dungy left behind a team developed around his and coordinator Monte Kiffin's zone defense that became known as the 'Tampa 2'. Where the scheme was believed to diverge from standard 'Cover 2' was in the use of a middle linebacker – the exceptional Derrick Brooks – in coverage as an intermediate centre-fielder/auxiliary third safety.

Its brainchild, however, discredits his own innovation somewhat, claiming it was the same tactic deployed by the Pittsburgh Steelers' 1970s squads on which he played. 'The Tampa 2 is a misnomer,' he admits. 'It was the "Pittsburgh 2" all the way, everything from the 1973 playbook, exactly the way we did it in Pittsburgh. No differences, no nuances, nothing new. I guess people, by the time I did it again in 1996, had lost the history.'

Whatever the reality, Tampa 2's reputation was cemented during the year after Dungy's departure, with Brooks, defensive tackle Warren Sapp, safety John Lynch, cornerback Ronde Barber and edge rusher Simeon Rice terrorising opposing offenses in a manner reminiscent of the 1985 Chicago Bears and 2000 Baltimore Ravens. The Buccaneers allowed just 12.3 points per game and 10 passing touchdowns during the regular season, cementing their legacy by winning Super Bowl XXXVII 48–21 over the Oakland Raiders.

Defeat was particularly galling for long-time Raiders owner Al Davis, given Tampa Bay's new head coach was Jon Gruden, a young offensive whizz he traded to the Buccaneers for two first- and second-round draft picks and $8 million the previous offseason. It sat among a catalogue of errors made by the legendary executive over the tail end of his career. By the point of Davis' death on 8 October 2011, the Raiders were the butt of many jokes, most centred around the team having had six coaches across the preceding eight seasons.

'He made a number of decisions that were criticised as not being in the long-term interests of the franchise,' says Amy Trask, by then Oakland's chief executive. 'Every time I heard someone say: "Wow, I don't really understand these decisions" – and sometimes the criticism was a lot worse – I bit my tongue. What I wanted to say is that when you're of the age he was, and in the health he was, confronting your own mortality, you're going to define long-term differently. It was apparent some odd decisions were being made, but it was just the desire to "win now".'

Unfortunately, the choices never panned out. The loss to Tampa Bay, under Bill Callahan, proved the final Super Bowl appearance for not one but two of the most legendary figures in league history. On the Raiders' offense, wide receiver Jerry Rice – nearly 40 years old – plied his trade with as competitive an edge as ever. 'I went through my media obligations, back to my hotel room and cried like a baby after that game,' he remembers. 'It meant a lot.' At the point of his retirement in 2005, Rice had played more games than any non-kicker in NFL history (303) and shattered the all-time receiving records with 1,549 receptions for 22,895 yards.

The clarity of his and Davis' feelings contrasted with Dungy, who watched a team he moulded earn the NFL's ultimate honour without his presence. 'It was bittersweet,' Dungy remembers. 'I was happy for those guys, but sad I wasn't there with them.'

By then, the head coach was settled in his new home of Indianapolis, ready – alongside Polian – to construct another team capable of lifting the Lombardi Trophy. As the years wore on, Polian began to complement the offensive weaponry with defensive additions. Most significant were Dwight Freeney and Robert Mathis, who arrived in back-to-back years to fashion one of the game's deadliest edge-rushing combinations.

Suddenly, Polian's Colts began to resemble his Bills: a

penetrative offense designed to get ahead complemented by men-acing pass-rushers capable of teeing off on opposing quarterbacks playing from behind. 'I'd seen it succeed there,' he admits, 'so why not replicate it?'

Moreover, Polian was in lockstep with Dungy, much like Marv Levy previously. 'Getting Tony was key,' he admits. 'He saw the game exactly as Marv did. When we interviewed him, I asked how he would prepare a team and started to laugh during his answer. I'd heard it verbatim from Marv years before.'

Unfortunately, the other similarity with Buffalo was Indianap-olis' ability to be good, but not good enough. In the Colts' case, their path to that elusive championship was blocked by an AFC rival fashioning a dynasty during an era in which they weren't meant to exist.

On 9 September 2002, New England played their first game at the privately funded, $325-million Gillette Stadium, a monument to Robert Kraft's devoted ownership and the NFL's newly crowned champions. Prior to the season-opening *Monday Night Football* match-up with the Steelers, the Patriots unfurled their Super Bowl XXXVI banner above the south end zone. Fifteen years later, Kraft would have to initiate further construction work because there was no longer space to fit the tableaus to their many championships.

The year that followed the first's introduction was the most disappointing of the Bill Belichick–Brady era, as the defending champions went 9-7 and missed the playoffs. What proved an exception was considered unsurprising at the time, a Cinderella Story coming back down to earth. But New England posted double-digit victories in each of the ensuing 16 years and only missed the playoffs when Brady suffered a season-ending injury in Week 1 of the 2008 campaign.

Their status as one of the NFL's finest-ever teams was estab-lished over two dominant campaigns, the first of which began, seemingly, in turmoil. On the eve of the 2003 season kicking off,

Belichick shocked the footballing world – including his own players – by releasing defensive heartbeat Lawyer Milloy. It preceded
arguably the worst loss of the coach's career, a 31–0 beatdown
by the Buffalo Bills – who featured former Patriot quarterback
Drew Bledsoe on offense and Milloy on defense – that prompted
ESPN analyst Tom Jackson to infamously declare: 'They hate their
coach.'

'It did make us think in the locker room,' admits Willie
McGinest. 'He was one of our best players, a little brother to me.
There was some uneasiness after he was let go. Belichick brought
us into a meeting room and said we all loved Lawyer, but he had to
make a lot of tough decisions and do what was best for the team.
It wasn't personal. Bill cared for Lawyer.'

As with the release of Bernie Kosar at the Cleveland Browns
and trading of Bledsoe following the Patriots' first Lombardi
Trophy, Belichick illustrated a cold-hearted approach to roster
construction. The head coach wasn't enamoured by Milloy's play
in 2002, nor his $4.5-million cap number. Furthermore, he had
signed hard-hitting San Diego safety Rodney Harrison to a six-
year $14.95-million deal that offseason, believing – counter to
general consensus – he had plenty left in the tank.

Harrison became one of three Patriots first-team All-Pros. He
starred alongside Ty Law and Richard Seymour on a defense that
led New England – following a 2-2 start – to 12 straight victories
to close out the regular season. Sweetest of all was number 12, a
31–0 mirror image against Buffalo that delivered a most remarkable bookend to the regular season.

When the postseason concluded, the streak hit 15. The club's
second Super Bowl was secured in XXXVIII, a thrilling, back-and-
forth second half ending when Brady hit wideout Deion Branch
on a clutch 17-yard, third-down pass with 10 seconds remaining
to set up Adam Vinatieri's 41-yard field goal that sealed their
32–29 victory.

The 2004 Patriots were even better. Running back Corey

Dillon became Belichick's latest reclamation project, justifying the second-round pick sent to the Cincinnati Bengals for his services by producing 1,635 ground yards and 12 touchdowns as New England again went 14-2. Their first defeat, to Pittsburgh, snapped pro football's longest-ever modern-day victory run at 21 games.

Not that it mattered to the Patriots in the end. They earned their third title in four years courtesy of a 24–21 Super Bowl XXXIX win over the Philadelphia Eagles. Brady delivered a clean, 236-yard passing day, Dillon rushed for 75 yards and a touchdown, Branch won the game's MVP award with 133 yards and the defense forced three Donovan McNabb picks.

As blue, red and white confetti again rained down on a team now officially in the realm of all-time greatness, many around the NFL contemplated whether or not New England could be stopped. Nobody was as acutely aware of how daunting a foe the Patriots were than Indianapolis, whose own playoff ambitions had been thwarted at the hands of Belichick and Brady over those 2003 and '04 seasons.

By now, at least, they didn't have to share a division. The 2002 introduction of the expansion Houston Texans saw the league's makeup finally fulfil a prediction made by Pete Rozelle some 30 years previously. When quizzed on the eve of the merger in 1969, Rozelle had outlined a vision for the organisation of 32 teams split into two conferences that each boasted four divisions. The Texans' creation brought that structure – the same as exists today – to pass.

AFC East

Buffalo Bills
Miami Dolphins
New England Patriots
New York Jets

AFC North

Baltimore Ravens
Cincinnati Bengals
Cleveland Browns
Pittsburgh Steelers

AFC South

Houston Texans
Indianapolis Colts
Jacksonville Jaguars
Tennessee Titans

AFC West

Denver Broncos
Kansas City Chiefs
Oakland Raiders
San Diego Chargers

NFC East

Dallas Cowboys
New York Giants
Philadelphia Eagles
Washington Redskins

NFC North

Chicago Bears
Detroit Lions
Green Bay Packers
Minnesota Vikings

NFC South

Atlanta Falcons
Carolina Panthers
New Orleans Saints
Tampa Bay Buccaneers

NFC West

Arizona Cardinals
San Francisco 49ers
Seattle Seahawks
St. Louis Rams

Upon their move to the AFC South, having previously resided alongside New England in the East, Manning's Colts were 0-2 against Brady's Patriots. It would be the start of an epic rivalry between the best two quarterbacks in football who, at least during the early part of their careers, were measured against one another. 'They were, without doubt, the pre-eminent quarterbacks of their time,' remembers Polian.

Adding extra spice were the contrasts between the two: Brady, the sixth-round pick with zero family sporting pedigree; Manning, the son of a long-time NFL passer taken first overall. Perhaps more pertinent were the similarities. 'Neither was athletic, but both made very few mistakes,' adds Dungy. 'And both were deadly accurate.'

If you passed judgement based on games against one another, there was no argument over the early rounds. At the conclusion of the 2004 campaign, Indianapolis' passer was 0-6 against his New England counterpart, with a pair of those defeats coming in the postseason. 'The problem with facing New England,' adds Dungy, 'is it becomes about scouting yourself. Bill Belichick changes his team so dramatically week to week that you need to look at the game through his eyes. He will always take away what you do best and attack your biggest weakness.'

Dungy and Manning finally scored victory over their nemesis during a 2005 campaign in which New England failed to scale previous heights, but it didn't change the ultimate outcome of Indianapolis's season. In the AFC divisional round, the number-one-seeded Colts snatched victory from the jaws of defeat then somehow handed it right back.

Down 21–18 at home, Indianapolis were staring down the barrel. Pittsburgh stood on their four-yard line, facing first-and-goal with just 1:16 remaining. Rookie quarterback Ben Roethlisberger handed off to Hall-of-Fame running back Jerome Bettis, who was met by linebacker Gary Brackett's ferocious hit on the ball and fumbled. Cornerback Nick Harper scooped it up and raced back the other way, only to be taken down – miraculously – by Roethlisberger one-handed near midfield. When Manning drove the Colts to Pittsburgh's 29, it seemed victory beckoned until Mike Vanderjagt – alongside Vinatieri as one of football's best kickers – struck wide right from 46 yards.

For the third straight year, Indianapolis were eliminated by the eventual champions. Pittsburgh reclaimed their status as the NFL's premier team by winning a fifth Lombardi Trophy, sending Bettis into happy retirement that year, and 15-year head coach Bill Cowher the next, courtesy of a 21–10 win over the Seattle Sea-hawks in Super Bowl XL.

One year on, the script seemed eerily familiar. At halftime of the conference title game, the AFC's top-seeded Colts – now boasting Vinatieri – were once again facing the prospect of a home playoff loss. The Patriots, beaten 27–20 by Indianapolis at Foxboro during the regular season, led 21–3 and appeared in complete control. Dungy gathered his offense on the sideline and, echoing centre Jeff Saturday's pregame sentiments, calmly spoke: 'It's still our time. I promise you we're going to win this game.'

His words found their audience. The Colts rallied to make it

21–21 in the third quarter, before Brady and Manning exchanged touchdown drives. Indianapolis' was completed when Saturday jumped on Dominic Rhodes' fumble in the end zone to avert disaster in a play which symbolised that, on that night, Indianapolis wouldn't be beaten.

Their winning score was delivered by the man who replaced James after the running back had departed that offseason, Joseph Addai rumbling over from three yards. It was set up, however, by some exceptional tosses from Manning, who spread the ball around his other weapons, with Belichick having shut down Harrison. One of those was another likely Hall of Famer: Reggie Wayne.

When Brady, who took over with just one minute left down 38–34, threw an interception to Marlin Jackson, Indianapolis knew they had conquered Everest. 'It was almost poetic justice,' remembers Dungy. 'We knew we were going to have to beat those guys to get there, and it was sweet when we did.'

'Jeff Saturday often says that that's the purest form of elation you can find because it's against a heated rival in your building for the right to go to the ultimate game,' adds Polian. 'To write your name, win or lose, in the history books. There's no joy like that.'

Polian knew only too well the pitfalls of the next game, having lost three Super Bowls in Buffalo before departing ahead of their fourth consecutive appearance. The script was different this time, the Colts overcoming torrential rain and the worst possible start – Devin Hester returned the opening kickoff for a touchdown – at Miami's Dolphin Stadium to beat the Chicago Bears 29–17 in XLI.

In the process, Indianapolis certified three Hall-of-Fame careers. Polian, following the heartache of Buffalo, finally lifted the Lombardi Trophy. 'It was so overwhelming,' he remembers. 'The best part was I received about 75 letters – and this still gets me choked up now – of congratulations from Bills fans.'

Manning, meanwhile, ended suggestions he crumbled in the biggest moments. 'I don't think he needed this to validate his career,' says Dungy. 'But I was happy for him.'

Yet Dungy's part was even more significant, for he became the first black head coach in NFL history to lift the Lombardi Trophy. 'As I mentioned in my Hall-of-Fame speech,' he says, 'my first year playing, in 1977, there were 10 African American assistant coaches in the league. So, in 28 teams, there were 18 teams that didn't even have an African American coach on their staff. Coming from that and watching guys evolve and not get an opportunity to be a head coach, to know I was representing all those men, felt very special.'

Dungy's mastery cleared a pathway for pro football's other black coaches in more ways than one. Such was the esteem in which many held the coach that his firing by Tampa Bay years earlier prompted attorneys Johnnie L. Cochran Jr and Cyrus Mehri to deliver a scathing critique of the NFL's poor hiring practices entitled 'Black Coaches in the National Football League: Superior Performance, Inferior Opportunities'.

Paul Tagliabue had previously illustrated his strong stance on discrimination in 1993, when making the landmark decision to strip Arizona of its first Super Bowl because of their refusal to establish a state holiday honouring Martin Luther King Jr. His reaction to the lawyers' report was similarly emphatic, founding a committee on workplace diversity that led to the rule named after its chair, Dan Rooney. 'We knew we had a problem,' the Hall-of-Fame owner said. 'But it should have been called the "Tagliabue–Rooney Rule".' The 'Rooney Rule', introduced in 2003, mandated that teams interview a minority candidate for head-coaching vacancies. Six years later, it was expanded to include all senior football operations positions and, in 2020, further broadened to demand two minority candidates are interviewed for head-coaching roles.

By that stage, Tagliabue – who Dungy also describes as a 'driving force' in the Rooney Rule's establishment – had brought down the curtain on his decorated 16-and-a-half-year commissionership.

In Week 3 of the 2006 season, Tagliabue sat in the stands of the Superdome as an invited guest of New Orleans and their Saints. It was a fitting tribute to a reign that had concluded only two months previously. Just as the repaired stadium playing host to the highly charged *Monday Night Football* contest was a symbol for the collective spirit of the people of New Orleans, it also embodied Tagliabue's legacy. Without him, the game might never have occurred.

The previous August, as Hurricane Katrina rampaged through New Orleans' streets to leave a trail of death and desolation in its wake, the Superdome became a life-saving sanctuary. In all, around 20,000 people congregated in the arena before it also succumbed under the relentless weight of the Category 5 storm. During its near-week-long ravaging of the city and surrounding areas, Katrina claimed the lives of more than 1,200 people, left 80 per cent of New Orleans flooded and forced the city's evacuation.

Once its destruction finally ceased, Tagliabue – as was the case a few years earlier following 9/11 – was forced to immediately view a crisis through his NFL lens. Water had seeped through the Superdome's walls and engulfed the field, while also settling in elevator shafts and other small openings, and winds had ripped off a portion of its roof. For all it passed structural tests, repair work would take an estimated two years.

The arena being unfit for the 2005 campaign was beyond doubt, but the Saints' very status in the Big Easy also came into question. Prior to Katrina, many people feared owner Tom Benson, whose automobile dealership business was located in San Antonio, desired relocation. So, when Benson announced the Saints would play the ensuing season in the Texas city, worries abounded. Tagliabue, however, stepped in. He insisted at least half the team's home games were played in LSU's Tiger Stadium

– located around 80 miles from New Orleans in Baton Rouge – and privately told city governor Kathleen Blanco the Saints would remain 'an integral part of the fabric of New Orleans'.

In order to back up that promise, Tagliabue leant on officials to perform the necessary building work in just nine months. The city upheld its end of the bargain and, on 25 September 2006, the Saints and Atlanta Falcons took to the field in front of 70,003 season-ticket holders – the team sold every seat for the entire campaign – and the then-largest-MNF audience ever.

Following an Atlanta three-and-out, the roof threatened to lift from the stadium again – only this time in a metaphorical sense. Special-teams ace Steve Gleason broke through the Falcons' protection and dived in front of Michael Koenen's punt, sending the ball rumbling into the end zone, where Curtis Deloatch completed the touchdown that set up New Orleans' 23–3 win. 'That's the coolest thing, as an announcer, I've ever experienced,' said former ESPN commentator Mike Tirico.

'I think we're all guilty of overstating the importance of football,' says former Saints linebacker Scott Fujita. 'But that was one of those special moments that was so much bigger than just football.'

Responding to the grave situation was one of Tagliabue's last acts as commissioner. He retired with a reputation that encroached the rarefied air occupied by Rozelle. Over the course of his tenure, the NFL enjoyed almost universal peace with the Players' Association, his 1993 Collective Bargaining Agreement being extended through the 2006 campaign. 'Paul took over at a time when we had serious problems,' said Rooney. 'But he was up to the challenge.'

Tagliabue also oversaw four expansion teams, significant growth in TV revenues, adoption of instant replay and overhauled the league's drug-testing policy. Finally, there were two major in-house innovations: becoming the first sports league with a website and, in 2003, launching NFL Network, the league's

24-hour television channel. 'Simply put, the most honest, genuine, kindest, smartest, most visionary person that I've ever met alongside Marv Levy,' says Polian. 'Bottom line, the things he did were incredible.' Full recognition of Tagliabue's achievements came with his induction in the Hall of Fame special Centenary Class of 2020, which ensured he joined predecessors Rozelle, Bert Bell and Joe Carr.

One hallmark of Tagliabue's run was the smart use of committees to oversee individual elements of league business. The last of these concluded its purpose on 8 August 2006 when, after only five ballots, career NFL executive Roger Goodell was appointed as the NFL's eighth commissioner/president.

As a 20-something studying at Washington & Jefferson College, Goodell sent a letter to his father Charles Goodell, a former senator, that outlined his life's ambition with remarkable clarity. The young economics student wouldn't rest, he said, until taking hold of pro football's highest office. Nearly a quarter-century later, Goodell fulfilled his promise.

That the 47-year-old inherited an organisation in such rude health owed plenty to his own efforts during a 24-year career learning under Rozelle and Tagliabue. Yet it quickly became apparent he, like those before him, would stamp his own mark on the league.

One of Goodell's first actions was to bring down the curtain on NFL Europe, a development league that hadn't captured the imagination in the manner anticipated. Clark Hunt, former chair of the league's International Committee, remembers: 'NFL Europe was designed to create NFL fans in Europe, and I think to some degree that happened, but probably not to the level everybody hoped – although it did end up being a pretty good development league.'

With an economic ceiling close to being reached in the United States, international avenues still appealed to the league. The NFL's solution was groundbreaking, Goodell announcing in 2007 that the Giants and Miami Dolphins would contest a regular-season fixture at London's Wembley Stadium. 'It was controversial,' adds Hunt. 'There were some teams and a lot of coaches very reluctant to think about playing a regular-season game overseas, because of the travel that's required and [the] logistics. It had never been done. And everybody knew it would be disruptive. But through Roger's perseverance and critical leadership of the International Committee, we were able to get that done.'

The International Series – which debuted with the Giants triumphing 13–10 amid a typically English rainstorm in front of 81,176 fans – has gone from strength to strength, expanding into Mexico and Canada alongside multiple annual contests in the United Kingdom. 'It was a huge success from a commercial standpoint,' adds Hunt. 'After a couple of years, we could see the needle starting to move in terms of the growth in the fanbase, particularly in the United Kingdom. The game has fans from all over Europe, but the majority come from the UK. It was doing exactly what the league wanted, creating relevance, and that's why it's now expanded to playing four or five games a year, as well as games in Mexico and Canada.'

Commercial success became a running theme of Goodell's reign. A decade into his tenure, annual revenues had doubled to an eye-watering $14 billion amid the NFL capitalising on interest surrounding its draft and free-agency periods to hold the fan-base's attention for longer. In 2015, three-day draft coverage drew an audience of 45.7 million, illustrating the attention that would make Goodell's decision to turn the event into a Super Bowl-esque yearly roadshow such a roaring success.

Various successful tweaks spoke of a leader performing the role he had spent decades preparing for. At the point Goodell took control, his confidante father had passed away, but the hallmarks of Charles' own career were illustrated in another of Roger's early moves.

The value of integrity was ingrained in Goodell from childhood, a natural by-product of his father's political career being
all but ended by an unwillingness to toe the Republican party
line in denouncing the Vietnam War, which ran counter to the
Republican line. So, it was no surprise that the I-word became an
ideological rallying cry for Goodell, who characterised guarding
the NFL's honour as 'protecting the shield'. Nowhere did that
aspiration show itself more prominently than in the announcement, seven months into his tenure, of a revised personal-conduct
policy that allowed the NFL to wade into uncharted waters by punishing off-field indiscretions. The intentions were undoubtedly
pure; Goodell, at his heart, was a man of his father's principles,
coupled with a deep-rooted love for the game he played in high
school.

When incidents surrounding misbehaving players came to
light, they hurt Goodell deeply. One such example occurred on
the day of his announcement, when Las Vegas police revealed
they would seek felony charges against Tennessee Titans cornerback Adam 'Pacman' Jones in connection with a fight at a strip
club that ended with a shooting (not by Jones) and left someone
paralysed. Less than a month later, Goodell implemented his new
policy and suspended the player for a year.

Later that year, star Falcons quarterback Michael Vick was
suspended indefinitely after pleading guilty to federal and state
charges of illegal dogfighting, which led to 18 months' imprisonment. Vick's case would also show Goodell's pragmatism, the
reformed signal-caller eventually receiving conditional reinstatement and playing another seven seasons as a model citizen.

It wasn't just players punished by the long arm of Goodell's
Law. Rooney recalled being fined for criticising an official during
the commissioner's first season, but that was a mere slap on the
wrist compared to the punishment meted out to New England
early the next year. That controversy, which became known
as 'Spygate', would loom large over the entire campaign as an

exceptional Patriots team fuelled by a siege mentally took football by storm once again.

If there is one word that marks Belichick out from his peers, it's adaptability. Throughout his coaching career, whether as an assistant or leading man, he has prospered not by perfecting one ideology, but by viewing football through a wider lens and adjusting to opponents or ever-changing football philosophies. It is why, unlike Vince Lombardi's Power Sweep and Bill Walsh's West Coast Offense, there is no defining innovation that hallmarks his work. Such is Belichick's football acumen that he has been able to adjust across decades and find alternate paths. New England operated in a 3-4 defense for much of their early success because other teams weren't running it and those players were therefore more readily available. When clubs began to emulate the Patriots at the end of the decade, Belichick reversed course again and deployed a 4-3.

The same is true on offense. In recent years, as defenses have become lighter in response to the proliferation of spread attacks, Belichick has been one of the few coaches to regularly use fullbacks. Which is ironic when you consider he played a significant role in the position's de-emphasis during the 2007 season.

Those who have worked with Belichick confirm he views each season through its own prism, and that public proclamations of turning the page after seasons – successful or otherwise – aren't just lip service. Each offseason is spent taking a broader view that informs roster building and tactical planning. Following the 2006 campaign, still smarting from New England's conference-title loss to Indianapolis, Belichick had a clear blueprint for returning New England to the NFL's top table. If 2006 exposed anything, it was the dearth of quality receiving options available to Brady. At the beginning of that year, Branch held out following a contract dispute and was traded to the Seahawks for a first-round pick. His absence was felt.

Informing the need to change was a special project undertaken by Josh McDaniels in 2005. The young coach, now offensive coordinator, spent time with Urban Meyer's Florida staff to better understand the minutiae of spread systems dominating college football. Two years later, his learnings would change the face of NFL attacks as the next stage of offensive development after the St. Louis Rams' Greatest Show On Turf.

In order to exploit the concepts studied, such as high-low route combinations* and the one-back sets that neutered fullbacks, New England required the correct personnel. During the first week of free agency, Belichick traded second- and seventh-round draft picks to Miami for a small wide receiver whose most significant impact with the Dolphins was as a returner. With the Patriots, Wes Welker would become an ace in the pack, his shiftiness redefining the NFL's slot wide-receiver position.

Welker's greatest trait, much like his eventual replacement Julian Edelman, was an ability to see the game through Brady's eyes. From the start, the pair connected almost telepathically, which, combined with the Patriots' penchant for option routes, sparked huge problems for defenses forced to devote extra resources to the middle of the field.

Which is where Part II of Belichick's offseason came in. With Welker sure to command extra attention inside, the coach determined that adding threats to challenge the deeper portions of the field would create an unstoppable combination. In the lavishly talented Moss, perceived as the archteypal diva receiver, Belichick got his man.

Moss had exploded into the NFL nearly a decade previously, his rare combination of size and 4.3-second, 40-yard dash speed immediately earning plaudits aplenty. In what would become an unfortunate career subplot, Moss starred on one of the greatest teams not to win the Super Bowl in 1998, he and fellow wide receiver Cris Carter catching passes from Randall Cunningham on a Minnesota team that went 15-1 and scored a league-record 556 points. But the Vikings were beaten in overtime of the NFC

Championship Game against the Falcons, Gary Anderson – having become the only kicker in league history to go an entire campaign without missing a field goal or extra point – bearing the brunt of responsibility for defeat when striking wide from 39 yards. Instead of holding a likely insurmountable 10-point lead, Minnesota allowed a game-tying score and lost in overtime.

Although the Vikings never recovered, Moss continued to shine as he racked up more than 1,000 yards in each of his first six years and still managed 767 in 13 games during his seventh. Come 2007, however, Moss was a lost soul, frustrated after a two-year run at the downtrodden Oakland Raiders. The wideout's previous year's output – 553 and three touchdowns – was the worst of his career. Moss was ideal as Belichick's latest reclamation project, especially when he agreed to forego the two years and $20 million remaining on his contract to pen a modest one-year $3 million pact with $1.75 million in incentives.

Afterwards, as hamstring issues plagued Moss' offseason and rumours swirled that he had lost a step, reports circulated that the Patriots were thinking of releasing him prior to Week 1. In reality, he suited up and signalled the ensuing devastation that would befall New England's opponents by roasting the New York Jets to the tune of 183 yards, including a 51-yard score in which he accelerated past three defenders to quell doubts about his speed. The notoriety that would become attached to New England's 38–14 beatdown didn't surround the spectacular reveal of Brady and Moss' connection, however.

During the game, Jets head coach, former New England defensive coordinator Eric Mangini, reported that Patriots staff member Matt Estrella was videotaping their defensive signals, which led to his equipment being confiscated. Though the practice wasn't illegal per se, such recordings were only meant to occur in designated areas. Mangini would later concede he didn't consider it any real advantage, but the ensuing storm was significant. For many people around the NFL growing tired of New England's success, it provided a 'gotcha' moment that could explain away their own club's inability to scale such heights. 'We were compromised by Spygate,' claims Polian. 'Without question, it was impactful on the outcome of games.'

Yet other observers disagree. Multiple former coaches and executives have since conceded the practice was common around the league, while Polian's right-hand man, Dungy, doesn't feel it provided a difference-making advantage. 'It's something they didn't need to do,' he admits. 'They were an excellent team, with great scouting, coaches and players. They are gonna win – a lot – no matter what. It wasn't something that took everybody by surprise, as a lot of people knew they were doing that. It's too bad, but, again, I think they've showed they didn't need to do that to win.'

Following that watershed incident, in a much-criticised move, three league officials visited the Patriots' facility and destroyed all their tapes. Goodell claimed it ensured no further competitive advantage was gained, but conspiracy theorists and critics alike – most notably Pennsylvania Senator Arlen Specter – questioned its haste. Either way, Goodell levied the most significant sanctions in league history upon New England, fining the club $250,000, Belichick $500,000 and removing their 2008 first-round pick.

For his part, Belichick pointed to a 'grey area' in the rules, stating his belief it would have only been illegal had the Patriots utilised the video at any stage during games – something stringently denied. The coach also emphasised the actions took place in plain sight. 'I interpreted it incorrectly, and I was wrong,' he said. 'If it was our intent [to cheat], we'd have done it in a more discreet way. We were open about it. We had instances where opposing coaches waved to the camera. Everyone can see the signals, and we've had coaches in the press box take notes of them. We videotaped them to do it in a way that was more convenient, but those signals were available to anyone.'

Although Belichick expressed public contrition, confidantes speculated he harboured resentment about the severity of the reprimand. Certainly, the 2007 campaign provided compelling evidence of bitterness as New England seemingly took their frustrations out on opponents week after week.

The opening two months saw the Patriots deliver as impressive a run of football as ever seen. Moss, Welker, the underrated Jabar Gaffney, tight end Benjamin Watson, third-down 'back Kevin Faulk and another new arrival with blazing speed, Donte Stallworth, provided targets for triggerman Brady's relentless stream of bullets. New England became the first team in NFL history to utilise the shotgun on 50 per cent of offensive plays, capitalising on their quarterback's growing understanding of opposing defenses and unique chemistry with pass-catchers.

Having won the opening eight games by a combined 204 points, the Patriots encountered their first real challenge against an old adversary: Manning's Colts. Down 20–10 with 9:35 remaining, Brady hit Moss for 55 yards to set up a Welker touchdown, then threw the game-winning score to Faulk after finding Stallworth on another big play.

Their 9-0 start would eventually become 16-0, with Brady – unsurprisingly – collecting his first Most Valuable Player award. Such was the coverage surrounding their quest to become the NFL's second perfect team after the 1972 Dolphins that many failed to notice the many cracks displayed over the second half of the campaign.

After sneaking past the Colts, New England required a late interception to beat the Eagles 31–28 and only overcame Baltimore after the Ravens called a timeout just before stopping the Patriots on a fourth-and-one play. Even then, Eric Alexander had to tackle Mark Clayton three yards shy of the goalline after he caught a Hail Mary.

A similar tale unfolded in Week 17 against the Giants, when Brady engineered a comeback by hitting Moss on a 65-yard bomb that saw both players set new marks for touchdown throws and receptions in a single season. When Stephen Gostkowski added the P.A.T. to Laurence Maroney's fourth-quarter touchdown, it set up a 38–35 win and the first undefeated regular season of the NFL's 16-game era.

Yet as Big Blue's players left the Giants Stadium field, they all agreed that – should the teams meet again – the outcome might well be different.

In hindsight, the 2007 Giants looked every bit a team of destiny. They began 0-2, reeled off six straight wins and then proceeded to deliver a series of close victories to sneak into the playoffs as a wildcard team. 'We would give you a heart attack,' said Strahan. 'We couldn't win easy.'

That trait was never more evident than during the postseason, where the Giants' four victories would, remarkably, come by a combined 20 points. The most comfortable was the 24–10 wildcard win over the Tampa Bay. Thereafter, Big Blue overcame the Dallas Cowboys 21–17 in a game where they were outgained 336 yards to 230, before memorably taking down the Green Bay Packers in freezing conditions at Lambeau Field.

The latter win was sealed in overtime by Lawrence Tynes delivering a unique first in league history. His 47-yard kick, seemingly headed wide right before the wind brought it back, was the first successful field goal over 40 yards in temperatures below freezing. 'He had missed two kicks in the game,' said head coach Tom Coughlin, who suffered frostbite during Big Blue's 23–20 win. 'I was looking for a sign that he could make it, and he just ran out there.'

For all the accomplishments in reaching the Super Bowl, and the career performances delivered by so many at University of Phoenix Stadium, few gave the Giants much hope with 2:40 left against the mighty Patriots. Eli Manning, despite the name recognition, was still more notorious for his pre-draft status. He famously 'pulled an Elway' by refusing to play for the Chargers, which heralded his journey to New York. As part of their deal with

San Diego, the Giants selected Phillip Rivers fourth overall and traded him alongside a third-round pick that year, as well as first- and fifth-round selections the next for Manning.

Three years into his run, the outlay seemed unjustified. Manning was a pale imitation of older brother Peyton and hadn't been much better over the course of the 2007 campaign, producing 23 touchdowns, 20 interceptions and 3,336 yards. Yet the outside perception differed from that inside the Giants' own building. Manning illustrated his toughness by playing through a shoulder injury early in the campaign, then repeatedly came up big in fourth quarters as Big Blue snuck into the postseason with a 10-6 record. Once there, he delivered clean performances against the Buccaneers, Cowboys and Packers to further cement internal confidence. 'His greatest skill was how steady he was,' says David Tyree. 'He came into his own as a leader and franchise quarterback.'

As such, when Manning took over at the 17-yard line with a shocking upset on the line, Giants players were confident in their quarterback. The same, however, couldn't be said of a receiving target submerged at the foot of their depth chart. Tyree might have caught a touchdown earlier in the quarter to put the Giants 10–7 ahead, but it was hard for players to ignore the Friday practice in which he dropped every pass except one. 'It was the worst day of practice I've ever seen,' says Umenyiora. 'He was getting beat up by the ball.'

'I dropped everything,' remembers Tyree. 'It was the worst practice of my life, but I closed the chapter on it and moved on.'

The play after a moment of fortune fell the Giants' way – New England's fine cornerback Asante Samuel dropped an easy game-winning pick after Tyree appeared to run the wrong route – the wideout's dreadful Friday would take on even greater resonance as he produced arguably the finest catch in NFL history.

It occurred on third-and-five, with Manning perched on the Giants' 44-yard line. After taking six plays and 85 seconds of game time to gain 17 yards, the underdogs needed something special. As he took the snap and became engulfed by Patriots blue, seemingly locked in the clutches of Jarvis Green, Manning's hopes looked dashed. 'I was running a post pattern,' remembers Tyree. 'As I turned around, Eli was under duress. I turned around and worked my way back towards the quarterback. I saw some green grass and settled into it.'

As Tyree headed back towards his passer, Manning somehow broke free of Green's grasp, evaded the flailing arms of Seymour and stumbled backwards towards the right sideline. With a moment's room to breathe, he spotted a white jersey and threw up a prayer. 'From that moment, everything is slow motion,' adds Tyree. 'It's that *Chariots of Fire* feeling. I was tracking the ball and timing my jump to high-point it. I can still feel the ball in both of my hands. I braced for contact.'

It came from the most physical defender in football, Harrison. The safety jumped alongside Tyree, grabbed his arms and pulled. But despite his left hand being briefly dislodged, the Giants wideout wouldn't relinquish the grip, pinning the ball against the back of his helmet with his left hand before holding it with both as he fell to the 24-yard line.

Tyree's catch became the signature play of the Giants' remarkable victory, illustrative of the team who simply wouldn't be beaten – no matter the opponent or circumstances. And nobody represented the unlikeliness of their achievement quite like Tyree, the blocking wide receiver who couldn't catch a pass in Friday practice but held on in the most improbable circumstances come crunch time. 'There's a miraculous element,' says Tyree. 'I knew my role but wanted to find a way to do something meaningful and make a mark. Most people never enjoy a moment like that – not just the greatest catch in Super Bowl history but the most forgotten winning touchdown too.'

Said touchdown came four plays later, Manning anticipating the Patriots' blitz and looping a throw over cornerback Ellis Hobbs and into the hands of Burress for a 14-yard score. The win meant the Manning brothers lifted the Lombardi Trophy and Super Bowl MVP awards in back-to-back years, while Strahan concluded his Hall-of-Fame career perfectly.

Yet, remarkably, this was a rare Super Bowl remembered as much for the losers as the winners. 'The Patriots were on the brink of history,' concludes Tyree. 'The all-consuming storyline was 19-0. Make no mistake, they were an 18-0 football team, every bit as good as we thought. But, on that day, we beat them. People turned up expecting sports history to be made, and it was – just not the way everybody anticipated.'

20

Peerless Patriots

Super Bowl LI

NEW ENGLAND PATRIOTS 34
ATLANTA FALCONS 28

---

5 February 2017

NRG Stadium, Houston

The darkness engulfing NRG Stadium masked the troubled expressions of New England Patriots fans whose silence betrayed their shock. When Lady Gaga appeared on the big screen, standing atop the stadium's roof to kick off her halftime spectacular, most in Patriots colours stared into the distance, as beaten as their iconic quarterback Tom Brady – who had spent the opening half looking every one of his near 40 years.

A game billed as the Atlanta Falcons' raw verve tackling the Patriots' veteran nous had gone off-piste, with the team who'd been there and done it shrinking under the gaze of the spotlight. They entered the break in a seemingly insurmountable hole, 21–3 down after an error-strewn opening half that hit its nadir with Brady throwing a pick-six to Robert Alford, a play defined by the image of this gridiron giant diving in vain as the young corner-back hopped over his arm on the way to glory.

Perhaps many of the players were just following the halftime entertainer's hit song and adopting their 'Poker Face' as Gaga's dulcet tones cascaded around the arena, but the Patriots in pads were behaving differently to those in the stands. As she charged around the stage with increasing ferocity, a calm descended on Bill Belichick's men in the locker room. Unheralded safety Duron Harmon sat on an exercise bike rallying his teammates. 'This is going to be the greatest comeback in NFL history,' he stated. Julian Edelman, the star slot receiver, added: 'It's gonna be a helluva story.'

New England returned with a noticeably renewed sense of purpose. Fans, disconsolate moments earlier, were suddenly alive. Their mighty Patriots, of Brady, Belichick and four Super Bowl titles, wouldn't just give up without a whimper . . . would they? A quick Atlanta three-and-out suggested there was life; an even quicker Patriots one indicated there wasn't.

By the time the quarter was six and a half minutes old, everybody seemingly had their answer. A dynasty was dying in front of millions. Belichick's men looked old and slow, feasted upon by younger, faster and hungrier opponents. Atlanta were not just beating New England, they were leaving an indelible mark, moving the ball at will on offense and causing key defensive turnovers.

The Falcons' fourth touchdown was emblematic of the night. Too fast and purposeful for the Patriots' ageing linebacker Rob Ninkovich, Tevin Coleman darted across the formation at dizzying speed, underneath the glare of Matt Ryan, and the MVP delivered a perfect pass into the flat for him to waltz into the end zone. Matt Bryant kicked the extra point without fuss.

As he did, one family, carrying two heartbroken children scarred by seeing their heroes left powerless on the most damaging night of a glorious run, passed the press seats and headed for the exits. They couldn't take anymore. New England were down and out, 28–3 behind on an evening where everything that could go wrong had.

Even Brady, who two years earlier had further cemented his sporting immortality in the face of improbable odds, had no answers.

At Arizona's University of Phoenix Stadium moments after winning his fourth championship, Brady sat by his locker, motionless, back to the room, struggling with how to act as he processed feelings as familiar as they were unfamiliar. It had been 10 long years since he had collected a third Lombardi Trophy in his first four seasons as a starter, seven since *that* David Tyree catch ruined his and the Patriots' perfect campaign in this very building, and three since the New York Giants denied New England a fourth title for the second time. But the dark memories of two brushes with Big Blue had finally been laid to rest alongside dynasty obituaries penned in the preceding hours.

Reporters had been sharpening their pencils as New England reached the fourth quarter of Super Bowl XLIX enduring another evening to forget in what was becoming their house of horrors. They were behind 24–14, struggling against an all-time great Seattle Seahawks defense and facing the ignominy of another loss on the biggest stage. New England – having begun their run under Belichick and Brady with a 10-0 playoff record, including three championships – were staring down the barrel of a third successive defeat in the Big Dance. The narrative on a two-decade reign was altering in front of everybody's eyes.

The preceding years had seen the Patriots endure untold frustration. Belichick's crew remained the NFL's blue-chip franchise, posting double-digit wins every year after their Super Bowl XLII defeat, but the magic touch that brought ample rings had disappeared. In the season following their brush with perfection, New England lost Brady to a torn ACL in Week 1, still won 11 games and somehow missed the playoffs. It was an ominous harbinger of things to come.

Number 12 was ever-present thereafter, but the story had seemingly altered irreversibly. In 2009, the Patriots were bounced in the wildcard round, humiliated 33–14 at home against the Baltimore Ravens. Fortress Foxboro was anything but that again the following season, the AFC East rival New York Jets – who New England had pounded 45–3 just weeks earlier – emerging with a 28–14 divisional-round success.

The 2010 season saw the Patriots return to the ultimate game. Again, however, the final hurdle brought a fall, Eli Manning producing yet another improbable pass on a title-winning drive – this time down the left sideline to Mario Manningham, who somehow toe-tapped in bounds – to set up Ahmad Bradshaw's score and the Giants' 21–17 Super Bowl XLVI win.

Worse yet for New England, Big Blue – once again roaring to remarkable victory as a wildcard team – seemingly summed up a modern NFL that was enjoying the true parity which it craved. Over eight seasons after the Giants consigned the 2007 Patriots to 18-1, the Lombardi Trophy was lifted by eight different franchises, all riding alternate formulas to glory.

The 2008 Pittsburgh Steelers were built in the club's traditional image, Dick LeBeau's zone-blitz defense – starring James Harrison and Troy Polamalu – conceding the fewest points in football to complement timely magic from Ben Roethlisberger. The Steelers went 12-4 and capped their campaign by edging a back-and-forth Super Bowl XLIII against an Arizona Cardinals team featuring veteran Kurt Warner at quarterback and the era's best wide receiver, Larry Fitzgerald. Pittsburgh's NFL-record sixth Lombardi Trophy owed much to two plays: Harrison's remarkable 100-yard pick-six to end the opening half and Roethlisberger's astonishing game-winning touchdown toss to Santonio Holmes, who held the ball and grounded his feet in the right corner of the end zone for a 27–23 win.

The next year's big game was no less momentous, a fascinating duel between the New Orleans Saints' Drew Brees and Indianapolis Colts' Peyton Manning. The clubs' 14-2 and 13-3 respective records illustrated that Super Bowl XLIV was a meeting of the leagues' outstanding sides, but it was the Saints who came out on top 31–17 thanks to Brees' clean performance, Manning's pick-six to Tracy Porter and New Orleans coach Sean Payton's successful gamble to begin the second half with an onside kick.

A resurgent Green Bay Packers' victory followed, heralding a run that truly illustrated why the NFL's popularity was soaring to an otherworldly stratosphere. As the calendar clicked into the 2010s, the league's annual TV revenues hit nearly $100 million per club. That broadcasters were so willing to empty the vault was thanks in no small part to week-to-week drama so often serving as a prelude to fascinating playoff races. No period illustrated that more than 2010 to '12, in which three successive unfancied teams emerged triumphant.

It began with Green Bay, shepherded to a league-record 13th championship by their latest likely Hall-of-Fame quarterback. Aaron Rodgers spent three years patiently backing up Brett Favre after slipping to the bottom of round one in the 2005 draft. By the end of his third campaign as starter, he had confirmed himself a worthy heir to Favre, who briefly sullied his God-like reputation among locals by signing for the NFC North-rival Minnesota Vikings having spent one season with the Jets.

While Favre fell just shy of leading the Vikings to the promised land when losing to the Saints in the previous year's NFC Championship Game, Rodgers endured no such problems in 2010. He led the Packers to road victories over the Philadelphia Eagles, number-one-seed Atlanta and, sweetest of all, arch-rival Chicago Bears before delivering an MVP performance as Green Bay beat Pittsburgh 31–25 in Super Bowl XLV. Favre, who paved the way for Rodgers to earn the job by claiming he was retiring in 2008

403

only to renege and be traded to New York, hung his cleats up for good that offseason.

Eli Manning's win over Brady in next year's edition meant five successive Super Bowls, remarkably, were contested between likely Hall of Fame passers. Yet the 2012 season finale would be all about Canton-bound defensive players. The Ravens' ageing unit was led by two who are now enshrined – linebacker Ray Lewis and safety Ed Reed – and one who will be on their heels: pass-rusher Terrell Suggs.

In what proved Lewis' last season, the Ravens – having over-come Indianapolis in the wildcard round – enjoyed back-to-back road victories against the generation's finest two quarterbacks. They rode into Mile High to take down a Denver Broncos squad now operated by Peyton Manning in the wildcard round, then knocked off Brady and the Patriots at Gillette Stadium. That set the stage for a thrilling Super Bowl XLVII, in which John and Jim Harbaugh went head to head in a suitably tough-fought battle of siblings. Having led 28–6 early in the third quarter, John's Ravens faced a stirring comeback from Jim's 49ers after a 34-minute delay due to the Superdome's lights going out. Fittingly, it was Lewis et al. who settled the 'Blackout Bowl' 34–31, defending four successive Colin Kaepernick passes from the seven-yard line in the final quarter.

Defense was to the fore again 12 months later, only Seattle's was incredibly youthful. The speed of linebacker Bobby Wagner terrorised Peyton Manning and the Broncos in Super Bowl XLVIII, while their 'Legion of Boom' secondary – starring safeties Kam Chancellor and Earl Thomas, as well as cornerback Richard Sherman – shut down statistically the greatest offense of all-time. Manning shattered Brady's single-season touchdown record of 50 by tossing 55 in the regular season but was powerless at MetLife Stadium. He managed just one score as the Seahawks, two-point underdogs, roared to a scarcely believable 43–8 victory.

Such was the Seahawks' vigour that when they followed that up by reaching the showpiece again the following year, people were beginning to utter the dynasty word. Complementing their excellent defense was fine young passer Russell Wilson, whose journey from undervalued third-round pick to superstar was eerily similar to that of Brady, and brilliant running back Marshawn Lynch.

The storyline being written, with New England's ageing signal-caller and the Patriots down 10 points entering the fourth quarter, was a changing of the guard. But Brady had other ideas. He completed 13-of-15 passes for 124 yards and two touchdowns on Seattle's famed secondary to give New England a 28–24 lead that they held onto thanks to perhaps the most famous play in Super Bowl history. With 26 seconds remaining, reporters stood with hands on head in the press box when head coach Pete Carroll – translating excellence as a college leading man with USC in his third stint in the NFL – shunned Lynch from the one-yard line and allowed Darrell Bevell to call a pass. The head coach could only watch as Wilson's throw, bound for Ricardo Lockette, nestled in the hands of unheralded cornerback Malcolm Butler. 'He made a great play and came out victorious,' admits Lockette.

Such was the stunning finale that even Brady remained flabbergasted when he stood by his locker, composing himself as reporters surrounded him, their phones and recorders transfixed by capturing greatness in the immediate aftermath of one of his most remarkable feats.

Despite the frustrations, the years between titles three and four were good to Brady in other ways. The unathletic kid became the metrosexual man married to the world's most famous supermodel, Gisele Bundchen. If the Brady of the early 2000s, with his goofy smile and innocent wonderment, was the nerdy kid who somehow coaxed the head cheerleader into a date, then this edition was the All-American jock turning heads on campus.

Certainly, his teammates were smitten. Once he left his trance, Brady was mobbed – first by reporters and then colleagues, who lined up for selfies with the veteran quarterback in the manner of excitable schoolchildren. Only the goofy expression as Brady held up four fingers hinted at the boy who won championships one, two and three.

It wasn't just the players, either. Team president Jonathan Kraft, son of owner Robert, was equally reverential when discussing his quarterback. 'Tom's career was already validated,' he said, 'but it's now very clear he is the greatest of all time. It's not even close. Four Super Bowls over that period and a couple more appearances. He's the greatest.'

Kraft's words reflected the mood of the occasion, most having agreed Brady surpassed childhood hero Joe Montana in the GOAT stakes, and the feeling extended to the other key architect of New England's run: Belichick.

It felt like all the good work of that night was being compromised slightly as the world's eyes rested on Houston, Texas. In leading his team back from that 10-point deficit against Seattle, Brady had engineered the biggest comeback in Super Bowl history. Now the hole was 25 and the heroes of that night were villains here. Coleman's touchdown came after Butler slipped to give up a 35-yard pass to Taylor Gabriel and then committed a key pass-interference penalty on third down.

Having watched helplessly from the sidelines as the hero of Super Bowls past became the zero, Brady gathered his composure and troops. He marched the team methodically down the field, converting to Danny Amendola on a fourth-down out route, then producing a rare scramble on third-and-eight, before finding James White in the left flat. The running back cut back inside and dived into the end zone. The touchdown, it was assumed, was a face-saving consolation, especially when Stephen Gostkowski missed the subsequent P.A.T. and saw his onside kick recovered by Atlanta.

But New England's defense followed their signal-caller's lead by forcing a three-and-out and Brady responded with a field-goal drive that stalled on the back of two Grady Jarrett sacks. It was a two-score game – even if only in name. With fewer than 10 minutes remaining, New England required two touchdowns and as many two-point conversions just to force overtime.

Yet the Patriots sideline remained weirdly at ease. 'The only issue is that we were running out of time,' said Belichick afterwards. 'We moved the ball all game without having the points to show for it. We just had to keep grinding it out and squeeze out some plays here and there. Hightower's play was a big one.'

With 8:31 remaining, Atlanta faced a third-and-one from their own 36. The Patriots, whose statistical chances of winning at that point were 0.3 per cent, sent five men. Left of that quintet, Dont'a Hightower wasn't seen by Atlanta running back Devonta Freeman and had a free run at Ryan. 'That was an unbelievable play,' said Ninkovich, champagne dripping from his nose, in the locker room afterwards. 'We've run it a lot. I'm kind of spying the quarterback to see if he's going to run out of the pocket, and High's coming off the edge at full blast, and sometimes they screw that up thinking he's in coverage, and then, boom, the 'back didn't pick him up . . . strip-sack. Game-changer.'

'I'd seen Matt Ryan with the ball in his hands and wanted it,' added Hightower. 'So, I hit him and took it from him.' Following Alan Branch's recovery, Brady re-entered the fray, hitting White for four yards, Malcolm Mitchell for 12 and Amendola back to back for eight and six, the second of which put six more points on the board. The two-point conversion call was identical to one New England had utilised on the same field 13 years previously in the 38th edition of the Super Bowl, and the result was too: whereas Kevin Faulk had taken the direct snap to rumble into the end zone in 2004, this time it was White.

If anybody expected a shell-shocked Atlanta to immediately fold, they were mistaken. For that touchdown only served to awaken their best player, Julio Jones, who seemingly put the game out of reach with one of the all-time catches, rising high above the outstretched arm of 6ft cornerback Eric Rowe and showing astonishing body control to get both feet down in play on the sideline. 'I had the challenge flag in my hand,' recalled Belichick, 'but then I saw the replay, and it wasn't even close. Unbelievable.'

Even as the air went out of a stadium filled mainly by Patriots fans, it didn't leave the defenders' lungs. On second-and-11 from their 22, Atlanta – already in field-goal range – made a critical tactical error by calling a pass. Ryan dropped back and Trey Flowers, stunting inside, got to the quarterback for the sack. New England's winning percentage stood at 1.4 per cent prior to the play – their hopes were still slim afterwards but enhanced. 'It was a good call,' said Flowers. 'I just went inside on the guard and kept getting vertical. We know he always likes to attack the spot and [Ryan] likes to step up in the pocket, so anytime you get some inside penetration, he was right there to get the sack.' Having seemed destined to kick a field goal, Atlanta failed to move the ball on third-and-33 and punted.

Brady would get the ball back, down eight, with 3:30 remaining. He stood on New England's sideline, where, like the whole night, the team operated in the mould of their head coach by displaying remarkable focus and poise. Belichick, of course, had been there and done it more than anybody else, including 24 months previously when Seattle were driving on his defense to the cusp of a game-winning touchdown.

Lynch had just rumbled down to the one-yard line, brought down only by an incredible Hightower tackle, and the clock was ticking towards 50 seconds left. 'Now New England has to think about taking a timeout,' said Al Michaels on commentary. Certainly, that was the conventional wisdom.

Yet Belichick has never been one to blindly follow convention. He stood coolly, observing the frantic scene on the opposing sideline. 'Something just didn't look right,' he later said. Assistant coaches were all on the headset asking if he wanted to call a timeout, and Belichick simply stated: 'Just play goalline.'

New England were utilising that personnel grouping for the first time all season, but it had been a big part of their planning. Belichick wanted a scheme that could stop the run out of passing formations – something increasingly problematic in the modern NFL – and now, for the first time, with a Super Bowl on the line, he'd find out if it worked.

The rest, as they say, is history.

Seattle, seeing the crowded defensive front, opted pass and Butler wrote his name into the history books. The whole sequence was the ultimate validation for Belichick, the team's coach and de facto general manager. A play that owed everything to his meticulous planning, executed by an unheralded undrafted rookie free agent, encapsulating the maniacal attention to detail he had built his whole programme upon – the Patriot Way.

It was no surprise, then, to see Belichick's face betraying signs of tiredness after the game as his hands formed the tightest of grips around the Lombardi Trophy, like a man who never wanted to let it go. It was particularly poignant given the turbulent times that had preceded that moment for the veteran head coach.

The challenges had been varied and complex, but they all fell under the category of Belichick's programme being attacked. That was most understandable in the case of Aaron Hernandez, the superstar Patriots tight end who caught a team-high eight passes for 67 yards and a touchdown in vain during Super Bowl XLVI, and was rewarded with a big-money contract. Because in the months after inking that deal, Hernandez was behind bars, charged and eventually convicted of murder.

For all New England could have never foreseen the level of trouble Hernandez would become embroiled in, they took a risk by selecting someone who slipped to round four of the 2010 draft due to character concerns – and their decision backfired spectacularly. As Belichick himself acknowledged: 'As the coach of the team, I'm primarily responsible for the people we bring into the operation. We will learn from this terrible experience that we've had and become a better team from the lessons.' He signed off by simply stating: 'Moving forward consists of what it's always been here: to build a winning football team, be a strong pillar in the community and be a team our fans can be proud of. That's what we're here for.'

The Patriots were certainly still winning, just not enough. The controversy heralded another frustrating year of playing brides-maid for New England, who were injury-ravaged and eventually beaten by the Broncos in the AFC Championship Game. That they were one of just three clubs to beat Manning et al. during the regular season – coming from 24–0 behind to do so – at least hinted at a brighter future.

Yet it didn't appear that promise would be realised amid a sluggish start to 2014 that hit its crescendo with Belichick facing the media again, this time on 29 September 2014. The Patriots had just suffered one of the worst defeats of his tenure, a 41–14 shellacking at the hands of the Kansas City Chiefs. Brady – who completed just 14-of-23 passes for 159 yards, one touchdown and two interceptions – was nearly 40, the age when most signal-callers fall off a cliff.

The performance prompted a question about whether his position would be evaluated, but Belichick laughed it off and, infamously, refused to address the game again after that night. 'We're on to Cincinnati,' he simply stated every time it was brought up the next day. But it didn't stop the noise. ESPN's Trent Dilfer declared New England a 'weak team' who 'just aren't good any more'.

He, and many others, would be made to look foolish as the Patriots brushed aside the 3-0 Bengals 43–17 and then won nine of their next 11 games, one of the defeats coming after the AFC's number-one seed was locked up. From there, Belichick's men – buoyed by finally having brilliant tight end Rob Gronkowski healthy when the year hit crunch time – twice came back from

14-point deficits to defeat Baltimore in the divisional round, before annihilating the Colts 45–7 in the AFC Championship Game.

That should have heralded a fortnight of Super Bowl preparation, but instead New England were forced to answer, once more, to accusations of cheating. This time, it was claimed the Patriots were purposely letting air out of footballs, against regulations, in an attempt to gain an advantage. Weight was added to suggestions by an erroneous ESPN report that claimed 11 of the 12 balls used by the Patriots – each team has their own set – were at least 2lb below the 12.5 PSI minimum. It later turned out none of the balls were so underinflated but, by that point, 'Deflategate' was the biggest talking point of Super Bowl XLIX.

Belichick attempted to quell the hysteria by addressing the matter head on prior to heading west, explaining his week of learning about Ideal Gas Law and running multiple dummy tests on footballs at Gillette Stadium. These would have been instructive, given science has since suggested the change in the Patriots' balls that night was in keeping with expectations in icy-cold temperatures.

The coach also illustrated his annoyance at a bizarre interruption to the season's biggest fortnight by offering rare thoughts on the last cheating controversy to hit his programme, Spygate. 'I mean, look, that's a whole other discussion,' he said, his voice signifying obvious irritation. 'The guy was giving signals in front of 80,00 people, so we filmed them doing it in front of 80,000 people, like there were a lot of other teams doing at that time. But forget about that. If we were wrong, we were disciplined for that. But 80,000 people saw it, everybody saw our guy in front of 80,000 people – there he is. It was wrong, we were disciplined for it – and that's it. We're never going to do it again, and if there's anything even remotely close [to crossing the line], we're on the side of caution.'

Belichick's performance hinted at a man who believed his team

411

was coming under attack from those preoccupied with explaining how New England – in the free-agency era – were sustaining their success. That had certainly been a running theme in recent years. Teams had been known to complain the Patriots supplied warm Gatorade, and even barricaded their locker room shut in Gillette Stadium out of fear the boogie man was lurking around the corner. All of which speaks to a culture of paranoia, fuelled by New England's immunity to year-to-year highs and lows endured by everybody else. Perhaps no statistic illustrates their consistency more than the Patriots reaching eight successive AFC Championship Games from 2011.

Combined with Spygate, their success left many around the NFL seeking other explanations for their excellence. Deflategate started, officially, with the Colts, who informed the league of their suspicions. But rumours suggested they received a tip from the Ravens, themselves incredulous that their playoff contest in Foxborough was lost due to Belichick's ingenuity. In that game, he installed 'Baltimore', a package of legal plays that saw the Patriots throw to a tight end lined up at left tackle while their actual tackle stood at receiver, staying on the line of scrimmage and declaring himself an ineligible receiver. Belichick spotted the ploy watching friend Nick Saban, arguably the greatest college coach in history, do so in a key game with LSU.

The Baltimore plays left opposite number John Harbaugh furious on the sideline – he drew a 15-yard penalty for his protests – but Belichick had already checked with the league office that it was legal. At least it was at that point. After the season, the NFL changed the rules.

The plays were key to victory and, like the subsequent Super Bowl, symbolic of the edge Belichick gives New England. They also combined to help him turn the page on the most challenging period of his career. He lifted his first title since becoming engulfed, directly or indirectly, in differing scandals and even staunch critics paid begrudging respect. 'I don't think you heal the wounds of Spygate,' says Bill Polian, 'but the later success since certainly cleaned up history.'

As Brady headed back onto NRG Stadium's field with 3:30 remaining of a dizzying contest, the Patriots' status as the NFL's best team lay in question. The scene was almost biblical, the battered-and-bruised quarterback, nigh-on 40 years old, rejoining his team once more in the huddle, somehow not blinded by the flashes of camera phones swarming around the stadium as he displayed the kind of 'laser focus' he had implored from his teammates moments earlier. 'C'mon, boys,' he screamed, his voice shaking with intensity. 'Let's go. You gotta lock in, now.'

Brady started inauspiciously, succumbing to pressure on first and second down to leave third-and-10. The Patriots had come so far but were still far from close. Brady dropped back on third down with 91 yards of field lying ahead, 16 of which were eaten up by wide receiver Chris Hogan, who cut on a dime and headed for the right sideline. Before he was out, the ball dropped in his hands. First down.

Another followed soon after, Brady hitting Mitchell on the left sideline after throwing incomplete to Edelman on first down. Then came the play that will be replayed in the minds of all involved for the rest of their lives. Brady dropped back once more, hop-stepped twice and drove the ball 23 yards downfield to the right hashmark, where Edelman waited, hands poised. Only it never arrived. Alford tipped it in the air and then, along with two other Falcons defenders, converged on the pigskin, scenting a game-sealing interception. Yet so too did Edelman, the scrappy 5ft 8in wideout – a former college quarterback – colliding with the blur of red and black but holding onto the ball as it nestled on top of Ricardo Allen's arm.

From there, the Patriots had momentum. Brady hit Amendola for a big gain, then threw twice underneath to White for 13 and seven yards to leave New England at the one. Brady stood under centre, called 'Alabama', turned around and handed the ball to White, who ran behind Marcus Cannon and Martellus Bennett's double-team block to score. The crucial two-point play was equally successful. Brady hit Amendola on a wide-receiver screen and watched as his wideout edged the football's nose over the goalline.

Atlanta still had 57 seconds with which to work but could do little with it. They looked cooked and, suddenly, reporters were writing a different story: of Brady's revenge. And a season that had begun with what was arguably his ugliest, most public, defeat ending in victory, concluded with the delicious irony of Brady receiving the Lombardi Trophy from the man he had spent months battling in the US court system: commissioner Roger Goodell.

Such a bizarre tale being reality was due to Deflategate, the saga having rumbled on far longer than anybody wanted or anticipated. It was a roller-coaster ride that eventually surrounded much more than the league's overzealous discipline or even Brady's guilt. The NFL was fighting to maintain wide-ranging powers enjoyed by Goodell that were upheld in the 2011 Collective Bargaining Agreement, which followed the NFL's first lockout for 24 years.

The biggest point of contention behind the NFL's longest work stoppage – it totalled 135 days but didn't include any games being missed – was the owners' desire to reduce the percentage of revenue given to the players. Their argument was that clubs earning a higher proportion would make investment in revenue drivers such as stadiums and international games more feasible and, therefore, grow the overall pot significantly. In essence, the players would gain a lesser percentage but greater amount overall.

Goodell eventually found agreement with DeMaurice Smith, the latest head of the players' association, albeit with concessions. Training camps and offseason team activities were reduced, retired players gained greater benefits via the establishment of a Legacy Fund and, perhaps most significantly, contracts given to rookies were significantly reduced – freeing more cap space for veterans.

A mere footnote was Article 46, which gave the commissioner carte blanche to initiate punishment 'for conduct detrimental to the integrity of, or public confidence in, the game of professional football' and also hear the appeals of any sanctions. The clause had existed since Rozelle's earliest days but – as the years wore on and Goodell began to serve as judge, jury and executioner more often – it became a bone of contention. In 2011, when the commissioner discovered the existence of the Saints' 'bounty' scheme – in which players were rewarded for injuring opponents – he brought the hammer down. Head coach Sean Payton was suspended for the 2012 season, defensive coordinator Gregg Williams indefinitely (he would be reinstated in 2013), general manager Mickey Loomis for eight games and assistant head coach Joe Vitt for six. The club were fined $500,000 and stripped of two second-round picks, while four current and former Saints players were also sanctioned. That the player penalties in 'Bountygate' – including linebacker Jonathan Vilma being banned for a year – were all quashed by Paul Tagliabue after he was appointed arbitrator spoke not only of the differing view between regimes, but Goodell's increasingly ham-fisted approach to discipline.

Another example was the case of Ravens running back Ray Rice, suspended for two games in 2014 and fined $529,000 after being charged with physical assault following an altercation with his fiancée in a casino elevator. On this occasion, Goodell was accused of being too lenient – something he later conceded was correct in a lengthy letter to the owners. As such, Goodell announced future violations regarding assault, battery, domestic violence or sexual assault involving physical force would carry a six-game ban with any second offence bringing banishment for at least one year.

Increasingly, domestic violence was becoming a touchstone

415

for criticism of Goodell's Personal Conduct Policy and muddled, reactionary thinking. When video of the Rice incident – showing him knocking Janay Palmer unconscious – circulated online, the commissioner announced an indefinite suspension that would later be reversed in federal court. Combined with another legal ruling in the NFLPA's favour surrounding likely Hall-of-Fame Minnesota Vikings running back Adrian Peterson, Rice's victory laid the foundation for further litigation, this time brought by Brady, who had been handed a four-game ban for his alleged involvement in Deflategate.

The argument against Brady featured some compelling circumstantial evidence: CCTV from the night showed Patriots equipment staff, one of whom referred to himself as 'the deflator' in text messages, going into stadium toilets with the balls. Brady and New England's strongest riposte was science. The PSI levels that night met forecasts based on temperatures, while the league has since tested the impact of weather on the air pressure of footballs but refused to publicise the findings.

What was published is independent investigator Ted Wells' investigation, which concluded it 'more probable than not' Brady was 'at least generally aware' of a scheme to deflate footballs. Based on the standard of proof required in the CBA, Wells gave Goodell licence to throw the book.

Most people considered the punishments, of both Brady and the club – they were stripped of first- and fourth-round picks and fined $1 million – heavy-handed. As such, many were stunned when Goodell upheld sanctions after personally hearing his appeal. Among those was Patriots owner Kraft, a long-time and powerful Goodell ally who 'reluctantly accepted' the club's penalties, publicly stating it was 'in the best interest of the full 32 [teams]' while privately believing the commissioner would reduce, or vacate, those against Brady. 'I was wrong to put my faith in the league,' he said at a press conference. 'The decision handed down by the league is unfathomable to me. I have come to the conclusion that this was never about doing what was fair and just.'

Brady was now a pawn in a wider game, with implications that extended beyond his own image. He pursued the matter with varied results. After scoring an unexpected victory when a federal court overturned the sanctions, they were reinstated by the United States Court of Appeals for the Second Circuit, with two of three judges adjudging Goodell's actions to be fair, and the other siding with the union and Brady.

While Goodell won that conflict, he lost in the court of public opinion, openly battling the NFL's most decorated player over the PSI of footballs based upon an insubstantial case. 'Goodell acted without nearly enough scientific evidence against the Patriots,' wrote renowned NFL writer Peter King. 'The NFL had some significant circumstantial evidence in the case, the kind that should have prompted a strongly worded letter and $250,000 fine. Instead, Goodell killed an ant with a sledgehammer.'

· The ultimate indictment of the episode came on the field, for Brady and the Patriots went on to prove that, even if such a scheme existed, it was inconsequential. They outscored the Colts 28–0 in the second half of the game that had originated the drama, when the balls had been pumped up again, then beat the Seahawks in the Super Bowl.

The next season brought another conference-title appearance, in which the injury-ravaged Patriots were defeated 20–18 on the road against Denver's exceptional defense. That game brought down the curtain on Brady's epic rivalry with Peyton Manning, who edged out his contemporary in their last meeting before winning Super Bowl 50 24–10 over the Carolina Panthers. Manning was a shadow of his former self during the campaign – even spending some time on the bench – but a deserved second ring brought further validation of an all-time-great career.

Although Manning triumphed in the final battle with his old adversary, Brady took the overall war. He returned from his four-game suspension with vengeance during the 2016 campaign, culminating one incredible night in Space City with a display that eclipsed anything seen in NFL history.

The coin landed on heads, and Matthew Slater was emphatic: 'We'll take the ball,' shouted the Patriots' star special-teamer and captain.

All eyes were suddenly back on number 12, the grizzled gladiator returning to centre stage of this gargantuan coliseum for what he hoped would be the last time. The task was simple: score another touchdown and become the first quarterback to win five Super Bowls. To achieve that, Belichick stuck with the plan that had got New England back in the contest, ignoring the running game and throwing outside the numbers.

Atlanta's defense, suffering from exhaustion having faced a remarkable 84 plays, had no answers as Brady took just an additional nine to precisely dissect them one more time to the tune of 75 yards. On the last of those, the Patriots utilised a call for which Belichick deserves the credit. Entering the game, the head coach instructed his staff to put extra effort into two-point plays, having an inkling they could form a key part of an anticipated high-scoring contest. New England subsequently installed three. Two had been utilised successfully to reach overtime and now, two yards from a fifth Super Bowl title, facing second-and-goal, they called the third, albeit for a touchdown rather than two-point play.

Brady lined up under centre with the Patriots in 11 personnel* and showing a stacked line* to the right. The signal-caller took the ball from centre David Andrews, made a step left and then tossed it back across his body to White, who began running right. As he did, right tackle Cannon came around the corner, replaced at the line by receivers Hogan and Edelman – who were executing crack blocks. From there, White – scenting the goalline – ran behind Cannon, but the tackle was outnumbered; Atlanta had played it well. Still a yard and a half separated White from the end zone, so he cut back between Deion Jones and Allen, riding the latter's tackle, and dived for glory. The line judge ran in and raised his two arms, prompting that familiar roar from the cannon and a shower of confetti.

Most of the Patriots were immediately jubilant, Mitchell and Hogan running off in a frenzy. But others, including Brady, knew better. He stood around, looking dazed, especially after Edelman jumped on top of him. Knowing all scoring plays are automatically reviewed, he waited. In the meantime, Edelman went to find Belichick, who extended for a hug. 'Is it over? They gotta review it,' the wide receiver said.

'They reviewed it,' replied Belichick.

'They reviewed it?'

'Yeah,' added the 64-year-old, his face breaking out into a rare smile as he screamed giddily, hugging one of the key men responsible for engineering the biggest comeback in Super Bowl history.

If Arizona represented New England reclaiming power, Houston was their coronation. 'Bill is guaranteed to go down as the greatest head coach in the history of the game,' says Brian Billick, himself a Super Bowl-winning leading man. 'The numbers support that. Whether you like or don't like him, he's the best.' Hall-of-Fame signal-caller Troy Aikman said: 'It was always an easy answer: Joe Montana was the greatest player ever. Now I've changed my tune: Brady is.'

The only remaining debate surrounded who was more responsible for New England's success: Belichick or Brady. The tenuousness of pursuing that question was best illustrated over the two campaigns that followed their fifth championship, both of which ended with the Patriots back in the Super Bowl.

In 2018, Brady was on the losing side despite arguably his finest big-game performance, a record 505-yard, three-touchdown night rendered irrelevant. The Philadelphia Eagles, playing backup quarterback Nick Foles after MVP candidate Carson Wentz suffered a late-season injury, went toe to toe with Brady to win LII

41–33. The result brought unfamiliar ire in Belichick's direction, compounded by his unexplained decision to bench XLIX hero Butler for every defensive series.

Yet Belichick's riposte the next season was emphatic. In the 2019 AFC Championship Game, his defense delivered a first-half road shutout against a Kansas City Chiefs offense piloted by second-year MVP sensation Patrick Mahomes and went one better by holding the Los Angeles Rams – who relocated in 2017 – to just three points in Super Bowl LIII. Ironically, one year after the highest-scoring showpiece came the lowest, New England's 13–3 win settled by Brady's game-winning drive, which featured a stellar sign-off from Gronkowski. The most dominant tight end in history collected Brady's arching 29-yard pass to set up Sony Michel's game-winning touchdown in what proved his final outing.

For all the Patriots' points were delivered by contributions from Brady, Gronkowski and game MVP Edelman, the game served as another distillation of Belichick's defensive genius. In shutting down a Rams offense that ranked second in football that year with 421.1 yards and 32.9 points per game, he delivered a masterpiece that sits alongside Super Bowl XXV and XXXVI gameplans. 'He doesn't need a lot of our help, but we try to do our best to serve him and this organisation,' says Belichick's long-time personnel right-hand-man Nick Caserio. 'He deserves all the accolades he gets.'

A sixth Super Bowl drew New England level with the Steelers, while putting Brady and Belichick's individual records for quarterback and head coach further out of reach. Where the numbers finish remains to be seen but the legacies are already sealed: the Patriots boast the greatest quarterback, head coach and dynasty in NFL history.

EPILOGUE

Week 1

GREEN BAY PACKERS 10
CHICAGO BEARS 3

---

6 September 2019

Soldier Field, Chicago

To think of the Chicago Bears versus the Green Bay Packers is to evoke images of the game's ultimate brutes colliding, kicking up clouds of dust in America's Midwest as they exemplify the very essence of the Black and Blue Division in which they sit. While the warriors provide sport on the battlefield, those observing create the iconic atmosphere, their screams visible as warm breath meets ice-cold air.

Yet the 2019 Week 1 kick-off showpiece, prior to the action at least, couldn't be further removed from the image conjured in the mind's eye. A tailgate sitting in the shadow of the Bears' illustrious arena plays out in 25 degrees Celsius temperatures, sun beating down on the hordes sporting orange and blue as they drink beers, down shots of Fireball and grill burgers.

Although the conditions are far from typical of pro football's ultimate match-up, evidence of the NFL's ingenuity in shunning the usual tradition of the reigning Super Bowl champion kicking off the campaign is provided at every turn – most symbolically by a family standing next to their pick-up truck, the youngest sporting a modern-day Khalil Mack jersey, his father in Mike Ditka fancy dress, complete with a moustache and cigar, and his grandfather wearing an old-fashioned Bears-coloured jumper in the style Red Grange might once have donned.

The NFL's 100th season kicks off with the 200th meeting between pro-football clubs who have played since its first (Bears) and second (Packers), and takes place in a stadium perfectly befitting their historic rivalry. Many writers mythologise NFL action, and it's easy – and natural – for them to resort to comparisons with war – to refer to players as soldiers in some grand conflict and the venues at which they play as Coliseums. Soldier Field is where fable meets reality. Not only is the structure a tribute to the United States' armed forces, it's unique in that a separate stadium sits inside that truly iconic outer shell, full of white pillars and stone that evoke immediate thoughts of Ancient Rome.

As kick-off approaches, fans begin their journey inside the walls, many stopping to take pictures of the recently unveiled statue celebrating an illustrious former son – Walter Payton – en route. Thereafter, all come together as they have so many times over the preceding 99 years, providing the unmistakeable noise that is just a little different when these rivals meet.

By the time legends from the 1985 Bears are paraded on the field – introduced as the 'greatest team in NFL history' – ahead of kick-off, the atmosphere is bubbling over. Fittingly, the modern-day Monsters of the Midway – having been compared to illustrious predecessors after fielding the league's best defense in 2018 – take to the field first, ready to make their mark on the Packers' all-time great quarterback Aaron Rodgers.

On the first play, Roquan Smith – the latest young linebacker following in the lineage of Bill George, Dick Butkus, Mike Singletary and Brian Urlacher – breaks into the backfield and brings down Aaron Jones by the ankles. On the next, it's a similar story, Smith perfectly diagnosing a screen play to deny the running back once again. Facing third-and-10, Rodgers retreats in the face of pressure and is sacked. The Monsters, like the stands, are roaring.

Despite that opening setting a suitable tone for the remainder of the evening, the fans' snarls were quietened by the game's conclusion. Smith's interventions set the stage for a bruising old-school battle that would have made greats from Butkus and Ray Nitschke to Vince Lombardi and George Halas blush. In the hyper-charged modern NFL, where passing is king and points come as quickly as the latest buck in the league's bank account, the teams manage 13 points in total. But it is the Monsters of the Bay, as opposed to Midway, who come out on top.

Which, when you think of it, is probably fitting too. The opening fixture of the NFL's 100th season somehow encapsulated all that had preceded it: the Packers of tiny Green Bay just emerging triumphant over their big-city rivals. The more things change, the more they really do stay the same.

Week 5

CHICAGO BEARS 21
OAKLAND RAIDERS 24

---

6 October 2019
Tottenham Hotspur Stadium, London

The highly anticipated moment occurred on Wednesday afternoon, hastily following English Premier League side Tottenham Hotspur's humbling 7–2 UEFA Champions League loss to Bayern Munich. A stadium that is quickly becoming iconic in the United Kingdom was a hive of activity, staff shuttling around to lay the groundwork for the hydraulic presses to kick in. As they did, events were being tracked closely by some of the NFL's biggest hitters either side of the pond. For all the successful tests, this would be truly significant. 'We followed it closely,' Christopher Halpin, the league's executive vice-president and chief strategy and growth officer, admits. 'I popped over mid-installation and at the end. We had done dry runs, but that first time it's real.'

They need not have worried. By the day's end, Tottenham Hotspur Stadium's grass football field had made way for gridiron turf, NFL logo painted into place and end zones gleaming under the glare of the floodlights. The first purpose-built American football stadium in England was, well, perfectly fit for purpose.

As he stood on the sideline four days later, Halpin beamed when I relayed to him that all 10 US sportswriters polled in the

424

press box felt the arena was not just akin to the stadiums in the United States, but up there with the crème de la crème. 'We want our teams to have best-in-class experiences,' adds Halpin. 'Tottenham have partnered with us and built something truly special. It is customised with the field and facilities all up to NFL standard. And, in terms of overall fan experience, we can do all of the things NFL fans have come to expect. Whether it's the viewing angles – that south end-zone ramp is like nothing else – or the two NFL-only locker rooms, or the field. The finished product is like nothing else in the world.'

When kick-off between the Oakland Raiders and Chicago Bears comes, the amphitheatre illustrates the value of the NFL's nearly $12-million investment in aiding the build. Pregame, one reporter observed the similarities between this ground and the Seattle Seahawks' CenturyLink Field, particularly the South Stand. Yet the comparison felt more apt once deafening roars – exacerbated by the unique shaping – filled your eardrums. It's a cauldron, far removed from the sometimes sterile atmosphere at the UK's other regular NFL venue: Wembley Stadium.

Were it not for the sight of an emblematic cockerel – representing Tottenham's club crest – perched on the South Stand roof, you might have forgotten that this wasn't just a place for gridiron. For the atmosphere was every bit as zealous as that for the season-opening tilt between the Bears and Green Bay Packers. There was something unmistakeable yet unquantifiable. An aura. A feeling that, 12 years on from the inaugural regular-season game on these shores, another new era was upon us.

'It feels momentous,' adds Halpin. 'This is the culmination of a decade of investment by [former head of international] Mark Waller, owners and commissioner Goodell. You pinch yourself, but we know it's taken an enormous amount of work and investment. So, you're pinching yourself, but on a lot of scar tissue. What we say is that we don't take for granted the investment made, nor the momentum we have.'

*

The league is at something of a crossroads. As celebrations of its 100th year continue apace, the question for pristinely dressed executives like Halpin becomes: 'What do the next 100 years look like?'

'We're a long-term league,' he says.

Central to that puzzle will be international expansion and, therefore, London. That Halpin's role encompasses that brief is telling, given there have already been reports that he has internal support as a potential future commissioner. An important man for an important job, you might say. 'This is one of the league's biggest growth areas,' he admits. 'It's always fun to have a fun job that has momentum and infrastructure behind it. The opportunities are significant. It's exciting to be in the growth part of one of the world's biggest sports.'

Where that growth goes might have been foreshadowed by the Collective Bargaining Agreement inked just a few months after Tottenham officially opened its doors to the NFL. It featured the introduction of a 17th regular-season game from the 2021 campaign, which will not only provide new revenue streams, but create a broader inventory for international efforts. 'There is a thought it may be best to continue playing between four and six games each year that feature different teams,' admits Kansas City Chiefs owner Clark Hunt, the former chairman of the NFL's International Committee. 'There are fans of every team in the UK, so rotating teams through there gives everybody an opportunity. If we just went with one team, it'd build the fanbase for that one team, but lessen opportunity for others. It's a fluid situation that could go either way.'

A backtrack on the previous rhetoric regarding the prospect of a franchise based in London? Not quite. As Halpin outlines, the UK already ticks three of the key boxes: stadiums that meet NFL requirements ('there are two'); passionate fandom; and media and corporate partners. If that isn't significant enough, Hunt vocalised a potentially grander vision than merely just playing games in London. 'In the UK and parts of Western Europe, you could have teams that are part of an expanded National Football League,' he admits. 'You could envision having a European division that plays in the NFL or having one team there. It's probably also possible to do the same thing in Mexico and Toronto because of the proximity to the US.'

Yet one lingering issue remains – and it's raised in a theoretical question by Halpin: 'What happens if the London team, were there one, has to host a playoff game on a short week?' It's one of many unanswered 'footballing logistics' questions sitting under the banner of 'competitive equity'.

'We've done a lot of analysis and continue to analyse it,' he admits. 'There's owner commitment to the market. We play four games now and could clearly play more based on ticket demand. But there are logistical issues that are different in an international market. We feel we have an opportunity for a team here. Now it's a question of if there's a team that wants to do it, and whether we can solve the football issues.'

Whichever way the NFL decides to go, don't be surprised if their international efforts expand quickly over the coming years. 'I think it's possible we could play a game in Asia – that's been discussed,' reveals Hunt. 'And we've also discussed South America. I think games there are possibilities to grow those markets.' The organisation has also done some fact-finding on potential venues in Germany. 'That is a phenomenal market for us,' admits Halpin. 'All of our numbers in terms of fandom, TV ratings, digital consumption, Madden, everything, are up. We want to keep serving that base.'

For all the potential that exists in new territories, however, none boast the infrastructure of London – a factor illustrated best by the Oakland–Chicago contest.

'This is one of, if not the best stadium I've ever played in in my

427

life,' enthused Derek Carr, having just made the short walk from one of the two giant locker rooms, designed to house 53-man rosters and support staffs, to the podium.

While he spoke, his teammates – buoyed by their surprising 24–21 win – were equally effusive. 'Wembley is great and has a load of history,' admits guard Richie Incognito, 'but this place is second to none. The locker rooms and field set-up was great. It's first-class. Wembley does feel like a soccer stadium; this feels like an NFL locker room.'

Even Bears head coach Matt Nagy, still licking his wounds, was expansive in his praise. 'Absolutely gorgeous,' he said of the stadium. 'You walk in here and you just see it is state of the art, top notch. It blows you away – phenomenal, absolutely phenomenal.'

As debuts go, this one was a dream. For the Raiders' victory over the Bears, played out amid a cacophony of noise and winning a seal of approval from everyone, confirmed that the NFL's future in the UK has never been brighter.

Week 11

PITTSBURGH STEELERS 7
CLEVELAND BROWNS 21

---

15 November 2019

FirstEnergy Stadium, Cleveland

A little more than 60 miles from where Ralph Hay first summoned the NFL's forefathers to the running boards of his Hupmobiles, the most violent game of its 100th season was underway. By the fourth quarter of the Cleveland Browns' regular-season meeting with the Pittsburgh Steelers, the occasion had already been marred by multiple flashpoints.

In the second quarter, young Pittsburgh wide receiver JuJu Smith-Schuster was walked from the field by medical personnel after being on the receiving end of a helmet-to-helmet hit from Cleveland cornerback Greedy Williams. After the interval, meanwhile, his teammate Diontae Johnson suffered the same fate, joined in the locker rooms by the player responsible for the contact: Browns safety Damarious Randall was ejected following the sickening impact. Neither Smith-Schuster nor Johnson would return.

As recently as 20 years previously, the incidents might not have warranted attention, let alone refereeing intervention or the need to safeguard the affected players. In fact, they would have been celebrated as 'football players playing football', with Smith-Schuster and Johnson encouraged to 'man up' and get back on the field. Yet, by the point of the NFL's centenary campaign, the landscape had altered dramatically and sensitivities were heightened. As such, when the game's final moments were blighted by an even more significant episode, the repercussions were severe.

With Cleveland up 21–7 and just eight seconds remaining, tensions boiled over one final time. Brilliant Browns pass-rusher Myles Garrett, following another play where he had Mason Rudolph in his clutches, lost control as he pulled the Steelers' quarterback towards the ground, yanking off his opponent's helmet and swinging it wildly onto his exposed head. The ensuing melee saw Pittsburgh centre Maurkice Pouncey respond by throwing Garrett to the ground and then repeatedly kicking him in the head.

The NFL responded swiftly. Garrett was fined nearly $50,000 and suspended indefinitely – he was reinstated after the season having missed six games – while Pouncey received a three-game ban that was eventually reduced to two. The league handing out such significant punishments can only be understood in the context of its wider response to the impact of head injuries on the game's future.

It was a journey that began with the autopsy of an all-time great player who had forged his legacy as a star for one of the teams on the field in Cleveland.

As he lay on Dr Bennet Omalu's stainless-steel table in 2002, Mike Webster bore few resemblances to the physically domineering centre who had starred on the Steelers' four-time Super Bowl winning teams of the 1970s. He was stripped down to just blue jeans and a frail imitation of the man who conquered all-comers in a career that ended, remarkably, only 12 years earlier. All he bore were the scars of a miserable few years leading up to him passing away aged just 50. 'My dad was not a complainer,' says son Garrett Webster. 'He didn't want sympathy, but the pain was horrible. There were times he would, or I would, use a mail-order taser that would paralyse him for 20 minutes to take the pain away. It's a horrible memory, but it gave him peace for that 20 minutes. I'd do anything for my dad.'

Having removed Webster's major organs, carefully weighing each, Omalu propped Webster's head on a rubber tee and began examining the brain. 'To my utter surprise and amazement,' he admits, 'it appeared normal. I was expecting a shrunken, dishevelled brain like in Alzheimer's disease. But there were no bruises, aneurysms or shrinkage. So, I reviewed the CT scans and the MRIs, but again nothing. However, my intellectual curiosity wasn't satisfied. There was no way this guy would have manifested this progressively deteriorating lifestyle with nothing in his brain. It wasn't scientifically feasible. So, I continued searching for an answer.'

His pursuit led to a discovery that would change the face of football and, increasingly, sports worldwide. After months of seeking answers, Omalu made a breakthrough when a batch of slides that had undergone a specialised staining process dropped on his desk: 'I remember it perfectly. I put the first one on the microscope and immediately I said, "Whoa, what is this?" and I had to go back and make sure they belonged to Mike Webster! I said, "No this cannot be." He was only 50. And yet his brain showed accumulations of very abnormal proteins that you would see in people with Alzheimer's. But, ironically, his brain was not atrophic like you would see in Alzheimer's. I'd never seen anything like this before. Ever.' The distinctive brown-and-red marks, responsible for killing cells in regions of the brain responsible for mood, emotions and executive functioning, would begin the process of Omalu naming it Chronic Traumatic Encephalopathy (CTE).

As the years wore on, and the condition was increasingly found in the brains of other former players, it became clear CTE and football were inexorably linked through the many collisions that occur on the field, under the term that still represents arguably the greatest threat to the NFL's future: concussions. 'I don't think

431

you can estimate how many concussions or brain injuries he suffered,' says Garrett Webster. 'A doctor who didn't know who he was or what he'd done for a living once asked, "What the heck happened to you? Have you been in a car accident?" And my father replied: "Yes, about 25,000 of them." My dad didn't miss a game for 25 years . . . 224 consecutive games. Add that up with full-contact practices and training camps. I don't think you can put a number on it.'

'I can remember playing against John Riggins,' says Hall-of-Fame former New York Giants linebacker Harry Carson. 'John was the kind of 'back that didn't try and run around you; he tried to run over you. One game we collided. You could hear the clasp of the helmets, and we both went down. I remember making my way back to the huddle, but I was struggling to make out what was going on. I was holding the hands of my teammates around me and everything faded to black. I sort of noticed that I was out on my feet, and so I squeezed the hands of the guys around me and my vision came back a little bit. I looked to the sidelines but couldn't see what Bill Belichick was signalling to me. And Washington were already breaking the huddle. One of my teammates, sensing I was in distress, called the defense. But I stayed in the game.

'Concussions were part of the game. Some players who sustain a concussion are out for the count. Others, like me, see stars or everything fades to black and there's no vision. It happened over and over again. You'd get a ding or [your] bell rung, phrases that really meant that you'd been concussed, but you always played through them. Only the weak didn't.'

For the vast majority of the NFL's 100 years, that was the prevailing attitude. It wasn't until 1994 that commissioner Paul Tagliabue set up a Mild Traumatic Brain Injury Committee, but the organisation's blasé mindset towards the situation was summed up when they appointed Dr Elliot Pellman, a rheumatologist with no expertise in brain injuries, as its chair.

432

That same committee were at the forefront of smearing Omalu upon the publication of his findings in the prestigious journal *Neurosurgery*. The league unsuccessfully demanded the article be retracted, but the weight of evidence would eventually become overwhelming. In 2005 and '06, Omalu found the same condition in the brains of Andre Waters, the former Philadelphia Eagles safety who shot himself in the mouth aged just 44, and another former Steelers lineman Justin Strzelczyk, who crashed into a tanker carrying corrosive acid at the age of 36.

Pandora's Box was open, especially as more former players began to speak about the issue. 'Around 1982,' adds Carson, 'I began to realise I was dealing with some very subtle issues mentally. At the end of practice or after a game, when approached by reporters I couldn't remember any of the words I wanted to use. So, I would search for these words I knew from childhood, but I'd find myself saying "ummm" or "you know". That really wasn't me. But I kept it to myself. It's the NFL. You learn not to share your weaknesses. I thought about ending it all. I drove to a bridge and thought about driving off. I was a professional football player, making big money, who shouldn't have had a care in the world. But I had those thoughts in my head. I had them a lot. And so when players started to commit suicide, I had a very firm understanding of what they were going through and why they were doing it, because I'd been there with the depression and suicidal thoughts. I wasn't surprised.'

With a groundswell of players coming forward – including nearly 5,000 who took part in a lawsuit alleging the NFL deliberately misinformed players by denying scientific data being presented in the medical community about concussion risks – attitudes needed to change. It was a gradual process, and the tide didn't truly turn until a few years into Roger Goodell's commissionership.

Having initially filed motions to have former players' lawsuits thrown out of court, the NFL agreed a $765 million settlement on 29 August 2013 – albeit without accepting liability. Seven months earlier, the National Institute of Health had determined that Hall-of-Fame linebacker Junior Seau was suffering from CTE when, a little less than a year earlier, he had committed suicide by shooting himself in the chest. Five months after the initial settlement, meanwhile, a federal judge declined the proposed amount and declared it insufficient. As of May 2020, the anticipated pay-out stood at close to $1.5 billion.

By that stage, many other important moments had occurred. Not least on 14 March 2016, when a senior league employee, senior vice-president of health and safety policy Jeff Miller, conceded for the first time that there is a link between football and brain conditions such as CTE.

Yet the key challenge, and one that remains, is to ensure that lessons are learnt from past failures. The NFL's attitude towards concussions over the 1990s and early 2000s was a rare blot on the otherwise exemplary tenure of Tagliabue, to such an extent that he wasn't enshrined into the Pro Football Hall of Fame until 2020 as part of a special centennial class. 'It was a fairly open talking point for many of those on the committee that Tagliabue and his response to head injuries, concussions, head trauma, was really a detrimental point in his career,' said long-time football writer and Hall-of-Fame voter Peter King. Tagliabue himself admitted missteps, most significantly his suggestion – in 1994 – that the problem was a media creation.

In reality, concussions were the greatest threat to the game in decades. Once realisation of that fact hit, the issue would fundamentally alter the way football was played in an attempt to ensure players of the present and future don't endure the health problems of their predecessors. Or, perhaps more significantly, to ensure that football actually has a future.

On 20 October 2010, Goodell issued a memo to all 32 teams warning 'violations of playing rules that unreasonably put the safety of another player in jeopardy have no place in the game, and that is especially true in the case of hits to the head and neck'. His sub-sequent threat of suspensions represented a powerful illustration of the NFL's evolving attitude towards enforcing new regulations created in the interests of player safety.

That campaign was the first in which hits to the head of a player deemed 'defenceless' after making a catch were penalised, while anybody who 'launched' to deliver a blow above the neck was also reprimanded. Those would prove to be just two examples of multiple alterations that have changed many aspects of the game, from kick-off returns becoming almost obsolete to the reduction of contact paving the way for a much more open game with greater scoring.

Although the latter represented a positive by-product in the fantasy-football era, the motive wasn't financial. With the understanding of concussions growing and the number of former players testing positive for CTE increasing, participation in the game has declined significantly. In 2020, studies showed that playing among those aged six to 12 is down more than 30 per cent from the peak, while the number is nearly 10 per cent less in high school. 'I told my daughter when my grandson was two that he will not play football,' says Carson.

The NFL's response has been multipronged. The league has launched initiatives to encourage correct tackling form in children, supported flag-football programmes, and spent millions of dollars investing in new research into head injuries and helmet technology. On the field, any player with a suspected concussion is tested in the locker room, while each game now grants an unaffiliated neurotrauma consultant seated in the press box, known as a 'spotter', the ability to initiate an examination on any player believed to be displaying possible symptoms. Anybody found to be suffering cannot return to a game and is entered into the NFL concussion protocol, which stipulates that he cannot return until all stages of a five-point progression have been completed. It was developed in conjunction with a panel of brain specialists and trainers, as well as the players' association.

There is no doubting the impact. Most players polled by this writer concede they are now more comfortable self-reporting concussion symptoms rather than shielding them to conform to tough-guy stereotypes, while others have retired earlier than they might have in previous generations. After the 2019 campaign, Carolina Panthers star linebacker Luke Kuechly called it a day. Aged just 28, he had suffered multiple concussions, including one in 2016 that forced him to miss six games.

Even amid the positives, however, concussions remain a looming shadow over the sport. Former star New England Patriots tight end Aaron Hernandez, who committed suicide in his prison cell in 2017 aged 27, two years after being convicted of murder, was found to have CTE. Researchers, meanwhile, are increasingly confident of being able to test for the condition in those living over the coming years. 'I think that could be huge,' said King. 'Every researcher thinks that's the golden ticket to the future of football. What this would tell us, especially in young people, is that if you come out of a big programme and do a baseline test, and there are signs you have CTE, obviously it's going to be hazardous to your health to continue playing. It could have a huge impact on football.'

Yet declarations surrounding the death of football are not a new phenomenon. In fact, they're nearly as old as the game itself. The most significant modification in the sport's history – the legalisation of the forward pass in 1906 – only came about after President Theodore Roosevelt demanded rules be applied to make the game safer following 18 players being killed and 159 injured during the previous year's college season. From that point onwards, if there is one word to describe both the sport and league that would popularise it so significantly, it's adaptability. Which is why, 100 years from now, the league will likely still dominate the American sporting landscape, even if the game is as unrecognisable from now as today's is from that of a century ago.

Super Bowl LIV

SAN FRANCISCO 49ERS 20
KANSAS CITY CHIEFS 31

---

2 February 2020
Hard Rock Stadium, Miami

As the Hard Rock Stadium lights, now fully in effect following a late-afternoon kick-off, shone down seemingly brighter than ever on a typically balmy Miami evening, Patrick Mahomes stood on the brink. The Kansas City Chiefs quarterback had just continued his troubling performance in the face of the San Francisco 49ers' menacing pass-rush, missing a simple pass to Tyreek Hill that was originally ruled complete before being overturned on review. Not only did the reversal mean Mahomes would again be squarely in the sights of San Francisco's quarterback hunters, it seemingly confirmed that a game beginning with such high expectations had veered permanently off course.

Prior to the action, the same field had been overrun with legends of now and yesteryear as living members of the newly crowned NFL 100 All-Time Team, featuring 100 players and 10 coaches, were paraded. During the ceremony – highlighted by the era's villain-in-chief Bill Belichick responding to boos by smiling and flashing the three Super Bowl rings (from his collection of nine) – one journalist in the press box suggested that, later on, we would bear witness to the league's next legend enjoying a crowning moment.

With the clock stuck on 7:13 in the fourth quarter, and Kansas City down 20–10, prophecies of that scribe and one of the league's outstanding players looked misguided. Earlier that week, super-star defensive lineman Aaron Donald had told me a story from the previous campaign, when he had consoled Mahomes after the quarterback threw a game-losing interception against his Los Angeles Rams. 'There are not too many times I give respect like that,' says Donald. 'But I had to let him know. Mahomes is special. He's going to be one of the greats.'

Yet the boy who would be king had looked little more than a court jester in Miami, succumbing to the 49ers' devastating rush and tossing two uncharacteristic interceptions, his first across four playoff games. After the aforementioned incompletion, Fox Sports' Troy Aikman said what everybody was thinking: 'He's not played well, Joe [Buck]. That should have been his easiest comple-tion of the night.' From reverence to ridicule.

Perhaps more significant than any acclaim Mahomes has attracted from those outside of the Chiefs' operation is the opin-ion of him inside the walls. Prior to the game, veteran passer Chad Henne lifted the lid: 'This early on in a career, I've never seen anyone better – but it's not just on the field. Off it, the way he prepares, takes notes and engages as a leader is special. I'm happy to have been with him these last few years. It's fun to watch.'

While the rest of the NFL world contemplated a damaging eve-ning for the young star at the worst possible time, those in Chiefs colours remained cool. 'It's like watching Denzel Washington in a movie or LeBron James in the playoffs,' says Kansas City safety Tyrann Mathieu. 'He has that glow, that spark. For him to be that young and keep his confidence in a Super Bowl against a tough defense who didn't really give him anything tells you a lot. He believes in himself, and we believe in him.'

Crucially, it wasn't just the players who felt that way – but his veteran coach Andy Reid as well. In one signature moment, that confidence paid off and altered the course of the biggest game of their lives. As the previous misfire was being reviewed, Mahomes asked offensive coordinator Eric Bieniemy: 'Do we have time to run "Wasp"?' For a play with so much riding on it, both in the context of the game and the careers of Reid, the league's winningest coach without a championship, and his young passer – the veteran head coach with arguably the finest offensive mind in football let Mahomes make the call. Like earlier in the contest, when Reid opted for a single-wing play on a crucial fourth down that led to Kansas City's first touchdown, it worked only thanks to the genius behind it. 'Their relationship is amazing,' adds Henne. 'Coach Reid is always asking Patrick what kinds of things he wants.'

Wasp, known as 'Gun Trey Right, 3 Jets Chip Wasp Y Funnel' to Kansas City's offensive players, would see the Chiefs deploy a three-wide-receiver set to the left side of the formation. On the far left, Sammy Watkins would run a 16-yard in-cut; to his right, Hill would run a deep post corner; and Travis Kelce a deep slant right from tight to the formation. Mahomes' key was to read San Francisco cornerback Emmanuel Moseley because, if he followed Watkins, Hill would be single-covered by safety Jimmie Ward. That the concept worked as designed, leaving one of the most dangerous weapons in the NFL to be covered one-on-one by Ward, illustrates the brilliance of Reid – that it led to a completion was down to Mahomes' equal skill.

The quarterback, battered and bruised after being feasted upon by Nick Bosa and Co., took what – in total – might have been a 15-step drop. Then, showing the physical gifts that have left the NFL world purring, delivered a ball that travelled 56 yards in the air – his longest all season – to hit Hill. From there, Mahomes continued his march down the field, then delivered another scoring drive and went from goat to furnishing his future GOAT resumé by being crowned Super Bowl MVP. If the fourth quarters of the showpiece are where careers are defined, Mahomes – having led the Chiefs back from a 10-point deficit and to their second championship – had got off to a pretty nice start.

Yet perhaps the greatest symbols of his place as the NFL's latest transcendent star, even more significant than images of Mahomes standing atop a podium clutching the Lombardi Trophy, would come over the course of the remaining offseason. Just days after a new CBA was agreed, confirming labour peace until 2030, Tom Brady, the six-time Super Bowl-winning New England Patriots quarterback, joined the Tampa Bay Buccaneers, breaking up his two-decade run of dominance with Belichick. Their respective fortunes would be among the biggest talking points when the NFL resumed later in 2020, albeit amid much change.

As well as the futures of Brady and Belichick, questions surrounded the success of the Raiders, with Las Vegas welcoming pro football for the first time; the sustainability of two Los Angeles clubs as the $5 billion SoFi Stadium opened its doors to the Rams and Chargers; and the league's new expanded 14-team playoff field. Separate to the standard footballing questions, meanwhile, were the spectres of two off-field items that would doubtless play a significant role in the league's future: the ongoing COVID-19 pandemic which had already forced the NFL to hold its first virtual draft and cancel its international slate for the coming season, and the racial tensions bubbling to the surface around the United States amid the riots that followed the death of George Floyd at the hands of police in Minnesota.

The latter hit at the heart of an issue that had drawn headlines four years previously, without a satisfactory conclusion, when then-San Francisco quarterback Colin Kaepernick chose first to sit, and then kneel, during the national anthem prior to games in protest of systematic racism and police brutality. 'I am not going to stand up to show pride in a flag for a country that oppresses black people and people of colour,' he said in a press conference after first sitting out during the anthem. 'To me, this is bigger than football, and it would be selfish on my part to look the other way. There are bodies in the street and people getting paid leave and getting away with murder.'

Kaepernick chose his method of action after speaking with Nate Boyer, a former NFL long snapper and United States Army Green Beret, who suggested kneeling made the point, yet still showed necessary respect. However, the issue would create a storm when President Donald Trump addressed it during a campaign rally in Alabama: 'Wouldn't you love to see one of these NFL owners, when someone disrespects our flag to say, "Get that son of a bitch off the field right now. Out. He's fired. He's fired".' With dividing lines being drawn in America and the NFL likely fearing conflict with the country's highest office, it reached what was considered a permanent compromise by advising players wishing to protest to stay in the locker room during the anthem. Kaepernick wasn't signed by a club after the 2017 season, and it seemed the number of players openly supporting his cause dwindled year-on-year.

But the death of Floyd, and subsequent riots across the United States, would lead to more players using their profile to raise concerns while readdressing the crux of Kaepernick's argument years earlier. The most powerful message came via a social-media video, in which a collection of the league's biggest black stars collaborated to call out the NFL's handling of the Kaepernick situation and implore it to recognise fault. To many people's surprise, the league listened. 'We, the National Football League, admit we were wrong,' said Goodell in a video reply. 'We, the National Football League, believe Black Lives Matter. The protests around the country are emblematic of the centuries of silence, inequality and oppression of black players, coaches, fans and staff. We are listening.'

Where the story goes next remains to be seen, but it was notable for many reasons. Not least that one of the men in the video that prompted the NFL's about-turn was the face of the organisation's future.

For as much as the league entered its 101st season facing considerably more uncertainty than in recent years, it did so amid the comfort of crowning its latest star months earlier. Mahomes, the youngest player to be named NFL MVP (2018) and win a Super Bowl (2019) in league history, had received the baton. 'He isn't going to do anything but keep getting better,' concludes Donald. 'That's the scary thing.'

GLOSSARY

THE PLAYERS

OFFENSE

Quarterback – The NFL's golden boy touches the ball on every play. He hands the ball to a runner, runs himself or throws downfield.

Offensive Line – Five big men up front are charged with protecting the quarterback on passing plays and blocking for running backs on rushing plays.

Running Back – One of the most versatile players on the team . . . must be able to run, catch and block. A variation of the running back is the fullback, who is usually tasked with leading the way and blocking for the ball-carrier, but can sometimes carry it himself.

Wide Receiver – Primary task is to get downfield as quickly as possible, find space in the defense and catch passes.

Tight End – This hybrid player lines up on the end of the offensive line and can be asked to block on running plays or act like a receiver and get downfield to catch passes.

DEFENSE

Defensive End/Outside Linebacker – This athletic defender spends every game in attack mode, chasing down the quarterback or attempting to destroy running plays.

Defensive Tackle – Huge and often an unsung hero, the defensive tackle is intent on stuffing opposing run plays and generally making life difficult for the offensive line.

Inside Linebacker – This hybrid defender can do a little bit of everything – tackle running backs, cover bigger receivers downfield and hunt down the quarterback.

Cornerback – Marks the fastest players on the field and must mirror the movements of the wide receiver. Being able to move at high speed while running backwards is one key job requirement!

Safety – As the name would suggest, the safety is the last line of defense and must be a good tackler.

SPECIAL TEAMS

Kicker – Handles all kicks at goal. Could be a spectator for three hours but his boot can win or lose games.

Punter – Called upon when the offense fails, the punter kicks the ball away for territorial reasons.

Return man – Can change field position in a hurry by running back the opposing team's kickoffs or punts.

*

A-formation – A variation of the single wing in which the centre could snap to any one of three backs.

Antitrust – In the USA, federal and state government laws that regulate the conduct and organisation of business corporations, generally to promote competition for the benefit of consumers.

Arena football – Eight-a-side version of traditional football, designed to be played at smaller indoor venues.

Base personnel – A team's most commonly used formation, offensively or defensively.

Blitz – When a defense sends a higher number of pass-rushers – five or more – than usual.

Bump-and-run coverage – Defensive tactic used by cornerbacks to disrupt a receiver's pass route by lining up directly opposite him and impeding him physically.

Bunch formations – Wide-receiver alignment that sees multiple receivers clustered together to one side of the formation in a bid to force the defense into a specific coverage.

Coming out of his break – The point at which a receiver makes a designed cut, or change of direction, on his passing route.

Crack blocks – A blocking assignment where an offensive player positioned near the sideline runs back towards the ball at the snap in order to block a defender and make room for a runner. Also known as a 'crack-back block', it must be made from the front and between the neck and waist to be legal.

Draft board – The order in which a team rates that year's draft prospects.

Draw play – A running play disguised as a passing play, in which the quarterback drops back and sets up to pass before delivering a late hand-off.

Drop-kicker – A player who chooses, or is able, to kick without the aid of a tee or holder by dropping the ball and kicking it after a single bounce on the ground.

Eagle defense – A 5-2 defensive alignment, formulated by Eagles coach Greasy Neale, with a tight five-man line and linebackers who jammed offensive ends. Unlike most units of the 1940s, it featured four defensive backs.

First read – The quarterback's first option on a passing play, whose viability he has to diagnose depending on the defensive coverage before moving on to other options.

Flea-flicker – An offensive play where the quarterback hands off to a running back, who then pitches the ball back to the quarterback for a pass downfield.

Franchise tag – A means of teams keeping designated players from free-agency by locking them into a guaranteed one-year contract that pays the average of the top-five highest-paid players at their position.

Goalline offense – Short-yardage formation used when close to the end zone, usually without wide receivers but with added running backs and/or tight ends – and occasionally linemen or defensive players reporting as eligible receivers in order to create a mismatch. Also known as the 'jumbo' or 'heavy' package in reference to the size of the players used.

Goalline defense – Player formation designed to deny or limit close-range scoring attempts, particularly running plays. Relies heavily on big defensive players being able to overpower their offensive counterparts, and often features six down linemen whose responsibility is to break into the offensive backfield.

High-low route combinations – An offensive passing play that gives the quarterback two routes that cross above and below a defender's zone, close enough to stay in view but vertically spaced enough (12–15 yards) that the flat defender can't cover either by splitting the difference.

Hitch – When a lineman stands up then returns to his stance.

I-formation – An offensive formation in which the fullback and halfback line up vertically behind the quarterback to form an 'I'.

Lighter boxes – The opposite of 'stacking the box', where a defense opts to position fewer players than usual in the area defined by the width of the offensive line and a depth of five yards from the line of scrimmage.

Man defense – Where a defensive player is responsible for covering a single offensive player.

Move the chains – The basic aim of an offense as it progresses towards its goal of scoring a touchdown. Each first down gained requires the sideline yardage markers – joined by a 10-yard chain – to be repositioned.

One-back offense – An offense with one running back and no fullback.

Nickel/dime defense – A defensive formation created by Philadelphia Eagles defensive coach Jerry Williams in 1960 that features five defensive backs, so named as a nickel is equal to five cents. Dime is an evolution of nickel, which adds a sixth defensive back.

Paydirt – an old mining term, defined as a source of success or wealth; in football terms, it means reaching the end zone for a touchdown.

Pick-six – An interception that is returned for a touchdown, earning six points.

Pick play – An illegal play in which a receiver intentionally hinders the defender covering another receiver.

Power sweep – Vince Lombardi's evolution of the sweep play relied on a hand-off or pitch to the halfback, who would run parallel to the line of scrimmage before turning upfield behind key blocks from both guards, who would move away from their usual assignments on the line to lead the way for the runner.

Reverses – A trick play in which the ball is transferred twice, first from quarterback to running back and then to a wide receiver travelling in the opposite direction. Sometimes turned into a double reverse if the receiver hands off to the other wideout, switching the direction again.

Routes

Option routes – A passing route in which receivers, rather than running to a predetermined position, read the defense and make a post-snap decision. They are incredibly tough to defend if quarterback and receiver read it the same way.

Passing routes – The specific paths run by receivers (including running backs and tight ends) in order to get into the right spot on the field to catch a forward pass. Each route will be determined by the play called by the quarterback and forms part of a wider 'route tree'.

Route tree

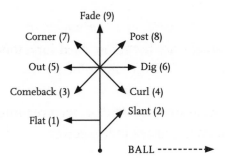

Run-and-shoot – Devised by high-school coach Glenn 'Tiger' Ellison and popularised by Mouse Davis in the USFL, the run-and-shoot offense operates from spread formations and relies on receivers being able to adjust their routes based on coverage and shifts in defensive formations.

Screen pass – A forward pass to a player protected by a screen of blockers, designed to create yards after the catch.

Shifts – One or more players changing position before the snap, leading to a change in formation.

Shotgun – A formation in which the quarterback lines up directly behind the centre, but usually five yards back, to receive the snap.

Single wing – Historical offensive formation featuring an unbalanced offensive line, with three linemen to one side of the centre rather than two, as well as four backs and two tight ends. The snap usually went to one of the running backs, with the quarterback often employed as a blocker. Precursor to both the wildcat and spread offenses.

Spread – Offensive system that typically sees the quarterback in the shotgun formation, and three-, four- or five-receiver sets designed to stretch the defense both laterally and vertically.

Stack defense – Variation on the nickel-defense alignments, featuring three down linemen and three linebackers, along with five defensive backs. Uncommon in the modern NFL but used to confuse the offense by applying various blitz options while still playing zone or man coverage with a faster defensive unit. Can be prone to conceding big plays but, equally, can yield the same for the defense.

Stacked line – A defensive line featuring more than the usual three or four players, commonly used to protect against scoring or short-yardage opportunities.

Stickum – Adhesive widely used by receivers and defensive backs to aid catching in the 1970s but banned, along with other similar substances, in 1981.

Sweeps – Any play involving a running back or wide receiver taking a pitch or hand-off from the quarterback while running parallel to the line of scrimmage.

The sticks – Alternative name for the yardage markers at either end of the chain, indicating the line of scrimmage and the point at which a first down will be gained. Origin of the phrase 'move the sticks'.

T-formation – Three running backs lined up around five yards behind the quarterback to create a 'T'.

Tackle-eligible plays – A passing play where an offensive tackle is declared as an eligible receiver, usually lining up in the tight end position.

Three-and-out – A short offensive possession consisting of just three plays that fail to yield a first down, forcing the team with the ball to punt.

Three-receiver sets – As the name suggests, offensive formations utilising three receivers rather than the historically more popular two.

To the house – Taking the ball all the way to the end zone for a touchdown, usually from a long way out. Can refer to offensive or defensive scores.

Two-minute warning – Stoppage in play when two minutes remain on the game clock at the end of each half or, less commonly, in overtime.

Umbrella – A 6-1-4 defense where the ends would usually drop into coverage.

Wildcard – A team handed a play-off berth despite not qualifying as a division champion. From 2020, each conference has three wildcards.

Winning percentage – Success rate in games of football, attributed to both coaches and players and measured by win-loss-tie records, dividing the number of games won by the number of games played. A tie counts as half a win. Always expressed as a decimal.

Zone – An alternative to man-to-man defense, in which defensive players are tasked to protect a certain area of the field.

Zone blitz – Evolution of the standard blitz play in which the defense disguises its intentions behind a standard zone-coverage formation before sending anticipated pass-coverage players to attack the quarterback.

11 personnel – With offensive formations designated by the number of running backs (first number) and tight ends (second number) involved, 11 personnel features one of each, along with three wide receivers. Alternatively, 12 would feature one back and two tight ends.

3-4 defense – Base defensive alignment designed to frustrate an offense's short-passing game, featuring just three down linemen and four linebackers, but flexible enough to become a nickel or dime defense if required. It remains susceptible to inside run plays.

5-3-3 defense – A defense with five defensive linemen, three linebackers and three defensive backs.

4-3 defense – The most commonly used defensive formation in pro football due to its flexibility. Featuring four linemen and three linebackers, hence 4-3, as well as four defensive backs, the alignment can be effective against both running and passing plays, while still providing the opportunity to blitz.

BIBLIOGRAPHY

A book of this nature is delivered only through significant research, but would also not be possible without the aid of some fine work from others. In particular, I'd like to credit my great friend Michael MacCambridge, whose exceptional book *America's Game* provided an incredible research tool. Furthermore, the level of detail provided wouldn't have been possible without ProFootballResearchers.org, whose archives are a gold mine for any budding historian, *Sports Illustrated*'s exceptional vault and an array of US newspapers, of which there are too many to name. I'd like to throw a particular spotlight onto the Pro Football Hall of Fame and, in particular, NFL Films – who opened their doors and vaults to me over the course of this process. Those days were some of the most fun I've had in my journalistic career and, in the case of NFL Films, I often found myself watching their documentaries that had little to do with what I was writing!

The greatest pleasure of all is derived from speaking to those involved. In all, I conducted around 100 interviews, with many Hall of Famers, and that wouldn't have been possible without the help of some exceptional PR people around the NFL. All have my eternal gratitude.

Below are quotes taken from other sources. Any not listed have come from author interviews or *Gridiron*, which is the magazine I edit.

PROLOGUE

Dayton Journal Herald – Two quotes in Prologue
The Canton Repository – Quote in Prologue
Canton Daily News – Quote in Prologue

CHAPTER 1

Chris Willis, Joe F. Carr, *The Man Who Built the National Football League* (Lanham, MD: Scarecrow Press, 2010), 136
- George Halas quote, 'He had what the rest of us lacked . . .'

CHAPTER 2

Red Grange, archival interview, 1973 (NFL Films)
- *Red Grange* quote, 'I would have been thought more of . . .'

CHAPTER 3

Chris Willis, Joe F. Carr, *The Man Who Built the National Football League* (Lanham, MD: Scarecrow Press, 2010), 303.
- Joe Carr quote, 'In fact, if we can give the offense . . .'

Films Encore: The NFL's First Playoff Game, December 2012 (NFL Films)
- Charles Miller quote, 'It was stinking . . .'
- Glen Presnell quote, 'He wasn't anywhere near . . .'

CHAPTER 4

Joseph S. Page, *Pro Football Championships Before the Super Bowl: A Year-by-Year History* (McFarland & Company, 10 December 2010), 53
- George Preston Marshall quote, 'The Bears are a bunch of cry-babies . . .'

Chicago Tribune, 'Meet Marshall, Pro Football's Modern Barnum' – 7 November 1940
- George Preston Marshall quotes, 'In 1931, I went . . .'; 'The first year I was in . . .'

Milwaulkee Sentinel, 'Hutson Recalls The Glory Years' – 18 September 1985
- Don Hutson quotes, 'I started before they had . . .'

James W. Johnson, *The Wow Boys: A Coach, a Team, and a Turning Point in College Football* (UNP – Bison Original, 1 November 2006)
- Clark Shaughnessy quotes, 'When George Halas didn't . . .'
- George Halas quotes, 'Before we began collaborating . . .'

Pro Football Hall of Fame biography: Sammy Baugh, ProFootball-HOF.com
- Sammy Baugh quote, 'Yep, it would have . . .'

CHAPTER 5

Gary Webster, *The League That Didn't Exist: A History of the All-American Football* (McFarland & Compan, 9 November 2018)
- Otto Graham quotes, 'Coach Brown should have . . .'; 'We were so fired up . . .'; 'There are times . . .'

John Eisenberg, *The League: How Five Rivals Created the NFL and Launched a Sports Empire* (Basic Books, 1st edition, 9 October 2018)
- George Halas quote, 'We owners were a tight . . .'
- Elmer Layden quote, 'There is nothing for the . . .'

Paul Brown with Jack Clary: *The Paul Brown Story* (Atheneum; 1st edition, 1979)
- Paul Brown quotes, 'I needed more than that . . .'; 'The laws of learning . . .'

A Football Life: Paul Brown (NFL Films)
- Bill Belichick quotes, 'There's nobody I have . . .'; 'When I think of Paul Brown . . .'

Bosh Pritchard, archival interview (NFL Films)
- Bosh Pritchard quote, 'We felt cocky . . .'

Chuck Bednarik, archival interview (NFL Films)
- Chuck Bednarik quote, 'He jumped on me . . .'

CHAPTER 6

ESPN Films, *50th Anniversary of the Greatest Game Ever Played*
- Gino Marchetti quote, 'If I wasn't a big guy . . .'
- Frank Gifford quote, 'Jim Lee never had anything . . .'
- Ray Berry quotes, 'When we got the ball'; 'Time and time again . . .'

Paul Schwartz, *Tales from the New York Giants Sideline: A Collection of the Greatest Giants Stories Ever Told* (Sports Publishing, 2011)
- Sam Huff quotes, 'Landry built the 4-3 defense . . .'; 'We had a defense that could . . .'

Baltimore Evening Sun, 29 December 1958, 'Baltimore Gambled, Giants Went Broke'
- Weeb Ewbank quote, 'I miscalculated . . .'

Detroit Free Press, 13 August 1957, 'Buddy Parker Says He's Quitting Lions . . .'
- Buddy Parker quote, 'The basic reason for my decision . . .'

CHAPTER 7

Harvey Frommer, *When It Was Just A Game, Remembering the First Super Bowl* (Taylor Trade Publishing; Reprint edition, September 2015)
- Frank Gifford quote, 'After Lombardi watched Kanas City . . .'

- Hank Stram quotes, 'We knew we had come . . .'; 'We felt we were doing . . .'; 'The interception changed . . .'

Baltimore Sun, 13 January 1967, 'Williams Calls Green Bay Highly Overrated'
- Fred Williamson quote, 'They're overrated . . .'

Full Color Football: The History of the American Football League (NFL Films)
- Bud Adams quote, 'We were doing all sorts . . .'

CHAPTER 8

The 1967 Ice Bowl (NFL Films)
- Referee Norm Schachter quote
- Bob Long quote, 'It was like an ice-skating rink . . .'

David Clarebaut, Bart Starr, *When Leadership Mattered* (Taylor Trade Publishing, 29 August 2007)
- Bart Starr quote, 'We were ready . . .'

A Football Life: Vince Lombardi (NFL Films)
- Vince Lombardi quote, 'A good teacher . . .'

A Football Life: Jim Brown (NFL Films)
- Jim Brown quotes, 'I was the only black player . . .'; 'I was not going to let'; 'I was set in my ways . . .'
- Bobby Mitchell quote, 'He would scream . . .'

Vince Lombardi, *Run To Daylight!* (Simon & Schuster; Anniversary edition, 13 August 2013)
- Vince Lombardi sweep quote, 'The pulling guards form . . .'

CHAPTER 9

Full Color Football: The History of the American Football League (NFL Films)
- Joe Namath quotes, 'We were told for 10 straight days . . .'; 'It was great to feel part of a league . . .'

Ron Jaworski with Greg Cosell and David Plaut, *The Games That Changed the Game: The Evolution of the NFL in Seven Sundays* (ESPN, 5 October 2010)
- Sid Gillman quote, 'The field is 100 yards long . . .'

Sports Illustrated, 2 September 1991, 'Sid Gillman, Screen Gem'
- Al Davis quotes, 'Sid Gillman was the father . . .'; 'The real treasure I got . . .'
- Bill Walsh quote, 'Much of what I did . . .'

Sports Illustrated, 19 July 1965, 'Show-Biz Sonny And His Quest For Stars'
- Sonny Weblin quote, 'When Joe Namath walks into a room . . .'

CHAPTER 10

A Football Life: Al Davis (NFL Films)
- Al Davis quotes, 'If there is anything we've ever done . . .'; 'I thought someone intelligent could . . .'; 'It's like having the bomb . . .'; 'Somewhere within the first five or 10 plays . . .'; 'I always say generals win . . .'; 'We may sign a player . . .'

A Football Life: John Madden (NFL Films)
- John Madden quotes, 'He spoke on one play . . .'; 'Anything that I ever wanted . . .'; 'We won every game that there is . . .'

America's Game: The 1983 Los Angeles Raiders (NFL Films)
- Howie Long quotes, 'We were practising . . .'; 'He was a tortured soul . . .'

Dan Rooney, *Dan Rooney: My 75 Years with the Pittsburgh Steelers and the NFL* (Da Capo Press, 2 September 2008)
- Andy Russell quote, 'Ray was first . . .'

CHAPTER 11

America's Game: The 1972 Miami Dolphins (NFL Films)
- Larry Csonka quotes, 'I don't think we should have . . .'; 'He treated a close victory . . .'
- Manny Fernandez quotes, 'I hadn't been blocked . . .'; 'For a bunch of no names . . .'

Winning is Living & Losing is Dying: The George Allen Story (NFL Films)
- Etty Allen quote, 'He said it was the most . . .'

CHAPTER 12

Greatness Cut Short For Greg Cook (NFL Films)
- Bill Walsh quote, 'I believe he was the greatest talent . . .'

Los Angeles Times, 'Living Legend', 22 December 2006
- Bill Walsh quote, 'All the way through . . .'

The Timeline, Tale of Two Cities, Part I (NFL Films)
- Bill Walsh quote, 'Looking back, that was Camelot . . .'

CHAPTER 13

ESPN 30 For 30, *The '85 Bears*
- Mike Ditka quotes, 'He resented authority . . .'; 'He was badgering me . . .'; 'What goes around . . .'
- Jim McMahon quotes, 'I screwed up my neck and back . . .'; 'As I regained by balance . . .'
- Richard Dent quote, 'He was a genius . . .'

A Football Life: Dick Butkus and Gale Sayers (NFL Films)
- Dick Butkus quotes, 'What got me . . .'; 'I loved the game . . .'

CHAPTER 14

Michael MacCambridge, *America's Game: The Epic Story of How Pro Football Captured a Nation* (Anchor Books; Reprint edition, 18 October 2005)
- Bob Waterfield quote, 'the best football player I ever saw . . .'
- Jackie Robinson quote, 'He had everything needed for greatness . . .'

Kansas City Star, February 1972, 'Otis Taylor Needs To Win'
- Otis Taylor quote, 'I'm a premier receiver . . .'

A Football Life: Doug Williams (NFL Films)
- Joe Gibbs quotes, 'I got real comfortable . . .'; 'I'll never forget . . .'; 'That year, I don't think . . .'

New York Times, 26 December 2005, '20 Years Later, Thiesmann Revisits Replay'
- Joe Theismann quote, 'It just went so suddenly . . .'

CHAPTER 15

CSNBC, 13 April 2017, 'EXCLUSIVE: Bill Belichick on leadership, winning, and Tom Brady not being a "great natural athlete"'
- Bill Belichick quotes, 'It was like having two or three . . .'; 'I learnt coaching at an early age . . .'

A Football Life: Lawrence Taylor (NFL Films)
- Joe Gibbs quote, 'We had to have a special gameplan . . .'
- Bill Belichick quotes, 'Taylor's the best player . . .'; 'He was so respected . . .'

America's Game: The 1986 New York Giants (NFL Films)
- Lawrence Taylor quote, 'From that time on . . .'

Joe Gibbs: A Football Life (NFL Films)
- Joe Gibbs quotes, 'I thought I was going to be the first . . .'; 'He could move all over . . .'
- Bill Walsh quote, 'He had a great technical . . .'
- Bill Parcells quote, 'Not to take away from . . .'

The Two Bills: ESPN 30 FOR 30 (NFL Films)
- Carl Banks quote, 'I thought it was a collective brain fart . . .'
- Bill Parcells quote, 'Nobody ever won with . . .'
- Bill Belichick quote, 'I was a detail person . . .'

Four Falls of Buffalo: ESPN 30 FOR 30 (NFL Films)
- Bruce Smith quote, 'I have no idea . . .'

CHAPTER 16

A Football Life: Jerry Jones (NFL Films)
- Jerry Jones quote, 'greatest PR disaster . . .'

The Timeline: Tale of Two Cities, Part 2 (NFL Films)
- Steve Young quote, 'We would watch each other . . .'
- Troy Aikman quote, 'We knew it was us . . .'
- Deion Sanders quote, 'It was great execution . . .'

CHAPTER 17

America's Game: The 1997 Denver Broncos (NFL Films)
- John Elway quotes, 'When I got to the line of scrimmage . . .'; 'After 15 years of work . . .'

Elway To Marino: ESPN 30 FOR 30 (NFL Films)
- Terry Bradshaw quote, 'He should play baseball . . .'

A Football Life: Terrell Davis (NFL Films)
- Gary Kubiak quote, 'To this day . . .'

CHAPTER 18

The Two Bills: ESPN 30 For 30
- Robert Kraft quote, 'My assistant came in . . .'

The Timeline: 9/11 (NFL Films)
- Paul Tagliabue quotes, 'The initial focus . . .'; 'Many owners were aware . . .'; 'In my mind . . .'

NFL.com, 22 September 2016, 'Tom Brady, Drew Bledsoe reflect on pivotal hit 15 years later'
- Drew Bledsoe quote, 'I couldn't think straight . . .'

CHAPTER 19

NFL 100 Greatest Plays, Part 3 (NFL Films)
- Mike Tirico quote, 'That's the coolest thing . . .'

'Eye To Eye: Bill Belichick', 17 May 2008, CBS News
- Bill Belichick quote, 'I interpreted it incorrectly . . .'

America's Game: The 2007 New York Giants (NFL Films)
- Michael Strahan quote, 'We would give you a heart attack . . .'
- Tom Coughlin quote, 'He had missed . . .'

AUTHOR INTERVIEWS

Dick Anderson, Ken Anderson, George Atkinson, Cliff Avril, Bobby Bell, Upton Bell, Brian Bilick, Rocky Bleier, Terry Bradshaw, Gil Brandt, Anne Marie Bratton, Tim Brown, Harry Carson, Nick Caserio, Byron Chamberlain, Cliff Christl, Roger Craig, Jimbo Covert, Charles Davis, Terrell Davis, Aaron Donald, Boyd

BIBLIOGRAPHY

Dowler, Tony Dungy, Kevin Dyson, Brett Favre, Marv Fleming, London Fletcher, Myles Garrett, Jerry Glanville, Victor Green, Joe Greene, Charles Haley, Dan Hampton, Chad Henne, Trey Flowers, Mike Haynes, Franco Harris, Mickey Herskowitz, Dont'a Hightower, Torry Holt, Clark Hunt, Michael Irvin, Richie Incognito, Tony Jefferson, Jimmy Johnson, Ted Johnson, Vance Johnson, Ed 'Too Tall' Jones, Mike Jones, Jonathan Kraft, Jim Langer, Marv Levy, Ricardo Lockette, Ronnie Lott, Steve Mariucci, Curtis Martin, Patrick McCaskey, Willie McGinest, Warren Moon, Rob Ninkovich, Jonathan Ogden, Joe Pisarcik, Jim Plunkett, Bill Polian, Frank Ramos, Andre Reed, Jerry Rice, Dave Robinson, Ken Rodgers, Bill Romanowski, Dan Rooney, Phil Savage, John Schmitt, Don Shula, Stewart 'Smokey' Stover, Leigh Steinberg, Jim Stuckey, Jason Taylor, Tom Thayer, Amy Trask, David Tyree, Dick Vermeil, Osi Umenyiora, Kurt Warner, Everson Walls, Paul Warfield, Marv Washington, Charlie Weis, Doug Williams, Ron Wolf, Rod Woodson

ACKNOWLEDGEMENTS

This book, and my career as an NFL journalist, would never have been possible without the support of my wife, Leah, and mum and dad, Ian and Judith. My parents got me started by paying for journalism training and all expenses of an 18-year-old living in London, as well as offering untold support over the years, while Leah didn't scoff when I suggested giving up a steady job to start an NFL magazine. I've also been aided at other times by other family members, particularly my grandpa Arthur and brother Daniel. For all of that help and confidence, I'll be forever grateful.

I'd also like to quickly acknowledge some others without whom this book would never have materialised. Without the belief of Matt Thacker, who owns the communications company, TriNorth, that produces *Gridiron* magazine, none of this would have occurred. As for the book itself, David Tossell, NFL UK's PR man and a prolific author himself, was crucial in making it happen and assisting the process, mostly by introducing me to his literary agent David Luxton – who actually secured a publishing deal! A book is never possible without good publishers, and the team at Orion have been exceptional. Special thanks to Isabelle Everington, Lucinda McNeile, Paul Murphy and Alan Samson. Finally, numerous colleagues and friends have helped me in various ways during the process: Liam Blackburn, Ben Burke, Simon Clancy, Will Gavin, Olly Hunter, Craig Llewellyn, Greig Norman, Josh Peacock and Neil Reynolds.

This book is for all of those listed above, my son Thomas and my second child – who has yet to be born! I hope that, one day, they enjoy reading it as much as I did writing it.

INDEX

465